THE MINOR LEAGUES

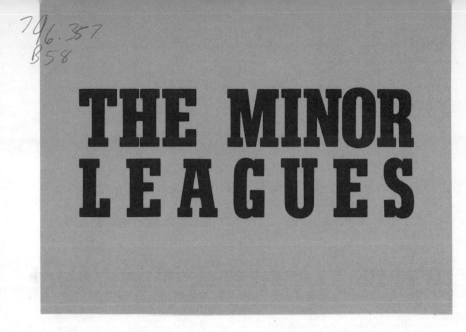

THE MINOR LEAGUES

MIKE BLAKE

WYNWOOD ® Press
New York, New York

Library of Congress Cataloging-in-Publication Data $\#$ 22660595

Blake, Mike.
    The minor leagues : a celebration of the little show / Mike Blake.
      p.   cm.
    Includes bibliographical references (p.) and index.
    ISBN 0-922066-60-4
    1. Minor league baseball—United States—History. I. Title.
GV875.A1B53   1991
796.357′64′0973—dc20   90-22957
                                                   CIP

Copyright © 1991 by Mike Blake
Published by WYNWOOD™ Press
An Imprint of Gleneida Publishing Group, Inc.
New York, New York
Printed in the United States of America

DEDICATION

To my wife Jan, who makes me whole, who gives me strength, support and love, and without whom there would be no works such as these. To Mom and Dad, who make me proud. To Cliff and Merle, who warmly took me into their family. And to Richard Re, who believed in me and in this project and who gave me room to work.

ACKNOWLEDGMENTS

My generous publisher, Wynwood Press, promised me that I would be able to thank everyone who made this book possible: the information providers; the friendly, cooperative, and helpful people who let me read their private files, probe into their personal lives, extract long-forgotten stories and provide me with information, contacts, and opportunities to research this tome. Without them, the lovers of baseball, there would be no book.

So, in what may be literature's longest, largest, and most deserved acknowledgments section, I wish to gratefully acknowledge that army of kind, generous people, whose help, real or imagined, was utilized in the organization and research of this book.

This people's army includes: Richard Re (Wynwood Press), the Pawsox fan who conceived of and focused this book; Nancy Jillard (Wynwood Press), a professional who really cares about her projects and her writers; Jon Miller (Baltimore Orioles and ESPN), who provided great stories; Al Conin (California Angels), another top storyteller; Mike Terry (San Bernardino *Sun*), who generously provided a plethora of interesting stories and contacts; and Miles Wolff (*Baseball America*, Durham Bulls, Butte Copper Kings, Carolina League), who was kind, generous, and instrumental in my receiving photographs, logos, and information—much of which appeared in various publications produced by *Baseball America*.

Also of great help to me were: Joe Black (ex-Dodger, MLB); Richard Levin (Major League Baseball—The Commissioner's Office); Phyllis Merhige (American League); Katy Feeney (National League); Nestor Alva Brito (Mexican League); Dave Cunningham (Long Beach *Press Telegram*); Bill Valentine (Arkansas Travelers); Phil Dixon (SABR), who provided much of the material and stories on the Negro Leagues; Joe Buzas (ex-New York Yankee, Portland Beavers, New Britain Red Sox); Julian John Portman (Portman and Associates of Chicago); Bobby Bragan (Hollywood Stars); Dick Clark (SABR); Stu Nahan (KABC radio/KTLA TV); Bert Blyleven, Doug Rader, Moose Stubing, Ken Brett, and John Sevano (California Angels); Dwight Evans and Rob Murphy (Boston Red Sox); Brook Jacoby and Mike Hargrove (Cleveland Indians); Don Mattingly (New York Yankees); Jolene Murcer; John Berardino; Julie Nathanson; Rudy Zaepfel (Newark Shellfish Co. and former Newark Bears batboy); Bob Hoie (SABR); Dave Kemp (SABR); Charles Hershberger (SABR and Old Tyme News); Bill Weiss (Howe Sports Data, PCL); George Brace (SABR); Jennifer McCarthy (*Baseball America*); Alfredo LaMont (USOC); Steve Rosenthal (Westwood One); Mark White (International League); Jimmy Bragan (Southern League); Carl Sawatski (Texas League); Ted Tornow (Memphis Chicks); Glenn Geffner (Rochester Red Wings); Brian Bane (Denver Zephyrs); Billy Johnson (Louisville Redbirds); Larry Schmittou (Nashville Sounds); Bill Wanless (Pawtucket Red Sox); Kyle Woodell (Rochester Red Wings); Mark Wilson (San Jose Giants); Pamela Gentry (Grand Hyatt on Union Square, San Francisco); Jeff Allen (Hyatt Regency San Francisco); and Ben Kaufman.

And the following organizations were instrumental in my research:

Albuquerque Dukes, American Association, Arkansas Travelers, Asheville Tourists, Birmingham Barons, Buffalo Bisons, Butte Copper Kings, Carolina League, Charleston Rainbows, Chattanooga Lookouts, Columbus Mudcats, Denver Zephyrs, Durham Bulls, Eastern League, El Paso Diablos, Florida State League, Frederick Keys, Greenville Hornets, Harrisburg Senators, Indianapolis Indians, International League, Louisville Redbirds, Madison Muskies, Memphis Chicks, Nashville Sounds, Northwest League, Oklahoma City 89ers, Pacific Coast League, Pawtucket Redsox, Phoenix Firebirds, Portland Beavers, Quad City Angels, Riverside Red Wave, Rochester Red Wings, San Bernardino Spirit, San Jose Bees, San Jose Giants, South Atlantic League, Southern League, Stockton Ports, Tidewater Tides, Toledo Mud Hens, Vero Beach Dodgers, Waterloo Diamonds, and Winston-Salem Spirits.

I wish to thank the Brea Public Library, Brea, California, for letting me keep and use reference books far longer than I should have.

I also humbly and gratefully offer special acknowledgment to all the members of SABR (Society for American Baseball Research) for their help and knowledge.

I additionally publicly praise and recognize Tim Mead, Director of Public Relations for the California Angels, the consummate baseball professional, who gave me a virtual carte blanche at Anaheim Stadium with home and visiting players, contacts, and information.

Finally, I sincerely bestow my supreme gratitude to SABR President Richard Topp, a funny, caring, and insightful man dedicated to research, facts, and humor at all costs, who talked me into joining SABR, and whose telephone bill and postage charges soared due to dozens of cross-country phone calls and reams of information sent to me in acts of generosity, all in an effort to help me complete the task that culminates in the following pages.

M.B.

TABLE OF CONTENTS

THE MINOR LEAGUES

PROLOGUE

Baseball has been tightly woven into the very fabric of America, or at least Americana, for 145 years, since Alexander Cartwright, not Abner Doubleday, conceived of the sport in 1845.

And if baseball is America, then Minor League baseball is grassroots America in its purest form. The diamond is, after all, American youth's genuine field of dreams, and those dreams that begin on the sandlots and schoolyards of this great land take real shape and gain honest purpose and unequivocal focus on the fields of the minor leagues.

This book, entitled *The Minor Leagues: A Celebration of the Little Show,* is just that—a celebration, or a *look* if you will; and to fully explain the author's frame of mind and frame of reference . . . an affectionate look . . . a salute. While we try to give an overview, an insight, and an entertaining treatment of the Minor Leagues, this is not the compendium to end all compendiums on the subject. This is not a cop-out, or an apology; it is a rationale.

According to the best-guess research provided by the Society for American Baseball Research (SABR) and its chief Minor League fact-checker, Bob Hoie, there have been an estimated 300–325 leagues, comprising some 3,000–3,500 different franchises residing in at least 1,414 different cities.

Hoie estimates that prior to 1910, maybe 20,000 players had toiled in the Minors, and from 1911 to 1990, another 130,000 players—an average of 1,600 new players per year—might have put on uniforms in the Bushes, bringing the total of Minor League players to some 150,000 (lower than some estimates but more logical than those who presume 250,000 athletes had laced up their cleats). This figure is tied to the belief that if there were an average of thirty leagues per year for the last 100 years—some stayed in business year after year, some went out of existence after a few weeks, and some new leagues emerged and disappeared, paring down to the eighteen leagues we have today—and an average of eight teams per league operated each year, there were some 24,000 clubs fielded over the period. Realizing that most players start from the bottom and work their way to the top, a low club might bring between twenty and twenty-five new players into the fold while an AAA or AA team might bring one new player, fifteen holdovers from last year and nine or ten players who were promoted from lower teams or demoted from higher teams. This works out to some twenty-three or twenty-four new players for every three teams (even considering that there were once AAA, AA, A, B, C, D, and Rookie Leagues with smaller rosters over the years than there are today), and a total between 150,000 and 160,000 players is a good guesstimate.

What all this means is that a compendium of Minor League history, the "Complete, Quintessential, All-encompassing Compendium of Minor League Baseball," would result in a work not unlike "The History of the World: The Whole Story." A Minor League treasury of that nature could run 10,000 pages or 100,000 pages, and aside from the marketing and printing difficulties involved, the hernia insurance needed, and the probability that very few copies of a book that size would be carried by bookstores or sold to fans, it might not prove as interesting or useful as the one we have put together here. That's not to say we are apologizing for the approach or scope of the present work. We are merely defining the parameters of this book, while not attempting to bite off more than we can chew or to provide the book to end all books on Minor League ball. What we have chosen to publish is a celebration—a good, entertaining, informative, easy-to-read look at the segment of professional baseball that retains the boyish fun that baseball was meant to be.

Why take this tack? To entertain, to inform, but also to pay homage to the institution known as Minor League baseball. After all, America has nearly always had a love affair with Minor League baseball. And what's not to love? Horatio Alger would have been hard-pressed to create fiction as rife with the rags-to-riches success that is daily reality in the Bushes. From the Ben MacDonalds who spend barely enough time in the Minors to get acquainted with teammates before becoming Major League heroes; to the Pete Coachmans and Rex Hudlers who spend six years or more on the Farm, aching for the chance to prove their worth in the Bigs; to the Jerry Reusses who give it one last shot in the lower level to convince the powers that be that they deserve one more chance in the Show; to the Glenn Davises, Benito Santiagos, and Mike LaCosses who spend rehab assignments giving "guest appearances" at Minor League ballparks. Add to this the George Brunets, Buzz Arletts, Jigger Statzes, and George Whitemans who spent decades on the Farm with little time to strut their stuff in the Show, and the Tony Lazerris, Joe DiMaggios, and Willie Mayses who performed with greatness at both levels—and you have one great saga of American perseverance and hard work designed to capture the pot of gold at the end of the rainbow. To some, that pot of gold might be the big bucks of the Big Leagues, and to countless others, it's the grand reward of being able to play this eternal kids' game—the wonder known as baseball—in front of adoring fans. That, the playing of the game, may be what the real field of dreams is. It is the *game* that survives and transcends. All else is incidental.

This approach to the subject includes some of the necessary facts and figures, though not so many (we hope) as to burden the reader; highlights, insights, and tidbits on great leagues, teams and players of the past, present, and future; remembrances of some of the great old ballparks of yesteryear; anecdotes designed to provide a tasty slice of Americana and some poignant entertainment; and enough historical information of the evolution of the game to satisfy the baseball purists, reviewers, and trivia freaks who love to dwell on each word and insertion as if the life of the baseball world depends on it.

So the author is not trying to be all things to all people. To repeat, he is presenting a *look.* A relatively thorough and diversified look using thumbnail overviews in some cases, but merely a *look,* our chosen look nonetheless, to celebrate the genre of Minor League ball.

Remember that baseball, for all its records, was not a great record-keeping concern at the Minor League level until only recently. So some leagues and players will receive somewhat less attention here than other leagues and players—there simply isn't as much accurate information available, and accuracy rather than bulk, as quality rather than quantity, is the goal. The Triple A Alliance (American Association and International League), for example, readily offered statistics since 1970, claiming that the leagues didn't compile histories (AA began in 1902, IL began in 1884) until recently. The Arizona Rookie League and Gulf Coast League take a low-key approach to public relations and purposely provide little or no information about their pasts (Arizona since 1988, Gulf Coast since 1964). The Mexican League provided its statistical catalogue, but it contradicts several other widely circulated and accepted versions of the same information. And Negro Leagues statistics are sketchy, inaccurate, and incomplete at best.

With all that in mind, and without being overly critical of what was included and what left out, the reader should find the enlightening anecdotes far more entertaining than page after page of statistics and rehashes of political in-fighting among league architects. That is part of the *look* that celebrates the sport.

The *look* includes the changing of the game on the Minor League level. Gone are franchises in Havana, Los Angeles, Hawaii, San Francisco, Newark (NJ), Seattle, Kansas City, Fort Worth, Milwaukee, Montreal, Duluth, Fargo, Kokomo, Joplin, Springfield (MA), and a thousand other villages, hamlets, cities, and metropolises that prospered and supported their hometown teams. In some cases, baseball passed by those places and in other cases, the Minor League fun and games were replaced with Major League big business. But gone from those places, too, perhaps, is the brotherhood and small-town spirit that was America of the 1920s, '30s and '40s, and gone is the small-town flavor and small-time atmosphere of the game.

Gone are the Piedmont League, Western League, Evangeline League, Ban Johnson League, Cotton States League, PONY League, Arizona Mining League (which had teams owned by brothels), and hundreds of other organized leagues that lasted from a week to decades and which lost out to evolution, shakeouts, redesigning of the sport, and the ravages of time and politics.

Where Minor League ball was once a nickel-and-dime operation in which anyone could own a team for little or no money down and operate same for gate receipts alone, most AAA and AA teams now go for millions of dollars per franchise and cost millions more to operate. Where local businesses and townsfolk used to take in the players and treat them to dinners and free suits and haircuts, now the chambers of commerce are responsible for helping to purchase blocks of tickets and pages of advertising in order to keep the Farm team down on their local farms.

And gone are the days when many cities aspired only to

Minor League franchises. Now, most look to the future, and Big League expansion or transfer.

Cities under consideration for a Major League award (from either expansion or an existing franchise move) include Denver, Buffalo, Phoenix, Louisville, Orlando, Miami, Tampa–St. Petersburg, Nashville, New Orleans, Santa Clara–San Jose, Sacramento, Vancouver, Washington, and Indianapolis. These cities think of themselves as Major League towns, deserving of Big League teams. Maybe that is so, and maybe it is neat and good and just that cities that have supported Minor League ball faithfully over the years get their turns at bat in the Bigs, but whenever a Minor League franchise leaves town and is replaced by a Major League operation, something is lost forever. What is irretrievably lost is that nostalgic link with the kinder and gentler and more naive and innocent days of America past. So while there is joy in Mudville for being named a Major League town, there is a sadness at the loss of a community friend, the "Nine" that had been a community brother and a part of the neighborhood lore.

Two aspects of this book which should be addressed involve inclusion of the Negro Leagues, and the title, in which the Minors are called "The Little Show."

Addressing the Negro Leagues . . . this book would be incomplete if it didn't include a chapter on the heroes, the stars, the teams and the regrettable circumstances surrounding the necessity of forming the Negro Leagues. It would be remiss not to explain that the Negro Leagues were considered "minor" only by the Major League baseball establishment, the biased press of the time, and the demeanor of an undeniably bigoted America of the period. This book is not a soapbox for deploring man's inhumanity to man in that era, since it is apparent from the perspective of talent—"Cool Papa" Bell, Satchel Paige, Judy Jones, Josh Gibson, Ray Dandridge, John Beckwith, Bullet Joe Rogan, Ghost Marcelle, Monte Irvin, Luke Easter, Hank Aaron et al.; the stadiums in which they played: Yankee Stadium, Ebbets Field, Comiskey Park, Crosley Field, Kansas City Municipal Stadium, among others; the organization behind the scenes and the caliber of play on the field—that the leagues were, in many ways, worthy of Major League distinction. But the fact is, to the baseball world of the day, in the media and the biases of America's citizenry of their era, the Negro Leagues were considered a separate Minor League. For those reasons, they are so treated here.

And, as this is a slice of Americana, Japan Leagues—both Major and Minor—Canadian Leagues, and European Leagues are excluded as they are vastly different versions of the art form we understand here as Minor League ball. So that can of worms, bucket of sushi, or box of Cracker Jacks will not be opened here.

The All-American Girl's Professional Baseball League (1942–54) merits only passing mention here, as none of its members ever climbed to the Major League level, and a full history of this circuit would open doors we have left closed to other leagues described above. So that gender-specific container of night-crawlers also remains unopened.

Finally, a word on calling the Minor Leagues "The Little Show." There is no slur intended here, just a reference to the baseball jargon of the day, in calling Major League ball "The Show," or "The Big Show." When compared to its big brother from economic, fan-supported, ticket-sales, degree of refined talent, or national recognition factors, Minor League baseball becomes the "little brother," or the "Little Show." But the way the game has evolved on the grassroots level of the Bushes, there's nothing very little about this show; it is big, and it is America. It is a link to a naive, young, easily excited and entertained, if a bit unsophisticated, America that knew how to have a good time without all the trappings and hype of the 1990s.

So enjoy the fun, the stories, and the brief histories. Our "Little Show" just may be Americana in its purest form, as between the white lines the game is the thing. It may be the most basic form of American entertainment and sport, one that can transcend all else that goes on in the world. From innings one through nine, within the friendly confines of the home park, nothing else matters but the final score. There's nothing more innocently pure than that.

As it was succinctly put by James Earl Jones, in the guise of author Terrence Mann in the film *Field of Dreams*, "The one constant through all the years . . . is baseball."

> America has rolled by like an army of steamrollers. It's been erased like a blackboard, rebuilt and erased again. But baseball has marked the time. This field, this game, is a part of our past. . . . It reminds us of all that once was good. And it could be again.

And, the history of this subject seems to prove that if you hold a Minor League baseball game, build a field of dreams for players past, present, and future, people will come. The players, the teams, and the cities they represent may all change, but the diamond . . . is forever.

Perpetuate the dream; keep America's ideal of sport pure and simple, and we keep the innocence of this nation alive.

Minor League Baseball keeps it pure and simple . . . and that is the reason for this book. Play ball . . . and go the distance.

Mike Blake

1
A BRIEF HISTORY OF MINOR LEAGUE BASEBALL

The drama and melodrama of sport, the paradigm of entertainment, with its fun, naivete, cold-hearted competition, big business and penny-ante operations, city slickers and country bumpkins, altruism and bigotry, success and failure, and the much-heralded thrill of victory and agony of defeat, are the flesh, the bone, and sinew of Minor League baseball.

The Minor Leagues are bus rides, dust, and signs in the outfield that say, "Hit Me and Win a $10 Suit." They are champagne wishes and caviar dreams, playing in dirty uniforms in the heat of summer, and going back to a non-air conditioned motel room.

The Minors are players like Johnny Berardino, now a television star, who survived on thirty-five cents a day in meal money, playing in Johnstown, Pennsylvania, just moments after a flood devastated the area in 1936.

Berardino recalls having to sleep in the nude after wetting down his motel room sheets with water in an effort to sleep during the suffocating summer nights of Dallas, Fort Worth, Oklahoma City, Beaumont, and Shreveport. And he and countless other ballplayers frequented air conditioned movie theaters—all-night ones if they could be found—to sleep "cool" for a quarter.

The Minors are more sophisticated now, and the players are more pampered, and more comfortable, but the dreams remain the same.

The Minors are the place where dreams start . . . and often end. Major League clubs see potential talents in a player and attempt to turn them into kinetic skills.

Such was the case with Morris H. "Moe" Solomon, nicknamed "The Rabbi of Swat." Solomon, property of the New York Giants, was a strong, stocky, five-foot-nine, 180-pound outfielder whom the Giants had hoped to groom into being "The Jewish Babe Ruth." Solomon responded by clouting 49 homers for Hutchinson of the Southwestern League in 1923.

He was called up to the Majors, but his booming bat was overshadowed by his ineptitude as a fielder, and, as designated hitters had not yet been invented, and pinch hitters were a dime-a-dozen, Solomon was exiled back to the Minors where he continued to pound homeruns for appreciative crowds in America's heartland.

Sometimes the Minors are the place where athletes on their way down make a last stop or two before they are entirely out of baseball. Sometimes they reach back for one more touch of glory.

In the 1919 Little World Series play-offs, former Major League pitcher Don "Rusty" Griner, who went 28–55 in the Bigs, pitched for St. Paul of the American Association against the Vernon, California, entry of the PCL. Throwing a curve, a "mudball," and a spitter, Griner completed three games without allowing an earned run, to vanquish Vernon.

The Minors are a place where boys are plucked from schools and farms and odd jobs, to play a boy's game for pay and fun and glory.

So it was with Freddy Leach, a railroad telegrapher who started with community teams in the Ozarks, circa 1920.

In 1922, he was seen by a baseball man who convinced him to try the Minors. Playing in the Missouri Valley league, Leach led the loop at .383. He finished the season with Rochester in the International League, and by 1923 was playing Big League ball with the Philadelphia Phillies. He bounced around, up, and down with several clubs for nine years, but the point was . . . he pursued his dream and it was the Minors that got him started.

And the Minors are the place where rewards are of a more "homey" nature, thanks to great community support.

The San Antonio Bronchos won the Texas League championship in 1908, and the community's city fathers decided to congratulate the players for bringing good fortune, good business, and good press to their town. They arranged to throw the champs a banquet at 410 Matamoros Street, the Alamo City's plushiest and most glamorous house of ill repute. In the dining room, the players were treated to a feast. After dinner, the players discovered that under each plate was a crisp, new $100 bill—a lot of money in those days. The players were told that the bills could be kept, or could be used "upstairs" as a key to a night of revelry with the lady of their choice. Legend has it that not a single player left the "house" with his $100 bill.

Similarly, the community of Klamath Falls, Oregon, is said to have rewarded its top homerun hitters of the '40s and '50s with paid-for romps with ladies of the evening. This merit system may have backfired, as the lucky players usually seemed to "play tired" the next day.

And of course, there was once an entire league, The Arizona Mining League, owned by brothels in the early part of this century.

That all seems to beat the oilman owner of the old Tulsa franchise, who celebrated his men hitting home runs by handing them dollar bills as they entered the dugout following a tour of the bases.

Sometimes the Minors are the place where older, experienced players are sent to find themselves, or the talent they once had that now is lost.

Such was the case with Hall-of-Fame shortstop Walter "Rabbit" Maranville.

Maranville was a star at every level, a steady, if not prodigious hitter, and an acrobatic, sure-handed fielder with lightning speed on the bases. But by 1926, his drinking had gotten the best of him and he had most definitely lost himself. The Brooklyn Dodgers dumped him in '26, and the St. Louis Cardinals picked him up and sent him to Rochester of the International League to get his drinking under control. The story ends happily as Maranville sobered up and was back in the Bigs in 1928, leading the Cardinals in the World Series.

Players are not born in the Minor Leagues; they are made there. Through coaching and practice, learning fundamentals and good work habits, and receiving game experience, a young athlete is fine-tuned and polished into a Major League talent.

Among the nuances taught to cocky, spirited ballplayers is hustle. Case in point: Enos "Country" Slaughter was known throughout his career as the original "Charlie Hustle," long before Pete Rose was born. It was Slaughter's mad dash from first base to home on a hit by Harry Walker that won the 1946 World Series for the St. Louis Cardinals.

But his hustle ethic was learned in the Minor Leagues.

In 1936, while being groomed by the Columbus (Georgia) Redbirds of the Sally League, Slaughter failed to run out a ground ball to short. As he returned to the dugout following the out at first, his manager, Eddie Dyer, chewed him up one side and down the other, dressing down the twenty-year-old in front of his teammates. From that point on, Slaughter vowed never again to walk on a ballfield and to always run everything out as if it were his last hit. His style of running to first base on every walk was copied and popularized by Pete Rose—who saw Slaughter run . . . and like the idea—some fifteen years after Slaughter had retired.

That vow went unbroken until his retirement from the Majors in 1959.

Often, the Minors are the first stop on the way up, in the days before fame, and the last stop on the way down before anonymity returns. And once in a while, it is a stop in the middle and a place to regain the touch and the limelight.

Johnny Lindell started it all as a crafty right-handed pitcher with Newark, the Yankees' top Farm club, in the International League, fashioning a 23–4 mark in 1941 while relying on a knuckleball and a curve.

Called up to New York, Lindell made the team but Yankee manager Joe McCarthy, a fastball devotee, decided Lindell didn't have a Major League fastball and moved him to the outfield—McCarthy liked his hustle, his bat, and his glove.

Lindell finished his pitching career with New York at 2–1 with a 3.76 ERA, and then it was on to the outfield.

Lindell spent ten years with the Yankees—twice led the league in triples and twice hit .300—from 1941 to 1950 and was rock steady in pinstripes. The six-foot-four, 217-pound athlete then was peddled to the Cardinals as his career looked to be on the downturn.

Hitting only .186, he was banished to the Minors, and the Hollywood Stars of the PCL. Manager Fred Haney returned Lindell to the mound, where in 1952 he responded by going a remarkable 24–9, earning MVP honors at the age of thirty-six. He had won another chance in the Majors.

His return in 1953 was a feat in itself, pitching in the Majors eleven years after last pitching in the Majors in 1942. His record of 6–17 got him booted from the Bigs for a final time, but his battle to get there, chronicled in the Minors, is a Rockylike struggle so typical of the Minors.

Sometimes the Minors provide a starting point for those who later on and in other places happen to be in the right place at the right time.

Worthy of note, in that regard, is the story of pitcher Steve Gromek. Gromek, a right-handed middle reliever for

the Cleveland Indians and Detroit Tigers in the 1940s and
'50s, was elevated to the Bigs after going 14–2 in the Michigan State League in 1941. A good season but not spectacular; nor was his career MLB mark of 123–108. What
makes the fastball, knuckleball, changeup pitcher memorable is that while playing for the Indians, Gromek started
and completed a 2–1 victory in the fourth game of the 1948
World Series. When teammate Larry Doby, the first black
in the American League, homered to win the game,
Gromek hugged him openly, creating a foundation for
successful and accepted integration of the sport.

Sometimes the Minors provide a platform for glory for
an athlete who reaches the zenith of his competence and
can't perform at a higher level.

Alan "Inky" Strange was a sure-gloved shortstop, the
Ozzie Smith of his day. In the Minors, he could hit like Ted
Williams (Inky blasted fifty-five doubles for Seattle in
1939, and had four years over .300), but in the Majors, he
hit more like Esther Williams (Strange finished at .223
with thirty-nine doubles, seven triples and one homer in
947 at bats with the St. Louis Cardinals and St. Louis
Browns.)—or, if you're of a more recent generation: he hit
like Reggie Jackson in the Minors and Janet Jackson in
the Majors.

Strange simply couldn't hit a curve ball. He got fastballs
in the Minors and curves in the Bigs, and once the pitchers
upstairs found he couldn't handle the bender, he never saw
heat.

And the Minor Leagues are the stage on which an after-
hours romp of a sexual nature resulted in a long winning
streak.

A former Texas League publicist who requests anonymity to protect the guilty, reported that several Texas
League ballplayers engaged in a midnight orgy in a home
team clubhouse, from shower to jacuzzi to tape room to
trainer's table. Following the free-love-for-all, a coed baseball game took place on the diamond. One of the women,

wearing perfume and nothing else, donned the manager's uniform for this impromptu ballgame.

The following day, the manager put on his sweet-smelling uniform and wondered what kind of flowery soap the clubhouse man had used. When the home team won, breaking a long losing streak, the manager kept the uniform unwashed and wore it again the next day. The winning streak reached twelve games and when it was finally over, the manager asked the bewildered clubhouse guy to use that "flower soap" on the uniforms again so they could start another streak. If only he had known, that Texas League team might have won a championship.

Often, the Minors are the theater of the absurd, where amazing displays of creative temper go forever into history.

On May 13, 1980, at Durham Athletic Park, a game between the hometown Bulls and the visiting, slumping Winston-Salem Red Sox (losers of 13 of its last 17) began as had countless others. The 2,011 fans in attendance could not guess what was to occur, when the game entered the top of the eighth with Durham leading 5–3.

With two outs, homeplate umpire Bob Serino called a close pitch for strike two on Winston-Salem's hitter, Juan Pautt. Without warning, Winston-Salem manager, Buddy Hunter, stationed in the third base coaching box, suddenly exploded in one of the most colorful cases of showing up an umpire in baseball history.

Hunter, aware that Serino had taken away a Red Sox home run the night before, with a controversial call—a ball that sounded and appeared to have hit a wooden addition to the metal barrier on the rightfield fence, over the home run line was incorrectly ruled in play by Serino—decided to get the umpire's goat. Knowing full well that questioning a ball-strike call would get him immediately thumbed from the game, Hunter decided to put on a show and get thrown out for something glorious. It turned out to be hysterical and historical.

First Hunter turned his hat backwards, went nose-to-nose with Serino and called him everything in the book. Then he ran to his own dugout, grabbed a baseball and sprinted to right field—spot of the blown-call "home run"—and fired the ball against the fence, directly on the spot the "home run" had appeared to hit.

Hunter then pantomimed a flip of a coin. After catching the imaginary coin and flipping it onto the back of his hand, Hunter danced around and waved his right hand in a circle to indicate that he had just called a homerun.

Then Hunter sprinted toward the infield and slid into first base, he stood up and signaled himself safe . . . then out. Then he sat on the bag and took off both baseball shoes. He took an imaginary bite out of the toe of one shoe, tossed it in the direction of Serino and pretended to blow him up with the "shoe-grenade" explosion.

Then he bit the "pin" off the toe of his other shoe and "blew up" base umpire Bob Duncan.

He left the field to a standing ovation . . . from opposing fans.

The tirade worked as Hunter's team won 27 of its next 41 games.

Sometimes the Minors are merely a stage on which to perform the same magic that players will perform at higher levels wherever they go, displaying talent that will surely be remembered.

Case in point is Joe DiMaggio, the Yankee Clipper. Joltin' Joe, graceful and classy in every uniform he ever donned, demolished Pacific Coast League pitching in 1933 as he went on a tear that saw him hit safely in sixty-one consecutive games—a PCL record and second-longest streak ever in the Minor Leagues—on his stop with the San Francisco Seals. Eight years and 3,000 miles later, Joe D. hit safely for a Major League record fifty-seven consecutive games for the New York Yankees, on his way to the Hall of Fame.

And sometimes the Minors provide a stage for the competitive spirit that will not die regardless of the circumstances.

In 1946, eight years after a pistol accidentally discharged severing the femoral artery of Monty Stratton's right knee, necessitating the amputation of his leg, Stratton was signed to pitch in the East Texas League. The former Major Leaguer responded with an 18–8 mark.

The Minors may also be small bonuses given to players for their services, unlike the millions being thrown to Major League players.

This case is exemplified by Satchel Paige. In 1926, Paige was hurling for the Chattanooga Black Lookouts in the Negro Leagues. For a salary of fifty dollars a month, Paige honed his fastball to such a flash that opposing hitters donned helmets to protect them from errant tosses. Control posed little problem for Paige, however, as he frequently told his fielders to sit down, declaring he would strike out the side . . . which he did. As to his bonus, well, when the New Orleans Pelicans offered Paige an ancient, dented jalopy for him to jump teams, he took the car and ran . . . to one of the estimated 250 teams for which he pitched during his long career.

And long ago, the Minors were the show that was re-created by studio announcers.

Stu Nahan, a television and radio broadcaster in Los Angeles, once did the re-creations for Pacific Coast League road games. He would get the results via Western Union, announce the games "live," using a wooden stick against a board to simulate the crack of the bat, and sound effects to suggest a cheering crowd. When a train went by the studio, Nahan announced it had stopped outside the ballpark bringing late-coming fans to the game. When Western Union suffered a communications breakdown, Nahan would ad lib, sometimes having hitters foul off fifteen or twenty pitches or make the manager and catcher go to the mound to talk to the pitcher, or announce that the pitcher had thrown fifteen pickoff attempts to first to keep the runner close. When the information started to flow again, Nahan would have to breeze through some nine or ten hitters who had come and gone since the ad libbing started.

On one memorable occasion, a cold night in the studio, Nahan revealed he had too much coffee to drink and it went right through him. With nowhere to go and no time to leave, Nahan heeded nature's call by relieving himself in a handy bucket in the cramped two-man studio. The sound of the liquid pelting the tin bucket was too loud to go unnoticed, so Nahan invented a pouring rain storm assaulting the stadium, and as far as the listeners knew, it was raining in San Francisco where the hometown team was playing the Seals.

And the Minors are the elements . . . for real.

California Angels broadcaster Al Conin remembered announcing games for the Pacific Coast League's Hawaii Islanders, in Honolulu's Aloha Stadium.

According to Conin, the prevailing winds blew from right field to left field and affected the ballgame as well as the people who listened to the games on radio. A severe wind shift could cause Island damage and send balls flying into the seats, so Conin had to continually give wind updates as the game progressed.

Another elements story dealt with Vancouver, an often rainy site. Mounties groundskeeper Rudd Haar often had the job of drying out the drenched sod before gametime, and he devised a way of tossing flammable fluid on top of the rain-soaked field, then setting it ablaze with a flame thrower. Somehow, he always dried the field and never scorched it. Home and opposing players alike praised the man for his infields.

The Minors are also players with time on their hands and fun in their hearts.

Another Hawaii story gives us Bobby Mitchell, who was at first base. He surreptitiously threw a fish in the first base coaches box between innings, then took out a fishing rod and trolled the infield until he "caught" his fish. He then returned it to the clubhouse where he hid it in the team's air conditioning ducts until the smell gave it away . . . and screamed for fumigation.

Or maybe the Minors are tactics . . . or even cheating . . .

honed in the Minors until the acts are refined enough to achieve success on the Major League level.

George Hildebrand, an outfielder who played only eleven games in The Show, is credited with being the Johnny Appleseed of saliva, spreading the invention of the spitball throughout the Minors.

As legend tells it, Hildebrand was warming up pitcher Frank Corridon, while both were playing for Providence in the Eastern League in 1902. Hildebrand watched the ball slow down and dip after Corridon licked the tips of his fingers prior to each pitch. At this point, there was no rule against foreign substances, and licking fingers or the ball was legal . . . it just wasn't done.

Hildebrand experimented with different amounts of liquid and studied how the ball dipped and darted. He soon showed Corridon how to master the pitch, and when Hildy traveled on to Sacramento in the Pacific Coast League in 1903, he taught the new pitch to Elmer Stricklett, who used it to win eleven straight games.

Stricklett, in turn, taught the pitch to his roommate Ed Walsh, when the two were rookies for the Chicago White Sox in 1904. Walsh learned it and won 195 games en route to the Hall of Fame. Walsh's success spread the spitter like wildfire until its banishment from the game sixteen years later.

Other Minor League "cheaters" who earned legitimate success in the Bigs include Earl Weaver, the venerable manager for the Baltimore Orioles, who learned the value of corking a bat.

Weaver was in New Orleans, a Double-A club, in 1954, and he hit six homers in a single month using a bat that had been bored out, filled with cork, topped off with wood putty, sanded, and stained with pine tar.

And Graig Nettles, the Golden Glove Yankee third baseman who was once caught using a bat filled with superballs, recalls a Minor League teammate who filled his hollowed-out bat with a vial of mercury, causing a centrifugal force strong enough to help propel a hit ball into the stratosphere.

Though neither Weaver nor Nettles' teammates made it to The Show, it is doubtless that their doctoring techniques survived and have found their way up the baseball ladder from the Minors to the Bigs.

And the Minor Leagues are humanitarianism.

During the 1908 Texas League season, members of the third-place Houston Buffaloes discovered a baby boy who had been abandoned on the team train. The ballplayers— particularly star third baseman Roy Akin—took it upon themselves to care for the infant. They started a fund for the child, passed the hat among themselves and among the fans during ballgames and raised money to support him. Before the end of the season, Akin adopted the child and raised him as his own.

All of these stories and countless others are what Minor League baseball is all about. And the story of the genre itself is every bit as exciting and improbable and poignant as the stories above and the tales to follow. The story may live on forever, but in its beginnings, one wondered if it would endure.

The beginning? As near as we can tell, the first league usually considered the initial Minor League was the International Association in 1877.

Others have suggested that there can't be a Minor League until there is a Major League, and the first Major League, the National League of Professional Baseball Clubs, was created in 1876.

However, the operative term is *league.* Previous groups of teams hardly constituted leagues though they were certainly "minor." And the co-op known as the International Association was so devoid of structure that it is hard by today's standards to call it a "league."

There were, in 1877, some fifty teams operating outside the auspices of the National League, but none was organized to the extent the National League was—an overseen business that tied up major markets and that had set up guidelines, a constitution, for its member clubs to follow.

That left only the International Association, the League Alliance, and the New England League as loosely described "leagues" that played a more or less set schedule of games among teams that adhered to the basic rules set up by league governors.

As for the first, it appears that the International Association, founded by the inventor of the curve ball, Arthur "Candy" Cummings, has that honor. For the sake of history, the league was organized on February 20, 1877, in Pittsburgh, Pennsylvania, and the first league-sanctioned game was played on April 26 at Lynn, Massachusetts, with the Manchester, New Hampshire, team (no nickname) defeating the Lynn Live Oaks, 14–3. The league championship was won by the London, Ontario, Tecumsehs, who posted a 14-wins, 4-losses, and 2-ties record to finish ahead of the second-place Pittsburgh Alleghenys by one-and-one-half games.

The International Association was a weekend warrior league in that it played games only on Saturday and Sunday—players had full-time jobs during the week—yet it issued a direct challenge to the National League for its professional ballplaying superiority and autonomy.

The Association reorganized in year number two as a ten-team union, and a short, twenty-game schedule was set, with Buffalo winning the title. Buffalo, by the way, played an impressive total of 116 games during the year, which included more than eighty barnstorming appearances and seventeen games against the Major League teams from the National League, against whom it won ten.

The International Association made it to 1879, when four surviving teams, Manchester, Pittsburgh, Rochester, and Springfield, joined the National Association (established in 1878) to form a twelve-team league.

A competing league that first year was the League Alliance, which also ran for two seasons. It boasted thirteen teams the first year, including teams based in Brooklyn, Buffalo, Indianapolis, Memphis, Minneapolis, Philadel-

phia, Providence, St. Paul, and Troy. By year two, the loop
was down to six teams.

The biggest ploy used by the Alliance was its kowtowing
to the National League. Alliance governors made it clear
that the National League was the only major league, that
the Alliance was not in competition with them and that the
National League had control over any and all players. Still,
this peaceful coexistence didn't help the loop survive.

The third league in operation in 1877 was the New England League, which ran, with brief periods of nonopera-
tion, until 1949. The league probably began as an
outgrowth of semiprofessional and amateur teams that
proliferated on the North Atlantic coast soon after the end
of the Civil War.

The New England League provided a happy medium be-
tween the subserviency to the National League of the
League Alliance and the thorn-in-the-side approach of the
International Association.

The first circumscribed league was probably the Northwestern League, which was established in 1879 but which
didn't really take hold until 1882. This creation led to an
immediate fear of pirating—the loss of its players and contracts to competing teams and leagues. Turning to the
existing National League for help, the TriPartite Agreement was penned, recognizing each club's players, forbid-
ding stealing or raiding of said players, setting territorial
rights, and establishing an arbitration system to settle dis-
putes.

The Northwestern League is also directly responsible for
strengthening the baseball industry as it eventually developed into the revered Western League, from which both
the original American Association and then the American
League were hatched.

Another important early league (1881) was the Eastern
Championship Association, which positioned three teams
in New York City and three others in major markets:
Brooklyn, Philadelphia, and Washington, DC. This, too,
lasted for only two seasons, but several of its teams went

on to join the Inter-State League in 1882 and survived until 1954.

The controversial and long-standing reserve clause was set up in 1887, to allow teams to "protect" (read that "imprison") their players from all leagues other than the National League and the American Association, and five years later, the National Agreement—a baseball constitution that was set up in 1885 and which was changed to reflect the times, much as the United States Constitution has been amended twenty-six times in 215 years—was modified to allow for Major League drafting and purchase of Minor League players.

Becoming "Organized Baseball," the Minor Leagues sought to run a money-making business while offering entertainment for fans and a workplace for athletes. The creation of reserve-clause restrictions may seem barbaric, unfair, and unconstitutional—and it can be successfully argued that they are—but the reserve clause might have been a necessary evil established to protect the Minor Leagues from outside competition while giving the players a chance to progress as they honed their skills. The enforcing of the contract gave the Minors the right to spend time and money developing a player within the system and reap the benefit from a future sale of the raw athlete they polished into a finished Major League talent. Cold? Yes. Materialistic? Of course. Capitalistic? Indeed. Unconstitutionally depriving a human being of his liberty and pursuit of happiness? Arguably so. Necessary at the time for the survival of the sport? Probably, just as the tearing down of the reserve clause became necessary in the 1970s, in keeping with the evolution of the sport and the sensitivity to human rights, probably decades after the clause should have been revoked. The leagues, Major and Minor, were healthy enough to withstand any outside raiding or competition as the monopoly or oligopoly pretty much had the market cornered following the Major League movement west in 1958, and its expansion in 1961 and 1962—those events single-handedly derailed the Pacific

Coast League's dream of becoming a Major League (see Chapter 5) and took out potential competitors in a proposed "Global League."

The National League was clearly in control by 1883, with the deaths of its Minor League tormentors, but the American Association, formed in 1882, was gaining steam as a Major League, and it outmarketed the older loop by charging only twenty-five cents per ticket, rather than the fifty-cent seat in the NL, and by playing games on Sundays, with liquor and beer available at the ballpark.

The National League declared war, began pirating players from the A.A., and staged a disinformation campaign, calling the fledgling Association the "Beer and Liquor Circuit."

With this, the Northwestern League, disbanded in 1879, came back to life, and to protect itself, proposed a nonraiding ordinance during a three-party meeting between the warring American Association and National League. Thus, "The Harmony Conference" established a relationship between the two Major Leagues and a Minor League counterpart, that is, in part, adhered to today.

In the antitrust atmosphere of the time—Sherman Anti-Trust Act of 1890—the reserve clause was under scrutiny. The creation of the draft of Minor League players by Major League clubs in 1892 helped diffuse the attack on Organized Baseball from trustbusters, and baseball operated while looking over its shoulder until freed from antitrust laws via 1922 legislation.

Until then, the Minor Leagues used the reserve clause, sales to other teams, and the draft setup to move talent around—up and down as mandated by the market—to create some amount of stability and profitability. Without it, it is doubtful that the Minor League game would have continued to exist as we know it . . . and that would have adversely affected the Major League game by denying it its proving ground on the Farm.

Thanks, in part, to Cap Anson, a star player and manager who echoed the prejudiced sentiments of America during the 1800s and the first part of the twentieth century, baseball apartheid was introduced. Anson refused to let his Major League Chicago White Stockings play Toledo of the Northwestern League in an exhibition game if Toledo played its black catcher Moses Fleetwood Walker. This 1883 game set the tone, and within four years an unofficial "color line" had been established.

On July 14, 1887, the International League instituted a nonintegration "gentlemen's agreement," effectively banning Walker, a solid and popular player, and all other blacks from playing Minor League and Major League ball with and against whites for sixty years.

At the time, there were an estimated sixty blacks playing Minor League ball, and after Bill Galloway played for Woodstock in the Canadian League in 1899, there were no blacks to play officially in the Bushes until Jackie Robinson in 1946. The exceptions were truly isolated cases of those who "sneaked" in. These included Jim Claxton, who was passed off as an Indian and who pitched two games for Oakland in the Pacific Coast League in 1916, and some Latin players who were part black, as in the case of Ramon Herrera, who played Negro League ball and eventually played for the Boston Red Sox in 1925–1926; ironic, because the Red Sox were the last Major League team to integrate—with Pumpsie Green in 1959.

The last two decades of the 1800s saw baseball come and go at a furious pace in cities around the nation.

The Eastern League, established in 1884 as a ten-team loop, fell to six teams and became the New York League, which in turn merged with the Canadian League in 1886 to form an eight-team circuit that was renamed the International League in 1887. This league fluctuated from ten teams to eight and saw cities enter and leave on a yearly basis. The International League, however, endured, and it survives today as the oldest Minor League in terms of continuous operation.

The IL had a tough go of it when a third Major League, the Players League, was formed in 1890 to make a one-year run before it disintegrated. But before it went, it lured away the franchise in Buffalo, while the American Association, in an effort to grab off major markets before its competitor did, took Rochester, Syracuse, and Toledo. With only six teams in operation, the IL withstood the bloodletting and in 1891 regained the Buffalo and Rochester teams and changed its name back to the Eastern League, a name it kept for twenty years.

The East Coast did not have a monopoly on Minor League ball during this period. In fact, baseball and the Minor Leagues mushroomed around the country at a prolific rate.

In the South, the Southern League was formed in 1885, covering all areas of the Civil War Confederacy.

Texas was also represented with the Texas League, established in 1888.

On the West Coast, the California League and California State League did battle in the mid-1880s, and each league placed three teams in San Francisco, much as all existing East Coast leagues saturated New York City.

The Northwestern League came back to life as the Western Association in 1888, covering the Midwest.

Other leagues that came and went included: Iron and Oil League (1884); Connecticut State League (1884); Northeastern Connecticut State League (1885); Virginia League (1885); Three-I League—Illinois-Indiana-Iowa (1886); Pennsylvania State League (1886); Central Pennsylvania League (1887); Kansas State League (1887); Hudson River League (1887); Central Atlantic League (1888); Central Inter-State League (1888); Central League (1889); Tri-State League—Ohio-Indiana-West Virginia (1889); Atlantic Association (1889); Eastern Inter-State League (1890); Central New Jersey League (1890); Michigan State League (1890); Keystone League (1891); Montana League (1891); Nebraska State League (1892); Pacific Northwest League (1892); Rhode Island League (1893); Naugatuck Valley League (1894); Puget Sound League (1895); a new Iron and Oil League (1895); Northwestern League—

Washington and British Columbia (1895); Atlantic League (1896); Pacific Interstate League (1896); Canadian League (1899); Utah (Intermountain) League (1901); Connecticut League (1901); as well as forty more that dotted the nation. Many leagues went unrecorded or had records lost through the years, so there is no way of finding out exactly how many popped up and out during those times.

At the end of the century, the National League had won the Major League war, and had dispatched the American Association and the Players League. The NL had become a twelve-team league, and a shaking out was required. About this time, the Northwestern League had evolved into the Western League, with teams in Detroit, Grand Rapids, Indianapolis, Kansas City, Milwaukee, Minneapolis, Sioux City and Toledo. The Western League moved to consolidate its Eastern franchises, began to compete successfully with the NL, and, under the guidance of early baseball architect Ban Johnson, began to directly challenge the monopoly of the surviving National League when it was accepted as a Major League (the American League) in 1900, leaving a hole in the Minor Leagues for Midwest representation . . . a hole that was filled by the founding of the new American Association.

By 1903, the American League and National League were at peace, and they decided to control the Minor Leagues in a peaceful fashion, using the Minors' governing body, the National Association of Professional Baseball Leagues, to accomplish the task.

The National Association was formed in 1901 following a meeting between the heads of seven different leagues: Pat Powers of the Eastern League; Tom Hickey of the Western League; John Farrell of the New York State League; Michael Saxton of the Three-I League; William Meyer, Jr., of the Western Association; W. H. Lucas of the Pacific Northwest League, and T. H. Murnane of the New England League. Proxies of compliance were also sent by representatives of the California League, the Connecticut

League, the North Carolina League, and the Southern Association.

This meeting, held in Chicago on September 5, marked the first time the Minor Leagues had joined together to accomplish anything and it set guidelines that were universally adopted.

The most important edicts of that day were the establishment of league classifications A, B, C, and D, based on talent level to ensure parity of competition; this talent level later was misused and abused to reflect market size and other vagaries rather than competition of athletes.

Roster size and salary levels were also determined, and fine schedules and adoption of a Major League-like reserve clause restricting player movement were initiated.

This new brotherhood spurred on additions to the Association: the restructured Texas League, Cotton States League, Iowa-South Dakota League, Missouri Valley League, Northern League, and Pennsylvania League.

A new prosperity hit the Minor Leagues, a run of good health that took it from the turn-of-the-century to World War I. New circuits included: The Cotton States League (1902), Northern League (1902), Central League (1903), the KITTY League—Kentucky-Illinois-Tennessee— (1903), Delta League (1904), Canadian League (1905), Copper Country–Soo League (1905), Northwestern League (1905); Wisconsin State League (1905), Virginia League (1906), Jobber's League (1909), Central California League (1910), Central New York League (1910), MINK League— Missouri-Iowa-Nebraska-Kansas (1910), Southeastern League (1910), Mountain States League (1911), California League (1913), and Eastern Michigan Border League (1913)—which were a few among many that sprung up to the delight of new fans.

As new forms of entertainment also sprung up about 1917, and the nation was plunged into World War I, interest in Minor League baseball waned. Where, in 1914, forty-two leagues were prospering, by 1917 only twenty leagues began the season and only a dozen made it through the year.

The 1918 season was just as bad, with only nine leagues beginning the season. Wartime travel restrictions and poor attendance added up to only one league, the International League, completing its season.

The National Agreement expired in 1919, and while the cat was away, the mice played—fourteen teams made the Minor League trip that year, without bullying from the Major Leagues, and soon baseball began to get healthy.

What the 1919 "Black Sox" scandal took away in 1920 Babe Ruth single-handedly brought back in 1921, and with the criminal degradation forgotten, baseball rallied. A new National Agreement was in force in 1921, and all was right with the baseball world. By 1925, twenty-five Minor Leagues were operating and they all made it through the season.

New leagues included: the Pacific Coast International League (1919), Piedmont League (1920), West Texas League (1920), Southwest League (1921), Western International League (1922), and the Middle Atlantic League (1925).

And in 1920, another league was born, the Negro National League, which was drawn and conceived by pitching great Rube Foster and which lasted, in various forms, until 1963.

Another reason for the health of Minor League baseball during this era was the man who reshaped baseball in The Show and the Little Show, Branch Rickey.

Rickey, of course, is credited with breaking the color barrier by bringing Jackie Robinson to the International League and then to the National League in the late 1940s. He was also a proponent of Major League expansion in 1960, both of which served to save the sport.

But more than this, he was responsible for the development of Farm systems as a means of developing players for Major League teams.

As general manager of the St. Louis Cardinals in the

'20s, Rickey saw the relationship between Major League and Minor League teams as much too informal. A Minor League club usually bore no allegiance to a Big League team and usually sold players to the highest bidder, if they cared to let a player go at all. Either that, or a player was drafted off their roster and they had little way to protect their own interests.

Rickey decided that the best way to control the relationship and the flow and development of young players was by ownership, so he began scouting entire leagues as most teams scouted players. He began a takeover campaign so that by 1928, his Cardinals owned seven Minor League teams. Using this ownership, Rickey saw to it that valuable players either ended up wearing Cardinal uniforms or were sold to other teams for a healthy profit.

Rickey's takeover mode bordered on the obsessive, and by 1940 the Cardinals owned thirty-two Minor League teams and had working agreements with eight additional teams—a total of 600 players at the Cards' disposal.

This situation got to be farcical, as in the Three-I League in 1938, the Cardinals owned the Danville club and also had a working agreement with at least one other team, Springfield, leading to a conflict of interest.

He openly decreed that the Minor League teams were being used strictly as a proving ground for his Cardinals, and he didn't mind exploiting his own teams to build a strong contender in St. Louis. At the time, though, the cash infusion by the Cards was necessary to the growth and development of the Minor League system.

Soon, other teams caught on and began doing the same, though on smaller scales. About the only competition Rickey and the Cardinals faced in those formative years was from George Weiss and the New York Yankees.

Weiss began formation of the Yankee Minor League system when he began operating the Newark Bears of the International League in 1931. He immediately sold Yankee owner Jacob Ruppert and general manager Ed Barrow on the virtues of a Minor League system. By the mid-

1930s, Weiss had developed arguably the most formidable Minor League system in baseball, with the Yanks either owning outright or working exclusively with fifteen teams from Class D to Double A. All their teams, it seemed, won pennant after pennant while Weiss carefully brought players up to help the Yankees win pennant after pennant. He didn't pillage his Minor League teams, he cultivated them. He even achieved a Minor League coup when his International League Newark Bears met his American Association Kansas City Blues in the Double-A championships, the Junior World Series, in 1938.

Thanks largely to the successes of Rickey and Weiss, Major League teams began heavily subsidizing their Minor League cousins, and the fortunes of the system rose spectacularly.

But every rise has a fall, and baseball was no exception. The Great Depression that ravaged America threatened to destroy Minor League baseball as well. While twenty-five solid leagues started the 1929 season, by 1931 the number was down to sixteen.

By 1932, Judge William Bramham, president of the Piedmont League, was named president of the National Association, and with the help of Branch Rickey, St. Louis Cardinals general manager, and Billy Evans, Cleveland Indians general manager, the men instituted reforms designed to prune away the weak and replace them with the strong. Bramham demanded guaranty deposits from franchise owners—knowing that underfinanced operations are destined to fail, he wanted only well-heeled ownerships. Bramham established the promotional aspect of the game, developing public relations departments and offering his promotional expertise to all media representatives and league members who wished to make use of this vital information.

Among the promotions Bramham initiated was night baseball, designed to increase attendance. The first night game in Organized Baseball history was played in the

Western League on April 29, 1930, at Independence, Kansas, as Muskogee defeated Independence 13–3.

And he approved the so-called Shaughnessy play-off plan for the International League in the early '30s, a plan named after Frank Shaughnessy, general manager of the Montreal Royals, who suggested a format in which the top four teams make the play-offs, thus keeping interest and attendance higher throughout the season.

His devices worked, and by 1940, there were forty-three leagues playing throughout the Minor Leagues.

New leagues formed during this era included the Evangeline League (1934), Penn State Association (1934), Alabama-Florida League (1936), Coastal Plain League (1937), North Carolina State League (1937), West Texas-New Mexico League (1937), Mountain State League (1938), Pioneer League (1939), the PONY League—Pennsylvania-Ontario-New York (1939), and Tar Heel League (1939).

Then the nation turned its attentions to the wars in Europe and the Pacific and diversions were slightly different in the States.

In 1942, begun, partially as a wartime diversion, the curiosity known as the All-American Girl's Baseball League was established. As stated earlier, it is arguable whether or not this is or was considered a Minor League. With all due respect to the female athletes who participated, the press, nevertheless, and most Americans of the era—from 1942 to 1954—seemed to give this circuit less than Minor League status, and few baseball fans of the day took the league seriously. One star of the league, Helen Callahan St. Aubin, mother of Montreal Expo and Houston Astro infielder Casey Candaele—she taught him the game—stole 354 bases in 388 games, and many other players provided thrills on the field by displaying extraordinary talent. Suffice it to say, for this treatment, that the league existed and produced some remarkable athletes and contests; and if a similar offspring of the loop were around today, it would most certainly be viewed with more respect and increased press coverage, perhaps opening the door to breaking gender barriers on professional diamonds around the nation.

Also in 1942, Minor League teams relished the opportunity to play their Major League parents on the Bush diamonds that dotted small towns across America. As had been the practice for many years, Big League clubs regularly scheduled exhibitions with their poor relations as a means of drawing some big crowds to help the Minor League franchises pick up some cash, while aiding the Big club in evaluating Farm talent.

One such exhibition nearly didn't come off, but when it did, it showed the grit and determination that are part and parcel of the Minor League fabric. The 1942 New York Yankees were reigning World Champions, with a fearsome pinstriped lineup that consisted of Joe DiMaggio, Bill Dickey, Tommy Henrich, Charlie "King Kong" Keller, Phil Rizzuto, Joe Gordon, George Selkirk, Frankie Crosetti, Red Rolfe, Red Ruffing, Lefty Gomez, Johnny Murphy, et al. And they had set up a mid-season game with the Amsterdam (New York) Rugmakers, a Class C affiliate in the Canadian-American League.

Amsterdam had just captured its third Can-Am crown in five years and seemed well suited to give the Bronx Bombers a good show . . . until fire struck. Just one week before the much-anticipated show and showdown, Amsterdam's Mohawk Mills Park, on the banks of the Mohawk River, had fallen victim to an arsonist, and the field was nothing but ashes. The game would have to be called off. Or would it?

Amsterdam's Can-Am League rival Gloversville offered the use of its home park, but the Rugmakers declined and went to work.

In less than a week, the demolished grandstand had been rebuilt, debris had been hauled away, every charred seat had been replaced, light poles bent from the heat had been straightened, and the infield and outfield had been restored to playing shape.

The game went on . . . and it was a barn-burner, with the Yankees pulling the game out with a run in the eighth and four more in the tenth inning to win 8–4 and fill the coffers of Amsterdam's city and team . . . a tribute to American hard work and dedication.

World War II slowed league growth as Americans were engaged in the war effort, and there were more serious things with which to occupy one's leisure time than going to a ballgame. Talent, too, was depleted as the healthy players went off to war, and the too young, too old, or too injured made up most of the rosters. And of those, the cream of the crop went to the Bigs, so fans didn't exactly flock to the parks to see Minor Leaguers perform.

Immediately following World War II, baseball prospered on all levels. But to do so, it had to withstand yet another scandal.

The Minors had withstood yellow fever, which wiped out an entire Cotton States League season; the financing of teams by gamblers in an Arizona League; and the ownership of teams by brothels in another league out West. But it was the circuit ironically named the Evangeline League that posed the problem in 1946.

The Evangeline League was a successful Class-D loop that was established in 1934, moving up to Class C from 1949 until its demise in 1957. The league was pretty much based in Louisiana, featuring teams from Houma, Abbeville, Alexandria, Opelousas, Lake Charles, Natchez, and New Iberia. It was a much-revered league, and its star of stars might have been sidearming right-handed pitcher Bill Thomas, who won thirty-five games in 1946. But the Evangeline League betrayed baseball, and Thomas was caught up in the scandal.

Thomas's Houma team had handily won the 1946 pennant by going 92–38, a .708 winning percentage to take the flag by six games over the Natchez Giants.

In the first round of the play-offs, Houma routed fourth-place Alexandria four games to one. And they repeated the carnage by taking Abbeville in the finals, four games to one. Thomas went a perfect 5–0 in the play-offs.

But following the Houma celebration, National Association prexy Judge W. G. Bramham received accusations that four Houma players (Bill Thomas, Lanny Pecou, Alvin Kaiser, and Paul Fugit) and one Abbeville player (Don Vettorel) had been in contact with gamblers who entreated them to throw games.

According to a SABR Research Journal article researched by George W. Hilton, in a closed hearing Thomas testified that Kaiser introduced him to a bookie who suggested that Thomas could lose a few games during the season. Thomas refused to comply.

Kaiser and Pecou were accused of working with and for a bookie and rigging some bets on horseraces.

Vettorel was accused of admitting he had won $600 by rigging the outcome of several games.

Fugit was alleged to have played too far off first base to allow baserunners to reach on throws by Kaiser. Pecou apparently let a ball drop in front of him.

There were no allegations of misplay by Thomas, but other allegations of association with gamblers widely circulated.

Judge Bramham found all the men guilty and suspended the lot of them in an effort to cleanse the game once again.

Thomas and Pecou were reinstated two years later, but the damage had been done. Even though the Evangeline League made a valiant run for another eight years, the public never seemed to trust the Evangeline game again, and attendance steadily dropped until the public found other things to do. And by the late '50s, the Evangeline League had been swept aside.

The damage seemed huge in 1948, but the rest of the Minor League world treated it as an isolated incident, and by 1949 all was forgotten, or at least forgiven.

But if 1946 was the year of scandal, then it was also the year that Minor League ball came out of the dark ages by admitting blacks to the diamonds for the first time in nearly fifty years.

On April 19, 1946, Jackie Robinson made his debut for the Montreal Royals of the International League, and he was followed five days later by teammate John Wright. On May 8, Roy Campanella integrated the New England League with Nashua, and on May 16, he was joined by teammate Don Newcombe. By the end of the year, six blacks were playing Organized Ball, and by the end of 1947, sixteen formerly restricted players were playing side by side with white players. That number jumped to twenty-seven in 1948, and the game became healthy morally as well as financially. And the fans understood and paid to see good baseball played by strong teams.

The high-water mark in terms of Minor League attendance occurred in 1949, when a record fifty-nine sanctioned leagues brought in an all-time-high paid attendance of a whopping 41,872,762. The crest was high and few thought a fall would occur ever, much less soon.

Just when all was well, the Minors suffered another setback. With the 1950s came televised Major League games and increased radio coverage. The Majors were so taken with broadcasting and the broadcasting dollar that a common occurrence saw as many as five games televised in a single day in certain markets from 10:30 AM to 11:00 PM.

Another Minor League killer was Major League franchise relocation. It seemed that in the '50s, the Majors would use up a location, throw it away, and go after a ripe new one. The Braves left Boston, which already had another Major League franchise, and went to Milwaukee, which it used up and then jumped to Atlanta. The Browns left St. Louis, which still had the Cardinals, and moved to Baltimore to become the new Orioles. The Athletics left Philadelphia, which still had the Phillies, and moved on to Kansas City, which it later left for Oakland. Milwaukee, Baltimore, and Kansas City were major Minor League markets that the Little Show now had to do without.

And by 1958, the Dodgers left Brooklyn and the Giants left New York, which still had the reigning top-drawing New York Yankees. These moves effectively knocked the Pacific Coast League off the roles of would-be Major League aspirants by nabbing its top two markets, Los Angeles and San Francisco.

All this served to cut Minor League attendance from more than forty million fans and fifty-nine leagues to a death knell of barely ten million fans and twenty-two leagues in 1961, a year in which the Majors expanded again and put another team in Los Angeles (the Angels) while taking away still another Minor League stronghold, Minneapolis, where the Twins supplanted the A.A. powerhouse Millers.

And there were also battles for fans within the Minor League family of the '50s. At the time, the undisputed king of the Mississippi Valley was the Three-I League. It had withstood challenges from upstart leagues for years, but in the late 1950s, the Three-I withered and died, as much from the challenge of the competing, but sanctioned Midwest League as from the increasing costs to run teams.

It cost substantially less to operate a Midwest League team than it did to run a Three-I team by 1958—$50,000 for profitability in the Class-D Midwest and $80,000 to $100,000 in the Class-B Three-I—and for many small towns, the class difference could not be rectified with the cost differential.

Another factor that helped kill the Three-I was shrinking attendance. Fans during the late 1950s began to look elsewhere to spend their entertainment dollars, and there simply seemed to be too many Minor Leagues and teams. With a total of six classes (from D ball to Triple-A) and the difference in talent from C to D or A to B seeming to be arbitrarily delineated, interest declined, attendance dropped, and belt-tightening as well as an industry shakeout was inevitable.

When Three-I members met in November 1957, they seemed resigned to that inevitable future. The league had shrunk to six teams as they prepared to do battle with the upstart Midwest League. When the Three-I went after two Midwest League cities, Clinton and Dubuque, in Iowa, they were chastised by the National Association, spelling the beginning of the end for the Three-I.

The Minor Leagues hit rock bottom in attendance in 1963, with the eighteen leagues in operation and accounting for only 9,963,174 fans, the worst figures of the postwar era. Among the casualties was the always solid-as-a-rock American Association. For sixty years, the Association thrived with a minimum of franchise shifts and interruptions, but as the Major Leagues absorbed all of its major markets, the Association disintegrated.

However, the Majors weren't about to pick the Minors clean. By the mid-'50s, baseball sages realized that a healthy Minor Leagues was important for the continued health of the Major Leagues.

What could be done to stop this accelerating slide toward death?

Brooklyn Dodgers' owner Walter O'Malley proposed Major League all-star games in major Minor League cities to raise contingency funds. This was voted down.

On August 2, 1956, a "Save the Minors Committee" was established by Major League leaders, and an ad hoc group decided to raise a $500,000 stabilization fund to be paid to those lower-level clubs who needed help. This amounted to a $31,250 stipend from each of the existing Major League clubs at that time. And, this was only the tip of the iceberg.

Baseball powers finally realized that there just wasn't enough talent or enough interest to go around to seven classifications of Minor League ball (Open, Triple A, Double A, A, B, C, and D). An agreement was drawn up in 1962 calling for guaranteed operation of at least 100 Minor League clubs (130 were in existence at the time) in four classifications. Triple-A remained the same, and Double-A and A leagues were joined to become Double-A. All of the surviving B, C, and D leagues were joined to become A leagues. And Rookie Leagues were formed to teach young players fresh out of school the complexities of Organized Baseball.

It also didn't seem much of a loss in eliminating Class D ball. Many Class D teams were bankrupt or near so, and most of the Class C and D leagues were not run well. And the talent there, with the exceptions of the Tony Olivas of the world who successfully made the jump from Class D to the Majors, was often just a step up from high school ball. This meant the top players could easily be assimilated into the new Class A leagues; if not, they probably shouldn't have been playing professional ball.

But of significance: those Class D leagues did have value . . . to the communities that supported them.

Both Robert Obojski, in his 1975 book, *Bush Leagues,* and Neil J. Sullivan in his 1990 work, *The Minors,* point out that baseball roots ran deep in the heartland of America's small towns.

Cases in point include: the Alabama-Mississippi League that favored such small towns as Anniston, Alabama, and Corinth, Mississippi, which gave pride to the residents of both villages when no other enterprise could during the oppressive 1936 despair, the Great Depression.

And while the Anthracite League lasted for only part of the 1928 season, the small Pennsylvania towns—Hazelton, Mahonoy City, et al.—were just as proud of their teams as Philadelphia and Pittsburgh were of the Phillies and the Pirates.

The same can be said for the Copper Country–Soo League (Minnesota, North Dakota, and Canada), the PONY League (Pennsylvania, Ontario, and New York), the KITTY League (Kentucky, Iowa, Tennessee), the Cotton States League (Mississippi and other Southern states), and countless other leagues that failed but were beloved by their host communities.

So while this pruning saved the Minor League baseball tree as a whole the amputation did adversely affect the lives of the residents of those small towns who enjoyed the halcyon days of Little Show baseball.

The Pacific Coast League, which had Open classification, also became a Triple-A League, but theirs is another story (see Chapter 5: Pacific Coast League).

Another victim during this time was the Negro American League, which had been slowly dying since the integration of the sport in 1946, but which fell victim to more sophisticated times and Major League expansion just as the members of the National Association did. For all intents and purposes, the NAL ceased operation in 1963.

Did the Major Leagues kill its weak Minor League children? Or did the small towns and hamlets and villages just become too sophisticated for the relatively unsophisticated D League genre? That's a moot point, but the fact is, that by 1962, the death knell had been sounded for the weak so that the strong might survive.

This 1962 plan also called for subsidization of Minor League teams by their Major League parents. The agreement called for the Big League affiliate to assume major portions of salaries and certain upkeep and upgrading costs.

That plan is substantially the same today, except that in many cases the Major League parent assumes all salary responsibilities plus a greater portion of operating costs— subject to a new MLB–National Association agreement.

From the 1960s to the 1990s, the Minor Leagues have thrived.

The American Association began operations again in 1969 and was immediately healthy, pulling in fans from across the nation who yearned for solid, Triple-A baseball in large cities without a Major League franchise.

In 1970, 10.9 million fans saw Minor League games in twenty leagues. By 1973, only eighteen leagues were operating and 130 teams finished the season, but attendance increased to 11.2 million. In 1990, there were more than 150 teams in the United States and Canada and fourteen in Mexico, at the A level and above, and twenty Rookie League teams in America with twenty-one more in the Dominican

Republic. That's 205 teams in operation drawing more than twenty million fans.

To save costs the American Association and International League joined forces in 1988 to form the Triple-A Alliance. This operation has saved administration costs, promotes inter-league play, and has generally added to the health of the division. Its agreement ends in 1991 but is expected to be reaffirmed.

An offshoot of this is the possible creation of a Double-A Alliance, joining the Eastern, Southern, and Texas leagues. While this has been discussed and could provide another shot in the arm to the industry, the adoption of this plan seems several years off at best.

Still, experts agree that the game has never been healthier and that the existing leagues and operating teams, franchise relocations aside, should remain intact for many years to come, and never have the Minor Leagues had such a rosy outlook on the future, as long as the MLB doesn't alter the financial balance.

Who would want to own a Minor League team today? Anyone with a little money, a love for baseball, and a desire to make a profit. Yes, profit. Minor League ball has come a long way since the shoestring days. In fact, it has been reported that in 1989, all but two privately owned teams—139 of those 141 teams not owned outright by the parent club—made a profit. How was that done?

In most cases, the working agreement between the parent MLB club and the Minor League affiliate states that the parent is responsible for all salaries of players and coaches, much if not all of the equipment expenses, much if not all of the lease expenses, and certain operating expenses. On top of that, the Minor League club owner gets to keep ticket, parking, and concession sales as well as logo and ancillary marketing profits. No wonder those including the Brett family (George, Ken, and Bobby), *Baseball America* publisher-owner Miles Wolff, former Major Leaguers Joe Buzas and Don Drysdale, and actor Bill Murray (to name a few) are multifranchise owners. They multiply their profits and get to play baseball mogul at the same time. And other baseball lovers such as singer Tony Orlando; actor Mark Harmon; and Los Angeles District Attorney Ira Reiner see this as a means of being part of the Little Show with little financial risk.

This Major League subsidization of the Minors works well—from a Minor League standpoint and to a certain extent from the Major League point of view as well—however, adopting an "if it ain't broke, fix it anyway" stance, the Major Leagues are currently moving toward lessening the level of subsidy based on increased costs at the Major League level and on the fact that the Minors seem to be healthy and in an economic boom.

In a late-year debate that got heated and nasty, the MLB threatened to start up its own Minor League system—severing an 87-year relationship by breaking completely from the existing teams—unless Minor League owners agreed to: pay a percentage of their profits back to the Major League parents; pay a fee for using an MLB parent's nickname (e.g., Quad City "Angels"); pay a greater percentage of operating costs; and kick in a percentage of attendance and concession grosses.

Minor League owners countered that the only reason they were eking out small profits was because of the current financial system in place. Nashville Sounds owner Larry Schmittou said that there were no extras to give up and that "there's no more blood in this turnip."

Most observers saw the MLB threat as a bargaining ploy, but the Majors actively sought out alternate sites to house a new Minor League setup of as many as 150 teams. Florida seemed to be the best location for such a maneuver, as existing Minor League franchises held a tight monopoly on most non–Major League cities and appropriate ballparks throughout the nation. Still, the threat was real and if an agreement was not reached, the structure of Minor League baseball could be inexorably changed for all time, with the familiar operations battling upstart leagues and teams which were more heavily financed by the same MLB coalition bent on lessening their financial burden.

The lose-lose situation was in the MLB's ballpark, as Minor League fans waited for cooler heads to prevail.

Apparently The Show would rather reap increased profits than assure economic stability on the Farm, preferring to wait and see if the Minors can make it in the 1990s on their own, then rescue them with more money if this strategy fails. Common sense did indeed return when in December 1990 the Major Leagues and the National Association of Professional Baseball Leagues, a.k.a. the Minors, reached a seven-year agreement that kept the status quo but that could be reopened for negotiation in 1994. Still, for now, Minor League ownership is profitable and glamorous.

So who would want to own a Minor League team? On the surface, the better question would be: who wouldn't? You've got glamour, prestige, sports, history, and profit . . . on the surface.

One multifranchise owner disagrees with the presumption that it's all peanuts and hot dogs on the Minor League front. Miles Wolff, publisher of *Baseball America* and owner of the Carolina League's Durham Bulls and the Pioneer League's Butte Copper Kings said, "If you get in this game for fun, you've gotten in for the wrong reason. It is not fun. It is sixteen hours a day of hard work. If you don't put in the time, you'll be out of business within two years."

Wolff was a Major League general manager when he scraped up $2500 to buy the Durham Bulls in 1980. Now, that team and all its merchandising is worth an estimated $9 million.

Wolff remarked, "The average guy can't buy a Minor League team now. Once, he could, but not anymore. The clubs aren't worth what they pay for them, anyway.

"In the old days, teams were community owned just to keep the franchise in town. But to operate them then, just as now, they needed to sell advance season tickets. To earn profits then, but especially now, teams need to advertise."

What makes a team money?

Wolff said, "Promotions make money. They pack a park and you always make enough to offset the promotion; otherwise it would make no sense to have it. If we give away an item, it always costs less than a seat costs the fan. Spending a dollar or a dollar-and-a-half to fill a $3.50 seat makes economic sense. If we spend $5,000 to bring the San Diego Chicken to our ballpark, we know we'll sell enough seats plus concessions and parking to make a profit on his appearance."

Why own a club?

It may be simply a case of ego.

Joe Buzas, a former shortstop for the New York Yankees (1945), decided thirty-four years ago, to own a Minor League team. Buzas said, "Ego played an important part. I didn't want to leave the limelight, so I decided to own a club. In thirty-four years, I have owned pieces of sixty-nine baseball operations."

Buzas, who currently owns the PCL Portland Beavers, the Eastern League New Britain Red Sox, and the California League Salinas Spurs, added, "Too many people want to own Big League baseball teams and those prices have skyrocketed out of reach for a normal businessman. Even in the Minors, an area in which I own teams to make a living . . . kind of a "living" hobby, the prices have gone out of sight. I have been offered $4 million for my New Britain Double-A team, and $7 million for my Triple-A Portland franchise which I bought for $1 million."

To become a success on the Minor League level, Buzas suggested, "Get to know your community. Become a part of it. Be visible, whether that's waiting on people, taking tickets, offering 'Back to School' nights, or 'Swingin' Summer' promotions, do what you can to attract people. We need people to show a profit. We get our profits on tickets, concessions, and parking and we need all of it to survive."

Wolff agreed, "The bigger the promotions, the better. But the days are gone when Minor League promotions were 'Minor League.' They're not very outlandish anymore. They are more conservative. The Minors started bat night and hat night and all the tried-and-true promotions that the Major Leagues now embrace. We've found out that the Major Leagues will take over and try all our successful promotions if they're not too offbeat. They do what we do . . . find ways to pack the ballpark."

Sometimes those attractions are rehabilitating Major Leaguers who make "guest appearances" in Minor League towns as they prepare themselves to reenter the Big League wars.

Sometimes, attractions are different. Camel races, horse-races, even people versus animal races—in 1977 at Modesto in the California League, speedster Rickey Henderson raced a horse . . . and lost. Many are tried and only the successful ones are repeated. Just last year (1990), the Cincinnati Reds closed out the regular season by initiating a promotion in which speedy infielder Billy Bates raced a cheetah. He lost, but escaped uneaten. Still, it was a take-off on similar Minor League attractions.

Promotion began as early as the 1890s when in Dayton, Ohio, a young woman in a parachute dropped out of a hot air balloon which had been circling the ballpark. She landed delicately on second base to the roar of the crowd . . . a feat duplicated more than ninety years later during the World Series at Shea Stadium.

Tacoma once hired a Brink's truck to haul $1 million in coins to the ballpark on "Dash for Cash" night. The winning fans had two minutes to put all the coins they could carry in buckets and take them home. The stands were packed and the winners took home about five dollars and fifty cents each, as nickels and quarters are heavy and tough to find, pick up, and carry.

The Orlando SunRays of the Southern League tried a "Blind Date" night in which single women were given even-numbered seats and single men were sold odd-numbered seats. Roses were provided for the women and strolling violinists serenaded the couples between innings. The crowd did increase, but the results were mixed. This may be one promotion that stays in the Minors and never surfaces in The Show.

To attract people in seasons past, Buzas has even hired Max Patkin, the reigning "Clown Prince of Baseball," and got entertainer Pia Zadora to be a vice president of the Portland Beavers.

Bill Valentine, the outspoken General Manager of the Texas League's Arkansas Travelers said, "We are an entertainment package. We have to attract grandmothers, mothers, kids, yuppies, hippies, and everyone in town to make it."

Valentine added, "To make ends meet, the owner and executives have to do it all. We sell tickets, watch the free pass gate, count the house, sell hot dogs, even sweep the field if it's necessary. You show me a Major League owner who'll do that. In the Minor Leagues, we are a hands-on operation. We all are. That separates us from the Majors . . . we seem to care more, but maybe it's because our livelihood may depend on that."

But now that profit is in the scheme of things for Minor League franchises, what of the future for the market?

Well, the Japanese are interested in buying in.

A Japan League Major League team recently offered Miles Wolff a bundle of yen for his Durham Bulls team. Wolff politely told the conglomerate that the franchise was not for sale.

Wolff reported, "They were really interested in a Triple-A franchise, and Durham is Single-A. So I've been helping them find out which Triple-A teams might be available."

And just last February (1990), the Birmingham Barons, a Double-A affiliate of the Chicago White Sox in the Southern League, were sold to Martin Kuehnert and Suntory Ltd., a Japanese food, beverage, and restaurant giant. Kuehnert, former owner of the PCL's Hawaii Islanders, has spent the last twenty years as editor of the Mizuno Japanese Baseball newsletter and as a Japanese baseball broadcaster, serves as club president and liaison to Suntory. The price was an estimated $3 million.

This followed a 1989 purchase of the Class-A Visalia Oaks by Japan Sports Systems U.S.A. The Oaks president is Don Drysdale, who reports a smooth operation with little interference from the Japanese parent.

There is certainly precedent for Japanese big businesses' love affair with baseball. In the Japan Leagues, large corporations own all of their teams. But in Japan, the company gets the press, so the city in which the team is located is not part of the official team name, and the corporation is. By way of example: there is no "Tokyo" Giants team even though the team is based in Tokyo and plays its home games in the Tokyo Dome . . . the official name is the Yomiuri Giants—the club is owned by newspaper giant Yomiuri Shimbun. The Seibu Lions, based in Saitama-ken, is owned by huge Seibu Ltd.; the Kintetsu Buffalos, based in Osaka, is owned by transportation conglomerate Kintetsu Ltd.; the Nippon Ham Fighters, based in Tokyo, is owned by food processor Nippon Ham; and the Hiroshima Toyo Carp, based in Hiroshima, is owned by tire manufacturer Hiroshima Toyo Ltd. They all bear the parent's name. That would be akin to re-naming the following clubs: Domino's Pizza (Detroit) Tigers, American Shipbuilders (New York) Yankees, Sun-Times (Chicago) Cubs, Schott's Brewery (Cincinnati) Reds, Levi Strauss (Oakland) Athletics, TBS (Atlanta) Braves, Baseball America (Durham) Bulls, or the Rich's Whip Topping (Buffalo) Bisons.

International business intelligence sources theorize that Japan's interest in American baseball is just beginning and that more purchases are on the Minor League horizon as foreign interest is frowned upon on the Major League level—Japanese share of the Yankees notwithstanding. All indications are that the new money and new blood may breathe new life into the Minor League industry. Time will tell.

And regarding existing teams and cities without Far East involvement, there is much movement on that front as well. From the rumor mill surrounding the futures of several Minor Leagues and Minor League cities, at least ten have submitted bids to the National League for consideration for the two expansion sites of the Senior Circuit in 1993. This gives birth to several ramifications.

First, the ten cities in question have been identified as: Denver, Colorado; Phoenix, Arizona; Buffalo, New York; Charlotte, North Carolina; Nashville, Tennessee; Orlando, Miami, and Tampa-St. Petersburg, Florida; Washington, DC; and Sacramento, California. All but Washington currently house Minor League teams, and current thought places Denver, Buffalo, and Orlando or Tampa–St. Petersburg as the front-runners. Phoenix had been in line for a franchise until Arizona voters rejected a proposition that would have recognized Dr. Martin Luther King, Jr.'s birthday as a state holiday. This angered civil rights leaders and effectively took Phoenix out of the running. All the winners need to do is pay $95 million to the National League as a franchise fee and secure $50 million more for estimated start-up fees. It may seem like a lot, but ownership conglomerates and limited partnerships have formed long lines to make bids for a piece of the MLB pie. Interested in the glamour of the Big League banquet were such celebrities as former players Don Drysdale and Ken Harrelson, with the St. Petersburg group; Mike Schmidt with a Miami partnership; Ernie Banks and Doug DeCinces aligned with a Denver bid; and owners of teams in other sports, most notably Dr. Jerry Buss of the Los Angeles Lakers.

The obvious result is that any city chosen for Major League status immediately loses its Minor League team, and cities close to the chosen community could also lose teams under region franchise exclusivity.

A second result is that the cities that are not chosen become ripe sites for franchise relocation. The most persistent rumors concerning Major League Baseball relocation involve Santa Clara, Buffalo, Indianapolis, and Vancouver. In what was apparently a "done" deal, San Francisco Giants owner Bob Lurie all but wrapped up a Giants move to San Jose–Santa Clara, effectively taking

Minor League ball out of San Jose (current home of the California League's San Jose Giants), but making Minor League baseball a real possibility in a city that had a remarkable Pacific Coast League (PCL) history . . . a return of the Little Show to San Francisco, former home of the storied San Francisco Seals. This double switch was complicated by the refusal of Santa Clara voters to approve a 1 percent utility tax hike to finance a proposed $153 million ballpark, and the fact that the Oakland A's would have to agree to allow a Minor League club to play in San Francisco. Lurie is still seeking a new ballpark in either San Francisco or Santa Clara. If neither city complies, he has indicated that he will relocate somewhere. With that desire now public knowledge, he is being romanced by officials from Denver, Buffalo, and New Orleans.

In late August 1990, the story circulated among insiders in the baseball world that Charles Bronfman, owner of the Montreal Expos, had his bags packed—or had potential new owners whose bags were packed—and headed for Buffalo, current home of the International League's Bisons. As Buffalo had been an early front-runner for an expansion club before the powers that be apparently soured on the choice, this northern New York city is ideal for relocation as a natural rival to the Mets, Phillies, and Pirates, though it was hoped by local officials that Buffalo would find its way into the American League to be closer to rivals such as the Yankees, Blue Jays, and Indians.

Another hushed and denied but lively rumor comes out of Seattle. It is known that the Mariners, owned by an Indiana-based contingent led by Jeff Smulyan and TV personality David Letterman, covet a move to the unrepresented, major Midwest city of Indianapolis, current home to the International League's Indianapolis Indians. Indianapolis had been a front-runner for an expansion franchise, virtually assured a team if minor improvements (a top-deck-high foul pole) in the Hoosier Dome were made. The fact that those overtures were pulled back may indicate that a Seattle-to-Indianapolis move is in the works.

Few obstacles remain, as the Mariners occupy King County's King Dome, but are not restricted by a lease and are free to move. A move would reopen Seattle for consideration in a Pacific Coast League expansion.

There is also some movement surrounding the city of Vancouver, British Columbia, Canada. Vancouver, currently the home to the Vancouver Canadians of the Pacific Coast League, has been mentioned as a future site of Major League baseball, as there is nothing else up there to compete with it during baseball season, and it is a major market. City leaders and businessmen have publicly and heartily gone after the Montreal Expos in an effort to keep the team in Canada yet relocate it to Vancouver. Two negative factors here include its distance from any other MLB team if Seattle departs—and Major League owners hate to spend more airline money than necessary—and the Canadian dollar-to-American dollar exchange rate. Still, it is a recurring piece of gossip.

But all expansion does not mean exclusion of Minor League ball. Quite to the contrary, Major League expansion means Minor League expansion. It is incumbent upon baseball to provide a farm system for its newest franchises, and that means that two new National League clubs will beget at least twelve new Minor League operations: two at Triple-A; two at Double-A; four at Single-A; and four Rookie league teams.

Where will those teams be located? Current guesses involve Edmonton (Pacific Coast League's Trappers), which was sold near the end of the 1990 season and which may sit dormant for a year as the California Angels look for a franchise more geographically suited to a parent club based in Southern California, and either the creation of a new league, or large expansion of an older one.

It seems apparent that the PCL, American Association, or International League will pick up an extra two teams to house the new MLB teams' Triple-A Farms, and Double-A will expand accordingly too. But the main thrust will be at

Single-A, where four affiliated teams and perhaps as many as two independent teams may spring up.

The Single-A expansion canard seems to be focused on the Midwest League or creation of a new circuit. The Midwest League is currently home to fourteen teams situated in Iowa (five), Illinois (three), Indiana (one), Wisconsin (five). Speculation has the league governors approving franchises in several of the following cities: Sioux Falls, South Dakota; Fargo, North Dakota; Deadwood, South Dakota; St. Cloud, Minnesota; and Winnipeg, Manitoba, Canada.

If that expansion plan is vetoed by league officials, there is a growing movement afoot to resurrect the old Northern League that first operated in 1902 and ceased operation, for the fifth and last time, in 1971. This Northern League may start with six teams chosen from among the five cities mentioned above as Midwest League sites, and Regina, Saskatchewan, Canada and Missoula, Montana, as well as any other city that puts together some money and a market plan.

Add to all that the allure of jumping to a higher league, and the Minor League city hopscotch becomes a Chinese checkers game, with one city leapfrogging over another. To illustrate: if the MLB chooses Denver, Phoenix, or Buffalo, then the Triple-A clubs in those cities must relocate elsewhere. As the International League is currently non-international, with all its teams in the United States, cities such as Ottawa, Ontario, and Winnipeg, Manitoba, become attractive. And several Double-A and Single-A cities want to make a move to Triple-A. So if Birmingham and Huntsville, Alabama; Charlotte and Durham, North Carolina; Jacksonville and Orlando, Florida; Memphis, Tennessee; Tulsa, Oklahoma; and Quad City (a four-city–two-state-region made up of Davenport and Bettendorf, Iowa, and Rock Island and Moline, Illinois)—all of which have inquired about just such an opening—move upward, their slots would have to be filled in the lower leagues.

And the PCL is looking for a few good cities, most notably Fresno and Sacramento, California—possible new homes for the California Angels' affiliate—and Eugene, Oregon and Spokane, Washington, currently with the Northwest League.

As of this writing, no front-runners have emerged, but speculation runs rampant and has created excitement for those who want to see professional baseball in their own backyards.

As a prelude to the endearing and enduring stories, amazing occurrences, and incredible performances that permeate later chapters of this book and tell the real story of the Little Show, we offer the following highlights that don't easily fall into the categories of those chapters but that warrant retelling to keep the tales and their participants alive.

⚾   ⚾   ⚾   ⚾

Inside the Minor Leagues (highlights, lowlights, anecdotes, quotes, and curiosities from the world of the Little Show):

- Tony Torchia, a coach for the Boston Red Sox, explained the difference between the Majors and the Minors, "In Kansas City, I had a phone in my bathroom. In the Minors I stayed at hotels where the fire escape was a rope."
- The 1905 Southern Association season was a tough one . . . particularly for the New Orleans Pelicans. A yellow fever epidemic ravaged the "Big Easy" and forced New Orleans to play all of its home games on the road during the second half of the season. That didn't seem to deter the Pelicans, who won the pennant anyway, running up an 84–45 mark.
- There is an unsubstantiated rumor—based on hearsay, look-alike photos and whispered story—that has been repeated for seven decades that a ballplayer named "Johnson," who played for the Abilene, Kansas, team in the Central Kansas League in 1909 and 1910 was really none other than Dwight David Eisenhower, the future

Supreme Allied Commander in World War II and thirty-fourth President of the United States, who played under an assumed name—baseball players were ill-thought-of—just prior to his appointment to West Point.

- In a pitching performance year to end all years, fastball thrower Walter "Smoke" Justis won 25 games for Lancaster in the Ohio State League in 1908. The amazing thing is that he won 21 of those by giving up hits. Four times that season, Justis fired no-hitters: shutting out Mansfield 6–0 on July 19, getting Portsmouth 6–0 on August 2, blanking Lima 3–0 on September 8, and white-washing Marion 3–0 on September 13. He had 293 K's that season and went on to record 20 or more Minor League wins three times. His fastball was erratic in his only stint in the Majors—Detroit in 1905—and he seldom did well in higher classifications. Still, his was one season in the sun that should be remembered, and one that has never been approached.

- Speaking of no-hitters, on May 10, 1909, Fred Toney pitched a gem of a ballgame; a seventeen-inning no-hitter for Winchester, against Blue Grass League opponent Lexington. Winning 1–0, Toney struck out nineteen and walked only one.

- In a stellar pitching performance stretching over two games, Harry Hedgepeth pitched both ends of a Virginia League doubleheader on August 13, 1913, leading Petersburg to a 1–0, 10–0 sweep over Richmond. Hedgepeth gave up an infield hit in the fourth inning of the first game, and threw a no-hitter in the nightcap.

- From the "Do I have to pitch? I'd rather hit." file comes a particularly strong performance on June 5, 1914, by John Cantley, a career Minor Leaguer who was pitching for Opelika in the Georgia-Alabama League. Cantley pitched a solid game in beating Talledega by a rout of 19–1. The story, however, was at the plate. Cantley, not known for his hitting prowess, blasted three grand slam homeruns and a single, driving in fifteen runs to ice the game.

- Following a four-year Major League career in which he hit .257 in 283 games, outfielder Joe Wilhoit was banished to the Minors. After being dumped for poor hitting by Seattle of the Pacific Coast League in 1919, Wilhoit settled in with Wichita in the Class-A Western League. He went on a tear that has never been approached. Wilhoit hit safely in 69 consecutive games, banging out 151 hits in 299 at bats for a .505 average. He never got another call in the Majors, and only Joe DiMaggio, "The Yankee Clipper," ever came close to Wilhoit's feat by hitting in 61 straight games in the PCL in 1933. Other top Minor League streaks include Roman Mejias: 55 for Waco in the Big State League in 1954; and Otto Pahlman: 50 for Danville in the Three-I League.

- Lyman Lamb belted 100 doubles for Tulsa in the Western League in 1922, twenty-five better than anyone has ever been able to hit anywhere else in Organized Baseball. Lamb had just been sent down by the St. Louis Browns after a lackluster .245 and nine doubles in forty-five games in 1921.

- In the May vs. December pitching duel to end them all, a May 11, 1925, Mississippi Valley League matchup saw fifty-five-year-old Joe McGinnity of Dubuque outpitch eighteen-year-old John Welch of Ottumwa, 7–3.

- The DiMaggio brothers, the Alou brothers, the Waner brothers, the Aaron brothers, and even the Canseco brothers may have gotten more ink for their sibling prowess, but no brother act ever hit them out with more regularity than did the Boone brothers in 1929.

  Isaac "Ike" Boone and his bro, Danny Boone, both rank on the all-time Minor League batting list (Ike at .370 and Danny at .356, both accomplished over fourteen seasons), but 1929 was something else, when they combined for 101 homers and 343 RBI on 514 hits, for a whopping 927 total bases. That year, Ike, playing for Mission (San Francisco) of the Pacific Coast League belted 55 homers, drove in 218 runs and hit .407, while connecting for 323 hits to total a professional baseball record of 553 total

bases—all tops in the league; and brother Danny, playing for High Point of the Piedmont League, blasted 46
homers, drove in 125 runs and hit .372 on 191 hits to
total 374 total bases.

* The 1936 Evangeline League season belonged to Alexandria first baseman Cecil "Dynamite" Dunn, who led the
circuit in batting (.378), homers (47), RBI (185), hits
(219), doubles (45), runs scored (162) and games played
(139). On April 29 of that year, Dunn hit 5 home runs
and drove in 12 against Lake Charles.

  Six years later, Dunn may have set a record in travel
and laundry as he played for six teams in five leagues:
Oakland of the PCL, Oklahoma City of the Texas League,
Louisville of the American Association, Atlanta and
Memphis of the Southern League, and Savannah of the
South Atlantic League.

* Nolan Ryan and Dwight Gooden each struck out more
than 300 batters in a single Minor League season, and
Ryan went on to do the same in the Majors. But no one
has ever punched out hitters with more frequency than
did lefty fireballer Bill Kennedy, for Rocky Mount in the
Coastal Plain League in 1946. Kennedy struck out an
unapproachable 456 batters in 280 innings, while giving
up 149 hits and fashioning a 1.03 ERA en route to a
28–3 season. Haunted by wildness, Kennedy lasted only
eight years in the Bigs, going 15–28 from 1948 to 1957
(breaking in with Cleveland), whiffing 256 and walking
289 in 464 innings.

* Another pitcher who mowed down the opposition in 1946
was forty-one-year-old right hander Bill Thomas, who
threw for Houma of the Evangeline League. Thomas won
35 games, lost only 7 and pitched 353 innings to fashion
a 2.88 ERA. Following the season, Thomas was issued a
two-year suspension from baseball for "conduct detri-
mental to baseball," a phrase used to deal with his alleged
conspiring with gamblers. Other teammates were suspended for their willingness to throw a few games in the
Evangeline League play-offs of 1946, but Thomas was

never accused of any misplay or intent to dirty the game. After a mediocre comeback-year in 1949, the forty-five-year-old Thomas came all the way back in 1950 by winning 23 and losing 8 for Houma and Lafayette.

- The 1947 Western League season was brightened by the power of Carl Sawatski, now president of the Texas League, who slammed 29 homers in 100 games for Des Moines; and by little Bobby Shantz, the Lincoln pitcher who set the league on its ear by going 18–7 with a 2.82 ERA and 212 strikeouts. Shantz was later to star for the Philadelphia A's and New York Yankees.

- Eddie Yost may have been "The Walking Man" during his eighteen-year Major League career. But in the Little Show, Gabriel "Pete" Hughes was easily the easiest to give a free pass. An outfielder with Phoenix of the Arizona-Texas League in 1948, Hughes, a career Minor Leaguer, walked 207 times. The next year, playing for Las Vegas in the Sunset League, he upped that mark by working for 210 walks in 123 games. He led his league seven times in free passes and during his career garnered more walks (1666) than hits (1566), though he did hit a solid .350 with power (284 homers) over his twelve-year sojourn, interrupted by a four-year hitch in the service.

- And 1948 was the year an outfielder named Bobby Crues dominated the West Texas-New Mexico League like few have ever dominated any competition. Crues, playing for Amarillo, hit .404, smashed 69 homeruns and drove in an all-time Minor League record of 254 ribbies in only 140 games.

- Also in 1948, a player who made his mark on baseball at the managing end rather than with athletic accomplishment gave the other team all it could handle on a night in Schenectady, when pitcher Tommy Lasorda struck out 25 batters in a 15-inning victory for his Schenectady Blue Jays over Amsterdam. Lasorda, of course, was a scrappy lefty hurler who is better known as the manager of the Los Angeles Dodgers.

- One Hall-of-Famer in another sport tried baseball and did rather well from 1947 to 1950. National Hockey League legend Doug Harvey played for four years with Ottawa of the Border League. The outfielder hit .344 with 18 homers, 187 RBI, and 58 stolen bases in 238 games before giving it up to concentrate on hockey.

  A basketball Hall-of-Famer also prevailed on the diamond, as Boston Celtics star Bill Sharman hit .288 playing in the Western League for the Pueblo, Colorado, franchise.

- Another of those men who is more famous in another arena than he was on the baseball field was a twenty-year-old centerfielder for the Class-D Brunswick Pirates in 1952. The outfielder, Mario Cuomo, led the Georgia team with a .353 average when he slammed into the centerfield fence while going full-out after a fly ball. The collision left him with an injured wrist, and, after finally regaining strength in the joint, was hit in the head by an errant fastball and was put in the hospital for two weeks. He never regained his swing and finished the season at .244 with only 26 RBI in 81 games.

  Remembering his roots, Cuomo, now governor of the state of New York, has spent much time and effort to bring an expansion franchise or relocation franchise to Buffalo, New York.

- Other celebrity Minor Leaguers include Johnny Berardino, the twenty-five-year veteran of TV's "General Hospital," who played the tough South and East; Charlie Pride, the Country Western singing star who toiled in the Negro American League and in the Reds and Yankees systems; Chuck Connors, TV's "Rifle Man," who played for the Montreal Royals, Newark Bears, and Los Angeles Angels; Kurt Russell, the hard-working motion picture star who was a prospect with the Sacramento Bees and Portland Mavericks before injuries overtook him; Randy Poffo, also known as wrestling star Randy "Macho King" Savage, who played for Orangeburg; and in a one-game stint with the Rochester Brownies of the

1897 Eastern League, former heavyweight boxing champion Gentleman Jim Corbett played first base, went 0-for-4 and committed two errors. Western author Zane Grey played for Zanesville, Ohio, in 1899 before leaving to enter dental school, and soap opera heartthrob Drake Hogestyn, who portrays Roman Brady on "Days of Our Lives," played third base for the Yankees' Oneonta affiliate in the late '70s under the name Donald Drake Hogestyn. Two others who toiled briefly in the Little Show were comedian-actor Dick Shawn, a pitcher in the White Sox organization in the early '50s, and *Bull Durham* screenwriter Ron Shelton, who rode the rickety Minor League buses for a few seasons before turning his talents to the written—and acted—word.

- Returning to 1952, it was also the year a twelve-year-old played professional baseball. Joe Relford, the youngest player to take part in a Minor League game, was a batboy for Fitzgerald in the Georgia State League, on July 12, 1952. In the eighth inning, with Fitzgerald being pounded by Statesboro 13–0, the fans started yelling. "Put in the batboy." Fitzgerald manager Charles Ridgeway talked with umpire Ed Kubick and young Relford was sent in to pinch hit.

  Relford grounded sharply to third for an out, then went out to play centerfield, handling a grounder with aplomb and then made a spectacular catch of a curving line drive.

  League officials were not amused, and fired Kubick and suspended and fined Ridgeway.

  Relford, a black youth who officially broke the Georgia State League's color barrier, was dropped from the team within a week.

- Also in 1952, former Negro Leagues star pitcher Connie Johnson led the Western League in strikeouts with 232.

- And 1952 was a year in which no-hitters were in vogue. Bill "Ding Dong" Bell threw three no-hitters for the Bristol Twins of the Appalachian League, and teammate Ron Necciai also tossed a no-no. That same season Frank

Etchberger of Bradford and Jim Mitchell of Batavia pitched a double no-hitter in a Pony League game. Bradford won the game 1–0 on an eighth-inning walk, a sacrifice, a wild pitch, and an infield error.

- In a case of too little too late—it's too bad he was given this little, this late—Negro Leagues legend Buck Leonard, age forty-six, made his only appearance in Organized Baseball by playing ten games for Portsmouth of the Piedmont League in 1953. The aging slugger only hit .333.

- Also in 1953, in the Evangeline League, Earl Caldwell, Sr., forty-eight, led the league in ERA with a 2.07 mark for Lafayette. Caldwell's batterymate that year was Lafayette catcher Earl Caldwell, Jr., his son.

- In 1955, John "Honey" Romano, a corpulent catcher in the White Sox chain, used his five-foot-eleven, 220-pound frame to his advantage by hitting a Three-I League-record 38 homers for Waterloo.

- In 1956, the first of a long line of "The Next Mickey Mantle" tags was pinned on Deron Johnson, a strong, right-handed thumper from San Diego, who blasted 162 Minor League homeruns. Johnson earned the sobriquet that year by bombing 24 homers, driving in 78 runs and hitting .329 in 63 games in the Nebraska State League. Johnson later had some big years with the Cincinnati Reds, but the California Angels batting coach could never live up to the impossible-to-live-up-to reviews.

- On January 4, 1959, only four days into the new regime of Cuban President Fidel Castro, the Havana Sugar Kings were playing the team from Marianao at Gran Estadio de la Habana (also known as Tropical Stadium and Gran Stadium) in the Cuban Winter League, when, midway through the third inning, machine-gun fire was heard throughout the ballpark. Players scrambled for safety and they were later told that several Fulgencia Batista supporters had been killed in the raid.

Later that year, July 26, 1959, the Havana Sugar Kings were hosting the Rochester Red Wings at Gran

Estadio de la Habana with the score tied 4—4 after 11 innings. At 12:30 a.m. gunfire poured out from the stands.

Dick Rand was at bat for Rochester and hit a grounder to Havana shortstop Leo Cardenas, who fired to first to get Rand just as the shots rang out.

Third base coach for the Red Wings was Frank Verdi, an infielder who had replaced manager Cot Deal, who was ejected earlier in the game.

On a whim, Verdi put on a batting helmet before stepping into the coaching box prior to that frame—an odd bit of behavior because he never wore a batting helmet unless he was hitting—and as he heard the gunshot, turned in the direction of the sound. A bullet whizzed in his direction and ricocheted off the helmet, saving Verdi from a potentially serious injury. Another shot nicked his ear and right shoulder.

Havana's Leo Cardenas was struck by another bullet, which grazed the infielder's right shoulder.

Verdi went down and umpire Ed Vargo screamed at the fallen player-coach, asking him if he was okay.

Once again the target of Castro's troops were some Batista diehards, and again, Castro's troops got the better of the former president's soldiers—several of whom were killed during the gunfight. The game resumed in what was the last year for Minor League baseball in Cuba, and the Wings hurriedly boarded a plane for the United States, leaving Cuba just as Castro was delivering a national address.

Digressing for a moment, into a game of "what if . . .", a Minor League pitcher (this point is arguable, as the player in question certainly pitched for his college team and in sandlot or organized pickup games, and some accounts have him playing for Cuban Minor League teams as well) named Fidel Castro may have thrown a little for Marianao in the early '50s and was scouted by the Washington Senators. Scouts concluded that Castro had a good change-up, a Major League-potential curveball and a strictly Minor League fastball. Still, his wicked curveball could have gotten the crafty hurler a shot in The Show if the Senators had not compared him to fellow countrymen Camilo Pascual (blazing fastball, great side-arm curve) and the young, athletic Pedro Ramos (quick pitch, quick feet). Castro reportedly turned down a $5,000 bonus to pitch for the New York Giants, deciding to continue his law studies, but the Senators intrigued him. One Major Leaguer who faced the Cuban president, former infielder and manager Dick Williams, reported that Castro had a great curve but that Williams "took him deep" anyway.

Imagine how history would have changed if the charismatic Cuban leader had turned to baseball instead of revolution. How would Cuba, Cubans, America, the Western hemisphere, world politics and the world of baseball be changed if in 1956, Castro was throwing curves in our nation's capital, rather than firing bullets in the jungles of his native land? Today, he might be the elder statesman of Latin American ball rather than the monarch with the longest reign in the West. And there might be a Major League or Minor League team in Havana, with hundreds of Cubans joining Jose and Ozzie Canseco, Rafael Palmeiro, and Nelson Santovenia in thrilling American baseball fans.

- In 1963, the controversial Dick Allen, after being signed to a $70,000 bonus—the largest amount ever paid at that time to a black athlete—was sent down to play ball in Little Rock, Arkansas, and he became the first black to play there. Allen played the entire season there and was subjected to abuse, including a sign which read: "Let's Not Negro-ize our Baseball." The next year Allen was National League Rookie of the Year with Philadelphia, hitting .318 with 29 homers.
- And as colorful nicknames are part of the fun that embodies the Minor Leagues, we offer the following as a small taste of the ingenuity of owners and namemakers from around the diamonds of the past:

New York Hercules (Independent), New York Quick-steps (Eastern Championship Association), Rochester Hop Bitters (International Association), Detroit Creams (Western League), Toledo Swamp Angels (Western League), Terre Haute Hottentots (Western League), Grand Rapids Gold Bugs (Western League), Omaha Babes (Western League), St. Joseph Rough Riders (Western League), Fort Wayne Kekiongas (Western League), Troy Haymakers (Western League), Charleston Charlies (International League), Dayton Ducks (Middle Atlantic League), Victoria Rosebuds (Texas League), Longview Cannibals (Texas League), New Orleans Pelicans (Southern League), Providence Clamdiggers (International League), Des Moines Demons (Western League), Sioux City Huskers (Western League), Beaumont Exporters (Texas League), Kansas City Monarchs (Negro Leagues), Homestead Grays (Negro Leagues), Baltimore Elite Giants (Negro Leagues), Indianapolis Clowns (Negro Leagues), Havana Sugar Kings (International League), Cedar Rapids Rabbits and Des Moines Prohibitionists (Three-I League), Sacramento Solons (PCL), Amarillo Sonics (Texas League), Waterloo Lulus (Central Association), Battle Creek Crickets and Adrian Infants (Southern Michigan State League), Chattanooga Choo-Choos (Southern Association), and others that are mentioned throughout the text of this book.

⚾   ⚾   ⚾   ⚾

As the preceding is the overview of the Minor League system as a whole, a league-by-league breakdown as well as player profiles follow in the succeeding chapters.

But before that . . . one more time—some records that deserve repeating:

(*Source:* SABR)

Single Season

Batting Average

Gary Redus	.462 Billings	Pioneer League	1978
Bill Krieg	.452 Rockford	Western Association	1896
Ike Boone	.448 Missions	Pacific Coast League (PCL)	1930

[*Author's note:* Walter Malmquist, who played for York in the Nebraska State League in 1913, has long been credited with a .477 average in 110 games. Recent re-calculations, however, dispute that mark, crediting Malmquist with something near the .350 level.]

Runs Scored

Tony Lazzeri	202 Salt Lake City	PCL	1925
Gus Suhr	196 San Francisco	PCL	1929

Hits

Paul Strands	325 Salt Lake City	PCL	1923
Ike Boone	323 Missions	PCL	1929

Doubles

Lyman Lamb	100 Tulsa	Western	1924
Paul Waner	75 San Francisco	PCL	1925

Triples

Jack Cross	32 London	Michigan-Ontario	1925
Walter Shaner	30 Lincoln	Western	1925
Dusty Cooke	30 Asheville	Southern Atlantic	1928
Eddie Moore	30 Fort Worth	Texas	1929
Pete Rose	30 Tampa	Florida State	1961

Home Runs

Joe Bauman	72 Roswell	Longhorn	1954
Joe Hauser	69 Minneapolis	American Assoc.	1933
Bob Crues	69 Amarillo	West Tex. New Mex.	1948
Dick Stuart	66 Lincoln	Western	1956
Bob Lennon	64 Nashville	Southern	1954
Joe Hauser	63 Baltimore	International	1930
Moose Clabaugh	62 Tyler	East Texas	1926
Ken Guettler	62 Shreveport	Texas	1956
Tony Lazerri	60 Salt Lake City	PCL	1925
Frosty Kennedy	60 Plainview	Southwestern	1956

Runs Batted In

Bob Crues	254 Amarillo	West Tex. New Mex.	1948
Joe Bauman	224 Roswell	Longhorn	1954
Tony Lazerri	222 Salt Lake City	PCL	1925
Ike Boone	218 Mission	PCL	1929

Stolen Bases

Vince Coleman	145 Macon	South Atlantic	1983
Donnell Nixon	144 Bakersfield	California	1983

Other 100-plus steal seasons include Alan Wiggins (120 in 1980) and Otis Nixon (108 in 1982), among many century-mark thieves.

Most Wins by Pitcher (Post-1900)

Stony McGlynn	41–11 York (36–10) Steubenville (5–1)	Tri State POM League	1906
Doc Newton	39–17 Los Angeles	PCL	1904
Harry Vickers	39–20 Seattle	PCL	1906

Most Strikeouts by Pitcher

Bill Kennedy	456 Rocky Mount	Coastal Plain	1946
Virgil Trucks	418 Andalusia	Alabama-Florida	1938
Harry Vickers	409 Seattle	PCL	1906

Career Records

Batting Average *(10 years minimum)*

Ike Boone	.370
Ox Eckhardt	.367
Smead Jolley	.366

Hits

Spencer Harris	3617
Harry Strohm	3486
Eddie Hock	3474

Games

George Whiteman	3282
Ray French	3278
Spencer Harris	3258

Doubles

Spencer Harris	743
Fred Henry	675
George Whiteman	673

Runs Scored

Spencer Harris	2287
George Hogriever	2046
Eddie Hock	2007

Triples

Joe Riggert	228
Fred Henry	200
George Whiteman	196

Homeruns

Hector Espino	484
Buzz Arlett	432
Nick Cullop	420
Merv Connors	400
Joe Hauser	399

RBI

Nick Cullop	1857*
Buzz Arlett	1786
Jim Poole	1785*
Spencer Harris	1769
Larry Barton	1751

Games Won (Pitcher)

Bill Thomas	383
Joe Martina	349
George Payne	348

Strikeouts (Pitcher)

George Brunet	3300*
Joe Martina	2770
Jackie Reid	2694

Incomplete records available

But these are just statistics. And the Minor Leagues are more than just stats. The Minors are a love of life . . . this life being the playing of a kid's game—baseball. Perhaps no one ever put it more succinctly than San Diego Padres broadcaster Jerry Coleman, a former New York Yankees infielder who has been associated with professional baseball for nearly fifty years. Coleman reflected on his 1942 season with a Class-D team from Wellsville, New York, and said, "It was a great, great summer, the best I've ever had in baseball. Only the game was important then. After that, winning and money became too important."

2
THE NEGRO
LEAGUES

In a game that was meant to be played by all, rules kept certain men out of the fun . . . the rules pertaining to race. An unwritten, often unspoken, agreement based on bigotry and apartheid simply and effectively stated that blacks and whites will be kept separate on the diamond. That meant no integrated teams will be formed and no white teams will be allowed to play black teams in sanctioned National Association games. Fearing economic reprisals, boycotts, or expulsion from leagues, surprisingly few team owners and players tried to buck the "good old boy network" and allowed the prejudice to permeate the sport for half-a-century.

In the early days of baseball, all men were allowed to play the game. Moses and Welday Walker, two black athletes, played for Toledo of the Major League American Association in 1884. And research has shown that no fewer than sixty blacks played in the Minor Leagues from 1883 to 1898, and more are being discovered all the time.

John W. Fowler is thought to be the first black to play on an otherwise all-white team, in New Castle, Pennsylvania, in 1872, three years after he began his career with an all-black team, the Washington, DC, Mutuals. By 1884, he had moved on to Stillwater, Minnesota, of the Northwestern League and it is thought that he played in at least seven different leagues around the country.

Speculation insists that Vincent Nava, who played for Providence and Baltimore from 1882 to 1886, and George Treadway, who was with Baltimore, Brooklyn, and Louisville from 1893 to 1896 were black, but evidence is not conclusive.

In 1887, in the International Association, Bud Fowler hit .350 for Binghamton and Frank Grant batted .366 for Buffalo, while Newark's George Stover won thirty-four games on the mound, where he and Moses Walker formed the first all-black pitcher-catcher battery in Organized Baseball.

In 1889, the Middle States League agreed that the bankrupt Trenton franchise would be replaced by the Cuban Giants, an all-black team that contained no Cubans, as the media of the day preferred to avoid the terms "Negro" and "black," choosing instead to call the teams "colored," or "Spaniard," or "Indian," or "Cuban." It was more readily accepted if the team was foreign than if it were black. Another black team, the New York Gorhams, also got into the league that year, and, oddly enough, George Stover pitched for both black teams that year.

In 1890, the Cuban Giants moved on to the Eastern Interstate League, representing York, Pennsylvania, but the team jumped in and out of fast-folding leagues and played more games as an independent team than as a league member.

There were numerous independent black teams at the time, and a black or Negro league was not even a dream then.

By 1895, several blacks were still playing in the Michigan State League—George Wilson of Adrian went 29–4, but few other blacks played on integrated teams.

In 1898, Harry Curtis, a white man, put together a talented, but young, all-black team and inserted them into the Oil and Iron League. Officially called the Acme Colored Giants of Celeron, New York, the team was derided and called simply "The Darkies," or the "Celeron Chocolates," by bigoted press members and opponents. And that same season, Bert "The Yellow Kid" Jones pitched well in the Kansas State League and may have been the last black to be officially welcomed into the Minors until Jackie Robinson in 1946, as the white players and owners network worked in concert to exclude blacks from the National Pastime, for, as one researcher puts it, "in the National census, blacks were only counted as two-thirds of a person anyway, so the sociological sentiments of the day almost made it a natural course of action, as convoluted as that thinking was."

Other blacks probably "passed" as either white, Latin, or Indian, and there is little doubt that some blacks were smuggled into lineups around the country, or pressed into service in outlaw leagues (leagues with no official National Association ties) or in Mexico, but other than that, the only way for a black to play baseball was with an independent team or barnstorming troop.

That was, until 1913, when, according to Negro Leagues researcher Phil Dixon, author of *The Negro Baseball Leagues: A Photographic History,* Rube Foster, thought of as one of the greatest pitchers in the game, wrote, " 'Organization is the only hope. With the proper organization, patterned after the men who have made baseball a great success, we will, in three years, be rated as other leagues are rated.' "

Calling for a league to be formed on the same basis as the Major League was formed, Foster's dream began to take shape in 1916 when the independent Chicago American Giants visited Kansas City to play the All-Nations Club.

One of the forces behind the Negro Leagues was the highly respected and innovative founder of the Kansas City Monarchs, J. L. Wilkinson. Wilkinson, the only white owner in the Negro Leagues, set up what was arguably the strongest and most secure franchise in the Negro circuit, creating the Monarchs as the All-Nations Club, an integrated multiracial, multinational team consisting of blacks, whites, Native Americans, Asians, Hawaiians, Hispanics, and a female second baseman.

It was Wilkinson who signed Jackie Robinson to his first professional contract, and in 1930, his club became the first to use a portable lighting system to introduce night baseball. Under his guidance, the Monarchs won twelve league crowns from 1923 to 1950.

And it was Wilkinson who initiated bus travel as a thrifty means of transportation for Minor League teams, which had used trains for most of their road needs. He was also one of the first owners to use promotional "days" as a means of drawing fans: Tennessee Day; Kids Day; Ladies Day; Alabama Day; et al. And he brought night baseball to the Negro Leagues, a move that increased his profits threefold.

But this 1916 game was the beginning, and within four years, Wilkinson and Foster had made believers out of investors and team owners in the Midwest.

On February 20, 1920, a meeting at the YMCA in Kansas City was presided over by Foster, which included such independent team owners as Tenny Blount (Detroit Stars), Joe Green (Chicago Giants), Wilkinson (All-Nations), C. I. Taylor (Indianapolis ABCs), Foster (American Giants and Cuban Stars), and Lorenzo Cobb (St. Louis Giants). John Matthews of the Dayton Marcos was too ill to attend but pledged his support. Members of the press and civic leaders also joined in this historic confab.

From this meeting emerged an eight-team "experimental circuit" called the Negro National League. Rube Foster was named president of the governing body, known as the National Association of Colored Professional Baseball Clubs.

The league opened in Indianapolis on May 2, 1920, and the host ABCs defeated the Chicago Giants 4–2. Attendance for the entire league reached nearly one million, and it is thought that several of the teams showed profits.

Subject to the same underfinancing that plagued its white counterparts, the Negro National League saw an influx of bankrupt teams and moved franchises over the next few years, and when the Eastern Colored League began in 1923, several teams pirated away top players from the older loop. The new league learned from the NNL's mistakes. The NNL's teams played nonuniform schedules and uneven numbers of games, whereas the ECL pledged to play set schedules . . . a pledge it failed to keep, as teams played anywhere from thirty-six to forty-nine games.

By 1924, however, an agreement was hammered out by the NNL's Foster and ECL prexy Ed Bolden to hold a World Series between winners of their respective leagues.

Playing in neutral Major League parks (Philadelphia, Kansas City, Baltimore, and Chicago) to assure larger attendance, the series went ten games as the Kansas City Monarchs, led by Bullet Joe Rogan, Newt Allen, Dobie Moore, and Hurley McNair, defeated the Hilldale club led by Judy Johnson, Rube Currie, and Nip Winters, five games to four with one tie.

Another league sprung up in the early '20s, the Negro Southern League, but that was considered a Minor League by Negro League officials and aficionados until about 1932, when it absorbed several NNL teams.

Rube Foster suffered a mental breakdown in 1926, and without his hand to guide the NNL, it was thought the league might fold. It didn't, but the ECL did, in 1928, due to financial burdens.

The American Colored League took its place, but that, too, failed by 1930.

And, because of the Great Depression, falling ticket sales, and the desire of the Kansas City Monarchs to become an independent team again, the Negro National League fell in 1932.

The East-West League made a one-year run in 1932, and

from 1933 to 1936, the Negro Southern League continued to run but was still thought of as a Minor.

A new Negro National League was formed and operated teams in the East, Midwest, and South and was successful for more than a decade.

In 1937, the Negro American League was established, running Southern and Midwestern franchises. The league flourished, and it absorbed the NNL in 1948, becoming the last survivor of the Negro League genre.

In an effort to break the color barrier and buy and operate a winning franchise, Minor League owner Bill Veeck found out in 1943 that the Philadelphia Phillies had been put into receivership by the National League and was up for sale.

Veeck wanted to buy the team and stock it with Negro League all-stars. With Major League teams pillaged by the military—World War II left many rosters bare—Veeck theorized that top black players could mean an instant pennant to his Phillies.

Veeck made one mistake. He called baseball commissioner Judge Kenesaw Mountain Landis and told him of the plan. He asked if there were any rule against such a move. Landis told him that legally, there was no rule prohibiting blacks from playing in the Majors and that such a rule would violate the nation's laws.

Veeck left the meeting convinced he would soon have a franchise, a pennant, and an integrated baseball world within days. He was naive.

As soon as Veeck left Landis's office, the commissioner engineered a quick sale of the Phils to lumberman William D. Cox, selling the team before Veeck had a chance to make his move.

The kicker is that ten months later, Landis expelled Cox from baseball for having bet on his Phillies to win ballgames, a violation of the no-betting rule.

Back to the Negro Leagues. Before the 1946 season, Branch Rickey reached into the Negro Leagues and plucked Jackie Robinson, Roy Campanella, Don Newcombe, and Roy Partlow from the circuit, making them property of the Brooklyn Dodgers and their Farm clubs.

This pretty much sounded the death knell for the loop.

Financially, the Negro Leagues were, for the most part, unaffected by the integration year of 1946.

But by 1947, when blacks began playing in the Majors, fans who had supported Negro teams began buying tickets for Major League clubs with black players. Attendance dropped in the major cities of the Negro Leagues—in 1946, the Newark Eagles drew 120,000 fans and by 1948, attendance was down to 35,000.

This forced several teams to play all their games on the road in areas where Major League baseball was not a threat. The New York Black Yankees became a traveling team called the Black Yankee Travelers in 1949, and they survived as a barnstorming show until 1955.

Negro League stars who made it to The Show in large cities, and who in effect helped the demise of the Negro Leagues included: Charlie Neal (Brooklyn from the Atlanta Black Crackers), Joe Black, Roy Campanella, and Jim Gilliam (Brooklyn from the Baltimore Elite Giants), Willie Mays (New York from the Birmingham Black Barons), Sam Jethroe (Boston from the Cleveland Buckeyes), Henry Aaron (Boston from the Indianapolis Clowns), Ernie Banks (Chicago from the Kansas City Monarchs), Monte Irvin (New York from the Newark Eagles), Larry Doby (Cleveland from the Newark Eagles), Minnie Minoso (Chicago from the New York Cubans), and Satchel Paige (Cleveland from the Kansas City Monarchs).

By 1950, uneven scheduling and weak franchises surfaced again—the Indianapolis Clowns played thirty-nine games in the second half of the season, the New York Cubans only eight, and the Philadelphia Stars, twelve.

When Elston Howard, a former Kansas City Monarch, made his first appearance for the previously all-white New York Yankees on April 8, 1955, it effectively took New York fans away from the Negro Leagues and exclusively to the Major Leagues.

The NAL tried to hang on, and into the early 1960s, teams played in small towns, as a traveling show, playing four-team doubleheaders and it officially disbanded after the 1963 season.

The Kansas City Monarchs, operating as an independent, with Satchel Paige, at age fifty-eight making guest appearances for them, failed after one more season on the road in 1964.

The final round was delivered by the Indianapolis Clowns, who struggled to play some barnstorming tours on an irregular basis in the early 1970s.

Many were saddened by the demise of the Negro Leagues, but, as Phil Dixon writes, "Their death was the ultimate victory," and indeed it was, as it was spawned out of bigotry and died when American baseball came to its senses.

⚾   ⚾   ⚾   ⚾

What were the Negro Leagues?

Books can be written about that, but maybe it was a credo: "Just play ball," or man's desire to play the game without sweating the small stuff . . . like color, or inane rules.

One rule ignored by the Negro Leagues was the banishment of the spitball. Trick pitches were part of the allure, innocence, entertainment and Americana of the Negro Leagues. Sam Streeter, "The King of the Spitball," and Smokey Joe Williams, "The Master of Sandpaper" (and a thick, sticky, black substance that defies description), often locked horns and pitched against each other in a "Battle of Butchered Balls." Such was the case in 1930, when Williams faced a scuffball ace, Chet Brewer. Williams, of the Homestead Grays, beat Brewer and his Kansas City Monarchs, 1–0, as Smokey Joe struck out 27 batters and Brewer fanned 19 in a 12-inning monument to sweat, spit, tar, scuffs, mud, and outrageous pitching.

The Negro Leagues were gamesmanship, competitive

spirit, win at all costs—but have fun doing it. It was allowing men to play a kid's game without concern over a man's skin color.

Inside the Negro Leagues:
- The 1909 Kansas City Giants set the all-time Organized Baseball record for consecutive wins, with an impressive 54-game win streak.
- In 1912, Dick "Cannonball" Redding, who perhaps threw the hardest, fastest pitches in the Negro Leagues, and who developed the hesitation pitch delivery before Satchel Paige got hold of it and popularized it, went 43–12, threw a 17-strikeout perfect game and 24-strikeout victory.
- In 1921, Dick "King Richard" Lundy, arguably the most graceful shortstop in Negro Leagues history, was a switch-hitter who could stick it. In 1921, with the Atlantic City Bacharach Giants, Lundy hit .484. Three years later, he led the Eastern Colored League with 13 homers.
- In 1925, Oscar Charleston won the league's batting crown at .430, besting John Beckwith, who came in second at .419.
- In 1927, John Beckwith led the leagues by belting 12 homers, but in the year of Babe Ruth's 60 homeruns, Beckwith is said to have wound up the year—including barnstorming games, all-star games, and exhibitions against industrial teams, city all-stars, and Major League teams—with 72. The top hitter that year was line drive smashing Jud Wilson at .408.
- In 1929, the Baltimore Black Sox employed their "million dollar infield," consisting of third baseman Oliver "Ghost" Marcelle, second baseman Frank Warfield, first baseman Jud "Boojum" Wilson, and shortstop Dick Lundy. The Black Sox won the Negro American League championship that year. The money title bestowed upon them was based on the conjecture that their collective talents would

have been worth that much to a Major League team had they been allowed to play at that level.

- In 1934, Jud Wilson again led the league in batting at .412 for the Pittsburgh Crawfords. Hitting equally as well with his fists as with his bat, Crawford was suspended during the 1934 play-offs for punching an umpire.
- In the mid-1930s, Gene Benson, a graceful, acrobatic outfielder with the Bacharach Giants and Pittsburgh Crawfords, popularized the basket catch . . . a technique that Willie Mays immortalized in the 1950s.
- In 1947, while pitching for the New York Cubans at the age of forty-one, Luis Tiant, Sr., father of Major League star pitcher Luis Tiant, compiled a perfect 10–0 record with eight complete games and three shutouts. This occurred twelve years after the ace junkball-screwball pitcher pitched and won two games against "The Babe Ruth All-Stars," a 1935 Major League barnstorming group. Tiant, Sr., held the forty-two-year-old Bambino to a lonely single in the two contests.

Tiant, Sr., who loved the mano-a-mano battle during the game, would often intentionally walk such speedsters as Cool Papa Bell, for the purpose of setting up a runner-pitcher dogfight. Tiant, Sr.'s pickoff move was so slick that legend has it he once picked a runner off first as the batter swung at a nonexistent pitch home for strike three. The kicker to this story is that the hitter insisted he fouled the pitch off.

⚾   ⚾   ⚾   ⚾

Despite the break in the color line, it wasn't easy by any means, and prejudice still was high among the "good old boys" of the baseball establishment.

When Robinson was officially admitted to the National League, Enos Slaughter, the same hustling athlete who never walked on a ballfield, and fellow Southerner Terry Moore, tried to organize their St. Louis Cardinal teammates into going on strike in protest against Robinson's inclusion into the Major League fraternity. When this revolt failed, Slaughter, showing his dislike of the situation, deliberately spiked first baseman Robinson in the leg after Slaughter had been thrown out by several steps on a ground ball.

And the physical abuse was nothing compared to the verbal abuse—the comments the early blacks had to withstand as they attempted to fit in. But then, baseball has recorded, bigotry always ran deep in the game, and blacks were merely a part of the mosaic from which prejudice reared its ugly head.

Blacks joined Jewish ballplayers, including Hank Greenberg and Moe Berg, who had to use their fists at times to stem the anti-Semitic tide of slurs leveled against them. Italians were cursed by the Irish—nearly all Italians were nicknamed "Dago," except for Joe DiMaggio, who was reverently referred to as "The Dago." Irish were verbally blasted. So were Catholics. And big city boys. And farmers. And the verbally impaired. And those who read books. And the offbeat. And anyone deemed by the establishment as being slightly different or out of the *accepted* mainstream.

This piece of bigotry, in some obscene, convoluted manner, actually created the result of showing that black ballplayers were indeed being assimilated into the baseball world. They were being allowed to play against those who took the position of hatred! In this violent and vile way, the blacks had gained a certain form of acceptance with those who also drew the wrath, the slings, and arrows of the WASPish leaders of the diamond.

While the statistics during the Negro Leagues era are sketchy—and, at times, downright inaccurate—thirty of those stars who passed this way, hit with the following success:

    Charlie "Chino" Smith (1925–30)—.423
    Jackie Robinson (1945)—.387
    Larry Doby (1942–47)—.378

John Henry "Pop" Lloyd (1914–32)—.368
John Beckwith (1920–26)—.366
Dobie Moore (1920–26)—.365
Oscar "Heavy" Johnson (1922–30)—.363
Norman "Turkey" Stearnes (1923–40)—.359
Oscar Charleston (1915–41)—.357
Josh Gibson (1930–46)—.354
Sam Jethroe (1942–47)—.347
Hank Thompson (1943–48)—.347
Monte Irvin (1939–45)—.346
Jud "Boojum" Wilson (1922–46)—.345
Ed "Huck" Rile (1920–31)—.344
Wilbur "Bullet" Joe Rogan (1920–38)—.343
"Cool Papa" Bell (1922–50)—.338
George "Mule" Suttles (1923–44)—.338
Luke Easter (1947–48)—.336
Ray Dandridge (1933–44)—.335
Howard Easterling (1937–50)—.334
Fats Jenkins (1920–38)—.334
Roy Campanella (1938–45)—.334
Willie "Devil" Wells (1924–48)—.331
Buck Leonard (1934–48)—.324
William Julius "Judy" Johnson (1919–36)—.303
Elston Howard (1949–50)—.289
Ted "Double Duty" Radcliffe (1928–45)—.282
Willie Mays (1948–50)—.263
Ernie Banks (1950)—.255

Negro League heroes (others including Oscar Charleston, Josh Gibson, Ray Dandridge, Jackie Robinson, Jud Wilson, and Luke Easter who are highlighted or profiled elsewhere in this book—(see Chapter 19: The Players: Yesterday, Today, and Tomorrow) were many, and include the following dozen stars, selected here, not for statistics alone, but as a representation of contribution, style, and manner that made them and those like them an integral part of Negro Leagues lore:

John Beckwith—John Beckwith, the third baseman-shortstop known as "The Black Bomber," was a six-foot-three, 230-pound block of granite in a baseball uniform, who pulled pitches with his huge thirty-eight inch log of a bat to distances rivaling anything fellow Negro Leaguer Josh Gibson, or white contemporary Babe Ruth, ever reached.

Beckwith pulled so consistently that many opposing managers aligned their infield in severe shifts—later used against Ted Williams and called "the Ted Williams shift"— in which all four infielders stationed themselves on the first base side of the second base bag, leaving the left side bare. Beckwith pulled hits through the right side anyway, finishing above .400 four times—hitting a whopping .480 in 1930 for the New York Lincoln Giants and Baltimore Black Sox—for a career mark of .366 over fifteen years.

As a nineteen-year-old, playing his second season for the Chicago Giants in 1921, Beckwith became the first player ever to belt a homerun over the laundry roof at Cincinnati's Crosley Field. His longest shot, however, may have been the one he blasted at Washington's Griffith Stadium—site of Mickey Mantle's legendary moon shot off Chuck Stobbs that came to rest 565 feet from home plate. Beckwith bombed one off an advertising sign some 460 feet from home plate and forty feet high. Unimpeded, the blast would have rivaled Mantle's.

Cool Papa Bell—James "Cool Papa" Bell was a switch-hitting, six-foot, 165-pound smooth-swinging outfielder blessed with blinding speed, a sure glove, accurate arm, quick bat, and nonpareil poise under pressure which earned him his nickname.

Bell's twenty-eight-year career (1922–50) saw him hit over .400 twice en route to a career average of .338. He never won a batting title, but had one in his grasp when, at age forty-three, in 1946, he was locked in a race for the crown with twenty-seven-year-old outfielder Monte Irvin (Newark Eagles). Bell, playing for the Homestead Grays, deliberately forfeited his chance at the title, allowing Irvin to win it, thereby enhancing Irvin's attractiveness to Major League owners who had just seen Jackie Robinson break the color barrier.

Regarding Bell's speed, roommate Satchel Paige often remarked, "Bell is so fast, he can turn out the light and be in bed before the room gets dark."

A popular story of the day involved Bell hitting a pitch during a game and driving a ground ball up the middle. The story ends with the sharp grounder bounding toward second base and striking Bell as the speedster slid in to the bag.

A more believable tale, documented, occurred during an interracial All-Star game played in California in the '30s. With Bell at first base, teammate Paige laid down a bunt. Cleveland Indians catcher Roy Partee ambled out in front of the plate, grabbed the ball, and as he prepared to throw to first to get Paige, Bell brushed by him to score—all the way from first.

It has been calculated (though statistics are sketchy) that during one 200-game season, Bell stole 175 bases.

He was offered a chance at Major League stardom in 1951 by the St. Louis Browns. Bell, then age forty-eight, turned down the chance, saying he was too old to do his team justice.

Rube Foster—Andrew "Rube" Foster was a six-foot-five-inch, 235-pound screwball pitcher who was widely regarded as the top black pitcher in America from 1902–26. In 1903, he pitched the Cuban X-Giants to four victories in the Black World Series over the Philadelphia Giants. Switching uniforms—and allegiances—he won both games the next year for Philadelphia in their two-out-of-three championship win over the X-Giants.

Foster, called by Honus Wagner "the smartest pitcher I've ever seen," is credited with an undocumented 51–4 won-lost record in one season early in the 1900s.

Foster, a father of the Negro Leagues, also earned raves as a manager, leading his Chicago Leland Giants to a 110–10 record in 1907. And in 1910, as his team's manager and best pitcher, he directed the team to a 123–6 record.

In 1919, while leading the Chicago American Giants, he helped form the Negro National League and, as a manager, is credited with inventing the bunt-and-run and several other strategies and tactics.

Monte Irvin—Merrill Monford Irvin was a six-foot-two, 200-pound outfielder who was a star on the Major League, Minor League, and Negro League levels. An athlete who could do the five things Leo Durocher said were the sign of a great player: "hit, hit with power, run, field, and throw," Irvin devastated Negro Leagues pitching to the tune of .403 for the 1939 Newark Eagles, and a reported .531 in a brief run with the Eagles in 1942, before he headed south of the border, continuing that success in the Mexican League, with a league-leading .397 average, top-ranked 20 homers in 63 games, loop-heading .772 slugging percentage, and run production at an RBI-a-game pace.

Following a three-year hitch in the U.S. Army, he returned to baseball and was rewarded for his performance by being named MVP in the Puerto Rican Winter League of 1945–46.

After leading his Kansas City Monarchs to a Negro League championship in 1946, Irvin was assigned to the Jersey City club in the International League, hit .373 there and then maintained his excellence in the Majors as a member of the New York Giants, hitting .312, with 24 homers and 121 RBI in 1951.

Sam Jethroe—Samuel "Jet" Jethroe, the six-foot-one, 178-pound outfielder, was a superb-hitting, poor-fielding speedster who hit .487 in his first year with the Cleveland Buckeyes (1942) and finished a six-year Negro Leagues career at .347.

And he had some power. Though never a monster home-run hitter in the same vein as Josh Gibson or John Beckwith, the switch-hitter is the only player ever to have hit a ball over Toledo's Swayne Field's 472-foot left-field fence and into the coal piles belonging to the Red Man Tobacco Company.

He was looked at by the Boston Red Sox in 1945 and was called "a gazelle in the outfield" by coach Hugh Duffy. Nevertheless, he was passed over for a spot on the BoSox . . .

the last Major League team to integrate (some fourteen years later).

Signed by the Boston Braves, he spent two strong years in the Minors, and following an eighty-nine-steal season in the International League in 1949, Jethroe was elevated to the Major Leagues, where, as the Braves' first black player, he won the National League Rookie-of-the-Year Award in 1950, based on a .272 average, 18 homers, 100 runs scored, and senior circuit-topping 35 stolen bases.

Judy Johnson—William Julius Johnson was as good a batting-fielding third baseman as there was in baseball, from 1919–36. At five-foot-eleven, 150 pounds, Johnson was quick, agile, and sure-handed, with a clutch bat and slashing style.

Called "The black Pie Traynor," Johnson got his nickname, Judy, because he resembled a Negro Leagues contemporary, Chicago American Giants' Judy Ganz.

Johnson hit .406 in 1929 in the Eastern Colored League for the Philadelphia Hilldales, and compiled an eighteen-year average of .303. Playing six winters in Cuba and Florida, Johnson batted .334, and his ninth-inning, two-out bases-loaded line-drive single in the sixth game of the 1935 Negro League World Series helped his Pittsburgh Crawfords defeat the New York Cubans and take the crown.

Johnson also gets a footnote in history as a player-coach for the 1930 Homestead Grays. When his catcher was injured, Johnson grabbed an eighteen-year-old catcher from the stands, signed him up, put him in uniform and coached the young man—Josh Gibson—into becoming one of the all-time greats in the game.

Buck Leonard—Walter Fenner Leonard was a five-foot-ten, 185-pound block of granite who played first base for the Washington Homestead Grays and Brooklyn Royal Giants from 1934 to 1950.

Leonard, who teamed with Josh Gibson on the Grays to win nine consecutive Negro National League championships (1937–45) earned the nickname "the black Lou Gehrig," as a companion to Gibson's "black Babe Ruth."

Together, the "Thunder Twins" smacked scores of home-runs; Gibson, with his tape-measure power, and Leonard, with his smooth Roger Maris-like lefty stroke.

A gifted first baseman, Leonard provided power and stability for the Grays for eighteen years, leading the league in home runs with forty-two in 1942. He went on to win three batting titles and another home run crown.

He was offered a spot with Bill Veeck's St. Louis Browns in 1949, but, at age forty-two, turned the job down saying he "didn't want to embarrass anyone or hurt the chances of someone who might follow him to the Majors."

Dobie Moore—Walter Moore, once called by Casey Stengel "one of the greatest shortstops who ever lived," the smooth-fielding infielder led his Kansas City Monarchs to three consecutive championships (1923–25) and hit at a .365 pace over a seven-year run with K.C.

Though a stocky five-foot-eleven, 200 pounds, Moore exhibited exceptional range and a rifle arm, and might have been elevated to legendary status had he not been accidentally shot in 1926.

Satchel Paige—Leroy Robert "Satchel" Paige may have been the greatest pitcher ever to throw a baseball . . . and tales about him could fill volumes. From 1927 to 1955, the six-foot-three, 180-pound Paige displayed uncanny ability, flashiness, style, brashness, braggadocio, and the power to back up his words with actions—all of which made him a folk hero. His presence served to thrill crowds and make him the most sought-after gate attraction in America after Babe Ruth.

He would rock into his legendary, high leg-kick windmill delivery and throw his hesitation pitch (stopping with one foot on the rubber and the other suspended in the air, midway into his delivery . . . a motion the Japanese have copied and often use in the Japan Leagues) or any of a number of pitches to which he gave names: "Little Tom" (a cut fastball), "Long Tom" (his blazing heat), and "The Two-hump blooper" (his moving change-up), displaying precise control and deceptiveness that won him (by estimation) 55 no-hitters and as many as 3,000 games.

He was finally allowed to pitch in the Major Leagues in 1948, and at the age of forty-two (or maybe forty-eight, as ex-teammate "Double Duty" Radcliffe asserts), went 6–1 with a 2.48 ERA in helping the Cleveland Indians win the American League pennant.

Ted "Double Duty" Radcliffe—The five-foot-ten, 212-pound athlete was given his nickname by Damon Runyan for performing "double duty" as both a pitcher and a catcher for several Negro Leagues teams from 1930 through 1946. The story goes that Runyan was watching the 1932 Negro League World Series at Yankee Stadium and saw Radcliffe catch teammate Satchel Paige in the first game of a doubleheader, which his Pittsburgh Crawfords won 5–0, then looked on as Radcliffe took the mound in the second game and proceeded to throw a shutout of his own to sweep the twin bill.

An excellent catcher with a strong arm, Radcliffe handled pitchers well and was steady enough at the stick—six times over .300 en route to a .282 career mark—to maintain a valued spot in the batting order.

But on the mound, Radcliffe at times exhibited greatness, using his emery ball and other trick pitches to fashion a .616 winning percentage, often going head-to-head with the top opponents' pitchers of the day, breaking even or better (he says) against the likes of Satchel Paige, Bullet Joe Rogan, Sam Streeter, Ray Brown, and Connie Johnson.

"Bullet Joe" Rogan—Another two-way player was five-foot-seven Wilbur Rogan, who played from 1920 to 1938 with the Kansas City Monarchs.

As a hitter, he was excellent enough to gain raves with his career mark of .343, including two .400 seasons and one homerun title—16 in 1922. And proficient with a glove, he played every position on the diamond at one time or another, all with successful results.

But on the mound, Rogan had no peer. He finished as the

top Negro Leagues winner of all time with a .721 winning percentage based on 111 wins and 43 losses. His repertoire on the hill included a blazing fastball (hence the nickname) that may have been second in speed only to that thrown by Dick "Cannonball" Redding, several curveballs and sliders, a forkball, palmball, and spit ball (legal in those days). And Rogan was renowned as one of the finest fielding pitchers of the era.

Rogan had been pitching for a U.S. Army team for nine years, when, at the age of thirty, he was discovered by Casey Stengel, who recommended him to Kansas City Monarchs owner J. L. Wilkinson, who signed him and watched him lead the Monarchs to several championships.

Mule Suttles—George Suttles was a six-foot-one, 212-pound hard-hitting outfielder-first baseman who played for twenty-one years, compiling a .338 career mark. Suttles won two batting crowns (including a .418 mark for the 1926 St. Louis Stars), and two home run titles (including 27 circuit-blasts for the '26 Stars).

A solid hitter, Suttles was an adequate fielder who might misplay an easy one early in a game, then make a game-saving circus catch of a tough one with the outcome on the line.

Just as Babe Ruth earned historical notoriety for blasting the first homerun in the Major Leagues' first All-Star game, Suttles accomplished the same feat in the Negro Leagues' first All-Star tilt. In five such contests, Suttles hit .412 with an .883 slugging percentage.

3
INTERNATIONAL
LEAGUE

The International League is the oldest Minor League alive today, having been established in 1884.

It is derived from three leagues: the Eastern League founded in 1884 (Richmond, Baltimore, and Newark were members), the New York State League (Rochester and Syracuse were teams) formed in 1885, and the Ontario League (Toronto made it to the reorganization) also founded in 1885.

The New York State and Ontario loops merged in 1886 to form the International League, and Buffalo, then in the National League, was also granted a franchise.

Final consolidation of the three leagues was effected in 1887 when the Eastern League was hit by dropouts and was down to two teams, Newark and Jersey City. The Eastern was then absorbed by the International League to form a ten-team circuit.

This group proved unwieldy and collapsed when Northern clubs withdrew, citing excessive distance from Southern teams. It quickly reorganized and was renamed the International Association, with teams from Buffalo, Rochester, Syracuse, Toronto, Hamilton, Albany, Troy, and London, and in 1889, Toledo and Detroit replaced Albany and Troy.

In 1890, franchise shifts, player pirating, and new leagues forced the league to disband, and it was reorganized again in 1891 as the Eastern Association. That name was changed to the Eastern League in 1892, a year that saw two teams fold, reducing the number of clubs to six.

The league grew stronger and in 1896, for the first time, there was not a single franchise shift—Rochester, Toronto, Buffalo, Providence, Scranton, Springfield, Syracuse, and Wilkes-Barre.

In 1897, when fire destroyed the Rochester home park, an agreement was reached to allow the Jingos to play their home games in Montreal, and by season's end, they had relocated there, with a group from Rochester purchasing the Scranton team to relocate back to Rochester.

Following some Minor League infighting in the early part of the century, the International League enjoyed prosperity until it was invaded by the upstart Federal League in 1914, putting teams in Baltimore, Buffalo, and Newark, taking away some IL fans and prosperity.

When the Federal League died in 1916 and the International League returned to health, World War I broke out and strapped the league. Revenues fell and the league was reorganized again as the new International League.

For the next decade franchise shifts became fewer and fewer as stability became the watchword of the IL.

Night baseball arrived on July 3, 1930, with a game at Buffalo, which the Bisons lost 5–4 to the Montreal Royals, and the next leap forward the IL experienced was the play-off plan offered by future IL president Frank Shaughnessy. It was a two-tiered play-off that kept up interest during the entire season: first place team plays fourth place team, second and third place teams square off, and the winners meet in the finals.

From 1937 to 1949, the IL remained steady without a single franchise shift, but as television popularity—and televised Major League games—took hold, the IL lost its New Jersey franchises and Ottawa replaced Jersey City while the popular Newark Bears club was resettled in Springfield.

The IL truly went international in 1954 when Havana was admitted to the loop. And when Baltimore was grabbed for Major League ball, the IL went back to Richmond.

In 1960, the league lost Havana due to the political climate in Cuba. When the circuit lost Montreal due to financial burdens in 1961, San Juan, Puerto Rico, was brought in to keep an international look. This proved to be an unwise move, and before season's end, the San Juan club relocated to Charleston, West Virginia.

After an ill-advised expansion to ten teams in 1963, the IL was down to eight clubs again the next year.

In 1965, Toledo returned to the IL fold after a seventy-six-year absence, replacing Richmond, which returned the next year when the IL lost Atlanta to the MLB Braves.

The next twelve years saw the league grow and prosper with franchise shifts again becoming fewer and farther between. League supremacy shifted between the Mets Tidewater club, the Orioles' Rochester team, and the Yankees' Columbus franchise.

The formation of the Triple-A Alliance (International League and American Association) brought a new look to the league structure as division play resumed for the first time in fifteen years, and interleague games were applauded by fans who filled stadiums to see teams they had not seen play before.

Attendance soared to 2,613,247 in 1989, to shatter the old mark of 2,358,270, which had stood since 1946, and with Major League expansion opening up possibly two new IL franchises, the future never looked brighter for the International League.

But gone is the "international" aspect to the league. There are no franchises outside the United States. Gone are Montreal, Toronto, Hamilton, and Winnipeg. Gone is Havana. Gone is San Juan, Puerto Rico.

Today, the International League is primarily an Eastern United States league, covering five states with teams from New York—Rochester (Orioles) and Syracuse (Blue Jays), Ohio—Columbus (Yankees) and Toledo (Tigers), Rhode Island—Pawtucket (Red Sox), Virginia—Richmond (Braves) and Tidewater (Mets), and Pennsylvania—Scranton/Wilkes-Barre (Phillies).

In 1990, the Rochester Red Wings took the Eastern Division by going 89–56, a whopping 21½ games better than second-place Scranton/Wilkes-Barre, while the Columbus Clippers took another title with an 87–59 mark, 8 games ahead of Tidewater. Rochester outlasted Columbus in five games to take the IL crown.

Among the IL's most interesting nicknames are: Toledo Mud Hens, Scranton Red Barons, and Rochester Red Wings.

What is the International League?

Tim McCarver, the former star catcher for the St. Louis Cardinals, reported that in 1959, his first year with the Rochester Red Wings, he was rookie-ized, which meant he was the brunt of jokes. A prank that the naive seventeen-year-old fell for: when Dick Rand, a twenty-eight-year-old catcher on his way down, told the rookie to "get the keys to the batter's box," and when McCarver asked for directions, Rand told him, "They're next to the glove stretcher," Mc-Carver spent quite a while looking for these non-existent items before he wised up and began to pull the same and more creative jokes on other teammates.

And if something else epitomizes the International League, it may be the combination of strategy and competitive spirit. These traits are illustrated by the mind game played by the thinking man's manager, Paul Richards, mentor of Buffalo. During one game in 1949, Buffalo was leading Montreal by a run, with one out, and no one on in the seventh. The Montreal pitcher was up at the plate, and on deck was the speedy Sam Jethroe, the former Negro Leagues great who set an IL record that season by swiping 89 bags. To keep Jethroe from getting on, stealing second and scoring on a fair single, Richards instructed his pitcher to walk the opposing hurler, clogging the bases, keeping a slow runner on first (or second if Jethroe got on), and maintaining a doubleplay situation on the bases. The strategy worked, and Buffalo came home with a one-run victory.

But the International League is also broken dreams . . . or broken ankles that end dreams.

Andy Cohen, a ballyhooed ballplayer who had several shots with the New York Giants—he replaced Frankie Frisch and Rogers Hornsby at second base for the Giants—was sent down to Newark following a .294 season in The Show in 1929. Giants skipper John McGraw felt that an old football injury had slowed Cohen down and at the age of twenty-five, Cohen had to re-prove himself to get another chance.

Cohen made the best of it and hit a solid .317 for Newark in 1931, and McGraw thought long and hard about bringing the ballplayer back to New York. Then a broken ankle and an illness in 1932 banished Cohen to toil in the Minors for the rest of his career, without another day in the sun at the Big League level.

And the International League is fun and games . . . and all-in-fun cheating, as Al Schacht demonstrated in 1913.

During a game against Buffalo, Schacht, a lanky (five-foot-eleven, 140-pound) pitcher for Newark, reached first base on a walk. When the opposing pitcher tried to pick him off, Schacht dove back to the bag and fell on top of the baseball. The first baseman, hearing the yells of the Newark fans who insisted the throw had rolled down the line, took off to find a nonexistent ball. Schacht, meanwhile, slipped the sphere into his pocket and took off for second, then third, and then home. Buffalo players looked frantically for the ball they could not find. Schacht slid into home and his crash sent the ball spinning out of his pocket and against the feet of home plate umpire Bill O'Brien.

O'Brien called Schacht out for interference and the league fined the hurler $50. This event got Schacht the laughs he yearned for and began a fifty-year career as "The Clown Prince of Baseball."

Later that year, Schacht found a cheap, imitation baseball made of pressed rags and oilcloth. He took this imposter to the ballpark with him and exchanged it for a real ball when he came in to relieve late in the ballgame.

This dead pile of rags served him well, as he got a power hitter to blast the ball . . . to short; another homerun type to kill the sphere . . . back to the mound; and a third batsman to belt one back to the mound for out number three. When the third hitter, rival pitcher Rube Parnham, demanded to see the ball, Schacht gave him the real one (hiding the faker) and Parnham exploded, taking the ball and throwing it over the roof and out of the ballpark. Parnham was thumbed out by the ump for his actions.

And, of course, the International League was the bigotry breaker.

Jackie Robinson's insertion into the Montreal Royals lineup on April 19, 1946, set aside the color barrier that had permeated the sport since the turn of the century.

And one opinion of the International League and the Minors in general comes from Wally Backman.

Backman, the ex-Met who played second base for the Tidewater Tides, summed up his feelings about Minor League ball and the IL, recalling that he had started the 1981 season with the Mets and was then sent down to the International League and Tidewater, when he said, "I'd rather be an unpaid Major Leaguer than a $3000 a month Minor Leaguer."

⚾   ⚾   ⚾   ⚾

Inside the International League:
- Babe Ruth made his presence felt by pitching to a 22–9 mark for Baltimore and Providence in 1914.

- The 1920 Baltimore Orioles won the pennant the hard way, if winning 110 games for a winning percentage of .719 is the hard way. They beat the Toronto Maple Leafs by only 2½ games and the Orioles had to win their final 25 consecutive games to produce a pennant. The Leafs never folded as they won 24 of their final 26 in a vain attempt to capture the flag.
- Deciding not to save the best for last, the 1922 Baltimore Orioles won 27 consecutive games in May to run away with the title—they won 119 games to take the championship by 20 games.
- The International League produced three 30-game winners in five years: John Ogden in 1921, Rube Parnham in 1923, and Tommy Thomas in 1925.
- Fred "Bonehead" Merkle, the maligned player who blew a crucial game for the New York Giants in 1908 by failing to touch second base when an apparent winning run had scored, made good in the International League when he drove in 166 runs for Rochester in 1923. He also reverted to poor form, when four years later, he managed the Reading entry that lost 31 straight games.
- With the good, there is some bad . . . some very bad. In 1926 Reading completed one of the worst seasons in baseball history by winning only thirty-one games and losing 129 for a meager .194 winning percentage. They finished seventy-five games behind first-place Toronto.
- Andy Cohen warmed up for his first shot in The Show—as New York Giants second sacker—by hitting .353 and driving in 118 runs for Buffalo in 1927.
- The 1937 Newark Bears went 109–43 to finish 25½ games ahead of second-place Montreal. The antithesis of the '26 Reading club, the '37 Bears are considered one of the greatest Minor League clubs in history.
- In 1938, Buffalo outfielder Bob Seeds put on a two-day hitting display the league has never seen before or since. On May 6 against the Bears, Seeds went 5 for 5 with 12 RBI, and hit homeruns in four consecutive innings (the

fourth, fifth, sixth, and seventh). On May 7, he hit three more homers and a single to run his two-day onslaught over Newark to 9 for 10, 7 homers and 17 RBI.

- Hank Sauer was named the IL MVP by virtue of his fifty homers, 141 RBI and .337 average in 1947 for Syracuse.
- Sam Jethroe, a stellar outfielder in the Negro Leagues, showed he could outrun anything in shinguards by stealing eighty-nine bases in 1949. A year later, he was in the Bigs, winning the Rookie-of-the-Year Award with the Boston Braves.
- Also in 1949, making his long-awaited debut in Organized Baseball, Monte Irvin broke in with Jersey City and batted .373. In 1950, the New York Giants, apparently not sure he was ready for Big League pitching, started him out in Jersey City again. Irvin showed he was, indeed, ready, by hitting .510 with 10 homers in 18 games. He was then called up and became a star with the Giants.
- Elston Howard won the 1954 MVP award for Toronto on the strength of his .330, 22 homers, 109 RBI season. Nine years later, he won the American League MVP for the Yankees.
- Satchel Paige, now aging and demoted from the Majors, made a pitch to hang on for three years with Bill Veeck's Miami Marlins (1955–58). Paige had limited success (give him a break, the man was close to sixty years old!), but he always drew big crowds.
- The 1958 International League Most Valuable Pitcher was Tommy Lasorda, now manager of the Los Angeles Dodgers. Lasorda, who was cut from the Brooklyn Dodgers' squad to make room for Sandy Koufax in 1955, is one of the winningest pitchers in International League history with 125 wins for the Montreal Royals. Lasorda is topped by Johnny Ogden, who won 213 games in his IL career from 1918–34.
- The year 1981 saw the longest game in baseball history, in which the Pawtucket Red Sox tangled with the Rochester Red Wings in a 33-inning, 8-hour-25-minute, 66-

day contest, resumed more than two months after the originally scheduled tilt.

On April 18, 1981, Danny Parks, the PawSox, hurler fired a fastball to Redwings lead-off man Tom Eaton, at 8 p.m.

By 4:07 a.m., Easter Sunday, April 19, the game had lasted 32 innings with the score tied 2–2. The game was suspended at that point.

On June 23, Red Sox hitter Dave Koza singled home Marty Barrett in the bottom of the 33rd, to ice a 3–2 victory for Pawtucket.

Among those "name" players to have performed in that longest day were winning pitcher Bobby Ojeda, Pawtucket pitchers Bruce Hurst and Mike Smithson, third baseman Wade Boggs, second baseman Marty Barrett, rightfielder Sam Bowen, and catcher Rich Gedman. On the Rochester side were third baseman Cal Ripken, Jr., and catcher Floyd Rayford.

[*Author's note:* On Sunday, April 19, the afternoon following the first 32 innings of the affair, Pawtucket and Rochester hooked up in a regularly scheduled game that was tied into the ninth, at 3–3. As players looked at themselves in a "here-we-go-again" disbelief, Rochester pulled it out 4–3.]

• And it was down on the farm at Pawtucket where Wade Boggs, the lefty third baseman and premier hitter for the parent Boston Red Sox, developed his superstition of running his laps at 7:17 each night. Boggs first took a look at the numerical clock and envisioned 7:17 as "seven for seven." Thinking that to be the very best performance a player could hope for—seven hits in one night is a career for many players—Boggs began his ritual as a means of pregame preparation and used it to win an Eastern League batting crown in his final Minor League season, 1981, with a .335 mark. It carried over into The Show, and Boggs has responded to a career average in excess of .350 through nine seasons, with five more batting titles.

Boggs was beaten for another International League Silver Bat in 1980, when, on the last day of the season, he was beaten out by .0007 to Toledo's Dave Engle at .307.

- Joe Lis, a first baseman for the Toledo Mud Hens (he also played eight years in the Majors with four teams—.314 for Cleveland in 1976) was given a series of awards for Minor League excellence, all resulting in the presentation of silver cups and bowls. His remark: "Even my dogs eat out of silver bowls, now."

- Showing that strange things can happen on the field on the Farm, Los Angeles Dodgers infielder Mike Sharperson, known more for his glove than for his bat, once whipped Detroit Tigers strongman Cecil Fielder in a homerun hitting contest when both were property of the Toronto Blue Jays and the IL Syracuse Chiefs.

In 1986, Sharperson won a set of airline tickets—he says they expired before he got to use them—by defeating Fielder 4–3.

Sharperson still brags about the incident while Fielder remembers it differently: "I got him. I won," he says.

Former Toronto Farmhand Dave Walsh, now also with the Dodgers, votes for Sharperson's memory, reporting, "Now I heard this third-hand because I was Double-A at the time, but that story was all over the organization— about how weak Mike Sharperson beat strong Cecil Fielder in that home run hitting contest."

To illustrate how big an upset the homerun contest was, on August 17, 1990, Sharperson hit his first Major League homer in his 446th at bat. On the same day, Fielder connected for his 37th homer in just his 423rd at bat in 1990.

- In 1987, after being sent down by the Detroit Tigers to the Minors, young-looking second baseman Jim Walewander, playing for Toledo, said "The only difference between the Minor Leagues and the Major Leagues was that in the Majors I had fewer bugs in my apartment."

He also admitted that when he was down on the Farm, he didn't think much of his play or his attire. "In the Minors I liked to wear a collared shirt under my uni. The shirts with the button-down collars. I figured if I'm going to play like a pussy, I might as well dress like one."

• Mike Marshall of the Boston Red Sox put in a guest appearance at Pawtucket in August 1990, on rehab assignment, just in time to get healthy for the BoSox pennant drive.

⚾   ⚾   ⚾   ⚾

The all-time International League career leaders list is a mixed bag of performers:

(*Source:* SABR)

Games played	Eddie Onslow	2,109
Runs Scored	Fritz Maisel	1,379
Hits	Eddie Onslow	2,445
Doubles	Jimmy Walsh	405
Triples	Eddie Onslow	128
Homeruns	Ollie Carnegie	258
RBI	Ollie Carnegie	1,044
Stolen Bases	Fritz Maisel	303*
Batting Average	George Puccinelli	.334
Games Won (pitcher)	Johnny Ogden	213
Strikeouts	Tommy Thomas	1,171

* *Maisel's total becomes 383 if Eastern League stats are included (old Eastern League became the IL).*

1990 Players to Watch

Phil Plantier, Pawtucket (Red Sox), belted out 33 homers and teammate Mo Vaughn knocked out 22.

Hensley "Bam Bam" Meulens connected for 26 roundtrippers and 96 RBI for Columbus (Yankees).

Leo Gomez ripped 26 four-baggers and 97 RBI for Rochester (Orioles).

Joe Johnson banged out 213 hits for the Pawsox.

Best Defensive Players to Watch (*Source: Baseball America*)

Catcher: Jeff Tackett, Rochester (Orioles)
First Baseman: David Segui, Rochester (Orioles)
Second Baseman: Luis Sojo, Syracuse (Blue Jays)*
Third Baseman: Scott Cooper, Pawtucket (Red Sox)
Shortstop: Travis Fryman, Toledo (Tigers)
Outfielder: Mark Whiten, Syracuse (Blue Jays)
Pitcher-Fastball: Kent Mercker, Richmond (Braves)
Pitcher-Control: Mark Leiter, Columbus (Yankees)
Pitcher-Relief: Jeff Innis, Tidewater (Mets)

traded to Angels

4
AMERICAN ASSOCIATION

The American Association was organized in 1901 and began play in 1902, following the failure of a Major League circuit by the same name.

It operated continuously as an eight-team circuit with relatively few franchise shifts in its first years, making it, as Robert Obojsky observed, "the epitome of stability in Organized Baseball."

From 1902 until 1952, the only change that occurred within the league's infrastructure was a shift of the Toledo franchise to Cleveland in 1914 and 1915 before coming back to Toledo for the next thirty-six years, with other charter franchises in Columbus, Ohio; Indianapolis; Kansas City; Louisville; Milwaukee; Minneapolis; and St. Paul remaining intact for half-a-century.

From 1954 to 1960, change seemed to be the order of the day, as the Majors took away Milwaukee and Kansas City and Toledo shifted again to Charleston.

Denver came into the league in 1955, as did Omaha, and when three Texas League teams joined the circuit in 1959

(Dallas, Fort Worth, and Houston), the A.A. became a ten-team loop.

Minneapolis was taken from the Minor League roles by the Twins in 1961, and the ten-team league dwindled to six that year, and by 1963, the American Association, devoid of its major markets, died a peaceful death.

In 1969, the Association was reestablished in an improved economic climate, and second charter teams were Denver, Indianapolis, Omaha, Tulsa, Oklahoma City, and Des Moines.

The year of expansion for the A.A. was 1970, one that saw Evansville and Wichita bring the league back up to eight teams.

There have been additional franchise shifts since then, but the circuit still maintains the reputation as the soundest loop in the Minor League system.

Attendance is the American Association hallmark, as the Buffalo Bisons have astounded the baseball world by drawing more than one million fans three consecutive times (1988–90), making it only the second franchise to draw one million ever—the other million-seat seller was the Association's own Louisville team in 1983—and the A.A. drew 3,578,710 fans in 1989, setting a new Minor League mark.

The American Association covers eight states, one in the East but mostly through the Midwest and South: New York—Buffalo (Pirates), Colorado—Denver (Brewers), Indiana—Indianapolis (Indians), Kentucky—Louisville (Cardinals), Iowa—Des Moines (Cubs), Tennessee—Nashville (Reds), Oklahoma—Oklahoma City (Rangers), Nebraska—Omaha (Royals).

The 1990 season came down to the Nashville Reds winning the Eastern Division with an 86–61 mark, one game over the Buffalo Bisons and the Omaha Royals running away with the West with an 86–60 record, fourteen games better than the Iowa Cubs.

Omaha needed five games to get past Nashville for the A.A. crown.

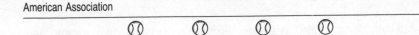

What is the American Association?

On the city of Buffalo's quest to obtain a Major League expansion or relocation franchise, the Bisons' Pilot Field is Big League all the way. Commenting on the field's status, however, was International League rival Rochester Red Wings' play-by-play broadcaster Josh Lewin, who jokingly remarked, "Pilot Field is indeed as beautiful and majestic as they say. However, it is not perfect. The press box Jacuzzi jets are a little weak and the pregame Zinfandel was tepid."

Or perhaps the American Association is where the young mature and acquire the seasoning needed to turn Minor League boys into Major League men. Such was the case with nineteen-year-old Mickey Mantle. In 1951, the Mick had been sent down by the Yankees after he had failed to live up to Casey Stengel's ballyhooed praise as "the second coming of Ruth, Gehrig, and DiMaggio." Mantle didn't handle the demotion to Kansas City well and fell into the morass of an 0 for 22 slump. In tears, Mickey called his father and told him he didn't think he could play baseball anymore. Mutt Mantle, the man who named his son after his own baseball idol, Mickey Cochrane, came to Kansas City from his home in Oklahoma, charged into young Mickey's hotel room, gathered up the kid's clothes, stuffed them into a suitcase and informed the lad that he was going home to work in the mines of Oklahoma. Since he couldn't play ball, he was to be a miner for the rest of his life.

Mickey argued with his dad and convinced him that he would work hard enough to stay in baseball. The Hall-of-Famer later said that this talk was the turning point of his life, and he proved it by raising his batting average to .361, and a second trip to the Majors . . . a ride that lasted eighteen years, 2,401 games, and produced 536 homers and 1,509 RBI.

And maybe the American Association is the place where

ex-Major Leaguers find they can't turn back the clock but they can have some fun.

While playing for Minneapolis in 1912, after his Big League days were behind him, the screwball's screwball, Rube Waddell, a 191-game winner in The Show, was set to pitch in a tough series against Toledo, with first place at stake. His manager, Joe Cantillon, instructed Waddell to refrain from drinking, as he would be pitching twice in the four-game series. His pitching foe, Toledo's ace, Earl "Chink" Yingling, was told the same thing by his Toledo manager.

The two flaky pitchers were set to square off on Monday and again on Thursday, but neither showed up at the ballpark—they were missing for four days. On Friday, after the series had been completed, Waddell showed up carrying a string of fish. He explained to Cantillon that he had kept Yingling from beating Minneapolis by taking him on a four-day fishing trip to Lake Minnetonka. Sometime later, Cantillon, who bought the story, got a bill from a local fish market for a string of fish purchased by Rube Waddell on that Friday.

And the American Association is certainly promotion.

When Bill Veeck bought the Milwaukee Brewers, he used every bit of promotional chicanery he could think of to enlarge the gate. He gave out door prizes: a dozen lobsters; six live squabs; a 200-pound block of ice; six ladders; free hotel rooms in Milwaukee; free breakfasts; a Rosie the Riveter Day game for the ladies; and free peanuts days. The come-ons worked, and Veeck packed them in.

⚾   ⚾   ⚾   ⚾

Inside the American Association:
- In a league known for its bats, Ulysses Simpson Grant "Stoney" McGlynn stands out as a pitcher who could handle the hitters. In 1909, he set a record, later tied, for most single-season shutouts in Minor League history. He threw 14 whitewashes for Milwaukee. As a Major

Leaguer, he went a hard-luck 17–33 with a sharp 2.95 ERA over three years. He had three MLB shutouts.

- Eccentric Major League pitcher Rube Waddell, sent down to Minneapolis in 1911 for "odd behavior," won 20 games for manager Joe Cantillon. The next season, off to a good start, Waddell came to the aid of a Kentucky community that had been deluged by a heavy rainfall and flooding river. While piling sandbags along the banks of a cresting river, Waddell stood in icy water and contracted pneumonia. He really never returned to health. He finished 12–6 for Minneapolis that year, and within two years, the thirty-eight-year-old Hall-of-Famer was dead.

- In 1931, pitcher Bob Logan made his debut with Indianapolis. He eventually set the career record for longest service in the A.A. with sixteen years in the Association.

- Left-handed hitting slugger Joe Hauser used the friendly confines of his home park, Nicollet Park, in Minneapolis, by crashing 69 four-baggers in 1933—50 of them at Nicollet. There must be something in the water in Minneapolis, or in the fences at Nicollet Park, because Minneapolis has been the home of seven single-season Minor League homerun leaders, though only Hauser, Buck Freeman with eighteen in 1907, and Gavvy Cravath with 29 in 1911, played in the American Association. Buzz Arlett, who led the Minors in homers twice, played long enough (116 games) at Minnesota to blast 41 homers in 1934. When added to the 7 he got at Birmingham in the Southern Association earlier that year, he wound up with a system-topping 48.

- Other A.A. homerun leaders who dominated the entire Minor League system included: Bunny Brief, Kansas City, 42 in 1921; Brief, K.C., 42 in 1922; Tom Winsett, Columbus, 50 in 1936; Ted Norbert, Milwaukee, 25 in 1943; Roger Freed, Denver, 42 in 1977; Champ Summers, Indianapolis, 34 in 1978; and Randy Bass, Denver, 37 in 1980.

- From July 9 to 12, 1940, Stanley "Frenchy" Bordagaray,

of the Kansas City Blues, hit safely 13 consecutive times, an Association record. On July 11, he went 6 for 6. Bordagaray showed his hitting skills in the Majors with an 11-year average of .283.

- In 1949, Minneapolis acquired Negro League star Ray Dandridge, who was signed by the New York Giants. At age thirty-five, he won the American Association's Rookie-of-the-Year Award by batting .362. The following year, batting .311 with 11 homers and 80 RBI, Dandridge won the Association's MVP Award.

- In 1951, having been sent down for extra seasoning, twenty-year-old centerfielder Willie Mays made the most of his stay with the Minneapolis Millers. In a 35-game stint with the Millers, Mays hit a blistering .477. He was called up by the New York Giants in late May, and the rest is Hall-of-Fame history. Mays credits the help he received from Dandridge, his teammate, who advised and coached the young Mays. On his election to baseball's Hall of Fame, Mays said, "Ray Dandridge helped me tremendously in Minneapolis . . . he was a part of me when I was coming along."

- Also in 1951, another young centerfielder phenom, nineteen-year-old Mickey Mantle, was sent down by the New York Yankees to get his swing together. Playing for the Kansas City Blues, Mantle slumped until a visit from his father set him right. Mantle regained his touch, and in 166 at bats, hit .361 with 11 homers and 50 RBI before being called back up to the Majors and a Hall-of-Fame career of his own.

- Golden Glove first baseman Vic Power, who might have become the first black player for the New York Yankees, led the Association in batting in 1953 with a .349 average for the Kansas City Blues, to follow up his 1952 campaign during which he batted .331. The Yanks peddled Power to the Philadelphia A's and waited for Elston Howard to develop (to become the first black player to wear Yankee pinstripes) after it was determined he didn't have "the right attitude." According to Power, he was brought up in Puerto Rico believing that all people were equal and that race and skin color had little meaning. That meant that in America, he felt he should be treated as an equal . . . eat wherever he wished, ride in whatever bus seat he wished, and date whomever he chose, regardless of race. This didn't sit well with baseball minds—particularly those in the South of the early '50's—and the Yankees chose to distance themselves from the potential problems of a free spirit and dealt him to the A's, for whom he starred before being traded to Cleveland.

Typical of Power's "behavior" was a trip to Little Rock, Arkansas, with his team. He went into a restaurant with the white players and the waitress told him, "We don't serve Negroes." Power didn't blink an eye and replied, "That's okay, I don't eat Negroes. I want rice and beans."

So Power often went back to the team bus, learned English and waited to do his talking on the ballfield . . . and he did, compiling a lifetime Minor League average of .330.

- One athlete more famous for his prowess in another sport, but who passed this way, was basketball star Bill Sharman. Sharman, more widely known as a star member of the multichampion Boston Celtics and as coach and president of the Los Angeles Lakers, was Brooklyn Dodger property when they assigned the outfielder to St. Paul. Sharman, a steady fielder and fair hitter, batted .292 for St. Paul in 1952, and .294 for them in 1955.
- The star of the season early in 1953 was stocky infielder Don Zimmer. Zim was leading the Association with 23 homers and 63 RBI on July 7, 1953, when a fastball got away from pitcher Jim Kirk and nailed Zimmer in the head.

The fiesty infielder was knocked unconscious and he remained in that state for two weeks. It took him six weeks to regain his ability to speak, and his time in the hospital cost him forty-four pounds. When he left the hospital, he had four screws in his skull.

By 1954, he was up with the Brooklyn Dodgers, and in

'55 was the Brooks' starting second baseman in the World Series.

* The 1955 season saw Indianapolis' Rocky Colavito belt 30 homeruns and Louisville's Frank Malzone hit .310.

* In 1956 and 1957, the Denver Bears ruled the basepaths, scoring runs at a record clip. Yankee prospect "Marvelous" Marv Throneberry, later to become a baseball immortal in ineptitude for the 1962 New York Mets, laid the thin air of Denver to waste by rocketing A.A. pitchers for 42 and 40 homeruns while driving in 269 runs. The free-swinging left-handed first baseman hit his stride in Denver, knocking in Bear teammates Tony Kubek, Bobby Richardson, Woody Held, John Blanchard, Norm Sieburn, Lou Skizas, and Whitey Herzog, but never lived up to his promise in The Show.

* In 1958, the Washington Senators sent prospect Harmon Killebrew down to Indianapolis for seasoning. Killer slumped, couldn't get untracked, and hit a feeble .215.

* In 1959, relief specialist George Spencer appeared in 85 games for Charleston and Gary Peters (Indy) and Juan Pizarro (Wichita) both tossed no-hitters. Bullet Bob Gibson prepared for The Show with a 9–9, 3.09 season for Omaha.

* In 1960, Carl Yastrzemski hit .339, second to Denver's Bo Osborne and his triple crown numbers: .342, 34 homers, 114 RBI. Houston's Billy Williams hit .323 with 26 homers and "Mr. Baseball," Bob Uecker, hit .147 for Louisville, some .053 under his Major League average.

* Howie Bedell tied the league record in 1961 by going on a 43-game hitting streak for Louisville. He was headed for the batting title when he broke his shoulder in late August and lost the crown by .001 when Denver's Don Wert went 4 for 7 in a final day doubleheader to edge Bedell .327 to .326.

* Bob Uecker liked 1961 and more than doubled his average, hitting a formidable .309.

* The 1962 season saw fireballer Herb Score go 10–7 for Indianapolis; reliever Phil Niekro fashion a 9–6 mark for

Louisville; and Mickey Lolich get pasted in an 0–4, 16.50 ERA season for Denver.

- The American Association disbanded in 1963 and didn't pick up again until 1969.

Indianapolis' Bernie Carbo led the way back in 1969 with a .359 average and Tulsa's Ted Simmons hit .332.

- In 1970, forty-eight-year-old Art Fowler picked up 15 saves and compiled a 1.59 ERA for Denver, as Chris Chambliss was the top hitter at .342 for Wichita. Cotton Nash belted 33 homers for Evansville to lead the league.
- Following a .337 mark the previous year, Richie Scheinblum led the league in batting in 1971, at .388 with 108 RBI for Denver—hitting over .400 until late August. On the mound, Oklahoma City's J.R. Richard was king of the hill with a 12–7 mark, 2.45 ERA and 202 K's.
- The 1973 season saw Indianapolis' Ken Griffey hit .327, Wichita's Tony LaRussa bat .314, and Omaha's George Brett come in at .284, as Jim Dwyer of Tulsa ran away with the silver bat at .387.
- Jim Kern blazed through lineups for Oklahoma City in 1974, going 17–7, with a 2.52 ERA and league-leading 220 strikeouts.
- In 1975, during his blaze through the Minor Leagues, Mark "The Bird" Fidrych, who had already whizzed through Bristol in the Appalachian League by going 3–0, before speeding in and out of the Florida State League and Southern League, made a stop in the A.A., impressing the parent Detroit Tigers by fashioning a 4–1 mark at Evansville with a 1.59 ERA.
- Mike Easler warmed up for The Show by hitting .352 for Tulsa in 1976, and Evansville's Steve Kemp blasted away at .386 in 52 games before being called up by the Tigers.
- Willie Wilson tore through Omaha with 74 stolen bases in 1977.
- On Minor League weather, Farm System hitting phenom (1977–78) Champ Summers, who spent 11 years in The Show, recalled his days at Indianapolis and said, "It was so muggy there, I spent $3500 on deodorant playing in the American Association one season."

When he was dry, he was hot, and in '78 Summers barely missed the triple crown, losing the batting title to Dane Iorg of Oklahoma City, .371 to .368, but taking the homer crown with 34 and the RBI title with 124.

- In 1980, strongman Randy Bass, who was later to become a homerun-hitting legend in the Japan Leagues, led the circuit and the entire Minor League system by belting out 37 homers at Denver while Tim Raines ran wild for the Bears with 77 steals, a .354 average, and 105 runs scored. Raines beat Oklahoma City's Orlando Gonzales in the closest batting race in American Association history, .3543 to .3541—by .0002!

Also in 1980, legendary Minor League star Hub Kittle, sixty-three, made a token appearance as a pitcher for Springfield, hurling one hitless inning, making him the oldest player to ever appear in a Minor League game, besting the mark of sixty-years-old by Satchel Paige (Peninsula of the Carolina League in 1966), who pitched two innings, and Kid Eberfield, sixty-one, in a token appearance for Fulton in the KITTY League.

- Ryne Sandberg left his mark on the Association in 1981 as an all-star shortstop (.293 with 32 steals), and Mike Richardt of Wichita nipped Terry Francona of Denver for the batting crown, .354 to .352.

- Ken Phelps was the loop's top offensive player in 1982, hitting .333 with 46 homers and 141 RBI for Wichita, Gary Redus hit a solid .332 and stole 54 bases for Indianapolis, and Iowa's Jay Howell won top pitching honors with a 13–4, 2.36 season.

- Andy VanSlyke made a short and sweet run by hitting .368 in 54 games for Louisville before being called up by the Cardinals in 1983.

- Vince Coleman of Louisville burned up the basepaths in 1984 with 101 steals, but Alan Kniceley stole the MVP award for Wichita with a strong .333, 33 homer, 126 RBI season. Daryl Boston led Denver with a .319 average, 21 doubles, 19 triples, 15 homers, 82 RBI, and 40 stolen bases.

In a case of local boy makes good and returns, sort of, Matt Winters, a New York Yankee prospect and native of Buffalo, New York, was signed by the Chicago White Sox and assigned to Triple A Buffalo. The Bisons heavily promoted the "prodigal son returns" angle for the 1986 season, but six weeks later, the ChiSox traded Winters back to the Yankees, who put Winters on their Columbus Clippers roster, killing the promo. Six weeks later, the Yankees loaned Winters back to Chicago, who sent the player back to Buffalo.

All's well that ends well? No. Winters slumped to a career low .088 for the Bisons and then was sent back to Columbus.

[*Author's note:* The day Winters left Buffalo for Columbus, he was being honored in Buffalo at a "Matt Winters Appreciation Day" ceremony.]

- Mickey Mahler, a journeyman pitcher for the Atlanta Braves, California Angels, and five other teams over an eight-year MLB career, was toiling for the Texas Rangers in 1986 when he said, "Every player who has played three straight years in the Majors should be sent back to Triple A for a month so he won't forget how good he has it."

  The following day, Mahler was sent to Triple A Oklahoma City.
- In 1989, Indianapolis beat Omaha in a tense five-game play-off to provide the Indiana club with its fourth consecutive A.A. crown.
- In 1990, the Buffalo Bisons (Pirates affiliate) gave aging hurler Jerry Reuss one last shot and he responded with 24 consecutive scoreless innings in late July and August.

⚾   ⚾   ⚾   ⚾

The all-time American Association career leaders list is a
Bunny Brief scrapbook:
(*Source:* SABR)

Games played	Harry Clark	1,834
Runs scored	Bunny Brief	1,342
Hits	Bunny Brief	2,196
Doubles	Bunny Brief	458
Triples	Joe Riggert	161
Homeruns	Bunny Brief	276
RBI	Bunny Brief	1,451
Stolen bases	Alex Reilley	330
Batting average	Bevo LeBourveau	.360
Games won (pitcher)	George Northrop	222
Strikeouts	George Northrop	1,176

1990 Players to Watch

Mark Ryal, Buffalo (Pirates), was hitting .373 in late August.

John Vanderwal, Indianapolis (Expos), had belted 26 doubles.

Juan Gonzales, the league MVP from Oklahoma City (Rangers)
  had blasted 18 homers, 16 doubles, and 59 RBI in his first 300
  at bats.

Chris Hammond pitched his way to a 15–1 mark for Nashville
  (Reds).

Best Defensive Players to Watch (*Source: Baseball America*)

Catcher: Gil Reyes, Indianapolis (Expos)

First Baseman: George Canale, Denver (Brewers)

Second Baseman: Jeff Small, Iowa (Cubs)

Third Baseman: Joe Redfield, Denver (Brewers)

Shortstop: D.L. Smith, Denver (Brewers) and Bien Figueroa, Louisville (Cardinals)

Outfielder: Ray Lankford, Louisville (Cardinals)

Pitcher—Fastball: Ken Hill, Louisville (Cardinals)

Pitcher—Control: Pete Filson, Omaha (Royals)

Pitcher—Relief: Mike Perez, Louisville (Cardinals)

5
PACIFIC COAST
LEAGUE

The Pacific Coast League is Triple-A, with a history of hitting prowess. It also came within a whisper—and Major League expansion—of becoming a third Major League.

After the on-again, off-again California League of the late 1800s became surprisingly robust around 1901, with a complement of Los Angeles, San Francisco, Oakland, and Sacramento, a move was afoot to challenge the Pacific Northwest League to achieve West Coast superiority.

When Portland and Seattle were pirated away from the PNL in 1903, the Pacific Coast League was formed and has run continuously since, making it the second-oldest extant league in the Minors.

This, however, did not occur without a fight. The PNL vowed to crush the upstart league and placed competing teams in San Francisco and Los Angeles, renaming itself the Pacific National League. As the PNL (same initials, different words) had been better entrenched prior to the showdown, Eastern observers were shocked when it was the PCL that prevailed, earning endorsement by the National Association.

All was still not rosy for the new league. Poorly financed operations, combined with lack of parity between teams— Los Angeles took the premiere season by a noncompetitive 27½ games over second-place Sacramento—forced owners to raise ticket prices to 35 cents (reserved seats were higher still) and reduce their rosters to 13 players.

It also forced questionable conflicts of interest, including the owning of two competing teams, San Francisco and Oakland, by a single owner, Cal Ewing. Ewing explained it was necessary in order for both clubs to survive.

The Bay teams did survive, but Sacramento's team fell victim to low finances and was replaced in 1904 by Tacoma, which crashed in 1906, as did Seattle.

By 1907 the PCL had withered to a mere four teams, and it appeared as if even God and the elements were opposed to the PCL's survival.

On April 18, 1906, the great San Francisco earthquake and fire wreaked havoc on the Bay area, and, among other things, obliterated the PCL's headquarters and the San Francisco team's home field, Recreation Park, forcing the league to suspend games for three weeks.

The National Association jumped to the rescue with much-needed funds that gave the PCL the shot-in-the-pocketbook it needed to weather the crisis. League headquarters were moved to Oakland, and the San Francisco franchise shared a home field, Idora Park, with Oakland for the remainder of the season.

In 1925, San Francisco's Paul Waner demolished league pitching by hitting .401 before being called up by the Pirates, but Salt Lake City's Tony Lazerri laid waste to the opposition by crashing out an amazing record of sixty homeruns (two years before future teammate Babe Ruth hit that many in the Bigs) and driving home an incredible 222 RBI. Lazerri's effort was the last Salt Lake City would provide the PCL for thirty-three years, as the franchise was transferred to Los Angeles to become the Hollywood Stars. That same season, the Vernon franchise (in a suburb of Los Angeles) moved north to San Francisco to become the Mission Reds, sharing home field (Recreation Park) with the Seals.

From 1927 to 1929, the Bay area fans had much to cheer about, as three teams skirting the Bay won three championships. In 1927, the Oakland Oaks took the flag with what was arguably the best team in their fifty-three-year history. Led by great-hitting but poor-fielding Russell "Buzz" Arlett (.351, 30 homers, 54 doubles, 123 RBI, and 20 steals) the Oaks romped home with 120 victories.

The year 1928 belonged to the San Francisco Seals, who also bagged 120 wins, and the bat of Smead Jolley (triple crown year of .404, 45 homers, 188 RBI) and arm of mound ace Walter "Dutch" Reuther (29–7).

Then 1929 was the year of the Mission Reds, who compiled the top record in the league (118 wins) before losing the play-off to Hollywood. The Mission club was led by Ike Boone's triple crown of .407, 55 homers, and 218 RBI.

The fans cried for lights, the PCL complied, and lo, there were lights in 1930 as Oakland, Los Angeles, and Seattle all installed lighting for night baseball.

In 1938, Mission was unable to compete with the San Francisco Seals for attendance—the Reds' top drawing card, Ox Eckhardt, was picked up then released by the Brooklyn Dodgers—and went south for the summer, to Hollywood to replace the team that had headed even farther south, to San Diego. And the Stars were reborn.

The PCL very nearly became a third Major League as attendance soared following World War II. With no Major League ball being played in the West, and with Los Angeles, San Francisco, and Oakland as its hubs, a campaign was soon under way to elevate the PCL to Major League status.

In 1952, the loop was awarded "Open Classification," considered just a half-step below Major League level.

By 1957, recognition was gaining steam, particularly with the notoriety achieved by slugging hulk Steve Bilko's assault on PCL pitching—.328, 37 homers, 124 RBI in 1955; triple crown in 1956: .360, 55 homers and 164 RBI;

and .300, 56 roundtrippers and 140 RBI in 1957—and the emergence of the West Coast as a viable market.

The Major League movement was killed in 1958, however, when the Giants and Dodgers moved West to capture the two biggest markets, San Francisco and Los Angeles, and the Los Angeles Angels followed two years later.

The Giants moved their Triple-A affiliate from Minneapolis to Phoenix that year, and the Phoenix Giants, also called the P-Gees (P. Giants) joined the league with a flourish. Dusty Rhodes (25 homers, 100 RBI), Willie McCovey (.319, 14 homers, 89 RBI), Andre Rodgers (.354, 31 homers, 90 RBI), and George Prescott (.310, 24 homers, 96 RBI) chipped in to propel Phoenix to a PCL record 205 homers—many blasted over Phoenix Municipal Stadium's short 320-foot left field fence.

The PCL's love affair with Phoenix was a short one, and in 1960, due to falling attendance, the franchise was shifted to Tacoma. The Firebird City was devoid of Triple-A ball until it returned to the PCL with the 1966 version of the Giants.

In 1969, due to the rebirth of the American Association, the PCL dwindled to eight teams.

In 1972, Albuquerque joined the PCL and began a strong run of success that has carried the franchise to five league titles in eighteen years.

From 1973 to the present, the league has regained its strength and has maintained a run of stability except for the required franchise shifts along the way.

Today, with a schedule of 144 games, the PCL runs from April 10 to July 21 for the first half, and then until September 3 for the second half, which determines the play-off combatants, a far cry from the 200-game schedules from March to October that it ran from the 1920s to 1950s.

That 200-game schedule combined with the extraordinary talents of Tony Lazerri (60 homers, 222 RBI, 202 runs scored in 1925), Ike Boone (553 total bases in 1929), and Paul Strand (325 hits in 1923) helped produce those inflated but incredible offensive marks that should last forever.

Today, the Pacific Coast League is a Triple-A League covering California, Arizona, New Mexico, Oregon, Washington, Colorado, Nevada, and Canada.

Teams and affiliations include: Edmonton Trappers (Angels), Portland Beavers (Twins), Vancouver Canadians (White Sox), Tacoma Tigers (A's), Calgary Cannons (Mariners), Albuquerque Dukes (Dodgers), Tucson Toros (Astros), Colorado Springs Sky Sox (Indians), Las Vegas Stars (Padres), and Phoenix Firebirds (Giants).

The 1990 season was dominated by the Edmonton Trappers and Tacoma Tigers in the Northern Division and Albuquerque Dukes and Colorado Springs Sky Sox in the Southern Division.

What is the PCL?

Perhaps it is stories of players who, through no fault of their own, are destined to spend their careers in the Minors.

In 1920, when Major League baseball banned the spitball from the game—excepting players who already threw the pitch; in a grandfather clause gesture—Chicago White Sox hurler Frank Shellenback, a wetballer who won 10 games for the ChiSox in 1918 and was sent down to Minneapolis for more experience, was inadvertently left off the grandfather clause list. The saliva throw was *his* pitch. As he was forbidden from throwing it in The Show, and the Pacific Coast League had no such restriction, Shellenback was destined to spend his career on the Coast, in the Little Show, where he won 295 games in fourteen years.

Or maybe the PCL is all about inspiration.

Lou "The Mad Russian" Novikoff, one of the greatest "good hit, no field" players in Minor League history, tore up the PCL for the Los Angeles Angels in 1939 (.452 and 37 RBI in 36 games) and 1940 (a triple crown year at .363,

41 homers, 171 RBI, 259 hits, and 147 runs scored in 174 games). He engaged in the ritual of having his wife, Esther, sit in a box seat behind home plate, and when Lou stepped up to bat, he had instructed her to yell, at the top of her lungs, "Novikoff, you bum! You can't hit worth a damn! You stink!"

Novikoff would get hot and would usually respond to the taunting by hitting prodigious homers. Novikoff explained that he used the nasty comments for inspiration. After a few off-years, when Esther was not allowed to accompany him to the Majors, he got permission from the Chicago Cubs in 1942 to let her do her act. Novikoff responded by batting .300. He finished with six years in the PCL, all well over .300.

The PCL was also the "Booze Cage."

In the 1920s, the Booze Cage, at San Francisco's Recreation Park, was an eight-row section of seats closed off by chicken wire. During the pre-prohibition days, a seventy-five-cent admission price got you a seat, and either a shot of whisky, two bottles of beer, or a ham and cheese sandwich. It has been reported that they nearly always ran out of beer and whisky and always had an abundance of ham and cheese left over.

The PCL was a "no frills" affair for the players.

At San Francisco, the clubhouses were located in center field, in a damp, dark, forbidding-looking, wooden cottage. As there were only two showers in each clubhouse (home and visitors), it made sense for players to finish the game and run quickly to the clubhouse. Admiring one's work after the game meant a certain cold shower, as hot water quickly vanished.

And sometimes the PCL was just entertainment.

Bobby Bragan, manager of the Hollywood Stars, had a penchant for making games fun for the crowd and nightmares for umpires.

One night in San Diego, with his Stars losing a close one to the Padres, Bragan, who was also a catcher at the time, protested an argument by taking off his chest protector, shin guards, mask, glove, and cap, throwing them, one at a time, onto the field. He finished this impromptu strip-tease by firing his uni top, shoes, "sleeves," and a towel on the heap of dirty laundry.

Another time, he stretched out and took a nap on home plate, casually reading a newspaper a fan had thrown at him.

A third time, he poked out a path with a baseball bat, while covering his eyes in an impression of a blind man—an obvious comment on the sight of an umpire.

On a fourth occasion, to get umpire Ed Runge's goat, the fiery Bragan sent in his teenaged batboy to coach third base.

And during another game, Bragan sent in a pinch hit-ter, replaced him with another before the pitcher had thrown a pitch, then replaced that hitter with another and another until nine men had been announced to hit for the original batter.

And finally, to protest umpire Jim Marshall's liberal use of a game clock—innings weren't supposed to start after 12:55 A.M., and at one minute to 1 A.M., with the score tied 2–2 in the 21st inning of a great pitching duel between Hollywood's Bob Hall and Oakland's Alan "Two-Gun" Get-tle (both of whom went all the way), Marshall said his watch indicated there was still time, leading to a 22nd inning in which Hollywood was defeated 5–2—Bragan sent coach Gordon Mosburger out to Marshall, wearing 10 watches and an alarm clock.

And throughout its history, the PCL is all about power.

In the past, the PCL was filled with the Tony Lazerris, Smead Jolleys, Ike Boones, Dave Barbees, Gene Lillards, Steve Bilkos, Bill McNultys, Ron Kittles, and Danny Tart-abulls, who bombed anywhere between 40 and 60 homers over the haul of a year. Now, the bombers don't stay in the PCL as long but may make more dramatic power splashes.

A case in point was the 1990 guest appearance rehab that Los Angeles Dodger outfielder Kirk Gibson did at Al-buquerque. Gibson was in the PCL for a twenty-day get-well assignment and he made the most of it one Friday night at Albuquerque Sports Stadium against Colorado Springs. As the Dukes beat the Sky Sox 10–5, Gibson strode to the plate in the first inning against lefty Kevin Bearse and took a called third strike. In the third frame, Gibson blooped a single to center to key a four-run rally. Then, in the fourth, Gibson came to the batter's box with none on and one out. He took the first pitch for a ball, then zeroed in on Bearse's next delivery and crushed it. Gibson knocked the ball over the right-field wall . . . past the back fence that surrounds the ballpark . . . and onto a service road well beyond the stadium . . . an astounding 600 feet from home plate. True, Albuquerque's thin air—5,200 feet above sea level—may have helped, but it goes down as a Ruthian blow of Mantleian proportion, and just another day at the office in the PCL.

⚾   ⚾   ⚾   ⚾

Inside the PCL:
- In a game that will live on in PCL history, the Oakland Oaks and San Francisco Seals met in the pitchers' duel to end all pitchers' duels on June 8, 1909, at Freeman Park in Oakland. Jimmy Wiggs of Oakland matched San Francisco's Cack Henley for twenty-three innings with the score knotted at 0–0. In the twenty-fourth frame, Nick Williams drove in the only run of the game with a single, to win it for San Francisco, 1–0.
- In a league dominated by hitters, a pitcher is tied for the all-time Minor League single-season shutout mark. In 1910, Vean Gregg threw 14 shutouts for Portland, tieing the mark set a year earlier by Stoney McGlynn, and tied again the same year by Major League Hall-of-Famer Grover Cleveland Alexander for Syracuse in the New York State League. Gregg made it to the Bigs as well as Alexander, but he didn't fare quite as well. He did stick around for eight years (with the Cleveland Indians and others) and put together three straight 20-win seasons

(1911–13). Gregg finished at 91–63 with a 2.70 ERA and 14 more shutouts. Alexander lasted twenty years, went 373–208 (mostly for the Philadelphia Phillies and Chicago Cubs) with a 2.56 ERA and 90 shutouts.

- In one of the most spectacular fielding plays in Minor League history, Walter "Rosy" Carlisle of Vernon pulled off an unassisted triple play as an outfielder on July 19, 1911. In a game against the Los Angeles Angels in L.A., with the score tied 3–3 in the bottom of the sixth, the Angels had Charlie Moore on second, George Metzger on first with none out, and Roy Akin at the plate. With the hit-and-run on, Akin hit the first pitch on a screaming line over second base. Speedy centerfielder Carlisle, running full-out, dove headfirst and made a shoestring grab just inches above the grass, robbing Akin of a sure hit. After turning three somersaults, he landed on his feet with the ball firmly in his glove.

  By this time, sure the line drive was going to fall in, Moore was rounding third on his way for home, and Metzger was past second, heading for third.

  Alertly, Carlisle stepped on second to nail Moore, and trotted to first to record the out on Metzger.

  Vernon came alive and beat Los Angeles 5–4, and in recognition of the achievement, Carlisle was presented with a diamond-studded gold medal by Vernon and Los Angeles fans.

  Carlisle, who stole 55 bases in 1911, was an England-born athlete who made it to the Majors only briefly, playing in three games for the Boston Red Sox in 1908

- In one of the oddest doubleheaders in Minor League history, the Oakland Oaks played two the hard way on April 13, 1913. Oakland was at home when they played the Portland Beavers in Oakland shortly before noon. As soon as the contest was completed, the Oaks packed up their gear and traveled across the bay to play an afternoon tilt against the San Francisco Seals.

- In 1920, Hal Chase, a former Big League first baseman who was implicated as a gambling figure in the Chicago

White Sox (Black Sox) scandal of 1919, was banned from all PCL ballparks for allegedly trying to bribe Spider Baum, a pitcher for Salt Lake City. Chase, who had been rumored to have thrown games during his career, was indicted in the Black Sox affair but as California refused extradition to Illinois, Chase was never brought to trial.

- Perseverance might have been the key for Portland pitcher Herman "Old Folks" Pillette. In a Pacific Coast League career that ran twenty-three years, Pillette lost 11 or more games 12 times and lost 20 or more, three different years. But in 1921, pitching for Portland, Pillette actually won a shot with the Detroit Tigers the following year by leading the PCL in losses, with a miserable 13-wins–30-losses season. He gave up 378 hits in 326 innings and had a 4.20 ERA, but Detroit talent scouts obviously saw something they liked, and in 1922, Pillette won 19 and lost 12 to start a three-year Major League career.

- In a move that seemed contrary to form, in 1922, tight-fisted, tight-walleted Chicago White Sox owner Charlie Comiskey purchased the fine-fielding third baseman Willie Kamm from the San Francisco Seals for an astronomical price of $125,000. Years later, when Kamm was managing the San Francisco Missions, he would smile as he passed a photostat of Comiskey's check, which was displayed, under glass, on a wall within the offices of Seals Stadium.

- On May 11, 1923, former pitcher Pete Schneider put it all together for one glorious day in the PCL. Playing for Vernon at Salt Lake City, Schneider blasted 5 homers and a double and drove in 14 runs. The outburst aided Schneider on his way to a season of 19 homers. In eleven Minor League seasons, Schneider wound up with only 88, and in 434 at bats in the Majors (Reds and Yankees), he totaled 5.

- In a precursor of greatness to follow, San Francisco Seals standout centerfielder Joe DiMaggio set the PCL on its ear from May 28 to July 25, 1933, when he went on a

61-game hitting streak, getting 104 hits in 257 at bats for a .405 average. He was later to nearly duplicate this feat by setting the all-time Major League record of hitting safely in 56 straight games for the New York Yankees in 1941. The only PCLer to come close to DiMag was Jack Ness, whose record he broke, a hitter in 49 consecutive games as a first baseman for Oakland in 1915. Ness didn't achieve Major League greatness, however, hitting only .253 during a two-year stay—1911 with Detroit and 1916 with the Chicago White Sox.

- In 1943, with a shortage of players due to the war, the Los Angeles Angels signed catcher Bill Sarni, fifteen. He often caught when ex-Major Leaguer Charlie Root, forty-four, was on the hill. Root's first year in the Majors—St. Louis Browns in 1923—occurred five years before his batterymate was born.

- In 1946, a man the Bay area fans regarded as a clown, Casey Stengel, earned the love and respect of Oakland Oaks fans when he guided the team to a second-place finish. Two years later, relying on the gutsy play of his top young soldier, second baseman Billy Martin, who made a reputation for himself as the street kid who always gave his all in hard-nosed, dedicated baseball, Ol' Case won the PCL flag for the Acorns. That victory prompted the New York Yankees to hire Stengel away to begin a dynastic twelve-year run with the Bronx Bombers.

- The PCL finally became integrated on March 30, 1948, when John Ritchey, the Negro American League batting champion of 1947, pinch hit for San Diego against Los Angeles. He was the starting catcher the next day and homered, to touch off a season that saw him bat .323 in 103 games.

- In 1953, first baseman Dale Long led the loop with 35 homers en route to an MVP award. Long of the Hollywood Stars would often thrill fans at Gilmore Field, a "friendly confines" park next to the Farmers Market on Fairfax Avenue, near CBS Television City. As TV stars of the day frequented the games, Long, a six-foot-four, 210-pound slugger who later starred for the Pittsburgh Pirates and set a Major League record in 1956 (tied by the Yankees' Don Mattingly in 1987) for hitting homeruns in eight consecutive games, sent shot after shot out of the old, wooden facility and onto the streets adjacent to the park.

- If Long were a star in 1953 and '54, then Steve Bilko was a superstar in 1955, '56, and '57. Bilko was the Mickey Mantle of the PCL, winning a PCL Triple Crown in '56 (as Mantle had done in the American League that year) by blasting 55 homers, driving in 164 runs, and hitting .360. He followed that up with 56 taters and 140 RBI in 1957. Bilko, who managed only 76 homers in 600 games in The Show, was more at home in the bandbox park of Wrigley Field (148 homers in three years) and against the fastball pitchers with Minor League curves that he faced in the Little Show, and against whom he blasted 313 four-baggers in 1,533 games.

    The hefty Bilko (he may have ballooned to over 240 pounds on his six-foot-one frame) often tried to keep his weight down—after a night of hard drinking—by locking himself in the bathroom, stuffing towels in the door and window cracks and turning the shower on to full hot. This steam bath served to sweat out the demons so he could play and wield his big bat and then go through the routine again the following day.

- Following Bilko on the scene as slugging king of the PCL was Willie McCovey. Big Mac dominated the 1959 season and he needed only half-a-year to do it. When the San Francisco Giants called up the big bomber on July 30, McCovey was hitting .372 with 29 homers and 92 RBI. He hopped on a plane and, in his first game, faced Hall-of-Famer Robin Roberts and responded by going four-for-four with two triples, three runs scored, and two ribbies. Mac went on to win the PCL homerun title and win the National League's Rookie of the Year trophy as well.

- An answer to a trivia question was Portland right-handed reliever Ed Bauta. The Cuban hurler was the PCL's top reliever in 1961, and notched some ignominious historical reference by becoming the losing pitcher in the first game ever played at Shea Stadium, April 17, 1964, as his New York Mets lost one to the Pittsburgh Pirates, 4–3.
- Satchel Paige, fifty-five, made a few starts for Portland in 1961 and brought in packed houses . . . he could still get hitters out, but two innings at a pop seemed to be his limit for sharpness.
- In 1963, Deron Johnson, the slugging, one-time "Next Mickey Mantle," belted out 33 roundtrippers for San Diego, as Chico Salmon of new PCL franchise Denver, led the circuit at .325, a mere .001 ahead of Jesus Alou of Tacoma, who hit .324. Carroll Hardy hit .316 for Oklahoma City and Tony Oliva of Dallas–Ft. Worth belted 23 four-baggers while batting .304.
- Basketball-baseball star Dave DeBusschere made his PCL mark for Indianapolis in 1964, pitching his way to a 15–8 year and Phil Niekro led Denver with an 11–5, 3.45 year, while Wilbur Wood knuckled his way to a 15–8, 2.30 campaign for Seattle. Top hitters included Denver's Lou Klimchock at .334, teammate Tommie Aaron with 21 homers, and San Diego's Tony Perez at .309, 34 homers, and 107 RBI.
- The 1965 season saw Andy Kosco go .327, 27 homers, 116 RBI for Denver; Lee May get .321 and 34 roundtrippers for San Diego; Sonny Jackson come in with .330 and 49 steals for Oklahoma City; and Ted Uhlaender lead the loop at .340 for Denver. On the mound, Tacoma's Bill Hands went 17–6, 2.19, and Arkansas teammates Fergie Jenkins and Dallas Green went 8–6 and 12–7 respectively.
- In 1967, the Portland Beavers employed a rightfielder destined for greatness . . . if only he could harness his already legendary temper. The rightfielder was Lou Piniella, later to be a World Series hero for the New York

Yankees, and manager of the Yanks and Cincinnati Reds, for whom he threw tantrums and bases in 1990. But while in Portland, Piniella developed both his hitting style (.291 over his MLB career) and his ferocity when things went awry.

On one occasion, with the Beavers trailing by a run in the eighth, "Sweet Lou" came up with the bases loaded and struck out. Frustrated, Piniella charged the outfield fence, gave it a huge kick, dislodging a fifteen-foot section of it. As it fought back, it fell on him and pinned him to the ground . . . taking the ground crew several minutes to extricate him.

After another whiff with the bags full, on another day in the Minors, Piniella took out his anger on a rain barrel filled with water. First he threw his glove in the barrel, then kicked it and then went in after his glove. The barrel got the last laugh by falling over on Piniella, soaking him to the skin.

And on a third occasion, he cursed so loud after striking out that some nuns sitting in the first row blushed to the point of near-collapse.

- Also in 1967, Willie Kirkland of Hawaii led the circuit with 34 homers and 97 RBI, and Roy White, on loan to Spokane, hit .343 before being recalled by the Yankees. Sal Bando hit .291 at Vancouver.
- Billy Martin made his presence felt again in the PCL in 1968. Twenty years after he had played on the PCL pennant winner in Oakland, Billy "The Kid" took over the Denver Bears in mid-season and guided them to a 65–50 finish to complete the season one game over .500. His run-and-gun style prompted the team to steal home seven times as Graig Nettles (22 homers), Bob Oliver (20 homers), and Pat Kelly (.306) led the hitters.
- Elsewhere that season, Bobby Bonds hit .370 in 60 games for Phoenix before the Giants called him up; Tulsa's Jim Hicks led the league at .366; and Portland's Richie Scheinblum batted .304.
- Former Major Leaguer Art Fowler made several appear-

ances on the mound for Denver in 1970. Fowler was 48 at the time.

- In 1971, Dave "King Kong" Kingman thundered onto the scene. He slammed 26 homers, 29 doubles, 99 RBI and added 11 stolen bases for Phoenix, as the "P. Giants" hit a record 89 triples.
- The Albuquerque Dukes came to the PCL in 1972, with Tommy Lasorda as its manager. The Dukes were royal from start to finish, winning 92 games and capturing the league title as they breezed through the play-offs. First baseman Tom Paciorek was named PCL MVP and Minor League Player of the Year, belting 27 homeruns; outfielder Von Joshua won the batting crown at .337; and infielders Davey Lopes and Ron Cey teamed with outfielder Larry Hisle, catchers Steve Yeager and Joe Ferguson, and pitchers Geoff Zahn, Rick Rhoden, and Charlie Hough to form one of the deepest teams in PCL history.
- In 1973, Steve Ontiveros was named Minor League Player of the Year thanks to a PCL season that saw the Phoenix slugger lead the league in hitting (.357), doubles (32), and triples (16). Phoenix reset the league record for triples by garnering 95.
- Jack Clark emerged as a star by pacing the second-place Phoenix Giants with a .323 average, 111 runs scored, 152 hits, 16 stolen bases, 16 triples, 17 homers, and 89 ribbies.
- Albuquerque's Henry Cruz put together a "triple-double" season in 1977 with 24 doubles, 12 triples, and 18 homers.
- Under Del Crandall, the Dukes won the title in 1978 with a potent offense led by Pedro Guerrero (.337 and 116 RBI) and Jeffrey Leonard (.365) and a hell-bent-for-speed squad that stole 260 bases—Rudy Law swiped 79, Leonard stole 36, Joe Simpson had 35, Rafael Landestoy took 22, and Claude Westmoreland picked off 21.
- In 1981, Mike Marshall, the six-foot-five, 215-pound slugger for Albuquerque, earned a "can't miss" label

from the parent Dodgers . . . a label he has not been able
to live up to at this point. All he did was win the Minor
League Player of the Year award by taking the first PCL
triple crown in twenty-five years (Steve Bilko) by slashing away at .373, with 34 homers and a solid 137 RBI in
128 games. His Dukes won 94 games and lost only 38,
for a .712 winning percentage, to waltz to the title with
an outstanding .325 team average aided by Candy Maldonado (.335, 21 homers, 104 RBI), Wayne Caughey
(.314), Larry Fobbs (.320), Rudy Law (.335), Bobby
Mitchell (.311), Jack Perconte (.346), Ron Roenicke
(.316), and Tack Wilson (.315). Ted Power led the Dukes'
pitching staff at 18–3, while teammates Brian Holton
(16–6), Dave Moore (12–5), Ricky Wright (14–6), and
Alejandro Peña (22 saves) provided a deep mound corps.

- Also in 1981, recently demoted Major Leaguer Jeffrey
"Hac Man" Leonard was so angered at being sent to Phoenix that he publicly declared he would swing at the first
pitch in every at bat. He kept his word, and the strategy
worked. Leonard hit .401 in 47 games.

- During the same year, former Major League star Luis
Tiant made another of his many comebacks a successful
one by throwing a no-hitter for the Portland Beavers over
Spokane. And Tiant was 41 (or more, depending on
which birth story you believe) at the time. The hurler's
performance came seventeen years after he set a PCL
pitching record by compiling a .938 winning percentage
with a 15–1 mark, also for Portland.

- In 1982, Albuquerque's Greg Brock shattered Mike Marshall's one-year-old club RBI mark by driving in 138 ribbies with his 44 homers.

- In the mid-1980s, Randy Ready was the best shuttle hitter in the PCL. A two-time batting champion in lower
classes, Ready shuttled between Vancouver and the Milwaukee Brewers (1984–86) and never hit below .325 in
the PCL, managing to get into a three-year total of 107
games in The Show.

- The Dukes again powdered the ball in 1983 with Sid

Bream's 32 homers, Tony Brewer's 24, German Rivera's 24, and Franklin Stubbs' 16.

- In 1984, Mike Bielecki won 19 games pitching for Hawaii.
- Pam Postema, a female umpire calling balls and strikes in the PCL in 1984, was involved in a piece of PCL lore, when during a game between the Portland Beavers and the Vancouver Canadians, Postema thumbed out four members of the home team Beavers. Beaver skipper Lee Elia was tossed out and retaliated by heaving a chair out onto the field. Postema waved her thumb and players were sent to the showers in hordes. Even the Beavers' fourteen-year-old batboy, Sam Morris, was tossed . . . for failing to retrieve the Elia-thrown chair.
- The 1985 season saw Sid Bream hit .370 for Albuquerque and teammate Dennis Powell fashion a 9–0 mark on the mound before his recall by the Dodgers.
- In 1986, as the Phoenix Giants renamed themselves the Firebirds, Jim LeFebvre was named Manager of the Year after leading Phoenix to a first-half title. Phoenix even overcame a 31–5 shellacking at the hands of Hawaii on May 23 in Phoenix to take the first-half crown.
- The league known for hitting became a one-man pitcher's paradise in 1989. Tom Drees, a twenty-six-year-old hurler for the Chicago White Sox affiliate Vancouver, was coming off arthroscopic surgery in 1988, and his 9–7 record, 2.79 ERA and 149 hits allowed in 158 innings for Birmingham in the Double-A Southern League did not prepare him or his followers for what was to happen in the PCL.

Drees opened the '89 season as a Vancouver Mounties starter but was unimpressive and was banished to the bullpen. Before missing a start, however, Drees was put back in the starting rotation when the White Sox called up Vancouver pitcher Jeff Bittinger.

On May 23, 1989, Drees fired a no-hitter, beating Calgary 1–0 before a sparse crowd of 289 at Vancouver's Nat Bailey Stadium.

In his next start, May 28, he sculpted a second consecutive no-hitter, also a 1–0 game at Edmonton against the Trappers.

Less than three months later, on August 16, Drees became the first Minor Leaguer since Bill Bell, in 1952, for Bristol of the Appalachian League, to toss three no-hitters in a single season, when he threw a no-no against Las Vegas.

Those three gems made Drees 12–11, with a 3.37 ERA and 142 hits allowed in 168 innings. His pitching has made history in the PCL but he's still waiting to make his mark in the Major Leagues.

With every story about prowess and success, comes an equal number of stories about performances of futility. Baseball fans and players remember them, too, and just hope that better days are to follow. That is the hope for Edmonton Trappers shortstop Karl Allaire, who had a game to forget on April 15, 1990, against the Las Vegas Stars. Allaire committed four errors in the first three innings of that game, then handled six chances without a miscue, before booting another one in the ninth inning for his fifth error of the night, tieing an all-time PCL mark by third baseman Ike Hampton (Salt Lake City vs. Spokane, August 23, 1978) and shortstops Charlie Zinssar (Portland vs. Los Angeles, April 29, 1905), Leo Kintana (Oakland vs. Portland, June 28, 1933), and Rigoberto Fuentes (Phoenix vs. Hawaii, May 22, 1969). Edmonton overcame the shoddy fielding and won the game 5–2.

- In mid-1990, Padres catcher Benito Santiago's rehab guest-appearance at Las Vegas went well, as he went 6 for 20 (.300) with a grand slam and 7 RBI.
- Late in 1990, the California Angels Triple-A affiliate, the Edmonton Trappers, was sold by Peter Pocklington (also owner of the NHL's Stanley Cup champs, the Edmonton Oilers) to Mike Nicklous for $5 million.

The Angels' working agreement with Edmonton ended after the 1990 season and the Angels were looking to pick up a franchise closer to Southern California for geographical (and player shuttle) reasons.

Look for Edmonton to go shopping or to be available as an affiliate for one of the new National League franchises in 1993.

⚾   ⚾   ⚾   ⚾

The all-time Pacific Coast League career leaders list is a Jigger Statz–Buzz Arlett testimonial.

(*Source:* SABR)

Games played	Jigger Statz	2,790
Runs scored	Jigger Statz	1,996
Hits	Jigger Statz	3,356
Doubles	Jigger Statz	595
Triples	Jigger Statz	137
Homeruns	Buzz Arlett	251
RBI	Buzz Arlett	1,188
Stolen bases	Billy Lane	468
Batting average	Oscar "Ox" Eckhardt	.382
Games won (pitcher)	Frank Shellenback	295
Strikeouts	Dick Barrett	1,866

1990 Players to Watch

Orsino Hill, Vancouver (White Sox), was hitting .353 in late August.

Dave Rohde, Tucson (Astros), was hitting .353.

Todd Haney, Calgary (Mariners), had knocked out 111 hits.

Jose Offerman, Albuquerque (Dodgers), was all-world at .344, with 111 hits and 48 steals.

Lee Stevens, Edmonton (Angels), had a .300 average, 28 doubles, 15 homers, and 57 RBI.

Tom Dodd, Calgary (Mariners), drove in 114 runs.

Best Defensive Players to Watch (*Source: Baseball America*)

Catcher: Bill McGuire, Calgary (Mariners)
First Baseman: Mike Laga, Phoenix (Giants)

Second Baseman: Jose Vizcaino, Albuquerque (Dodgers)
Third Baseman: Dave Hansen, Albuquerque (Dodgers)
Shortstop: Mike Benjamin, Phoenix (Giants)
Outfielder: Mike Huff, Albuquerque (Dodgers)
Pitcher—Fastball: Rafael Valdez, Las Vegas (Padres)
Pitcher—Control: Scott Lewis, Edmonton (Angels)
Pitcher—Relief: Joe Bitker, Tacoma (A's)

6
MEXICAN LEAGUE

The Mexican League is considered a Triple-A League that has been in operation since 1955, though earlier leagues have operated south of the border since the first years of this century, most notably from 1933 to 1953 under the direction of millionaire businessman Jorge Pascual.

Occasionally thought of as an outlaw league—it had no status with the National Association—it allowed all people to play on its teams, regardless of race, skin color, or laws or suspensions that kept them from playing professionally in the United States.

In 1946, the Mexican League put together a concerted effort to lure high-priced players away from the American game, much as some Japanese League teams tried to do in the 1960s—Sandy Koufax, Don Drysdale, and Mickey Mantle were offered huge contracts to jump to the Far East.

In '46, Hank Greenberg, Bob Feller, and Stan Musial refused lucrative offers, but Sal Maglie, Mickey Owen, Max Lanier, and Danny Gardella took the money and ran south.

These league-jumpers were suspended from Major

League ball for five years by Commissioner Happy Chandler, but that didn't really correct the situation, and by 1949 Chandler rescinded his ban.

Over the years, several teams based in Mexico played in American Minor Leagues—Nogales and four other cities housed teams that played in the Arizona-Texas League in the 1940s and 1950s.

In 1949, the Mexican League rewrote its charter and began operating with only native players on its rosters. Prior to that, and prior to the integrating of professional baseball, the Mexican Leagues would often staff their teams with top Negro League stars. Due to poor finances, the league succumbed in 1953.

By 1955, a new Mexican League emerged, was given proper recognition as a stable league, and was welcomed into the National Association as a Class-AA loop.

The Mexican Central League was established in 1960 as a Class-A loop and was joined by the Mexican Northern League, Mexican Pacific League, and Mexican Rookie League.

That classification of Double-A for the Central League was raised to Triple-A in 1967.

By 1979, only one single league existed; the others being merged into the remaining Mexican League, which had twenty teams. Following some pruning and some bankruptcies, fourteen strong teams remain.

Today, Mexican League rosters may contain seven foreign-born members, and occasionally a former American Minor League player will travel south to give it one more shot. Case in point is Willie Mays Aikens, who, playing for his third team in four years, nearly won the Mexican League triple crown in 1989, posting league-leading numbers of .395 and 131 RBI, but coming in second in homers with 37, two off Leo Hernandez' 39.

Today, there are seven teams each in the Mexican League's two divisions.

The North is made up of the Los Dos Laredos Owls, Union Laguna Cotton Pickers, Saltillo Serape Makers,

Monterrey Sultans, San Luis Potosi, Monclova Steelers, and Monterrey Industrials. The South consists of the Campeche Pirates, Leon Braves, Yucatan Lions, Mexico City Red Devils, Mexico City Tigers, Tabasco Cattlemen, and Aguascalientes Railroadmen.

Inside the Mexican League:
- In 1937, Alfonso Nieto of Agricultura led the league with a .476 average.
- James "Cool Papa" Bell took the 1940 hitting title at .437, the RBI crown with 79, and the homerun leadership with 12 for Torreon-Veracruz.
- Josh Gibson won the Mexican League homerun crown in 1941 for Veracruz with 33 and took the RBI top spot with 124.
- Monte Irvin won the 1942 batting crown with a .397 mark for Veracruz, while also capturing the homer title with 20.
- Ray Dandridge tied for the RBI title at 70 with Burnis Wright.
- Bobby Ortiz won four straight homerun titles for Mexico from 1945 to 1948.
- Danny Gardella, a Major League outfielder for the Giants and Cardinals, hit 18 homers for New York in his sophomore season of 1945. When Giants management offered Gardella a paltry $4,500 for the 1946 season, Gardella jumped the Giants and signed with Vera Cruz of the Mexican League for a salary of $10,000.

     Baseball Commissioner Happy Chandler took a dim view of the situation and suspended Gardella and all other league-jumpers for five years. Gardella sued baseball in a historical antitrust case—*Gardella* v. *Chandler*—but the case was dismissed by a district court in 1948.

     Gardella's attorney, claiming that Gardella was only bound by an "illegal" reserve clause, won an appeal before the Second Circuit Court a year later, forcing Major League powers to settle out of court, ending Gardella's suspension, and awarding him damages of $29,000.

Gardella signed with the Cards in 1950 but only made a token appearance before he was unceremoniously dumped.

His case, unpopular across the nation, in the press, and among players and the hierarchy of baseball at the time, is thought to have been a major legal step toward the declaring of free agency more than two decades later.

- The 1948 batting leader was Ray Dandridge at .373 for Veracruz.
- Rene Gonzalez took three straight batting titles for Aguila (1952–54).
- Alfred Pinkston won four straight batting titles from 1959 to 1962.
- In 1960, Luis Tiant went 17–7 in 180 innings.
- All-time homerun king and local hero Hector Espino took his first of five batting titles with a .371 effort in 1964 for Monterrey. Espino also took the title in 1966 (.369), 1967 (.379), 1968 (.365), and 1973 (.377).

  In 1968, Hector Espino won his second of four homerun titles with 27.
- Vic Davalillo won the batting title for Aguascalientes with a .384 mark in 1977.

  Also in 1977, George Brunet of Poza Rica threw a no-hitter against Durango.
- In 1986, Willie Aikens broke Josh Gibson's forty-five-year-old RBI record by driving home 154 runs. He followed that up with an RBI crown in 1989.
- Nick Casteneda, of Yucatan, led the Minor Leagues with a .390 average in 1990. And Saltillo's Trench Davis topped the Minors with 189 hits, while Saltillo's Armando Reynoso won 20 games on the hill, losing only 3.

Career Mexican League leaders include:

Hits	Hector Espino	2,752
Doubles	Jesus Sommers	379
Triples	Gonzalo Villalobos	132
Homeruns	Hector Espino	453
RBI	Hector Espino	1,573
Stolen bases	Antonio Briones	490
Batting average	George Puccinelli	.334
Games won (pitcher)	Ramon Arano	332
Strikeouts	Ramon Arano	2,370

7
EASTERN LEAGUE

The Eastern League is a Double-A group in its sixty-eighth year of continuous operation. While several other leagues have been called the Eastern League over the years—the International League grew out of one of the early Eastern Leagues—the current league was established in 1923, with circuit teams now based in Canada, Connecticut, Maryland, New York, Ohio, and Pennsylvania.

The latest Eastern League was originally known as the New York–Pennsylvania League, not to be confused with the New York–Penn League, which is still in operation but which didn't begin until 1939.

The league, formed as a Class B circuit, played its first game on May 9, 1923, with Williamsport defeating Wilkes-Barre 10–4 at Williamsport. Scranton, York, Binghamton, and Elmira were other charter members, and when Hartford replaced Scranton in 1938, the league changed its name to the Eastern League. By that time, the loop had been upgraded to Class A status, which it retained until 1963, when it became Class AA.

In terms of continuous operation, the Eastern League

trails only the International League and the PCL, as through sixty-eight years, the loop has been represented by forty-three cities in eleven states and two Canadian provinces.

Among Eastern League alumni are Rabbit Maranville, Whitey Ford, Heinie Manush, Lefty Gomez, Juan Marichal, Bob Lemon, Warren Spahn, Ralph Kiner, Early Wynn, Robin Roberts, Wade Boggs, Eric Davis, Wally Joyner, Nolan Ryan, and Andre Dawson—there were some 335 Eastern League grads who saw action in the Majors in 1989.

Running a 140-game schedule from April 9 to September 0, the Eastern League adheres to the Shaughnessy play-off structure.

Its eight current teams are: Albany-Colonie (Yankees); Canton-Akron (Indians); Hagerstown Suns (Orioles); Harrisburg Senators (Pirates); London (Tigers); New Britain (Red Sox); Reading (Phillies); and Williamsport Bills (Mariners).

In 1990, Albany led the league for the third straight year, this time with a 79–60 record, 3 games ahead of London. However, the Yankees were beaten in the first round of the play-offs by New Britain, which faced off in the finals against London after the latter dispatched Canton-Akron.

Holding true to the recent development doctrine of putting its top prospects at Double-A then jumping them, when ready, to the Majors, bypassing Triple-A entirely, some of the best Minor League players in the system come through the Eastern League as their last stop before MLB stardom.

⚾   ⚾   ⚾   ⚾

What is the Eastern League?
Maybe it is former Major League greats who coach in the Minors and show frustration at the not-yet-developed youngsters playing the game.

In the late '40s, former Yankee great Lefty "Goofy" Gomez managed the Yanks' Eastern League farm club at
Binghamton, and while coaching third base one day, he
had runners at first and second when his batter singled to
center. He watched, dumfounded, as the lead runner
rounded third, came to an abrupt halt and slid back into
third. Meanwhile, the runner at first legged it all the way
to third and slid in on the opposite side of the sack at the
same time. The throw came in and the third baseman
tagged both runners, who had now both vacated the bag.
Gomez, unable to restrain himself, let out a cavemanesque
roar and slid into third himself.

And the Eastern League was, as all other leagues were,
a contributor to America's war effort, with the old as well
as the young.

As the nation became embroiled in World War II, Andy
Cohen was hanging on as an infielder for Elmira in 1941
and 1942. During both of those years, Cohen was the oldest player on the Elmira team by more than four years—
Cohen was thirty-eight in 1942—yet he was the first to see
military service, leaving his team, his new wife, and his
family behind to serve in a U.S. Army Engineering Corps
platoon that took part in the invasions of Northern Africa
and Italy, where he rose to the rank of squad sergeant.
Following his discharge, Cohen became a player-manager
and part owner of the Mexican National League's El Paso,
Texas, franchise.

And the Eastern League is the home of a grand prank,
"The Great Potato Hoax."

On August 31, 1987, a weak-hitting catcher named Dave
Bresnahan, grand-nephew of Hall-of-Famer Roger Bresnahan, pulled off a hidden spud trick with two outs in the
ninth and a runner at third in a game between Williamsport and Reading.

With a peeled potato tucked in his glove, Bresnahan
caught a pitched ball, and fired the tater over the third
baseman's head in an apparent errant pick-off attempt.
When runner Rick Lundblade tore for the plate, Bresna-

han produced the real ball and tagged the bewildered Reading runner out.

For his trick, Bresnahan was thumbed out, fined, and released . . . his .149 batting average cited for his expulsion.

A year later, however, his uniform number 59 was "retired" by Williamsport in a "night" promotion given in his honor.

⚾   ⚾   ⚾   ⚾

Inside the Eastern League:

* Joe Hauser, the homerun terror who twice blasted more than 60 roundtrippers in a season, began his Minor League career with Providence in 1918. In his sophomore year, 1919, he led the Eastern League in homers with the un-Hauserlike total of 6, and also blasted a circuit-topping 21 triples.
* In 1932, New Haven's thirty-eight-year-old catcher Clarence "Yam" Yaryan stopped by long enough to hit .366.
* Jack Graham lit up the Eastern League for Binghamton in 1939 and 1940. The six-foot-two, 195-pound outfielder played in 118 games in '39 and that was all he needed to lead the league in homers (29) and triples (16), while driving in 94 runs and hitting .326.

    Following a demotion from the Newark Bears' International League team, in 1940, Graham played in 126 games and led the loop in homers again, with 20.
* Rip Collins set the Eastern League batting mark in 1944 with a .396 average.
* In 1945, ex-Major Leaguer Wally Schang became the oldest player to participate in an Eastern League game by catching for Utica. Schang was fifty-four, and continued to play in other leagues until he was fifty-seven.
* In 1948, one-armed outfielder Pete Gray made a stop in Elmira. Gray hit a solid .290 in 82 games following a year of voluntary retirement.

    Also in 1948, homerun king Joe Bauman visited the

Eastern League with Hartford and found hitting home-runs rather difficult. Following seasons of 48 and 38 homers in the West Texas–New Mexico League, and pre-ceding years of 50, 53, 72, and 46 homers in the Long-horn League, the first baseman only managed 10 circuit blasts against Eastern League pitchers.

• And 1948 was the year Fred Thomas (Wilkes-Barre) and Al Smith (Wilkes-Barre) broke the color barrier in the Eastern League and the year Jimmy Piersall led the loop with 92 RBI.

• Ken "Hawk" Harrelson blasted through 1962 with a league-record 138 RBI and a league-leading 38 homers.

• Eddie Watt threw two no-hitters for Elmira in 1965.

• Gerald Hannahs became the league's first 20-game win-ner since Dave Leonhard in 1965, when he won 20 in 1976 for Quebec City.

• In 1979, Rick Lancellotti of Buffalo became the first East-ern League player in seventy-nine years to lead the en-tire Minor League system in homeruns by belting out 41. The last Eastern League player to accomplish the feat was Kitty Bransfield, who slammed 17 roundtrippers for Worcester in 1900.

• Cory Snyder led the league in both homers and RBI in 1985, with 28 four-baggers and 94 runs driven across.

• Tommy Gregg feasted on Eastern League pitching in 1987, batting a robust .371.

• Jerome Walton warmed up for The Show by leading the league with a .331 average in 1988.

⚾   ⚾   ⚾   ⚾

Players to Watch

Baltimore Orioles No. 1 draft choice Mike Mussina, pitcher, went 3–0 at Hagerstown with 40 strikeouts and only 34 hits and seven walks in 42 innings. He jumped to Rochester (International League) for one start before the season ended.

Scott Taylor, a hurler for New Britain (Red Sox), had whiffed 138 batters by late August.

Mike Wilkins, a right-handed pitcher for London (Tigers), went 13–5 with a 2.42 ERA in 25 starts. He led the league in shutouts with 3 and will move to Triple-A with a shot at The Show in 1991. After the season, Wilkins was traded to the Dodger organization for lefty relief prospect Mike Munoz.

Best Defensive Players to Watch (*Source: Baseball America*)

Catcher: Chris Howard, Williamsport (Mariners)
First Baseman: Rico Brogna, London (Tigers)
Second Baseman: Pat Kelly, Albany (Yankees)
Third Baseman: Don Sparks, Albany (Yankees)
Shortstop: Carlos Garcia, Harrisburg (Pirates)
Outfielder: Moises Alou, Harrisburg (Pirates)
Pitcher—Fastball: Rudy Seanez, Canton (Indians)
Pitcher—Control: Mike Gardiner, Williamsport (Mariners)
Pitcher—Relief: Rudy Seanez, Canton (Indians) and Joe Ausanio, Harrisburg (Pirates)

8
TEXAS LEAGUE

As barnstorming teams gained in popularity in Texas in 1887, several businessmen who were also baseball enthusiasts met in December to form a state baseball league. On April 8, 1888, the first Texas League game was played, and the league began with six teams in operation: Austin, Fort Worth, Houston, San Antonio, Galveston, and Dallas. Before the end of the season, only four teams survived, having to reorganize the following year.

Barehanded ballplayers (no real men wore gloves in those days) played in hot, dusty weather, but fans were few, teams were underfinanced, and by 1892, the league had folded.

In 1895, a new eight-team circuit was established, thanks to the organizational skill of a former baseball manager, Ted Sullivan, but low receipts caused four teams to fall out by 1896. The teams that did finish, however, played a Minor League record 130 games plus play-offs, showing a smattering of stability.

The 1898 season was a tough one. The Spanish-American War decimated teams whose players went to fight for their country, and the league, known as the Texas Association, barely made it to the twentieth century.

Sullivan put the league back on its feet in 1901 with teams from Corsicana, Dallas, Waco, Fort Worth, Paris, and Texarkana. By 1902, given a National Association classification of D ball, the league looked fairly stable, but there was a huge disparity in talent as Cosicana ran other teams off the field in several memorable hitting outbursts that totaled well into the double figures.

From 1902 to 1920, the league thrived and only weather—hurricanes, rainstorms, dust storms, and blazing heat—kept fans out of the ballparks. Along the way, Texas League talent was being more highly thought of and in 1907 was ranked Class C; in 1911 that was raised to Class B, and in 1921 the Texas League had achieved a Class A ranking.

The Texas League became known as a tough league . . . a league of survivors. That became apparent on the field, as team rivalries often manifested themselves in the form of fistfights, especially between Texas teams and those based in Oklahoma.

In fact the only negative that can be leveled at the league in the early '20s was the lack of parity in teams, as the Fort Worth Panthers rolled off six straight league championships from 1920 to 1925 by a minimum of 12 games and a maximum winning margin of 30½ games over second-place Houston in 1924.

As with all other Minor Leagues, the Great Depression weakened but did not kill the circuit, which fought off low incomes to draw people to the parks using promotional schemes including night baseball, ladies days, giveaways and play-offs to spur interest.

With the Depression behind it, the Texas League remained stable and prosperous, withstanding the challenge from border towns in Mexico and rival leagues along the outskirts of Texas League operations.

The Texas League virtually sailed through World War II and the economic slowdown of the Minors as well as more bad weather in the '50s and '60s—there were forty rainouts in 1950 as attendance fell by 300,000—and past television intrusion and the Korean War to remain sturdy enough to survive until conditions proved more favorable.

In 1959, a reorganized six-team circuit entered into a type of Double-A Alliance with the Class-AA Mexican League to form the Pan-American Association, but by 1962 the league stood on its own again.

Despite losing Houston and Dallas to Major League ball in the 1960s, the Texas League survived and stands out today as a staple in the business of Minor League ball.

Today, the Double-A Texas League runs a 136-game schedule from April 10 to September 1, broken down into two halves to form a play-off structure.

Covering six states, the Texas League has teams in Arkansas (Little Rock), Texas (El Paso, Midland, San Antonio), Mississippi (Jackson), Louisiana (Shreveport), Kansas (Wichita), and Oklahoma (Tulsa).

In 1990, the Shreveport (Giants) and Jackson (Mets) won their halves of the Eastern Division pennant, and the El Paso (Brewers) and San Antonio (Dodgers) split the Western Division. San Antonio and Shreveport squared off in the finals.

Some colorful current team nicknames include: Arkansas Travelers, El Paso Diablos, San Antonio Missions, and Wichita Wranglers.

In what must be the definite example of *carpe diem*, no one has ever seized the day as did J.J. "Nig" Clarke on June 15, 1902. Clarke, an excellent defensive catcher who was an adequate hitter, was batting seventh for Corsicana in a game against Texarkana, at Ennis, Texas.

As written above, the Corsicana Oilers were solid up and down the lineup and romped off to a 58–9 mark— including a 27-game winning streak—through the first two months of the season (they finished the season at 88–23, a .793 percentage).

So on this hot, clear June day, the Oilers faced a weak

team from Texarkana, a club that had just relocated from Sherman-Denison.

Local ordinances prohibited Sunday baseball, so the June 15 game was moved to a bandbox park in Ennis, Texas. Still, Texarkana's owner and pitcher, C. B. DeWitt, had no idea of what was to come. True, Texarkana was in last place, but who could have guessed that Corsicana would explode for a record 51 runs to annihilate Texarkana, 51–3?

The topper to this day to end all days wasn't Corsicana's 51 runs on 53 hits; it wasn't Nig Clarke's perfect day to end all perfect days—eight homeruns in eight at bats and 14 RBI—and it wasn't the fact that this 51–3 slaughter took only two hours and ten minutes to complete; it was the absurd reality that the losing pitcher, C. B. DeWitt, went all the way. One man threw the entire game and gave up 51 runs on 53 hits. True, only 26 runs were earned—five Texarkana errors aided the onslaught—and DeWitt only walked three and hit three Corsicana hitters, but going 9 innings and giving up 21 homeruns, 4 doubles and 2 triples is just one of those strange but true tales that forever make baseball scholars shake their heads in wonder.

One sidelight on the game was that some telegraph operators reporting the game heard (by code) the score and assumed there must have been some mistake. They reported the score as 5–3.

⚾   ⚾   ⚾   ⚾

What is the Texas League?

Perhaps it is communication between Major League parent and its affiliate.

When Bobby Bragan was manager of the Fort Worth team (in the Dodger system), he received instructions from Dodger GM Branch Rickey to cut costs on all levels. Bragan was annoyed and showed his dismay after receiving a telegram from Rickey that asked the Texas League manager if his club needed a shortstop, or if it could play well enough

BOX SCORE: CORSICANA VS. TEXARKANA AT ENNIS, JUNE 15, 1902

Corsicana	AB	R	H	Texarkana	AB	R	H
Maloney, cf	6	5	3	Deskin, cf	5	1	2
Alexander, 2b	8	5	8	Mulkey, 2b	4	0	1
Riupley, rf	8	6	5	Welter, 3b	4	0	1
Pendleton, lf	8	6	8	Wolfe, c	4	1	1
Markley, 3b	7	7	6	Murphey, lf	4	0	1
O'Connor, lb	8	7	7	DeWitt, p	3	0	1
Clark, c	8	8	8	Tackaberry, lb	4	1	1
Morris, ss	8	6	6	Gillon, rf	4	0	1
Wright, p	4	1	2	Burns, ss	4	0	0
	65	**51**	**53**		**36**	**3**	**9**

Stolen Bases: Maloney, Alexander, Morris, Clark, Ripley. **Home Runs:** Clark (8), O'Connor (3), Alexander (3), Ripley (2), Pendleton (2), Maloney, Markley, Morris. **Triples:** Markley, O'Connor. **Doubles:** Morris, Alexander, Maloney, Pendleton, Deskin, Welter, LOB: Corsicana (15), Texarkana (5). **Errors:** Corsicana (0), Texarkana (5). **Double Plays By:** Corsicana (4), Texarkana (1). **Walks By:** Wright (1), Dewitt (3). **Struck Out By:** Wright (2), DeWitt (1). **Hit By Pitcher By:** DeWitt (3). **Earned Runs By:** Corsicana (26), Texarkana (1). **Umpires:** Method and Cavender. **Time:** 2:10.

Texarkana	010	000	020—3
Corsicana	629	275	488—51

Source: The Texas League

with the existing alignment. Bragan cut costs by sending back a one-word reply telegram that read: "Yes."

Rickey sent back another telegram with the question: "Yes, what?"

Bragan got in the last word by wiring back, "Yes, sir!"

Bragan may be worthy of a volume or two on his exploits alone. He often baited umpires, sat down on home plate as they argued with him, offered them bottles of soda during debates and engaged in striptease shows to demonstrate his disgust. In five years as a manager in the Texas League (Fort Worth: 1948–52), Bragan was tossed out of sixty games—a record as near as anyone can tell.

One night in Oklahoma City, Bragan bumped and yelled and shouted with the men in blue who called a cop and had Bragan arrested. The lawman chased Bragan from home plate to center field and back to the dugout before grabbing him. Bragan also performed his act in the Pacific Coast League and in the Majors, but as a player-manager—he was a catcher in 1949, catching in 111 games, hitting .295, throwing out more than 50 percent of the would-be base-stealers who tested him, and did not allow a passed ball—and league president (1969–75), he might have been at his best in Texas.

Maybe the Texas League is all about promotions.

Bill Valentine, General Manager of the Arkansas Travelers, who have copyrighted the slogan "The greatest show on dirt," said, "We do a lot of advertising on television. We tell the kids to come on out and have fun. We (the Minors) did all the promotions first. When we did it, it was called 'bush league.' Now all the Major League clubs have copied us. We did bat night, ladies night, hat night, radio giveaways, t-shirts, jerseys, discounts to families, community nights, business nights, and free food. We do it to survive. We have to compete for the entertainment dollar, and our ticket sales is what makes us our profits. When we think up a night and it's successful, you can see it the next year in the Majors."

And the Texas League is a league that respects accomplishments, regardless of religious persuasion.

In 1925, Andy Cohen, a five-foot-eight, 160-pound infielder, began his professional career with Waco. Cohen, one of the few Jewish ballplayers at the time, and a rarity in Texas, was accepted by his teammates—though fans were not so gracious and shouted deplorable anti-Semitic epithets at him, and opponents seized the ethnic difference to try to rattle the player—but to no avail as he hit .321 in 106 games to earn a shot with the John McGraw-led New York Giants (he was eventually to replace Hall-of-Famer Rogers Hornsby).

With typical Texas League hospitality, to honor Cohen's Texas League accomplishments, his Major League efforts, and the Major League pitching career of Andy's brother Sid Cohen (Washington Senators—1934–37), and Andy's successful Minor League managing career following his World War II stint as an army squad sergeant, the Texas League named Cohen's mother, Lena Cohen, "Baseball Mother of the Year."

The Los Angeles Dodgers, parent of the San Antonio Missions since 1977, have threatened to leave their Double-A affiliate over the city's unwillingness to build a new ballpark.

In a weird play that typifies the Minor League experience, on August 16, 1990, the Midland Angels (Angels) defeated the El Paso Diablos (Brewers) 5–4 and pulled an odd triple play as well. In the eighth inning, with runners at first and third, El Paso's Rafel Skeete hit a ball to left field that was deep enough to score Shon Ashley from third. Left fielder Johnny Monell made the catch and fired home, but his throw skipped past catcher Doug Davis. Backing up the play, Midland's pitcher Mark Zapelli corralled the errant toss and threw to first to nail Casey Webster, the El Paso runner who had wandered off the bag.

The ball was then flipped back to Zapelli, who took the mound, fired to third and appealed to umpire Red Morrow, who ruled that Ashley was out for leaving the base too soon on the fly ball. Score it a typical triple play: 7 to 1 to 3 to 1 to 5 (left to pitcher to first to pitcher to third).

⚾   ⚾   ⚾   ⚾

Inside the Texas League:
• Texas Leaguers who went on to further glory and election to the Major League Hall of Fame include: Grover Cleveland Alexander (Dallas 1930), Dizzy Dean (Houston 1930–31, Tulsa 1940), Hank Greenberg (Beaumont 1931–32), Chick Hafey (Houston 1924), Rogers Hornsby (manager at Oklahoma City 1940–41, Fort Worth 1942, and Beaumont 1950), Carl Hubbell (Fort Worth 1927, Beaumont 1928), Ducky Medwick (Houston 1932–33, 1948), Joe Morgan (San Antonio 1964), Branch Rickey (Dallas 1904–05), Brooks Robinson (San Antonio 1956–

57), Frank Robinson (Tulsa 1954), Al Simmons (Shreveport 1923), George Sisler (Shreveport-Tyler 1932), Duke Snider (Fort Worth 1946, manager at Albuquerque 1967, Alexandria 1972), Tris Speaker (Cleburne 1906, Houston 1907), and Bill Terry (Shreveport 1916–17).

- Some great, colorful team nicknames of the past include: Alexandria Aces (with Johnny Grubb, Mike Ivie, and Dave Freisleben, managed by Duke Snider); Amarillo Sonics (with Joe Pepitone, Jim Bouton, and Phil Linz, managed by Rube Walker); Beaumont Blues (also Millionaires, Orphans, Exporters, and Roughnecks—the Exporters had Dizzy Trout, Schoolboy Rowe, Dixie Howell, and Frank Secory); Dallas Hams (also Submarines, Steers, Rebels, and Spurs—with Snipe Conley, Eddie Knoblauch, Buzz Clarkeson, and Pete Burnside); Galveston Sandcrabs (also Buccaneers, with Wally Moses, Joe Gibbs, and Beau Bell); Houston Lambs (also Red Stockings, Babies, Buffaloes, Buffs, and Moore's Marvels—the Buffs had Dizzy Dean, George Payne, Ducky Medwick, Homer Peel, and the manager was Joe Schultz); Lake Charles Creoles (with Casey Horn, Lefty Logan, Dick Latham, and Charles Blackburn); New Orleans Pelicans (with Abner Powell, Farmer Works, and Frank Behan); Paris Eisenfelder's Homeseekers (also Red Peppers, with Homer Peel, Paul Martin, Frank Carswell, and James Walkup); Shreveport Gassers (with Hyder Barr, Hack Eibel, and Tony Thebo); Temple Boll Weevils (with Rick Adams, Hickory Dixon, and Prince Ben Shelton); Victoria Rosebuds; Wichita Falls Spudders (with Lyman Lamb, Tut Jenkins, and George Payne).
- Patrick Newman became the first Texas Leaguer to lead the Minor Leagues in home runs by hitting 18 for San Antonio in 1908.
- On May 9, 1912, a scant ten months after he hit into an unassisted triple play in the Pacific Coast League, third baseman Roy Akin, playing for Waco against Houston, achieved a measure of revenge by completing an unassisted triple play himself.

On a double-squeeze attempt, with runners on second and third both trying to score on a bunt down the third base line, Akin grabbed the bunt in the air, stepped on third for out number two, and tagged the incoming runner for the third out, erasing the bad taste he had from being on the receiving end the year before.

- In 1923, right-handed hurler Ulysses Simpson Grant "Lil" Stoner won 27 games and dominated the league with a no-hitter, an 18-strikeout performance and a 13-inning shutout en route to a league-low 2.70 ERA. The following year he won 11 games for the Detroit Tigers.
- Clarence Kraft led the Texas League and the entire Minor Leagues with 55 homeruns for Fort Worth in 1924.
- With the 1931 season nearing an end, Houston skipper Joe Schultz sent in his son, thirteen-year-old Joe Schultz, Jr., the team's batboy, as a pinch hitter against Galveston. Schultz, Jr., later a Major Leaguer, went 0 for 1.
- In 1939, thirty-nine-year-old former home run king Nick Cullop won his first swatting crown in nine years by belting 25 and driving in a league-leading 112 runs for Houston.

That year Edward "Bear Tracks" Greer was the pitching king. The thirty-eight-year-old Fort Worth right-hander went 22–11 with a 2.29 ERA.

- Pepper Martin, coach for Tulsa in 1958, became the oldest pinch runner in history, taking over first base for a pitcher. Martin was fifty-four.
- In a part-time stint with Victoria in 1959, Frank Howard boomed out 27 homers before being promoted to Spokane of the Pacific Coast League, where he blasted 16 more for a Minor League leading 43 four-baggers.
- In 1963 Arlo Engel led the entire Minor League circuit in homers by belting out 41 for El Paso.
- Hall-of-Fame second baseman Joe Morgan won the 1964 Texas League MVP award after hitting .323 with 90 RBI, 47 stolen bases and 113 runs scored as he led San Antonio to the league title.

- Total league attendance hit 770,070 in 1970.
- From 1973 through 1978, six consecutive members of the El Paso Diablos won the batting title: 1973-Morris Nettles at .332; 1974-Jerry Remy at .338; 1975-Butch Alberts at .342; 1976-Fred Frazier at .363; 1977-Tom Smith at .366; and 1978-Danny Goodwin at .360.
- Willie Mays Aikens won the 1976 homerun crown with 30 for El Paso.
- Steve Sax took the 1981 batting title with a .346 mark for San Antonio.
- Darryl Strawberry stirred the crowds for Jackson in 1982 with a league-leading 34 roundtrippers.
- Rob Deer hit 35 in 1983 for Shreveport to gain the title.
- In 1990, in a throwback to the J.J. Clark days of 1902, pitching took a night off in Midland. The final score that night was Wichita Wranglers 33, Midland Angels 17, as 50 runs, 47 hits and 9 errors etched the game for the 3,527 fans in attendance. It was the highest score in the circuit since Beaumont and El Paso combined for 56 runs in a game in 1983.

⚾   ⚾   ⚾   ⚾

The all-time Texas League career leaders list is a Paul Easterling one-man show:

(*Source:* Texas League)

Games played	Paul Easterling	1,777
Runs scored	Paul Easterling	1,134
Hits	Paul Easterling	1,922
Doubles	Paul Easterling	378
Triples	Harold Epps	112
Homeruns	Paul Easterling	223
RBI	Paul Easterling	1,136
Stolen bases	Pat Newman	422
Batting average	Homer Peel	.325
Games won (pitcher)	Paul Wachtel	231
Strikeouts	Oyster Joe Martina	1,412

1990 Players to Watch

Eric Karros, San Antonio (Dodgers), hit 45 doubles by late August.
Henry Rodriguez, San Antonio (Dodgers), had driven in 72 runs.
Tom Goodwin, San Antonio (Dodgers), had stolen 80 bases.
Pete Schourek, Jackson (Mets), had nailed down 13 wins.
Terry Bross, Jackson (Mets), had picked up 22 saves.

Best Defensive Players to Watch (*Source: Baseball America*)

Catcher: Todd Hundley, Jackson (Mets)
First Baseman: Eric Karros, San Antonio (Dodgers)
Second Baseman: Rudy Hernandez, Jackson (Mets)
Third Baseman: Steve Finkin, San Antonio (Dodgers)
Shortstop: Kevin Baez, Jackson (Mets)
Outfielder: Chuck Carr, Jackson (Mets)
Pitcher—Fastball: Terry Bross, Jackson (Mets)
Pitcher—Control: Rod Beck, Shreveport (Giants)
Pitcher—Relief: Terry Bross, Jackson (Mets)

9
SOUTHERN LEAGUE

The Southern League is a Double-A circuit in its fifth time around organized baseball. Originally established in 1885, it operated sporadically until 1899. A new league sprang up in 1904 and ran until 1917. Since then, it has had reigns of 1919–30, 1936–42, 1946–61, and its current run, which began twenty-seven years ago in 1964.

The original Southern League, in 1885, was made up of six teams: Atlanta, Augusta, Columbus, and Macon, Georgia; Birmingham, Alabama; and Chattanooga, Tennessee. But poor attendance and the common bugaboo, underfinanced operations, killed the loop by 1899.

Other strong starts followed but failed—during World War I, the Great Depression, and World War II—the Southern Association began again in 1946 and did well, drawing a record-high attendance of 1.8 million, which was surpassed in 1947 with an all-time high of 2.1 million.

But once again, the times caught up with the game, and lower attendance plagued the league in the late '50s, and when the National League took Atlanta in 1962, the Association had had it.

In 1964, however, the South Atlantic League, commonly called the "Sally League," changed its name to the Southern League and over the next twenty-seven years has taken back under its wing the old cities of the South that had been part of the many Southern League predecessors of the past, including Birmingham, Nashville, Charlotte, and Chattanooga.

Television and the Atlanta Braves Superstation definitely hurt attendance in the early '80s, but more than 1,650,000 fans went through turnstiles in 1989, and the outlook seems bright for the future of this Southern hospitality version of the Minor League game.

The current Southern League runs a schedule of 144 games from April 6 to September 1, broken down into two halves for play-off consideration.

The Southern League covers Alabama—Birmingham (White Sox) and Huntsville (A's); South Carolina—Charlotte (Cubs); Tennessee—Chattanooga (Reds), Knoxville (Blue Jays), and Memphis (Royals); Georgia—Columbus (Astros); South Carolina—Greenville (Braves); Florida—Jacksonville (Expos) and Orlando (Twins).

In 1990, Jacksonville took the second half Eastern Division crown after Orlando won the first half, and Birmingham nailed down the second half in the Western Division after Memphis won the first half. After Orlando took three of four from Jacksonville and Memphis won three of four from Birmingham, Memphis and Orlando hooked up in the finals.

The Southern League's most interesting nicknames include: Chattanooga Lookouts; Memphis Chicks (named after the Chickasaw Indians); Columbus Mudcats (also nominated for best logo, a catfish staring ahead from out of a large "C"); and Orlando SunRays.

What sums up the Southern League?
Perhaps it is the rags to riches to rags to riches to rags

story of Walter "Boom Boom" Beck, a journeyman pitcher if ever there was one.

Beck was an active ballplayer for twenty-seven years, from 1924 to 1950. During that time he pitched for 23 teams in 13 leagues. In the Majors, he earned his nickname for the sound that belted baseballs made when his pitches were hit and the spheres came crashing against tin fences making a resounding "Boom."

Beck went only 38–69 in the Majors, but in the Minors, working in such leagues as the Three-I League, Texas Association, Western League, American Association, International League, Pacific Coast League, Interstate League, Southeast League, Central League, and Middle Atlantic League, as well as the Southern Association, he compiled a strong 199–167 record.

But it was in the Southern Association in 1932 that he had his moment in the sun. As the leading pitcher in the league he had a 27–6 mark for the Memphis Chicks, by far a surprise season for a twenty-eight-year-old who was considered through four years earlier by the St. Louis Browns, who had banished him to the Minors. Beck struggled, fought back, and earned a trip to Brooklyn in 1933. True he lost twenty games in '33 and pitched poorly in '34 before another Minor League sentence, but for Walter Beck, 1932 in the Southern Association was the year to end all years. He was a hero in Memphis from start to finish and it earned him a first class ticket to play with the Boys of Summer at Ebbets Field. For Beck, the Southern Association was the field of dreams on which he put it all together.

Or maybe the tale that exemplifies the Southern Association is one of innovation.

In 1910, the entire league decided to see just how fast a professional game could be played, so on September 19, all teams in the league were under instructions to play the game as quickly as possible—batters swinging at every good pitch; pitchers getting the ball over and not playing a waiting game against hitters; fielders running on and off the field.

In the fastest game ever played in professional baseball history, Mobile defeated the Atlanta Crackers 2–1 in Atlanta in a mere thirty-two minutes. There were no strikeouts, one walk, ten hits (six by Mobile, four by Atlanta) and a triple play (by Mobile).

The game set the mark by ten minutes, as on the same day, Chattanooga played Nashville in a forty-two-minute whirl.

Or maybe the Southern League is a compendium of colorful players, such as Casey Stengel. In 1912, while playing left field for Montgomery against Pensacola, twenty-two-year-old Stengel, in his final Minor League season, discovered a box containing water pipes hidden beneath the field. Casey lifted the lid and crawled into the container. The inning began and there was no left fielder, yet no one noticed . . . that is, until the third batter hit a soft fly to left. Stengel, watching the play from underground level, mysteriously appeared from nowhere to make the catch.

⚾   ⚾   ⚾   ⚾

Inside the Southern League:
• The Southern League, like its predecessor, the Southern Association, is the quintessential mix of great pitching and great hitting. The great hitters have often dominated the statistics—Danny Taylor's 81 extra base hits for Memphis in 1928; eight players with 40 or more homers (see Jack Harshman and Bob Lennon stories in this chapter); Elliot Bigelow's career Southern League batting average of .359; Eddie Rose's career Southern League mark of 866 RBIs; Andy Reese's 1,641 Southern League hits; and so on—but in one streak, Irvin "Kaiser" Wilhelm got even. In September 1907, Wilhelm, who also played for nine years in The Show compiling a credible 3.44 ERA with 12 shutouts, put Southern Association hitters on their ears . . . or back in their dugouts. Pitching for Birmingham, Wilhelm threw six consecutive shutouts, fin-

ishing up with a two-complete-game doubleheader shutout sweep over Shreveport to end the year with 56 consecutive shutout innings. Wilhelm finished the '07 season at 22–13, and by 1908, he was up with the Brooklyn Dodgers for whom he went 16–22.

- The Minor Leagues is the epitome of highs and lows . . . dreams and nightmares . . . absolute ecstasy and unparalleled agony. And all of that happened to right-handed pitcher Tom "Shotgun" Rogers within a span of eleven days.

  Pitching for Nashville against Chattanooga, June 11, 1916, Rogers got his fastball in high gear and threw a perfect game. Elation was still his when, eleven days later, on the mound again, he faced former Major League infielder John Dodge and his fastball got away from him, striking Dodge in the face. Dodge died the following day.

  Though he was called up to the Majors the next year by the St. Louis Browns, the accident haunted Rogers and he was never able to throw high and hard inside again, limiting his effectiveness in a four-year lackluster career.

- Beginning a longevity mark for Southern Association performers, Rube Robinson, a pitcher for Little Rock, pitched his first game in 1916. He lasted thirteen years, one more than second baseman Henry Knaupp—New Orleans from 1910 to 1917 and 1919 to 1923.

- In 1924, Johnny Dobbs, a Southern Association manager for twenty-four years from 1907–31 won his fourth of six pennants by leading Memphis to a 104–49 record.

- For a two-year period from 1929 through 1930, Nashville's first baseman Jim Poole ruled home plate. The left-handed hitting six-footer won back-to-back homerun and RBI crowns, driving in a combined total of 294 runs on 83 homers while hitting better than .350 over that span.

- Striking a blow for the fair sex, the Southern League may have been six decades ahead of its time, thanks to a 1931 performance by seventeen-year-old Jackie Mitchell.

  On April 2, 1931, Joe Engel, owner of the Chattanooga

Lookouts, inked lefty hurler Jackie Mitchell to a contract for the '31 Southern Association season.

Mitchell's auspicious debut came in an exhibition game against the barnstorming New York Yankees, making a trip northward to open the regular season. The Bronx Bombers opened the first inning with two hits, when Chattanooga manager Bert Niehoff pulled his starter, made the wave to the bullpen and called in the lefty, Mitchell, to face the Yankees' lefty hitter, Babe Ruth.

Ruth, who was preparing for a big season—he hit .373, 46 homers, 163 RBI and a .700 slugging percentage in 1931—stood in against the sidearmer and on a 2–2 count, The "Sultan of Swat" watched the sidearm delivery sail in on the corner for a called strike three. Making like Muhammad Ali, Ruth opened his eyes and shook his fist in mock anger before slamming into the dugout.

Lou Gehrig was next for Mitchell, and "Columbia Lou" was on his way to a .341, 46 homer, 184 RBI season. The left-handed "Iron Horse" swung and missed at a strike three curveball for out number two.

Minor League superstar (60 homeruns for Salt Lake City of the PCL in 1925), and Major League hero, Tony "Poosh 'em up" Lazerri was next. The right-handed hitting second sacker worked Mitchell for a walk and Niehoff yanked Mitchell.

The Yankees won that day, 14–4, but Mitchell gained a spot in baseball lore.

[*Author's note*: Baseball Commissioner Kenesaw Mountain Landis soon ruled Mitchell's contract void, dealing a blow to female rights in sports.]

• Also in 1931 comes this story from the SABR files involving a meeting of great pitchers, one on the way up, the other on the way down.

The opening game of the 1931 Dixie Series saw Birmingham of the Southern Association against Houston of the Texas League. On the mound for the Barons was forty-three-year-old star of another era Ray Caldwell. His opposing number for the Buffs was twenty-year-old star of the future, Jerome "Dizzy" Dean.

Caldwell began his Major League career with the New York Yankees in 1910, a year before Dean was born. Caldwell went 133–120 in twelve years in The Show and had been hanging on in the Minors for nine years—though "hanging on" may not do "Slim" justice, as he went 19–7 for Birmingham in '31.

Dean, of course, who lived a storied life and went 150–83 in an injury-shortened twelve-year career in the Bigs, and was on his way up—26 wins and the Texas League MVP when the two met in 1931.

Caldwell outdueled Dean that day, 1–0, and nine years later, when Dean's Major League career was ostensibly over, Caldwell was still hurling in the Minors, pitching for Fremont in the Ohio State League—and working one inning of the league's all-star game.

- In 1934, Minor League great Buzz Arlett made a stop in Birmingham and hit 7 homers before being promoted to Minneapolis of the American Association, where he hit 41 more. His combined total of 48 four-baggers led the Minor Leagues that year.

- But 1934 and the Southern League proved kinder to first baseman-outfielder Phil Weintraub of Nashville. Batting in lefty-friendly Sulpher Dell, the six-foot-one, 195-pound Weintraub led the league with a .401 average, and drove in 87 runs before being called up in August to play for the New York Giants—for whom he hit .351 with 15 RBI as a rookie in 31 games.

- The toughest to fan in Southern League history must have been Knoxville catcher Lee Head. In 1935, Head whiffed only once in 122 games and 402 at bats. That bettered his 1933 mark when he K'd three times in 131 games. Head never made the Majors, but in the Little Show, playing from 1920 to 1933, Head struck out only 140 times in 1,943 games . . . six times fanning five times or less.

- On August 11, 1935, Edward Rose, the career-Minor

Leaguer who holds the Southern Association record for runs scored (858) and RBI (866), and who banged out 2,517 hits during a fifteen-year career, got his strangest hit. Playing for the New Orleans Pelicans against Birmingham, he popped one up near second base. As the infielders camped under the fly, the ball struck and killed a pigeon who had decided to fly across the field. The ball fell untouched, and Rose was given a single. He scored on a double by teammate Bud Connally, later that inning.

- Another Nashville Vol left-handed hitter who used the home park to great success to build imposing numbers was an outfielder for the 1948 club, Chuck Workman. The thirty-three-year-old six-footer led the loop with 52 homers and 182 RBI, and followed it up the next year in another hitter-friendly park—Nicollet in Minneapolis— to bomb 41 roundtrippers in the American Association.

- In 1941, Leslie Burge, playing for Atlanta, slammed 38 homers to tie Howard Murdeski of Johnstown in the Pennsylvania State Association for the Minor League leadership in homers.

- In 1943, a second-year pro named Pete Gray played in the league for Memphis. Gray, an outfielder who stood six-foot-one and weighed 169 pounds, had only one arm. After losing his right arm in a childhood accident, Gray, a natural right-hander, taught himself to be proficient with his left hand and developed a slashing, spraying batting style to go with his speed and smart base running. In the field, Gray would catch the ball, tuck his glove under his right arm stump, roll the ball across his chest and throw, all in one graceful motion.

  Following a .381 season in the Canadian-American League, Gray came on to bat .289 with Memphis. He followed that up with an MVP year, hitting .333, with 5 homers and a record-tying 68 stolen bases. This performance earned him a spot on the talent-depleted (due to World War II) St. Louis Browns of 1945.

- In 1945 the Southern Association was taken by storm by

Mobile catcher Harry Chozen, who went on a 49-game hitting streak. And it wasn't easy. After hitting safely in his first 33 games, Chozen walked in game 34 (July 6) and left the game due to an injury before taking a second trip to the plate. The injury occurred when Chozen was in the on-deck circle. The batter preceding him swung and missed at a pitch and his bat slipped out of his hands. The errant stick flew through the air and slammed into the head of the kneeling Chozen, knocking him unconscious.

League President Billy Evans ruled that since Chozen hadn't been charged with an official at bat, his streak would continue. The catcher then hit in his next 16 games to bring the streak to 49, breaking the previous S.A. record of 46 set by Johnny Bates in 1925. And Chozen, who homered in his first at bat in game 47 to set the mark, finished up the hard way. Inserted as a pinch hitter in four games, and getting only one at bat, Chozen came through with a hit each time to keep the streak alive. "Choz" made only one trip to The Show, a one-game, 1 for 4 appearance with Cincinnati in 1937.

- Jack Harshman led Nashville, the Southern Association, and the entire Minor League chain in homers with a 47 four-bagger performance in 1951. He also knocked in 141 runs. The next year, he began to transmogrify, leaving his bat behind to become a pitcher. Two years later, Harshman set a Chicago White Sox record by recording 16 strikeouts in a game at Boston, July 25, 1954.

- The 1951 season will also be remembered as the last great year of Herbert "Babe" Barna, an outfielder who toiled in the Little Show for sixteen years. In his next-to-last season, the thirty-six-year-old Nashville Vol led the league in hitting at .358 and drove in 94 runs in 131 games.

- Bob Lennon set the baseball world on its ear by crashing out 64 homers for the Nashville Vols in 1954, the fifth highest single-season total ever. The six-foot, 200 pound outfielder made it up to the Bigs for 38 games over the next three years and managed only one dinger.

    Many critics attributed Lennon's homerun onslaught
to his home ballpark, Sulphur Dell. The rightfield fence
at the foul line was only 250 feet from home plate, perfect
for Lennon's lefty swing. Additionally, right field was
set on an embankment that made a rightfielder run
downhill to get ground balls. To support the friendly
confines theory, seven other left-handed hitters who
played for Nashville at Sulphur Dell hit 40 or more homers and never again approached that total elsewhere. The
magnificent seven: Chuck Workman—52 in 1948; James
Poole - 50 in 1930; Jack Harshman—47 in 1951; Carl
Sawatski - 45 in 1949; Charlie Gilbert—42 in 1948; Babe
Barna - 42 in 1949; and Jay Partridge—40 in 1950.

• In 1961, Howie Koplitz, pitcher for Birmingham, went
  23–3, an .885 percentage, and threw a no-hitter. In the
  Majors, with Detroit and Washington, he won his first
  seven decisions, but arm ailments limited his career accomplishments.

• A one-year wonder (three years if you consider his two
  big years in the Little Show and one blaze-through season in The Show), was Chattanooga Lookouts right-
  handed hitting sensation Joe Charboneau. The flaky
  outfielder hit .352 in 1979, before becoming a rookie hero
  with the Cleveland Indians in 1980. Charboneau
  marched to a different drummer, as illustrated by his
  naming his dog "Diarrhea" and his daughter "Dannon"
  (after a brand of yogurt), and by his drinking beer
  through a hole in his nose. He also delighted Chattanooga fans by meeting them at bars after games and
  putting on shows: he opened bottles of beer with his eye
  socket, ate cigarettes (lit and unlit), displayed countless
  scars all over his body, and fought anybody over anything. He was out of baseball within five years, but in
  1979, he was a hitting machine.

• Another Chattanooga Lookout of note was Kevin
  Rhomberg, the great-hitting outfielder who finished at
  .367 in 1981. Rhomberg went 187 for 509, with 17 triples and 76 stolen bases. He was at .400 for most of the

year before slumping in late August.

He was a "can't miss" who did miss with the MLB Cleveland Indians because of some superstitions that got out of hand. It seemed that Rhomberg was neurotic about touching people and having people touch him and felt fearful of making right turns. These and several other habits took his mind from the game and before he was thirty, he was out of the sport in which he excelled.

- In 1982, Otis Nixon stopped by Nashville long enough to steal 59 bases, en route to leading the Minor League with a total of 108 thefts. He also swiped 49 playing for Columbus in the American Association.
- In 1990, among the name players to serve guest appearance rehab assignments in the Southern League was Houston Astros homerun leader Glenn Davis, who spent two weeks at Columbus, following his recovery from a torn rib cage muscle.

After going 6 for 12 in a three-game rehab stint, he suffered a strained back, setting his return to the Majors back more than three weeks.

⚾   ⚾   ⚾   ⚾

The all-time Southern Association (League) career leaders list is represented by many players:

(*Source:* SABR)

Games played	Freddie Graff	1,527
Runs scored	Eddie Rose	858
Hits	Andy Reese	1,641
Doubles	Andy Reese	320
Triples	Tommy Taylor	120
Homeruns	Ralph Atkins	142
RBI	Eddie Rose	866
Stolen bases	Stuffy Stewart	370
Batting average	Elliot Bigelow	.359
Games won (pitcher)	Rube Robinson	211
Strikeouts	Roy Walker	1,240

1990 Players to Watch

Chicago White Sox No. 1 draft choice phenom Alex Fernandez cut a swath across the Minors with a two-month sprint to the Majors. Stopping by with Birmingham after his start in the Gulf Coast and Florida State Leagues, Fernandez's combined Minor League totals were 5–1, 1.81 ERA with only 10 walks and 66 strikeouts in 49 innings.

Jeff Conine, Memphis (Royals), hit .320 with 15 homers and 95 RBI.

Scott Brosius, Huntsville (A's), hit .296 with 23 homers and 88 RBI.

Matt Stark, Birmingham (White Sox), hit .309 with 14 homers and 109 RBI.

Brian Barnes, Jacksonville (Expos), fanned 213 hitters in 201 innings.

Danny Neagle, Orlando (Twins), had K'd 138.

Best Defensive Players to Watch (*Source: Baseball America*)

Catcher: Kelly Mann, Greenville (Braves)
First Baseman: Mike Bell, Greenville (Braves)
Second Baseman: Williams Suero, Knoxville (Blue Jays)
Third Baseman: Sean Berry, Memphis (Royals)
Shortstop: Freddie Benavides, Chattanooga (Reds)
Outfielder: Darren Lewis: Huntsville (A's)
Pitcher—Fastball: Willie Banks, Orlando (Twins)
Pitcher—Control: Blaise Ilsley, Columbus (Astros)
Pitcher—Relief: Steve Chitren, Huntsville (A's)

10
CALIFORNIA
LEAGUE

The California League is a Single-A organization consisting of ten teams within California and Nevada.

The California League first began operations in 1941, and after a one-year trial run, reopened in 1946, and has been operating ever since—a forty-five-year performance.

The league was given Class-A status in the 1960s and has been a model of healthy growth ever since.

Running a 142-game schedule from April 6 to August 29, the current roster of teams consists of: the Bakersfield Dodgers, Modesto A's, Palm Springs Angels, Reno Silver Sox (Independent), High Desert Mavericks (Padres), Salinas Spurs (Independent), San Bernardino Spirit (Mariners), San Jose Giants, Stockton Ports (Brewers), Visalia Oaks (Twins).

In 1990, San Jose and Stockton each won half of the Northern Division, while Visalia and Bakersfield split the Southern Division.

The 1990 California League Championship series made history, and took its time doing it. The Series opener pitted the Bakersfield Dodgers against the Stockton Ports and, after 21 innings covering 5 hours and 57 minutes, the score was tied 3–3. Finally, at 1:30 the next morning, the umpires, on direction from league president Joe Gagliardi, called it a suspended game, to be completed the next night.

The game restarted and action was quick and often as the Dodgers prevailed by outscoring the Ports 2–1 in the 22nd inning for a 5–4 victory.

This affair tied for the second longest game in terms of innings in Cal League history, losing only to a 23-inning tilt played on August 31, 1966. The final in that one, Reno 6, Lodi 5. In terms of time, even this one had a long way to go, as on June 20–21, 1971, Visalia took 22 innings and 7 hours to outlast Bakersfield 11–9.

Stockton prevailed in the finals, topping Bakersfield three games to two.

Some of the more colorful nicknames in the league belong to the exiled Red Wave of Riverside, the new High Desert Mavericks, and the Spirit of San Bernardino.

From a logo point of view, an interesting one belongs to the Stockton Ports, who feature an old-time, mustachioed ballplayer with an "M" on his cap, signifying "Mudville." Stockton was the location of the historic Mudville Nine, immortalized by Ernest Lawrence Thayer in his poem "Casey at the Bat." As Stockton was affectionately known as Mudville some one hundred years ago, the Stockton Ports play upon that heritage and proudly proclaim they are the current-day Mudville Nine.

What is the California League?

It is two men on the same team hitting for the cycle on the same day. On May 20, 1984, at Visalia, Kevin Stock and Bob Loscalzo of Modesto each hit a single, a double, a triple, and a homerun as the A's walloped the Oaks 23–4. According to SABR researchers, that was the first time in Minor League history that the dual cycle had been accomplished.

Three years later, on June 3, 1988, at Fresno, two members of the Stockton Ports duplicated the rare double cycle. As Stockton bombed Fresno 26–0, Shon Ashley and Sandy Guerrero each picked up the four necessary hits.

Or maybe it is one man hitting two grand slams in the same inning. According to researchers, this rare feat had been accomplished twice, once by Kenny Myers in a Sunset League game in 1947, and the other on June 30, 1983, at Reno by Redwood Pioneers outfielder Lance Junker in the ninth inning of a 16–5 victory.

After two walks and an infield single, Junker, who had not hit a homer in 52 games that season, blasted Tom Biko's 1–0 delivery some 370 feet, over the right field fence.

With two out and two on in the same inning, an error prolonged the frame, and Junker came to the plate and blasted Greg Steffanich's 0–2 pitch to almost the same spot he placed the first.

As a note of interest, Junker hit 21 homers in his 300-game Minor League career . . . and 5 of them were grand slams.

Or maybe the California League is a great stunt.

In 1977, Modesto had its fleet-footed outfielder Rickey Henderson race a horse out in center field. Henderson lost but gained the cheers of the crowd.

And there is certainly a Far East flavor to the California League.

For seven consecutive seasons, the San Jose Bees, now called the Giants, have been stocked with players from the Japan Pacific League's Seibu Lions, and while athletes such as Nori Tanabe (San Jose MVP in 1986), and Tad Hanyuda have been partially responsible for San Jose's recent run of play-off teams, this symbiotic relationship has developed more than twenty players for use by the Seibu Lions, in their back-to-back Japan League championships seasons of 1987 and 1988.

Celebrity ownership is also a California League trait.

Singer Tony Orlando owns a piece of the Palm Springs Angels, NBC's Brandon Tartikoff and actor Robert Wagner own part of the Reno Silver Sox, George and Ken Brett own the High Desert Mavericks, actor Mark Harmon has a piece of the San Bernardino Spirit, and Don Drysdale is part owner of the Visalia Oaks.

And the California League is countless stories of dedication. Sam Favata, a prospect from California State University, Fullerton, rated "can't miss" by the Milwaukee Brewers, was a hot-hitting, base stealing second baseman for the Stockton Ports. In 1982 a high-inside fastball shattered his hopes and his skull. Favata, unconscious for several days, was left unable to walk or talk, and a return to the diamond was said to be impossible. After intensive work, one year and eleven days after his fateful beaning Favata earned his way back into the Ports' starting line-up, and on his first trip to the plate, before cheering fans, stroked a single to right, earning him a spot forever in the lore of Minor League baseball.

Inside the California League:
• An all-star list of California League players who made names for themselves on the Major League level might include the following:

 Catchers: Bob Boone, Ted Simmons, and Benito Santiago.

 First Basemen: Will Clark, Jack Clark, Mark McGwire, Kent Hrbek, and Mike Epstein.

 Second Basemen: Joe Morgan, Davey Johnson, and Billy Grabarkewitz.

 Third Basemen: George Brett and Ron Cey.

 Shortstops: Bobby Grich and Bud Harrelson.

 Outfielders: Vince DiMaggio, Reggie Jackson, Jose Canseco, Rickey Henderson, Kirby Puckett, George Foster, Irv Noren, Rob Deer, Kevin McReynolds, and Vada Pinson.

 Starting Pitchers (right-handed): Don Drysdale and Don Sutton.

 Starting Pitchers (left-handed): Fernando Valenzuela and Bob Knepper.

Relief Pitchers: Rollie Fingers, Mike Marshall, Tex Clevenger, Hal Reniff, and Dave LaRoche.

- In 1946, the first season following the war, Irv Noren drove in 125 runs to lead Santa Barbara and the league.
- Vince DiMaggio won the California League homerun crown in 1948, belting 30 for Stockton, and Fresno's Rip Repulski won the RBI battle with 125.
- In 1949, Jess Pike set the all-time Cal League RBI mark with 156 for Bakersfield.
- In 1956, the Cal League homerun mark was set at 51 by Visalia's Bud Heslet.
- Reno's Francis Boniar set the league's batting mark in 1957 at a lofty .436.
- In 1959, Willie Davis hit .365 for Reno, to lead the league.
- In 1965, the top hitter was Mike Epstein, who hit .338 and 30 homers for Stockton.
- Rudy Law was number one in 1977 at .386 for Lodi, but Rickey Henderson ran wild on the basepaths for Modesto, swiping a league-record 95 bases.
- In 1980, Lodi's Alan Wiggin topped Henderson's theft mark with 120.
- Kent Hrbek had it all his way in 1981 for Visalia, hitting .379, while Rob Deer won the homerun title, belting 33 for Fresno.
- In 1982, Kevin McReynolds led the loop at .376 and 28 dingers for Reno.
- The stolen base mark fell again, to the speedy feet of Bakersfield's Donnel Nixon, who nailed 144 in 1983.
- Mark McGwire had to settle for a tie in the homerun race in 1985. McGwire got 24 taters for Modesto and Eric Hardgrave hit the same for Reno.
- And in 1990, Hide Koga, a Minor League pitcher in the 1960s, was named manager of the Salinas Spurs, becoming the first Japanese manager of an American baseball team.

One final note: the Riverside Red Wave, owned by George, Ken, John, and Bobby Brett, and an affiliate of the San Diego Padres, struggled financially in 1990 despite drawing 82,000 fans, in part because it could not acquire a license to sell beer at the Riverside Sports Complex. So the Red Wave has drifted north and inland, and will play in the small village of Adelanto, California, in 1991, where it will be known as the High Desert Mavericks.

Adelanto, a town of 7,000, may be the smallest town in America to house a professional baseball team . . . getting back to the roots of the Minor League version of America's pastime.

⚾   ⚾   ⚾   ⚾

1990 Players to Watch

The San Diego Padres first round draft choice, pitcher Robbie Beckett, tempered velocity with wildness at Riverside. He used his crisp fastball to strike out 65 in 66 innings, but he walked 56 and allowed 58 hits over the same duration, as he went 4–6 with a hefty 5.05 ERA.

Dave Slaton, Riverside (Padres), hit 19 homers through late August.

Ken Whitfield, Reno (Independent), hit 18 homers.

Ellerton Maynard, San Bernardino (Mariners), had stolen 65 bases.

Pat Listach, Stockton (Brewers), had stolen 49 bases.

Chris Johnson, pitcher for Stockton (Brewers), had won 13 games.

Rich Garces, reliever for Visalia (Twins) had picked up 28 saves.

Best Defensive Players to Watch (*Source: Baseball America*)

Catcher: Dave Nilsson, Stockton (Brewers)
First Baseman: Bo Dodson, Stockton (Brewers)
Second Baseman: Matt Howard, Bakersfield (Dodgers)
Third Baseman: Frank Bolick, San Bernardino (Mariners)
Shortstop: Royce Clayton, San Jose (Giants)
Outfielder: J.T. Bruett, Visalia (Twins)
Pitcher—Fastball: Rich Garces, Visalia (Twins)
Pitcher—Control: Danny Neagle, Visalia (Twins)
Pitcher—Relief: Rich Garces, Visalia (Twins)

11
CAROLINA LEAGUE

The Carolina League is a Class-A operation that was begun in 1945 with Danville, Raleigh, Martinsville, Burlington, Leaksville, Winston-Salem, Durham, and Greensboro all fielding teams.

Over the years, the strong and healthy league has operated in twenty-two cities, a relatively small number for a forty-six-year-old circuit.

The league has generally had eight teams in the loop, but that dropped to six in 1957 and again from 1959 to 1961.

In 1963, the Carolina League split into two divisions of five teams each, and by 1966, the league had twelve teams.

Whatever builds up seems to tear down, and by 1970 eight teams made up the complement of the circuit, with a low-water mark of four teams making it through the 1976 season.

The current group of eight teams has been fairly constant since 1980, and the league has grown, with every team in the loop earning a profit for the past three years.

Opening its season April 12 and running through September 2, the league schedules 140 games, broken down into two halves of the season for play-off consideration.

The league, as its name indicates, has roots in Carolina, but is not limited to the two states bearing that name. Only three of the eight current teams have homes in North Carolina, with four in Virginia, and one in Maryland.

The current roster of teams includes the Durham Bulls (Braves), Durham, North Carolina, in its eleventh year in the league; Frederick Keys (Orioles), Frederick, Maryland, in its second year in the league; Kinston Indians (Indians), Kinston, North Carolina, in its twenty-seventh year in the league; Lynchburg Red Sox (Red Sox), Lynchburg, Virginia, in its twenty-fifth year in the league; Peninsula Pilots (Mariners), Hampton, Virginia, in its fifteen year in the league; Prince William Cannons (Yankees), Woodbridge, Virginia, in its seventh year in the league; Salem Buccaneers (Pirates), Salem, Virginia, in its twenty-third year in the league; and the Winston-Salem Spirits (Cubs), Winston-Salem, North Carolina, in its forty-sixth year in the league.

The 1990 Carolina League provided two runaways, with Frederick winning the Northern Division in both the first and second halves of the season—beating Prince William by 5½ games in the second half, and Kinston winning both halves of the Southern Division season, taking the latter half by 3½ over Winston-Salem. Frederick took the whole pie in the play-offs, winning in five games.

Colorful Carolina League nicknames of the past include: Fayetteville Scots (1953–56), Leaksville-Draper-Spray Triplets (1945–47), Raleigh-Durham Triangles (1970–71), Reidsville Luckies (1948–54), and Wilson Tobacconists, also the Tobs (1956–68).

⚾   ⚾   ⚾   ⚾

What is the Carolina League?

According to Durham Bulls owner Miles Wolff, "The

movie *Bull Durham* pretty much sums it up," in competition, pranks, silliness, history, and content.

⚾   ⚾   ⚾   ⚾

Inside the Carolina League:
- The 1948 Greensboro club finished eighth despite a 27-game hitting streak by outfielder Ernie Showfety, and a league-leading 13 triples by James Lamb.
- Greensboro pitcher Luis Arroyo, later to become the Yankees' top reliever (saving Whitey Ford on a seemingly game-after-game pace in 1961), tossed a no-hitter for Greensboro in 1949.

  Also in 1949, Leo "Muscle" Shoals lived up to his nickname by slugging 55 homers and driving in 137 ribbies while batting .359 for Reidsville.
- In 1954, Guy Morton hit a circuit-topping .348 with 120 RBI and Joe "Peppy" LaMonica burned up the basepaths with 34 steals that year and 13 triples the next.
- Carl Yastrzemski won the batting title for Raleigh at .377 in 1959.
- Jim Bouton stopped by in 1960 to help Greensboro to a league championship. Bouton led the loop with a 2.73 ERA and Phil Linz (of harmonica fame) led the league in batting .321.
- In 1962, Negro Leagues star Buck Leonard helped found the Rocky Mount franchise, and served as its first vice president.
- Bobby Murcer won the Carolina League MVP award in 1965 for Greensboro.
- On May 15, 1966, two pitchers for the Rocky Mount Leafs ganged up to toss no-hitters in both games of a doubleheader against the Greensboro Yankees. Dick Drago tossed his no-no in the 5–0 first game, while teammate Darrell Clark matched the pitching performance with a no-hitter of his own in the 2–0 nightcap.
- Tolia "Tony" Solaita, the New York Yankees' prospect

from Samoa, was reputed to be the strongest man in the Minor Leagues when, in 1968, he hit .302 with 49 homers for High Point-Thomasville. However, he also made 20 errors at first base, and his fielding deficiencies plus a wrist injury limited his Major League playing time. He wound up as a successful *gaijin*, or foreigner in the Japan Leagues, belting 155 homers in four seasons in the Far East.

- Rocky Bridges, manager of the Prince William Pirates (now the Cannons—Yankee affiliate), was talked into a promotion before a game and came in second in a milking contest.

  After his failure to win the challenge, Bridges alibied, "I didn't try too hard. I was afraid I'd get emotionally involved with the cow."

- In 1983, Dwight Gooden won 19 games for Lynchburg as he earned the name "Doctor K" by operating on hitters to K 300 of them in only 191 innings. His win total was the highest since Rich Fusari won 19 for Peninsula in 1971.

- Lenny Dykstra ran wild in 1983 for Lynchburg and stole a Carolina League record 105 bases.

- Dave Magadan showed he was ready for the Bigs by hitting .350 in 1984 for Lynchburg.

1990 Players to Watch

Cleveland Indians No. 1 draft choice Tim Costo, first baseman, hit .325 in 53 games with Kinston. Shifting from his college position, shortstop, to one in the outfield, Costo fielded his spot well and found time to belt homers and drive in 42 runs.

Frank Seminara, a pitcher for Prince William (Yankees) had a 1.36 ERA through late August.

Roger Hailey, a pitcher for Durham (Braves) had picked up 128 strike outs.

Best Defensive Players to Watch *(Source: Baseball America)*

Catcher: Brad Ausmus, Prince William (Yankees)
First Baseman: J.T. Snow, Prince William (Yankees)
Second Baseman: Rouglas Odor, Kinston (Indians)
Third Baseman: Russ Davis, Prince William (Yankees)
Shortstop: Rickey Gutierrez, Frederick (Orioles)
Outfielder: Roy Gilbert, Frederick (Orioles)
Pitcher—Fastball: Arthur Rhodes, Frederick (Orioles)
Pitcher—Control: Rick Balabon, Peninsula (Independent)
Pitcher—Relief: Mike Gardella, Prince William (Yankees)

12
FLORIDA STATE
L E A G U E

The Florida State League is currently a Class-A loop that was established in 1919.

Following a short run that ended in 1927, the league was reorganized in 1936 for a five-year try that ended with World War II in 1941. The current Florida State League setup began in 1946 and has enjoyed forty-five years in the sun.

In the 1940s, the FSL expanded to eight teams, with Orlando and St. Augustine capturing the most titles. And Daytona Beach's sterling pitcher Elvin Stabelfield was the talk of the league in 1940, when he pitched two no-hitters, en route to a 28-win season.

The 1950s brought stability to the league as Major League teams began to use the FSL as a pipeline to The Show.

In the 1960s, Fort Lauderdale, Miami, Tampa, and St. Petersburg dominated play. Miami left the International League to join the FSL in 1962, and two of its initial stars that year were Ferguson Jenkins and Alex Johnson.

The 1970s saw Pompano Beach, Key West, Dunedin, and

Fort Myers enter the fray, and when Coco, Winter Haven, Orlando, Lakeland, and Daytona Beach joined, the FSL was acknowledged as the strongest Single-A circuit in the Minor League system.

The 1980s offered a change in thinking, as Class-A players were no longer thought of as projects or prospects who needed years of seasoning. Jose Rijo, Brett Saberhagen, and Jack Fimple all made the jump from the FSL directly to the Majors, and the league is now used to prepare athletes for The Show, and for that call that might be made sooner rather than later—from A-ball rather than from Triple-A.

The fourteen teams making up the 1990 loop were all based in Florida, and most carry the names of their parent affiliate, as most are owned and operated by the Major League club bearing the nickname.

The 1990 roster of teams was: Baseball City Royals, Charlotte Rangers, Clearwater Phillies, Dunedin Blue Jays, Fort Lauderdale Yankees, Lakeland Tigers, Miami Miracle (Independent), Osceola Astros, St. Lucie Mets, St. Petersburg Cardinals, Sarasota White Sox, Vero Beach Dodgers, West Palm Beach Expos, and Winter Haven Red Sox.

The 1990 season saw West Palm Beach capture the first- and second-half pennants in the Eastern Division, while Lakeland took both halves in the Central Division and Charlotte and Dunedin split the Western seasons. But it was wild card team Vero Beach that picked up all the play-off oranges with victories over St. Lucie, Charlotte, and West Palm Beach, to capture the title.

A relationship of nearly a quarter-century will soon end, leaving a Florida city at least temporarily without a team for the first time since the Lyndon B. Johnson administration was in power. Winter Haven, home of the Winter Haven Red Sox and the Spring Training home of the Boston Red Sox, has apparently lost its team as the BoSox have cited "unfulfilled promises of the city officials" as the reason for seeking a move. The Red Sox have announced they

will move following the 1991 Florida State League season.
Possible new sites for the Red Sox and possible new ten-
ants for Winter Haven are currently being explored.

What is the Florida State League?
    Some owners think the league is for fun.
    Comedian-actor Bill Murray owns the Miami Miracle.
    Perhaps it is innovation and a crossing of the gender
barrier.
    Kathy Gillespie, the wife of former MLB player Bobby
Molinaro, serves as color commentator for the Miami Miracle radio broadcasts. She is believed to be the only female
announcer regularly working professional baseball. Miami is an independent club owned by Marvin Goldklang,
one of the limited partners of the New York Yankees.
    It is friendly games of Home Run Derby played at Miami
Stadium by Cal Ripken, Jr., Eddie Murray, and Jim Fuller,
and it is the young strongmen such as Steve Balboni blasting them for real—26 homers for Fort Lauderdale in 1979.

Inside the Florida State League:
• Babe Bigelow, an outfielder for St. Petersburg, dominated the Sunshine State in 1922 by leading the league
  in batting (.343), triples (21), doubles (27), hits (150),
  and at bats (437).
• Lyle Judy, a second baseman, spent eight years in the
  league for St. Augustine from 1938 through 1950, in a
  career interrupted by military service and stints with
  other teams. As a twenty-six-year-old in 1939, Judy, who
  captured the imagination of the baseball world by stealing 107 bases for Springfield in the Western Association
  in 1935 (a hitter's league with little emphasis on running), stole 51 bases, and hit .304 to create excitement in

the league unheard of for non-homerun hitters—he didn't hit a four-bagger all season.

- In 1940, pitching hopeful Stan Musial went 18–5 from the mound for Daytona Beach. They didn't know just how well he could hit then.
- Myril Hoag put together a complete season for Gainesville in 1947. He led the league with a .350 average and was also the loop's top pitcher at 17–3.
- In 1949, pitcher Chester Covington, a thirty-nine-year-old journeyman, came to Palatka in mid-season to start in 14 games and post an 11–2 mark with a 1.71 ERA, and St. Augustine's Stan Karpinski won a league-record 29 games.
- From 1949 through 1951, Gainesville's Al Pirtle was Mr. Clutch, winning three straight RBI crowns with 110, 124, and 119 ribbies.
- Sanford's Ed Levy set an FSL mark with 33 homers in 1950, a mark that was tied twenty-one years later by Miami's Jim Fuller.
- First baseman-pitcher Linnel Roberts put together a great double-duty season on the mound and at the plate in 1952 for Deland. Roberts hit .356, drove in 129 runs, and led the loop with 16 triples, while also leading the league's pitchers with a 15–2 record and 1.94 ERA.
- Felipe Alou won the FSL batting title in 1956 at .380 for Coco.
- Big Nesbit Wilson, a six-foot, 200-pound first baseman-outfielder for St. Pete, led the league with a .373 average, 47 doubles, and 192 hits in 1957. Strangely, he only hit 9 homeruns, down from the 42 he hit a year earlier in the Alabama-Florida League and the 24 he went on to hit the following year, back in the Alabama-Florida circuit.
- Mike Mattiace threw back-to-back no-hitters for Palatka in 1960.
- In 1961, playing for Tampa, Pete Rose smacked 30 triples, an FSL record.
- Dick Jensen of Tampa threw three no-hitters over a two-year period in 1973–74.

- Gene Nelson dominated the circuit for Fort Lauderdale in 1980, chalking up 20 wins while losing only 3.
- Tampa's Danny Tartabull only hit .310 in 1981, but it was good enough to take the batting crown.

1990 Players to Watch

Brian Romero, a pitcher for Charlotte (Rangers) had compiled an ERA of 1.30 by late August.

Dave Telegheder, a pitcher for St. Lucie (Mets) had a 1.39 ERA.

Randy Marshall, a hurler for Lakeland (Tigers) had picked up 7 of his season-high 20 wins. (He went 13-0 in the South Atlantic League.)

Barry Manuel, a reliever for Charlotte (Rangers) had nailed down 36 saves.

Nikco Riesgo of St. Lucie had pounded out 14 homers with 94 RBI, and teammate D.J. Dozier, a professional football player (a Bo-wannabe?), blasted 13 taters and hit .297.

Best Defensive Players to Watch (*Source: Baseball America*)

Catcher: Ivan Rodrigues, Charlotte (Rangers)
First Baseman: Adam Terris, West Palm Beach (Expos)
Second Baseman: Jeff Kent, Dunedin (Blue Jays)
Third Baseman: Fred Samson, Charlotte (Rangers)
Shortstop: Keith Kimberlin, Lakeland (Tigers)
Outfielder: Gerald Williams, Fort Lauderdale (Yankees)
Pitcher—Fastball: Robb Nenn, Charlotte (Rangers)
Pitcher—Control: Dennis Boucher, Dunedin (Blue Jays)
Pitcher—Relief: Mike Timlin, Dunedin (Blue Jays)

Ted Williams, "The Splendid Splinter," tore apart the American Association for the Minneapolis Millers as a nineteen-year-old in 1938. He hit .366 as a prelude to his Major League prowess.
(George Brace photo)

Russell "Buzz" Arlett was the Minor Leagues' top all-time switch-hitter, connecting for 432 homers and 598 doubles while knocking in 1,768 runs and batting .341. (George Brace photo)

Nick "Tomato Face" Cullop holds the Minor League record for career RBI at 1,857. In twenty-three years, Cullop hit 420 homeruns — third on the all-time list — while compiling a .312 average. (George Brace photo)

Joe "Unser Choe" Hauser is the only player in professional baseball history to twice top the 60-homerun barrier. He blasted 63 homers for Baltimore in 1930 and 69 for Minneapolis in 1933. (George Brace photo)

Smead Jolley spent sixteen years in the Minors (four years in the Majors) and compiled a .366 career average. He won the PCL Triple Crown for the San Francisco Seals in 1926, batting .404, hitting 45 homers, and driving in 188 runs. (George Brace photo)

A young Johnny Bench is shown in his pre-Hall of Fame days in a Buffalo uniform. Later, with the Peninsula Grays (1966) of the Carolina League, he slammed 22 homers and had his uniform number retired.
(George Brace photo)

J.J. "Nig" Clarke, an excellent defensive catcher but a mediocre offensive threat, had the single greatest day in baseball history when he hit 8 homeruns in 8 at-bats in a single game for Corsicana in the Texas League in 1902.
(George Brace photo)

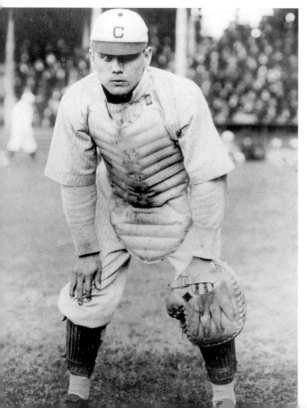

Grover Cleveland Alexander is shown on his way back...as a member of the barnstorming House of David team. Years earlier, in 1910, Alexander tossed 14 shutouts for Syracuse of the New York State League.
(George Brace photo)

Leroy "Satchel" Paige, shown here in his Kansas City Monarchs uniform, was arguably the best pitcher of his day...a day that lasted more than thirty years. After playing for twenty-one years in the Negro Leagues, Paige finally pitched in the Majors at the age of forty-two.
(George Brace photo)

This 1956 photo shows Vince, Joe, and Dom DiMaggio (left to right) in their old San Francisco Seals uniforms, as they got set to play in an Old Timers Game. Joe hit in 61 consecutive games for the Seals in 1933...the second-longest hitting streak in Minor League history (Joe Wilhoit's 69-game skein in 1919 for Wichita, of the Western League, stands as No. 1).

Mile-High Stadium, home of the Denver Zephyrs, was formerly called Bears Stadium. Erected in 1948 as a single-level ballpark, it has been expanded to a three-tier, multisport stadium. It sits on what was once a dump site, and its underground spring, beneath what is now second base, creates an eternal wet spot, slowing down the infield. (photo by Gary Warner)

Ned Skeldon Stadium, stomping grounds of the Toledo Mud Hens, was built in 1963 as Lucas County Stadium. It was renamed following the death of Mud Hens president Ned Skeldon, who was responsible for building the new yard to house the Minor League franchise.
(Courtesy of the Toledo Mud Hens)

George Herman "Babe" Ruth won 22 games as a left-handed hurler for Baltimore and Providence in the International League in 1914. Even then, his bat and arm awed onlookers.
(George Brace photo)

In a Pacific Coast League opening day game on April 9, 1944 at Gilmour Field, Connie Creeden of the Seattle Rainers is tagged out at home by Hollywood Stars' catcher Jim Hill, as umpire Dewey Widner prepares to make the call.
(Photo by Tom Courtney)

John O'Donnell Stadium, in Davenport, Iowa, serves as friendly confines for the Quad City Angels. Built in 1931, it has been remodeled several times. The wind, whipping off the water and through the bridge, makes for tough-to-catch pop flies.
(Boyd Fitzgerald, Inc. ©1989. Courtesy of the Quad City Angels)

13
MIDWEST LEAGUE

The Midwest League is a Class-A league covering America's breadbasket of four states: Iowa, Illinois, Indiana, and Wisconsin.

The Midwest League was officially born in 1956, but its roots go back to 1949 and the Mississippi-Ohio Valley League, a circuit that had all of its members located in small towns throughout Illinois, with the exception of Paducah, Kentucky.

The MOV League expanded into Indiana in 1950, into Missouri in 1952, and into Clinton and Dubuque, Iowa, in 1954.

In 1956, the MOV League was reorganized, and the Midwest League was created. This birth created quite a stir within the Three-I League, which had long dominated the middle Minors in the upper Mississippi Valley, and when Three-I's Terre Haute franchise jumped ship to join the Midwest circuit (its membership was rejected by Midwest leaders), the Three-I directors reacted with a vengeance and attempted to pirate away the Dubuque and Clinton franchises.

This brought a strong protest from Midwest directors . . . a protest that was upheld by the National Association, which decreed that the Iowa teams must stay put.

Waterloo and Keokuk, Iowa, joined the loop in 1958, as Mattoon, Illinois, and Lafayette, Indiana, went bankrupt.

Black players had been allowed to be a part of the Minor League experience for more than a decade when the 1958 Midwest season opened, but some scattered leagues still refused to comply, choosing instead to gauge a man on his skin color rather than his talent. It was largely due to that circumstance that the Waterloo Hawks, a Red Sox affiliate, wound up with a black athlete named Zeke King.

King played Class-B ball at Eugene, Oregon, in 1957 though Eugene was not a Boston Farm club. King was forced to play there because the BoSox's B-League team in North Carolina refused to welcome blacks on their team.

Since the Sox had Class-C Waterloo, King was assigned to play in the Midwest circuit.

The move paid off and King came through to the tune of .318 and 24 homeruns to lead Waterloo to a league title.

During the 1962 season, Dubuque was the only Midwest League city to have two teams in operation (two Dubuque-based franchises in the same league), when Keokuk lost its franchise on August 7 and the club was moved to Dubuque under the name "Midwest Dodgers."

The 1965 season featured future MLB stars Sal Bando, Joe Rudi, Billy Conigliaro, and Fran Healy.

The last twenty-five years showed steady growth and success, with few defections but numerous franchise shifts. Prosperity has seen the loop swell to fourteen teams.

The current league setup is a 140-game schedule from April 6 to August 29, featuring fourteen teams in two divisions.

The 1990 roster of teams included: Appleton Foxes (Royals), Beloit Brewers, Burlington Braves, Cedar Rapids Reds, Clinton Giants, Kenosha Twins, Madison Muskies (A's), Peoria Chiefs (Cubs), Quad City Angels, Rockford

Expos, South Bend White Sox, Springfield Cardinals, Waterloo Diamonds (Padres), and Wausau Timbers (Orioles).

In 1990, the A's affiliate, Madison, won the first half in the Northern Division, while South Bend (White Sox) took the second half.

Quad City, the Angels' entry, grabbed the second half in the South, while Cedar Rapids (Reds) won the first half and missed the second by a mere game.

Quad City took the play-offs with a three games to one victory over South Bend.

ⓑ   ⓑ   ⓑ   ⓑ

What is the Midwest League?

Lately, it seems to be much ado about nothing.

In the 1990 scandal of the year the Wausau, Wisconsin, Timbers (Baltimore Orioles affiliate) convicted five of its own team members—aka "The Wausau Five"—for watering.

It seems that the Timbers were in South Bend, Indiana, to play a doubleheader against the South Bend White Sox (Chicago White Sox affiliate), August 13, 1990. The weather was poor with heavy rains forecast, and five Wausau players, hoping to force a cancellation of the doubleheader, which would move it to Wausau's home turf a week later, did what they could to make the field unplayable.

In a prank taken from out of the frames of *Bull Durham* (similar scenario, different result), the five Timbers sneaked into Stanley Coveleski Regional Stadium in South Bend sometime after midnight, and, as the heavens opened and rain fell on the field, rolled back the infield tarpaulin. The rains came, but adroit South Bend groundskeepers worked overtime and put the field back in order and the scheduled doubleheader was played. The teams split the twinbill. In the opener, Wausau won 4–3 after South Bend hurler Lenny Brutcher slipped and fell on the wet turf, injuring his knee and precipitating his removal from the game.

The players' actions resulted in double suspension, fine, and outright releases . . . by the Wausau management (personnel director Doug Melvin) and by Midwest League president George Spelius. Spelius suspended the quintet for the remainder of the season and the first ten games of 1991. As happened in the Great Potato Hoax (see Chapter 7: Eastern League), the perpetrators were not deserving of star status, and like the potato thrower Dave Bresnahan, the Wausau Five may be remembered more for this ill-advised prank than for their abilities on the field. The hoax that backfired was conceived and executed by shortstop Brad Heldreth, catcher Jimmy Roso, and pitchers Jim De-drick, John Boothby, and Kip Yaughn.

Spelius remarked, "Somewhere down the line, two or three years down the road, we'll probably smile a bit, but now the smile comes harder when you think of what could have happened (someone getting injured)."

> [*Author's note:* This watering act will be the last item for Wausau fans to recall for some time. Beginning in 1991, the Orioles are moving their Midwest League act to Kane County, Illinois.]

⚾   ⚾   ⚾   ⚾

Inside the Midwest League:
• The team from Michigan City, Indiana, used a Dominican Republic hurler named Juan Marichal (21–8) to earn a spot in the 1958 league play-off finals. Marichal won two starts against Waterloo, but 'Loo took the series three games to two.
• Galen Cisco went 15–7 with 165 K's to lead Waterloo to another title in 1959.
• While 1961 was the year of the homerun in the Major Leagues—Roger Maris hit 61, Mickey Mantle belted 54, and the New York Yankees blasted an MLB record 240—the same was true in the Midwest League, which saw Waterloo connect for 155 four-baggers in 125 games.

Bob Lawrence hit 30, while driving in 127 ribbies to go with his .305 average, to star for the Hawks.

- Graig Nettles, playing for Wisconsin Rapids, won the league homerun crown in 1966.
- In 1968, Burlington's Vida Blue showed what was to follow in the Bigs, when he struck out 321 batters in 152 innings while compiling a 2.49 ERA.
- Chris Wren became the first female umpire in Midwest League history in 1975, and when she completed her first game and went on to her second, set the record for longevity by gender at her position. A solid ump, Wren lasted three years, resigning after the 1977 season to take a better paying job with the United Parcel Service.

1990 Players to Watch

Chicago Cubs No. 1 draft choice Lance Dickson, pitcher, jumped from A to Double-A to the Majors and then down to Triple- A in a period of three months. Playing for Geneva in the New York-Penn League, at Peoria in the Midwest League, and Charlotte in the Southern League, Dickson blazed a path with a 7–3 mark, 0.94 ERA, 18 walks, and 111 strikeouts in 76 innings, while allowing only 8 earned runs. After struggling with the parent Cubs, Dickson was sent down to Iowa in the American Association to gain more experience. He'll be back in Chicago in 1991.

Ramon Carabello, with Burlington (Braves), hit 11 triples by late August.

Alan Newman, a pitcher with Kenosha (Twins), had an ERA of 1.35.

Clyde Keller, a reliever with Springfield (Cardinals), had 21 saves.

14
SOUTH ATLANTIC
L E A G U E

The current South Atlantic League, first established in 1948 (it ran until 1952) and reestablished in 1960, has run consecutively for thirty-one years. Previous tries at loops called the South Atlantic League began in 1888 and operated sporadically. Those circuits were affectionately known as "The Sally League" in earlier morphoses, which eventually became the Southern League.

The current league sprang up during the postwar boom, but collapsed during the period of increased interest in TV and the Major League mishandling crisis of the early '50s. This led to poor attendance and failed clubs. Revived in 1960, attendance has steadily swelled until the 1989 season saw the S.A.L. draw more than one million fans.

The South Atlantic League is a Class-A circuit with twelve teams covering North Carolina, South Carolina, Georgia, and West Virginia.

Running a 144-game schedule from April 5 to August 30, the South Atlantic League team roster currently includes: Asheville Tourists (Astros), Augusta Pirates, Charleston Rainbows (Padres), Charleston Wheelers

(Reds), Columbia Mets, Fayetteville Generals (Tigers), Gastonia Rangers, Greensboro Hornets (Yankees), Myrtle Beach Blue Jays, Savannah Cardinals, Spartanburg Phillies, and Sumter Braves.

In 1990, the Charleston (Reds) took the second-half crown in the Northern Division, after the Fayetteville (Tigers) grabbed the first half. In the Southern Division, Savannah (Cardinals) ran away with the second half after Columbia (Mets) nabbed the first half.

What is the South Atlantic League?

Well, it is the only league with two teams representing two different cities of the same name—Charleston. The Charleston Rainbows hail from South Carolina and the Charleston Wheelers come from West Virginia.

Inside the South Atlantic League (including earlier leagues bearing the same name):

- Pitcher Bugs Raymond went 35–11 for Charleston in 1907.
- Maurice Archdeacon, who later starred for the International League's Baltimore Orioles, stole 42 bases for Charleston in 1919 and 44 the next year.
- George Rhinhardt had back-to-back seasons of quality in 1923–34 with Greenville. The outfielder put together years of .370, 100 RBI, 22 steals, 40 doubles and 28 triples in 1923; and .404, 92 ribbies, 32 steals, 45 doubles the following campaign.
- In 1927, Walter Tauscher, a right-handed pitcher who won 259 Minor League games during a twenty-five-year career, lost 19 games for Columbia despite a solid 3.04 ERA. His earned runs seemed to matter to scouts more than his losses, as the Pittsburgh Pirates snatched him up for the 1928 season.

- The 1930 season belonged to twenty-one-year-old outfielder for Greenville, Murray "Red" Howell. Howell led the league in RBI (147) to follow up his league-leading 135 in 1929 and also was number one in hits (193) and runs scored (123), while maintaining his batting consistency—he hit .341 in 1929 and .340 in 1930.
- In 1939, forty-five-year-old journeyman pitcher Red McColl found his way to the South Atlantic League and walked only 21 batters in 154 innings on his way to a 2.81 ERA.
- Greensboro entered the South Atlantic League in 1980, and outfielder-first baseman Don Mattingly was named MVP as he led the league with a .358 batting average while bashing 32 doubles and driving in 105 runs.
- In 1981, for Spartanburg, Jeff Stone swiped 123 bases.

⚾   ⚾   ⚾   ⚾

1990 Players to Watch

Cincinnati Reds No. 1 choice Dan Wilson, catcher, made Charleston, West Virginia, his home and hit .248 with 2 homers and 15 RBI in 31 games. A contact hitter, he struck out only 18 times in 109 at bats.

Tim Howard, with Columbia (Mets), had knocked out 112 hits by late August.

Brian Cornelius, Fayetteville (Tigers), had slammed 11 triples.

Austin Manahan, Augusta (Pirates), had hit 10 triples.

Pat Howell, Columbia (Mets), had stolen 58 bases.

Jeff Hoffman, Greensboro (Yankees), fashioned a 1.47 ERA.

15
NEW YORK–PENN
L E A G U E

The New York–Penn League is a college-dominated Single-A loop in its fifty-second year of operation. It was established in 1939 but had earlier beginnings as several East Coast Leagues, with teams that bounced in and out of various loops before joining up on an irregular basis during the less-structured days of the Minor League system. Today's circuit covers New York, Pennsylvania, Massachusetts, and Canada, with most of its players first-year athletes who have just completed their college careers.

It was a Class-D circuit until the 1962 reorganization gave it Class-A status.

Its current fourteen members are: Oneonta (Yankees), Auburn (Astros), Batavia (Phillies), Elmira (Red Sox), Jamestown (Expos), Niagara Falls (Tigers), Utica (White Sox), and Watertown (Indians) in New York; Erie (Independent) in Pennsylvania; Hamilton (Cardinals), St. Catherines (Blue Jays), and Welland (Pirates) in Ontario, Canada; and Pittsfield (Mets) in Massachusetts.

Running a seventy-eight game schedule from June 19 to September 3, the New York–Penn League is divided into three divisions. In 1990, Oneonta ran away with the four-team McNamara Division-East with a 52–26 mark, 8½ ahead of both Watertown and Pittsfield. The McNamara Division-West, also a four-team loop, was won by Geneva, on its 51–26 record, 9½ games ahead of Batavia. The Stedler Division was taken by Erie with a 44–33 record, 3 games better than Jamestown at 41–36. Oneonta took all the marbles by defeating Geneva in two straight and Erie in a best-of-three.

The most interesting nicknames in the NY–Penn League include: Elmira Pioneers, Erie Sailors, and Niagara Falls Rapids.

What is the New York–Penn League?

It is John Elway trying to make the grade as a first baseman in 1981, then giving it all up to play pro football.

And it is small towns and bus rides between those towns that cause the vibrations young males love.

Many a young athlete has taken the rides up and down the Atlantic states that make up the New York–Penn League, and as the buses motor along, and the vibrations cause stirring sensations within the players' loins, these fresh-out-of-college free spirits will cry out with glee, "Hey, bus driver . . . how much do you want for this bus? I'm in love."

It seems to be a baseball right of passage, as that conversation has been employed by ballplayers for more than fifty years.

Inside the New York–Penn League (including earlier variations and predecessors of the league):
• In 1923, following a year of voluntary retirement from the sport, thirty-seven-year-old hurler Thomas "Lefty" George, began a fifteen-year run with York by going 19–

10 in 260 innings. He followed that up with 25 wins in 1924 and 27 wins in 1925. Over his long Minor League career, George won 327 games.

- Joe Munson, who also played under the same Joe Martin and who was born Joseph Martin Napoleon Carlson, was an outfielder for Harrisburg in 1925. He won the triple crown in '25 by hitting .400, 33 homers and 129 RBI before being called up by the Cubs.
- After seventeen years in Organized Ball, Jack Bentley came to the NY–P as a first baseman for York, and hit .363 while leading the loop in doubles with 46. He followed that up in 1930 with a .368 average and 103 ribbies.
- And 1930 was a strong year for National Football League star Ken Strong. The NFL Hall-of-Famer hit four homers in one game for Hazleton in 1930 and played the outfield while compiling a hefty .373 average with a league-leading 41 homers and 130 ribbies.
- Bill "Chink" Outen caught for Scranton in 1931 and hit .325 before being promoted to Jersey City of the International League.

    That year, another catcher, Bill Steinecke, led Binghamton with a .361 average and 84 RBI before being called up by the Pirates.
- Outfielder Ray Flood, on a tour with Reading, capped off the 1933 season by hitting .338 with 24 doubles, 20 triples, 189 hits, and 110 runs scored.
- Following a Spring Training injury that left him with a broken leg, forty-four-year-old Rabbit Maranville rehabilitated with Elmira in 1935 and hit .323 in 123 games.
- In 1972, the New York–Penn League broke the gender barrier by hiring Bernice Gera to umpire. She was the first female ever to umpire a professional game in America. Her career lasted nine innings—she resigned after the final out of her first game, apparently having her fill of the job.
- In 1974, Jorge Lebron, a gifted fourteen-year-old, played two games at shortstop for Auburn, making him the sec-

ond youngest Minor League player in Minor League history.

- A celebrity in another sport had a fling with Oneonta in 1981. The New York Yankees' No. 1 draft choice, John Elway, "tried" Minor League baseball before deciding to take his athleticism to the gridiron. Elway hit a creditable .321 and fielded his position well, but the Yankees lost him to Denver's football Broncos. Undaunted in their quest for the perfect football-baseball player, the Yanks later drafted Bo Jackson out of high school and lost him to four years at Auburn University and later to the Kansas City Royals and Los Angeles football Raiders. They picked up "Neon" Deion Sanders, also, but have lost him to the Atlanta football Falcons.

- Proving that some Minor League teams will do anything as pregame promotion, on July 30, 1990, the Hamilton Red Birds signed up Richard Topp, president of SABR, to throw out the first ball prior to the scheduled game against the Auburn Astros. Most fans in the stands had never heard of Topp or his organization—the Society for American Baseball Research—and were largely confused by the action taking place in the infield. Some left the park thinking a baseball card company was involved, others thought SABR was an English razor manufacturer, and still others only heard that a "President" was throwing out the ball and wondered what country he was from.

⚾   ⚾   ⚾   ⚾

1990 Players to Watch

New York Mets first rounder, outfielder Jeremy Burnitz, spent most of the year in Pittsfield before moving up to St. Lucie (Florida State League). He hit .301 with 6 homers, 22 RBI, and 12 steals in 51 games in Pittsfield, but the Mets look for him to increase his power numbers.

Pittsburgh Pirates No. 1 draft choice Kurt Miller, pitcher, came out of high school to pitch at Welland. He went 3–11 with a 2.60 ERA and 58 strikeouts in 62 innings while giving up only 52 hits.

St. Louis Cardinals first rounder Dave Osborne, pitcher, began his career with Hamilton before being shipped to Savannah (South Atlantic League). His combined totals for 1990 showed a 2–4 record with a 2.93 ERA in 61 innings.

Robert Katzaroff, an outfielder for Jamestown (Expos), led the league in hitting at a .364 clip.

16
NORTHWEST
LEAGUE

The Northwest League, first established in 1879, is in its third run of operations: 1879–1922; 1937–42; and 1946–present.

Its initial enterprise as the Northwestern League reorganized as the Western Association in 1888. The Western Association became the Western League and challenged the National League for baseball supremacy.

A more direct line to the current Northwest League can be traced back to the Pacific Northwest League of 1901 and 1902, which became the Pacific National League in 1903, which reorganized into the Northwestern League and ran from 1905 to 1918. Another reorganization transformed the circuit into the Pacific Coast International League, which collapsed in 1922.

Picking up again in 1937, the Western International League surfaced and operated until 1942 when the war shut down operations. It was revived in 1946, and following a name change to the Northwest League in 1955, has run smoothly ever since.

The circuit is another league dominated by first-year

players fresh out of college competition, and it currently covers Idaho, Oregon, and Washington. Its eight Single-A teams include the Bellingham Mariners, Bend Bucks (Co-op), Boise Hawks (Angels), Eugene Emeralds (Royals), Everett Giants, Southern Oregon Athletes, Spokane Indians, and Yakima Bears (Dodgers).

Running a seventy-six-game schedule from June 18 to September 3, the league is divided into two divisions of four teams each.

In 1990, Spokane took the Northern Division with a 49–27 record, 13 games better than second-place Yakima, while Boise ran away with the Southern Division with a 53–23 mark, 13 games ahead of Southern Oregon.

Spokane prevailed in the playoffs, two games to one over Boise.

What is the Northwest League?

It *was* a less sophisticated organization that is *now* big business. But in the old days . . .

Bob Frietas was the president of the league in 1970, and following the departure of the American League's Seattle Pilots (to Milwaukee), the Seattle market opened back up for possible inclusion in the Northwest League.

Frietas was at his Oregon home watering his roses, when a car drove up. A well-dressed man got out of his automobile and said to Frietas, "I'm looking for the baseball guy."

Frietas politely answered, "You mean me."

The man then asked Frietas, "I want to run a team. Can I have one?"

Frietas, still watering his roses, and barely looking up at the stranger, asked, "Do you have a credit card?"

"Yes," the man answered.

"Fine," said Frietas. "You've got the franchise."

That was then. Now, according to current league president Jack Cain, "You need a lot of money in the bank and you must go through an extensive background check. But then, it was easy."

Inside the Northwest League:

• In 1887, Tom Lovett, the only pitcher to win 20 games in one season in two different leagues, started his summer in the sun by going 21–3 with Bridgeport in the Eastern League. Moving on to Oshkosh in the Northwest League, Lovett went 20–2 for an incredible 41–5 Minor League season. From 1886–88, Lovett won 103 games.

  Carrying that winning habit to the Majors, Lovett won 30 for Brooklyn in 1890, pitching 372 innings; and he won 23 more for the Brooks in 1891, throwing 365 innings. During his six-year Big League stint, he went 88–59.

• In 1955, Tom Agosta banged out 18 triples for Salem.

• Bobby Bolin whiffed 271 hitters for Eugene in 1959, and also posted 9 shutouts.

• Glenn Beckert went to the plate a record 560 times for Wenatchee in 1963, before the league went to a short season.

• John Warner smashed 37 homers for Tri-City, a long-season record, in 1964.

• In 1965, Dave May scored 129 runs for Tri-City.

• Bob Davis drove in 83 runs in the short-season of 1971, for Tri-City.

• Reggie Thomas set the league stolen base mark with 72 for Portland in 1974.

• Ron McNeely set an all-time batting mark by hitting .403 for Boise in 1976.

• Willie Darkis hit a short-season record 25 roundtrippers for Central Oregon in 1980.

1990 Players to Watch

The Oakland A's sent both of its first round draft choices to Southern Oregon, but only one lasted there all summer. Pitcher Todd Van Poppel, everybody's All-American, went 3–2 with 49 strikeouts in 37 innings split between Southern Oregon and Madison of the Midwest League. He may see action with Oakland in 1991. His teammate, pitcher Don Peters, went 1–1 in nine games and saw limited action due to a tender shoulder.

San Francisco Giants also sent two first rounders to the Northwest League and its affiliate, Everett. Top choice Adam Hyzdu, outfielder, hit .250 with 6 homers and 34 RBI in 64 games in his first stiff competition after high school. Fellow first rounder, Eric Christopher, catcher, hit .272 with 1 homer and 23 RBI in 51 games and was moved to San Jose in the California League.

17
THE ROOKIE
LEAGUES

Since those operations that make up the classification known as "Rookie" Class are, for the most part, newer than those more-historically experienced upper class leagues, and since several Rookie Leagues refuse to publicize their operations due to region-sharing with upper classification teams, we have chosen to lump the five short-season leagues together in this chapter.

Generally speaking, Rookie Leagues are June-to-September operations run for the benefit of training and coaching newly graduated high school and college players while introducing them to Organized Baseball.

These leagues provide the first taste of professional competition for athletes who aren't deemed as being ready for upper classification competition.

Seldom does a ballplayer return to Rookie ball. If he can't make it here . . . he can't make it anywhere, is the parent team's judgment. But from these stepping stones, often do tomorrow's stars emerge.

Appalachian League

The Appalachian League fills out its roster of teams with franchises from North Carolina (Burlington), Tennessee (Elizabethton, Johnson City, Kingsport), Virginia (Bristol, Martinsville, Pulaski), and West Virginia (Bluefield, Huntington, Princeton).

The Appalachian League has been active from 1921–25, 1937–55 and its current reign, which has now reached thirty-four years, began in 1957.

With a season running from June 21 to August 31, the Appalachian season is 72 games long, enough time to introduce young players to the rigors of everyday baseball.

In a league in which all but one team carries the nickname of its parent Major League owner, the Elizabethton Twins (Twins affiliate) cruised to a championship by going a remarkable 51–15 (.773 percentage), some 12½ games ahead of Huntington Cubs. The ten-team league has no postseason play-offs, and while the Kingsport Mets, Bluefield Orioles and Pulaski Braves finished above .500, there was nowhere to go but up for the athletes who played their first seasons on the Farm.

In 1990, Appalachian League members (with parent club in parentheses) were: Elizabethton (Twins)—seventeen years in the league; Huntington (Cubs)—one year in the league; Kingsport (Mets)—thirty-two years in the league; Bluefield (Orioles)—thirty-four years in the league; Pulaski (Braves)—nine years in the league; Burlington (Indians)—five years in the league; Princeton Patriots (Co-op)—three years in the league; Johnson City (Cardinals)—thirty-two years in the league; Martinsville (Phillies)—three years in the league; and Bristol (Tigers)—forty-eight years in the league.

The 1990 Appalachian League season saw Elizabethton go an incredible 51–15, for a .773 winning percentage, 12½ games ahead of second-place Huntington.

⊗   ⊗   ⊗   ⊗

Inside the Appalachian League:

- Lew Flick dominated the then-Class D Appalachian League hitting stats from 1938 through 1942 while playing the outfield for Elizabethton, winning two batting titles, four hit leaderships, a doubles crown, triples title, and RBI championship. His best year was 1941 when he hit .418, drove in 116 runs, hit 37 doubles, and scored 127 runs while stealing 20 bases.

- Leo "Muscle" Shoals won five Appalachian League home run titles over a span of twenty-six years with time out for military service and stints in seven other leagues. Shoals was number one as a first baseman-pitcher for Johnson City in 1939 when he hit 16 roundtrippers, for Kingsport with 21 in 1946 and 32 in 1947, for Kingsport again with 30 in 1951—a triple crown year in which he also hit .383 and drove in 129 runs. And in 1955, at the age of 39, he hit 33 homeruns and drove in 134 runs in his last year with Kingsport.

- In one of the greatest pitching performances ever, six-foot-five-inch, 185-pound, nineteen-year-old "Rocket" Ron Necciai, pitching for the Bristol Twins, threw a no-hitter over Welch (West Virginia) on May 13, 1952. During the contest, Necciai struck out 27 batters in nine innings. Only one hitter hit the ball fair for an out, as one ground out was recorded. Necciai faced one extra hitter when his catcher allowed a runner to reach base via a passed ball on a third strike, as Necciai had to whiff four batters that inning. The only other Welch players to reach base that day were on a walk, a hit batsman, and an error.

  In Necciai's next start, he struck out 24 and won with a two-hit shutout. For the season, he recorded 109 strikeouts in 43 innings at Bristol, and 172 more in 126 innings after a call up to the Carolina League at Durham.

  Falling victim to arm trouble and ulcers, Necciai lasted only one season in The Show, going 1–6, with a 7.08 ERA, 31 strikeouts in 54 innings for Pittsburgh in 1952.

  Necciai's teammate that year, Bill "Ding Ding" Bell

threw back-to-back no-hitters May 22 and May 26, and finished the season with three no-hitters, only one behind the record of four set in 1908 by Walter "Smoke" Justus.

⚾   ⚾   ⚾   ⚾

1990 Players to Watch

Detroit Tigers' No. 1 draft choice Tony Clark, an outfielder, played poorly with Bristol—.164, 1 homer and 8 RBIs in 25 games, but Detroit didn't care. They reported they just wanted Clark to get his feet wet before beginning classes and varsity basketball at the University of Arizona.

Minnesota Twins No. 1 draft choice Todd Ritchie, pitcher, went 5–2 with Elizabethton, with an impressive 1.94 ERA. In 65 innings he allowed 45 hits, walked 24 and whiffed 49.

Philadelphia Phillies No. 1 draft choice Mike Lieberthal, catcher, had a tough time at Martinsville, hitting .217 with 4 homers and 21 RBI in 48 games. He did, however, impress the Phillies with his catching ability and will move up in 1991.

St. Louis Cardinals first rounder Aaron Holbert, shortstop, was only seventeen years old when the Cards subjected him to Appalachian League pitching. While with Johnson City, Holbert hit just .171 with 1 homer and 18 RBI in 53 games; although he made 23 errors in the field, he figures to get better with age. Cardinals player development director Ted Simmons said, "Holbert has the tools to play Major League ball . . . but he's five years away."

Arizona League

Established in 1988, the Arizona League is the first new league to be formed in thirty years.

With all of its teams operating in Arizona, this Rookie League runs from June 24 to August 31 and schedules fifty-six games per season with no postseason play-offs. Begun in 1988, the league houses six teams from Tempe

(Mariners), Scottsdale (Athletics and Padres), Peoria (Brewers and Cardinals), and Mesa (Angels).

The Arizona League takes such a low-key stance on operations that it charges no money for tickets and has no concessions. It doesn't advertise and tries to keep its existence as quiet as possible, allowing parent clubs to run the operations while they inauspiciously groom their players. This isn't done out of shame or lack of confidence; it is done because the Phoenix Firebirds of the Pacific Coast League own the territory and forbid the Arizona League to publicize its existence.

In 1990, the Brewers won the league championship with a 36–17 mark, 3½ games ahead of the Mariners and 7½ on top of the Cardinals.

1990 Players to Watch

Seattle Mariners' No. 1 draft choice Marc Newfield, first baseman, played for the Mariners' squad in Arizona, hitting .326 with 6 homers and 38 RBI in 48 games. Look for a switch to the outfield for Newfield.

Dominican Summer

This is a Rookie Class League with little or no data coming from organizers. It runs scrimmages as well as regular games and all of its games are played in the Dominican Republic, with about 99 percent of the players coming from Latin American countries.

The Major League teams that participate include: Atlanta, Baltimore, Boston, California, Chicago White Sox, Detroit, Houston, Kansas City, Los Angeles, Milwaukee, Montreal, New York Mets, New York Yankees, Oakland, Pittsburgh, San Diego, San Francisco, Seattle, Texas, and Toronto.

Suffice it to say that several Major League GMs swear that some of the best talent in baseball may come from this league in the next few years.

Gulf Coast

The Gulf Coast League, in its twenty-seventh year of operation (established in 1964), runs a sixty-three-game schedule from June 20 to August 31, covering fourteen teams and eight cities in Florida.

The Rookie League is divided into two divisions, with the Northern Division made up of the Dodgers and Astros based in Osceola, Reds based in Plant City, Red Sox and Indians based in Winter Haven, and Royals based in Baseball City.

The Southern Division has teams from the Braves and Expos based in Bradenton, Rangers based in Port Charlotte, Yankees and White Sox based in Sarasota, Twins and Mets based in another complex in Sarasota, and the Pirates based in Pirate City.

As a draw to the beach-going crowd, and as a means of teaching a 9 to 5 work ethic to its young athletes, all games start at noon.

In 1990, the Dodgers won the North with a 38–25 mark, beating the Reds by 2 games and the Red Sox by 4. The Southern Division was taken by the Expos, 4 games ahead of the Rangers and 6½ up on the Braves.

The Dodgers swept a two-game play-off series from the Expos.

In 1992, look for the Red Sox to leave Winter Haven all to the Indians. The BoSox are still looking for a replacement site. The Dodgers are headed for Kissimmee.

Inside the Gulf Coast League:
- Kyle Rote, the football hero for the New York football Giants—and a former All-American at Southern Methodist University—gave baseball a shot in 1952 when he joined Corpus Christi in April after missing Spring Training.

  Rote wasted little time and smacked out three homers

in a game against Galveston en route to hitting .348 with a .712 slugging percentage in 22 games before he left the team to report for football training with the Giants.

- Before it became a Rookie League, the Class-D Gulf Coast League welcomed forty-two-year-old journeyman pitcher Vallie "Chief" Eaves to Brownsville, where he won 19 games and posted a 2.61 ERA. It marked his fourth stop in the Gulf Coast after a long Minor League and Major League career.
- Omar Moreno, later to be a base-stealing whiz in the Majors, was only fifteen years old when he played 25 games for the Bradenton Pirates in 1969.
- Pam Postema became the first female umpire in Gulf Coast League history in 1977, and when she was still umpiring in 1981 in the Texas League, became the all-time female career umpiring leader, besting the three-year run by Chris Wren (1975–77).

1990 Players to Watch

Chipper Jones, a shortstop, the Atlanta Braves No. 1 draft choice—and first player chosen overall in the June draft—hit only .228 with 1 homer and 18 RBI in 43 games at Bradenton while committing 18 errors. He looks to improve with confidence and experience.

The Chicago White Sox did a little better a little faster with their first rounder, pitcher Alex Fernandez, who made three brief stops in the Minors, going a combined 5–1 with a 1.81 ERA in the Gulf Coast League and Florida State League before moving on to Birmingham in the Southern League on his way up to the White Sox in Chicago, where he became a pennant-drive stopper.

Houston Astros first rounder, Tom Never, shortstop, jumped from high school to Gulf Coast pitching and hit .238 with 2 homers and 32 RBI and 13 stolen bases in 50 games. Nervous, he committed 21 errors. He'll get better.

Montreal had two first rounders in the Gulf Coast League in 1990. Third baseman Shane Andrews hit .238 with 3 homers and

24 RBI in 53 games while committing 15 errors. Outfielder Rondell White, his teammate, showed early poise by batting .295 with 5 homers and 34 RBI in 54 games.

The New York Yankees used their first first round draft choice since 1980 to pick outfielder Carl Everett. He fared decently, hitting .261 with 1 homer and 14 RBI while stealing 14 bases in 46 games. The Yankees see rapid development on the horizon for Everett.

Pioneer League

The Pioneer League, which began operations in 1939 (inactive only during the World War II years of 1943–45), is the oldest of the current Rookie Leagues.

Running from June 20 to August 31, the Pioneer League offers a seventy-game schedule for its eight teams, which it divides into two divisions.

Covering a regional area that reaches Alberta, Canada (Medicine Hat); Idaho (Gate City-Pocatello, Idaho Falls); Montana (Billings, Butte, Great Falls, Helena), and Utah (Salt Lake City); the Pioneer League is considered by many scouts as the toughest and best, in terms of talent and competition, of the Rookie Leagues.

The current roster of teams includes the Billings Mustangs in its twenty-second year (Reds); Butte Copper Kings in its fourth year (Rangers); Gate City Pioneers in its fourth year (Co-op); Great Falls Dodgers in its twenty-second year (Dodgers); Idaho Falls Braves in its forty-eighth year (Braves); Medicine Hat Blue Jays in its thirteenth year (Blue Jays), and the Salt Lake Trappers in its sixth year (Independent).

In 1990, the Great Falls Dodgers ran away from its Northern Division neighbors with a 48–20 mark, 9½ games better than Helena, while Salt Lake City, the independent team, went 42–26, 3½ ahead of Idaho Falls and 4½ over Butte.

○○   ○○   ○○   ○○

Inside the Pioneer League:

- Pocatello first baseman Tony Robello had a dream season in 1939, by hitting .404, with 58 homers, 179 RBI, 205 hits, and 168 runs scored in 124 games. During a four-year Pioneer League career that ended with his enlistment during World War II, Robello hit 106 four-baggers and drove in 402 runs.

    The 1939 season was also good to Pete Hughes, an outfielder for Ogden. Hughes hit .409 with 41 homers and 133 RBI, and also walked a league-leading 101 times.

- Returning to baseball in 1946, following a three-year hitch in the military service, Harry "Bud" Heslet, a catcher for Twin Falls, led the Pioneer League in home runs with 29 and RBI with 124 while batting .308.

- The all-time Minor League record for strikeouts by a batter was set by rookie outfielder Jim Lankford, for Ogden in 1954. A power-hitter, if he didn't miss, Lankford fanned 216 times in 133 games, batting only .226. His mark was in jeopardy as recently as 1985, when Toronto Blue Jays outfielder Glenallen Hill whiffed 211 for Kinston in the Carolina League in 1985.

- In 1980, Rafael Montalvo, fourteen, became the youngest pitcher in Minor League history to play ball when he went 4–2 for Lethbridge.

- The Salt Lake Trappers are owned by comedian-actor Bill Murray.

- At Idaho Falls, the Atlantic Braves Rookie Class affiliate, pitchers Don Dease and Bill Bates combined for a 23-strikeout performance on July 23, 1990. Dease whiffed 12 and Bates 11 in the tilt.

1990 Players to Watch

Texas Rangers first round draft choice Dan Smith began the year pitching for Butte, before jumping to Double-A Tulsa (Texas

League). His combined totals were 4–2, 4.18 ERA, and 55 strike-outs and 19 walks in 56 innings.

Los Angeles Dodgers first rounder Ron Walden, pitcher, pitched in four games for Great Falls and posted a 3–0 mark before straining his elbow. Rest should put him on the mark in 1991.

18
A LOOK AT SOME GREAT BALLPARKS, TEAMS, AND MINOR LEAGUE CITIES

Minor League baseball begins with its teams and the wonderful cities and towns and communities that support them. As with other sections of this book, a complete compilation of *all* the great teams would require thousands of pages. Therefore, included in this *look*, is a selection of *some* of the great teams and franchises that have become part of Minor League lore, and *some* of the cities that have made their marks on the fabric of the Farm System.

An attempt has been made to include all of the thousands of cities who proudly proclaim their contribution to the game in another section—Chapter 22, "Minor League Cities in Operation 1877–1990."

Meaning no disrespect to cities from Des Moines to Durham, Havana to Honolulu, Minneapolis to Memphis, Niagara Falls to New Orleans, Pawtucket to Portland, Tulsa to Tucson, or Walla Walla to Wausau . . . or any other glorious Minor League hamlet, what follows, then, is not an oversight or slight of those franchises and communities left out, but rather a celebration of a few teams and towns that have participated in the legend of the Little

Show, with a footnote: These teams and towns live on and are forever bound with the countless other teams and towns that define Minor League baseball.

Ballparks
(*Source: Green Cathedrals*)

Part of the wonder and innocence that are Minor League baseball are its ballparks.

Bandbox parks? Certainly the Minors were filled with them—204 feet down the line and a measly 300 feet to center—but how about distances that only golfers could appreciate: an astronomical 1,200 feet to dead center, 900 feet down one line, and 600 feet down the other. Yes, the Minor Leagues had those, too. Parks with personality.

Most newer parks are the antiseptic concrete and steel engineering marvels that show progress and uniformity but are devoid of personality. Some of the more endearing parks of the past include those with irregular, short, or long dimensions.

Short Dimensions

Hodges Field in Memphis went only 204 feet down the right field line. Hodges was used after the Memphis Chicks' Russwood Park burned down. After eleven home runs were hit in one game (May 2, 1960), the Southern League decreed that all balls hit over the fence and its forty-foot screen would be doubles. Right center was only 279 feet away, and left field was a more reasonable 335 feet from home plate.

The Mooresville, North Carolina, ballpark went only 210 feet to left.

Rome, Georgia, had a field that was 225 to right.

Athletic Park in Vancouver, British Columbia, Canada, went 232 to right, a paltry 318 feet to center, and 383 to left.

Sulphur Dell, home of the Nashville Vols, had its right

field foul line stretch out to 250 feet, which was shortened to 235 when overflow crowds sat behind ropes there. It had a forty-six-foot-high fence and screen above the short porch. It was such a left-handed hitters homerun park that eight Nashville lefties hit the top eight homerun marks in Southern Association history . . . all making Sulphur Dell their home: Bob Lennon (64 in 1954), Chick Workman (52 in 1948), Jim Poole (50 in 1930), Jack Harshman (47 in 1951), Carl Sawatski (45 in 1949), Charlie Gilbert (42 in 1948), Babe Barna (42 in 1949), and Jay Partridge (40 in 1930).

Borchert Field, a wooden ballpark in Milwaukee, Wisconsin, served as home to the Negro National League Bears in 1923 with hitter-friendly dimensions of 266 down the left field and right field lines and 395 to center. The park, also called Milwaukee Athletic Park, was used as an ice rink in the winter.

Nicollet Park in Minneapolis, home of the Minneapolis Millers of the American Association, offered a short porch, 279 feet in right and 328 to the "power" alley in right. The center field scoreboard was topped by a forty-foot fence, and the short right field barrier was home to a sixteen-foot screen on top of a thirty-foot wooden fence.

The Beatrice, Nebraska, field was brutal to lefties but forgiving to righties: only 280 to the left field wall but a tough 420 to the right field foul pole.

The Johnstown, Pennsylvania, Point Stadium, home of the Pittsburgh Crawfords and Homestead Grays, was a hitter's delight . . . 270 to the left field wall and 280 to right. Center field was a pitcher-friendly 475 feet from home and housed a ticket booth.

The Cleveland, Ohio, League Park (II), home of the Negro American League Bears in 1939 and 1940, and the Buckeyes from 1943 to 1948 and 1950, favored lefty hitters, with a short 290 feet to right (240 feet when roped off to house overflow crowds), but a deep 465 to dead center, and a tough 374 feet to left. It was the home of the Negro

Leagues champion Cleveland Buckeyes in 1945, and a historical marker was erected to note the event.

Long Dimensions

The most unbelievable dimensions in ballpark history belong to Leeman, in Huntington Gap, Virginia, with an unreachable 1,200 feet to dead (and we mean dead) center, 900 feet to the left field marker, and a "porch" of *only* 600 feet to right. Not exactly your typical Minor League bandbox.

College Hill Park, in Montgomery, Alabama, boasted a park with 600-foot totals to center and right and 420 feet to left. It was home to the Negro Southern League Grey Sox in 1932.

The Dothan, Alabama, stadium went 700 feet to dead center and a mere 475 down the left field line.

The Newport, Arkansas, park was a deep 650 to dead center, 550 to left, and 440 down the right field foul line.

In Fairbury, Nebraska, the yard went 620 to center, 590 to the foul pole in left, and 490 to right.

Athletic Park of Terre Haute, Indiana, also known as Memorial Stadium and Triple-I League Park, was 440 down the lines and a monstrous 592 to dead center.

Watt Powell Park in Charleston, West Virginia, once topped out at 528 to right center and 527 to center. Home of the South Atlantic League Charleston Wheelers, center field is now a more liberal 406 feet from home plate.

Ponce deLeon Park, Atlanta, home of the Negro American League Atlanta Black Crackers in 1938, had a two-foot hedge as a wall in left field, 330 feet from home plate, a Magnolia tree as a wall by the 321-foot right field marker, and a "death valley" to left center of 525 feet. Affectionately called "Poncey," the facility was torn down in 1967 and is now a parking lot opposite a Sears department store.

Parkway Field, in Louisville, Kentucky, is the current home of the University of Louisville baseball team. But the

1931 Negro National League White Sox and the 1932 Negro Southern League Black Caps used the park as their home, and hitters had to contend with a 512-foot expanse to dead center field, flanked by a 350-foot distance from home to right, and 331 from home to left.

The San Diego Padres' Pacific Coast League home from 1936 to 1958, Lane Field, went 500 feet to dead center, 390 to left and 350 to right.

Some other unreachable seats down the foul lines include:

Monahans, Texas—600 feet to the left-field foul pole.

Roswell, New Mexico, home of homerun king Joe Bauman (72 homers in the Longhorn League in 1954) was 425 down the right-field foul line.

Famed Yankee Stadium, in the Bronx, New York, served as home for the Negro National League Black Yankees from 1946 to 1948, and had the original "death valley" of 466 to left center, 461 to dead center, and a reachable porch of only 296 down the right-field line and 301 down left.

Swayne Field, also known as Mud Hen Park, in Toledo, Ohio, went 472 down the left-field line and 482 to center, but was a reachable 327 to right. The Toledo Mud Hens and Negro League Tigers and Crawfords played home games there. It is now a shopping center.

Highest fences and barriers:

Remember, Fenway Park's Green Monster fence and screen in left field is a devastating 37-feet high. Compare that to:

The Savannah, Georgia, Grayson Park—90-foot-high light tower in left field.

The Johnstown, Pennsylvania, Point Stadium—70-foot-high left-field screen.

The Buffalo, New York, Offermann Stadium—60-foot-high wooden scoreboard in center field.

In Milwaukee, Wisconsin, Borchert Field—60-foot-high screen in right.

The Durham Athletic Park had a 50-foot high right-field wall consisting of a 15-foot embankment on atop which sat a 35-foot brick wall. That wall now totals a mere 31 feet.

In Minneapolis, Minnesota, Nicollet Park, a homerun paradise, had a 46-foot-high screen in right field and a 40-foot-high scoreboard in center.

In Chattanooga, Tennessee, Engel Stadium has a 42-foot-high scoreboard in left field.

Other Parks Worth Noting

Rickwood Field in Birmingham, Alabama, former home of the Birmingham Barons, was opened on August 18, 1910, and served the team for nearly eighty years. It went 405 to left, topped by a 35-foot-high scoreboard, a dreaded 470 to center, and a comfortable 334 to right. The park was named after Barons' owner Rick Woodward.

McCormick Field, in Asheville, North Carolina, serves as home to the Asheville Tourists of the South Atlantic League. Built in 1924, the ballpark boasts the thickest vines on any baseball wall in America. Its fence dimensions go 328 to left, 404 to center, and 301 to right, and Asheville enthusiasts maintain that their 3,500-seat facility is the oldest continuous use baseball stadium in America, now that Comiskey Park has shut its doors.

Arguing that stand are devotees of Greensboro, North Carolina's War Memorial Stadium, also known as World War Memorial Stadium, home of the South Atlantic League Greensboro Hornets. Reportedly built in 1926, and dedicated on Armistice Day, November 11, War Memorial has dimensions of 327 to left, 401 to center, and 327 to right, but it began as a short porch-death valley park at 243 down the line and 500 feet to center. It seats 7,500 fans. The age dispute revolves around the Greensboro contention that Asheville's McCormick Field was torn down and rebuilt on the same spot years after War Memorial was long used. Original plaques honoring World War I soldiers killed in action, listed local deceased veterans. In the 1930s, the names of black soldiers were chiseled off and listed separately from the white soldiers.

The Chattanooga, Tennesee, Engel Stadium, home of the Chattanooga Lookouts of the Southern League, goes 355 feet to left, 413 to center, and 324 to right. The 8,000-seat stadium once topped out at 471 to center, and today, there are arguments that the right-field fence, marked 324 feet, is actually measured at 318 feet. Built in 1930, the name "Lookouts" was often painted on the outfield grass in chalk. Engel Stadium has been the site of free Christmas Eve turkey dinners, a Donald Duck Egg Laying Contest, a wild elephant hunt, a jackrabbit chase, and a home for fifty cages filled with canaries.

The Durham, North Carolina, Athletic Park, home of the Durham Bulls of the Carolina League, seats 5,000 with dimensions of 330 to left, 410 to center, and 305 to right. Dedicated in 1938, the fences once reached 460 to center and 390 to left, with a tantalizing 290 feet from home to right field. Center field once housed twelve bushes, a tree, and eight telephone poles.

The El Paso, Texas, Dudley Field was home of the El Paso Diablos from 1945 through 1989. With dimensions of 340-395-340, the 7,000-seat park was abandoned for 10,000-seat Cohen Stadium in 1990. Dudley was endearingly constructed with steel, brick, and adobe, with straw, rocks, mud, and twigs mixed into the unique texture of this ballpark.

Russwood Park in Memphis, Tennessee, home of the Memphis Chicks of the Southern League for decades, burned down twice, the second time in 1960. Now used as a medical center, the park once had dimensions of 424 to left field, a short 366 to center, and 301 to right.

Nicollet Park in Minneapolis was home to many sluggers. Joe Hauser hit 50 homers there in one season in 1933, en route to his 69 four-bagger year, Ted Williams hit .366 in 1938, and Phil Weintraub blasted a total of 60 homers in two years, 1939–40. Nicollet was home to Art Ruble, Babe Ganzel, and Joe Mowry, who feasted there.

The park, which was home field to the Minneapolis Millers of the American Association, went 279 feet to the right-field foul pole, 328 to the power alley in right, 432 to center, and 334 to left—tailor-made for hard-swinging lefties, but right-handed hitting Willie Mays (.477 in 1951) made a successful stop there, too. Home of seven Minor League-leading home run kings: Dell Darling (21 in 1891), Perry Werdon (25 in 1894 and 42 in 1895), Buck Freeman (18 in 1907), Cliff "Cactus" "Gavvy" Cravath (29 in 1911), Joe Hauser (69 in 1933), and Buzz Arlett (48 in 1934). Built in 1896 and torn down in 1956, Nicollet was memorable with its chimney sitting high atop its wooden roof. It currently is the site of the Norwest Bank building.

Newark, New Jersey, location of Ruppert Stadium (also known as David's Stadium, Bears Stadium, and David's Folly) was home to International League powerhouse Newark Bears, as well as Negro National League monster Newark Eagles. It was said during the late 1930s that Ruppert Stadium housed the two greatest Minor League teams of the era, the Bears and Eagles, and when the touring House of David used Ruppert as its home, local baseball enthusiasts called it a hat trick . . . the three top non-New York Yankee teams of the period. Ruppert's dimensions were 305 feet down each line and 410 to center. The park was built in 1926 on the site that had housed Wiedenmayer's Park from 1902 to 1914. Ruppert Stadium, named for its owner who was a beer magnate and owner of the New York Yankees, Col. Jacob Ruppert, was torn down in 1967 to make way for an industrial park.

McCoy Stadium in Pawtucket, Rhode Island, home of the Pawtucket Red Sox of the International League, was built as part of a 1930s WPA project. Current dimensions go 325 to left, 380 to center, and 325 to right. The park seats 6,010.

The Rochester, New York, Red Wing Stadium, home of the International League's Rochester Red Wings, was built in 1928. It was renamed Morrie Silver Stadium in 1968 and once went 445 to left center, 322 to left, and 315 to right. Currently seating 12,503, the yard goes to 320-400-315. Its endearing qualities included little wooden rectangular distance markers sitting atop the green right-field fence and a huge scoreboard in center.

The Denver Zephyrs of the American Association call Mile High Stadium home. Built in 1948 over what had been a city dump, Mile High was first called Bears Stadium. Originally equipped with uncovered single-level stands, right-field bleachers were added in 1961, second and third decks were added in 1968 and 1976, and football stands were added in 1977. The park goes 348-420-365 and seats 76,000. An underground lake runs beneath the stadium, and history tells us that once upon a time, the area around second base became a soggy swamp at least several times during each season.

The Toledo Mud Hens of the International League play their home games in Ned Skeldon Stadium. Built in 1963 and known as Lucas County Stadium, the 10,025-seat park was renamed for former Toledo owner Ned Skeldon, who pushed through the financing to replace the Hen's antiquated Swayne Field, a half-century old when replaced. Skeldon has dimensions of 325 down each line and 410 to center.

Davenport, Iowa, is the home of the Quad City Angels (Midwest League) who play at John O'Donnell Stadium. O'Donnell has dimensions of 340 down each line and 390 to center, and it seats 5,000 fans. Built in 1931, on land that was reclaimed from the Mississippi River in an area that had been the site of a rubbish heap, the park has recently undergone a $2.3 million renovation. The upgrading was apparently done to keep the parent affiliate California Angels happy and to put it in line to become the home of a proposed Triple-A franchise.

The ballpark designed with the future in mind is Pilot Field, home of the Buffalo Bisons of the American Association. Built with a Major League franchise as a motive, Pilot Field, erected in 1988, seats 19,500 but is expandable to 40,000. Its dimensions of 325 down each line and 410 to center seem likely to remain. Pilot Field replaced War Memorial Stadium, the site of moviedom's *The Natural.* Pilot's 50-foot by 80-foot scoreboard is fully animated, in full color, and is seen as state-of-the-art. The park has thrice drawn over one million fans and the construction price was $42 million. On the food front, Pilot Field boasts a varied menu found in specially designed sections of the park (a different taste treat in each section). This food court sends up Italian sausage, fried bologna, pizza, submarine sandwiches, Polish sausage, Buster burgers, roast beef sandwiches, barbeque specialties, chicken sandwiches, steak hoagies, and Grand American ice cream, in addition to the normal baseball fare of hot dogs, peanuts, Cracker Jacks, popcorn, and beverages.

Wrigley Field, home of the PCL Los Angeles Angels, and later, the Major League Los Angeles Angels, was dedicated September 27, 1925 and torn down in 1966. During its forty-year run, Wrigley was a homerun launching pad, serving as a batter's friend for such Minor League stars as batting champions Lou Novikoff, Frank Demaree, Johnny Moore, Andy Pafko, Frank Baumholtz, and Steve Bilko. Power kings including Gene Lillard, Demaree, Ripper Collins, Novikoff, John Ostrowski, Lloyd Christopher, Max West, and Bilko fondly awaited each home stand. The park made a hero of Bilko, who used it to help him win three consecutive homer crowns (1955–57). Wrigley Park saw the Angels fashion the longest winning streak in PCL history (19 games in 1939) and the longest undefeated streak (21 games—20 wins and 1 tie—in 1941) and it helped gain the Halos a league record 14 PCL championships.

The park, which served as the location for television's "Home Run Derby" series in 1960, earned its name as it became a Major League ballpark, yielding a record 248 roundtrippers in 1961. Its dimensions were 340 feet to left, only 345 to the left-field power alley, 412 to center, 345 to the right-field power alley, and 338.5 feet to right.

Great Teams and Cities

Some of the scores of great, not-so-great, mediocre, and downright terrible teams of the past and present deserve to be remembered somewhere, to preserve them in the minds of those who saw them perform, and to bring them alive to those who weren't so fortunate. This salute represents an attempt to do just that.

The 1937 Newark Bears

Arguably the greatest team of all time was the powerhouse Triple-A Farm club of the New York Yankees, the Newark Bears. Long the last Minor League stop for its superstars before they donned Yankee pinstripes and exchanged the "N" on their caps for the "NY" were the Newark Bears.

In the late 1930s and early '40s, the Bears were the class of the International League, seven times earning the top record in the loop and five times topping the 100-win plateau: 109–59 in 1932; 102–62 in 1933; 93–60 in 1934; 109–43 in 1937; 104–48 in 1938; 100–54 in 1941 and 92–61 in 1942. Like the '37 Newarkers, the 1932 Bears also won 109 games and even beat the powerhouse Minneapolis Millers in the Junior World Series in six games, outscoring them 39–23, but they are not thought of historically with the same reverence bestowed upon their successor. The 1938 squad may have been just as talented as the '37 team, but their loss in the Little World Series to another Yankee Farm Club, the Kansas City Blues, (4 games to 3) deprives them of mention as an all-time great Minor League platoon. Suffice it to say that, for a solid decade, no team in the Little Show had dynasty associated with its logo as did the bear wearing the big "N."

Newark regularly stocked its teams with such future Major League stars as Larry "Yogi" Berra, Ike Boone, Red Rolfe, Spud Chandler, Gene Woodling, Spec Shea, Tommy Henrich, Andy Cohen, Dusty Cook, Johnny Neunn, Dixie Walker, George Selkirk, Johnny Murphy, George Puccinelli, Myril Hoag, Roy Schalk, and countless others who gained an air of invincibility wearing the big "N".

But the cream of the Bears' crop was the 1937 club, which has earned immortality for its exploits. The kings of the International League, the '37 Newark Bears, managed by Ossie Vitt, finished with an amazing 109–43 mark, an astonishing .717 winning percentage in a tough league, and 25 1/2 games ahead of the second-place Montreal Royals. This outweighs the 94–38 mark (.712) by the 1981 Albuquerque Dukes of the Pacific Coast League, the 137–50 record (.733) by the PCL Los Angeles Angels in 1934, and other teams with better records in weaker divisions. By compiling a 12–3 mark in the play-offs (4–0 over the Syracuse Chiefs, 4–0 over the Baltimore Orioles, and 4–3 over the Columbus Red Birds), Newark ran its mark to 121–46, a .725 percentage. And the dominating World Champion New York Yankees only went 106–53 that year, including their 4–1 Series mark against the New York Giants.

The '37 Newark Bears were well-stocked, as they were manned by Willard Hershberger and Buddy Rosar behind the plate, George McQuinn at first, Joe Gordon at second, Babe Dahlgren at third (he was a first baseman being groomed to take Lou Gehrig's spot with the Yankees, but was learning other positions to help him jump to the Majors more quickly . . . he ended up at third for Newark), Nolen Richardson at shortstop, Jimmy Gleeson in left, Bob Seeds in center, and International League batting leader Charlie "King Kong" Keller in right. They were backed up by utilityman Frank Kelleher. Of these, McQuinn, Gordon, Dahlgren, Richardson, Keller, Seeds, Hershberger, and Rosar were named to the International League all-star team that year.

In the IL batting race, Keller (.353), Dahlgren (.340), Rosar (.332), McQuinn (.330), and Hershberger (.325) finished 1-2-4-5, and Kelleher (.305) and Seeds (.303) gave them seven hitters over .300. And while Gleeson hit only

.299, he led the league in doubles with 47. Gordon only hit .276 but spanked a team-leading 26 homers.

On the mound, Atley Donald finished at 19–2, a .905 winning percentage, Joe Beggs went 21–4, Steve Sundra 15–4, and Vito Tamulis 18–6, for a four-man rotation total of 73–16, an .820 percentage. They were backed by Marius Russo, Johnny Niggeling, and Kemp Wicker.

The four-game sweeps in the play-offs were imposing in that they occurred over teams with talented lineups of their own. Syracuse met the Newark challenge with future Major Leaguers Harry Craft, Eddie Joost, Al Glossop, Frank McCormack, Dee Moore, Lee Gamble, and Johnny VanderMeer, the pitcher who would throw back-to-back no-hitters in the Majors the following year. They were no match for the Bears, who outscored them 20–4.

The Baltimore Orioles got the IL finals by defeating Montreal in five games (4–1). Baltimore had Ab Wright (37 homers), George Puccinelli (24 homers), Joe Martin (22 homers), Les Powers (21 homers), and Woody Abernathy (21 homers), with sure-gloved Chet "Wimpy" Wilburn at short and Bill Lohrman and Hy Vandenberg on the mound. The Birds were shot down in four straight, with Newark outscoring the powerful O's, 25–17.

In the Junior World Series, the Bears met the Columbus Red Birds, kings of the American Association. Columbus had a strong outfield, with Enos Slaughter (who hit .382 that year) in right, Johnny Rizzo (.358) in left, and Lynn King (.302) in center.

In the infield, Columbus had Dick Siebert (.318) at first, Jimmy Jordan (.285) at second, Jimmy "Skeeter" Webb (.286) at short, and Justin Stein (.272) at third.

On the mound, the Red Birds had Bill McGee (17 wins, 7 losses), Max Lanier (10–4), Max Macon (21–12), John Chambers (12–7), and Mort Cooper (13–13).

The Birds came in tough and got tougher, winning the first three games of the best-of-seven series, by scores of 5–4, 5–4, and 6–3. Then Newark flexed its muscles and swept the final four games by scores of 8–1, 1–0, 10–1, and 10–4.

The Bears hit .299 in the regular season with 285 doubles, 81 triples, and 142 homeruns. They led the league in double plays turned with 159, and their home record was 60–16 at Ruppert Stadium. They went undefeated (8–0) at home during the play-offs to finish at 68–16.

When the Yankees sold their Newark franchise to the Cubs in 1950, and the Cubbies transferred the team to Springfield, Massachusetts, that was pretty much it for baseball in New Jersey's largest city. But for eighteen years, it was glorious.

Other teams with better won-lost percentages but without the history, color, and legendary status reserved for the '37 Newark Bears include:

Full Season (*Source:* Bill Weiss)

Year	Team	League	Record	Percentage
1922	Enid	Western Association	105–27	.796
1902	Corsicana	Texas League	88–23	.793
1920	Tampa	Florida State League	79–27	.745
1941	Wilson	Coastal Plain League	87–30	.744
1905	Pittsburgh	Missouri Valley League	75–46	.743
1903	Jersey City	Eastern League	92–32	.742
1951	Hazard	Mountain States League	93–33	.738
1949	Stroudsburg	North Atlantic League	101–36	.737
1907	Wichita	Western Association	98–35	.737
1939	Sanford	Florida State League	98–35	.737

Short Season

Year	Team	League	Record	Percentage
1979	Paintsville	Appalachian League	52–13	.800
1989	Great Falls	Pioneer League	53–14	.791
1975	Rangers	Gulf Coast League	41–12	.774
1990	Elizabethton	Appalachian League	51–15	.773
1985	Great Falls	Pioneer League	54–16	.771
1974	Oneonta	New York-Penn League	53–16	.768
1986	Oneonta	New York-Penn League	59–18	.766
1973	Kingsport	Appalachian League	53–17	.757
1971	Royals	Gulf Coast League	40–13	.755
1974	Bristol	Appalachian League	52–17	.754
1926	Crisfield	Eastern Shore League	63–21	.750

The 1934 Los Angeles Angels

If the East Coast kings were the Newark Bears, then their West Coast counterparts had to have been the Los Angeles Angels, particularly the 1934 version.

It may have been tougher for the Angels to dominate the Pacific Coast League than it was for the Bears to annihilate the International League because the Bears were fed by the Yankees and the Angels were more or less an independent team fueled by the Chicago Cubs.

The Angels ran roughshod over the PCL from its beginning, winning the first PCL title ever (1903) en route to a league record of fourteen championships through 1956.

PCL all-time statistical bests are a "who's who" of Angels' talent, thanks in part to the home launching pad known as Wrigley Field: Angels won 11 batting championships and 12 homerun titles as well as 7 Earned Run Average crowns and had 14 leaders in won–lost percentage.

All-time Angel heroes included outfielder Jigger Statz, who played a record eighteen years with the same team (the Angels) and lead the PCL in runs four times, hits once, triples twice, and stolen bases three times; catcher Truck Hannah, who played twelve years with Los Angeles; outfielder Dixie Carroll, who stole 80 bases in 1922–23, and the following stars: outfielder Hiram Carlyle drove in 100 in 1935 and hit .339 in 1936; Pop Dillon starred at first base for eleven years; Frank Sigafoos drove in 103 runs in 1930; "Jittery Joe" Berry pitched in 258 games in six seasons; Doc Crandall won 213 games in eleven seasons; John Salveson went 21–7 in 1936; Ripper Collins hit .334 with a league-leading 26 homers and PCL best 128 RBI in 1939; Harl Maggert won two triples titles; Lou "The Mad Russian" Novikoff won the PCL triple crown at L.A. with a 1940 performance of .363, 41 homers, 171 RBI, after hitting .452 in a short run the previous year, and Steve Bilko demolished PCL pitching from 1955 to 1957.

The 1934 Halos went 134–50, a .733 winning percentage, under manager Jack Lelivelt, a superb player in his day as well, batting .416 in 659 at bats for Omaha of the Western Association in 1921. Lelivelt won 346 games in three years (1933–35) at the Angels' helm, and was on board for seven seasons. The 1934 Halos were manned by outfielders Marv Gudat (hit .319, with 125 RBI, and 43 steals); Frank Demaree (a league-topping .382, 45 homers, 173 RBI, and 190 runs scored); and Statz (.324, 61 stolen bases, and a league-leading 13 triples).

First baseman Jim Oglesby hit .312, second baseman Jimmy Reese (now, at age eighty-five, a California Angels' conditioning coach) hit .311, third baseman Gene Lillard banged 27 homers, shortstop Carl Dittmar hit .294, and catcher Gilly Campbell hit .305 with 17 four-baggers.

On the Angels' hill were Fay Thomas at 28–4, Louis Garland and Ernie Meola with 20 wins each, and J. Millard Campbell with 19 wins.

To top off the season, the '34 Angels defeated a formidable team of PCL all-stars—including Joe DiMaggio, Ox Eckhardt, Smead Jolley, and '37 Bear Babe Dahlgren— four games to two.

Angel glory died in 1958, when the Dodgers moved west from Brooklyn, and the Los Angeles franchise was relocated to Spokane. Three years later, Los Angeles got another franchise, in the Majors' American League. Out of reverence—and as a marketing ploy, owner Gene Autry named his new team the Angels . . . but it never did recapture the magic the original Angels brought to Los Angeles.

The Baltimore Orioles

Another of those franchises that has been deified over the years is the Minor League Baltimore Orioles, an International League power by virtue of their winning seven consecutive pennants from 1919 through 1925.

They were owned by Jack Dunn, a former player, who came to Baltimore as a player-manager in 1907 and led the team to a title in 1908.

He built the team from scratch, plucking Doc Adkins (three-time twenty-game winner), Lefty Russell, and Rube Vickers, all top pitchers, from obscurity. His eye for talent is legendary.

In 1914, Dunn signed nineteen-year-old left-handed pitching phenom George Herman "Babe" Ruth to a contract. Ruth got a $600 bonus for his signature, and paid it back in his first start, a shutout against Buffalo. Just four months into the season, Dunn sold Ruth to the Boston Red Sox for $2,900 and the BoSox sent Babe to Providence (also in the International League), where he finished the season with a 22–9 mark before being called up by Boston in September. That year Dunn also sold off Ernie Shore and Ben Egan.

By 1920, Dunn had created one of the strongest teams in baseball. The Orioles not only won the Little World Series (defeating St. Paul of the A.A.) but also took the Major League New York Yankees and Babe Ruth 1–0 in an exhibition game.

In 1911, the O's went 115–49, and they followed it up with a 111–53 mark in winning their fifth straight flag in 1923, and they won 117 games for title number six, in 1924.

Dunn continued his knack of finding players, honing their talents, then selling them to the Major League teams for big profits. He did this with Jack Bentley for $72,500 in 1923, and Max Bishop for $25,000 in 1924.

Lefty Grove pitched five years for the O's, twice winning 27 games en route to a 109–36 mark. Dunn then sold Grove to the Philadelphia Athletics for a record $100,600 in 1924.

Before Dunn's sudden heart attack and death in 1928, he had made twenty deals that netted him a profit of more than $400,000 . . . not exactly chump change in those days. He had gone from penniless dreamer in 1916 to millionaire sportsman by 1928.

Dunn was gone, but Baltimore continued to attract top players who responded with record-shattering performances.

In 1930, Joe Hauser had a dream year for Baltimore, with a .313 average, record-setting 63 homers, 443 total bases, 173 runs scored, and 175 RBI in 168 games.

On June 1, 1932, outfielder "Buzz" Arlett smacked four homers in a game at Reading. On July 4 the same season, Arlett victimized Reading for another four-homer game, this time at Baltimore. That season, Arlett led the IL with 54 homers and 144 RBI.

Other O's stars included two-time batting king Dick Porter; batting leaders Julius "Moose" Solters, George Puccinelli, Murray "Red" Howell, and Sherm Lollar. Other Baltimore heroes included John Gill (.344 in 1931); Jake Jaconsen (.404 in 1920); Fritz Maisel (13 years with the O's, and a .336, 44 doubles, 63 stolen base year in 1920); Johnny Ogden (a pitcher who won 191 games in eight years with the O's); and Rube Parnham (won 33 games in 1923, 28 games in 1919). Parnham also gained International League immortality by winning 20 consecutive decisions in 1923.

A great two-way player for the O's was Jack Bentley, who hit a loop-leading .371 in 1920 while pitching to a 16–3 record and a league-leading 2.11 ERA. The following year he hit .412, led the league in hits, homers, and doubles, and went 12–1 on the mound, and in 1922, he went 13–2 with a 1.73 ERA while batting .351. Bentley became known as "The Babe Ruth of the International League," as early as three years after Ruth had been peddled by the Orioles.

The Baltimore Minor League experience ended at the end of the 1953 season, when the American League's St. Louis Browns shifted their franchise to Baltimore and assumed the name Orioles. Jack Dunn, Jr., the O's owner, was paid $350,000 for the regional rights.

The Minneapolis Millers

If ever there was a hitter's team—or a hitter's paradise, it was the combination of the Minneapolis Millers and Nicollet Park.

Feats of batting strength seemed to go on forever, from the late 1890s to the late 1950s.

Minneapolis lost Minor League ball when the Minnesota Twins moved from Washington, DC, to bring The Show to the "Twin Cities" in 1961. But for the Millers, their hitters seemed to always be putting on a big show.

Some of their batter's box heroes include the following: outfielder Buzz Arlett bombed 41 homers for the Millers at age thirty-five in 1934 in only 116 games, and followed that up with 25 the following year; Babe Barna played five years in Minneapolis and hit 121 homers; Joe "Unser Choe" Hauser bombed out 69 homeruns for the '33 Millers and belted 208 roundtrippers in five seasons; former Negro League star Ray Dandridge spent four years in Minneapolis, winning a Rookie-of-the-Year award and MVP award, batting .318 in his Millers career; Joe Mowry set a league mark for runs scored with 175 in 1932; infielder David Altizer spent nine years with the Millers, leading the A.A. in steals twice and runs scored four times; first baseman Zeke Bonura hit .366 in 1941; third sacker Buck Fausett starred for three seasons; Showboat Fisher hit .350 in 1925; Earl Smith patrolled the outfield nine seasons and hit 173 homers; Jim Middleton won 20 games for the 1926 Millers; Henry Rondeau played twelve years in Minneapolis; Spence Harris played eight years and hit .337; Bob Lennon slammed 31 four-baggers in 1955; Phil Weintraub averaged .340 and 30 homers a year; Moose Werden hit .428 in 1895; Chuck Workman bombed 41 four-baggers in 1949; Ab Wright won the A.A. triple crown in 1940 with a .369, 39 homer, 159 RBI year; Walt Tauscher pitched in 386 games during his nine-year Millers career and went 21–7 in 1934.

Still more batting bombers were: Ted Williams, on his

last stop before tearing up the American League (.366); Babe Ganzel; Joe Mowry; Art Ruble; Gavvy Cravath; and in his last Minor League tune-up before reaching Major League stardom . . . Willie Mays (.477 in 1951).

And just before the Twins robbed Minneapolis of the Minor League experience, Orlando Cepeda hit .309 with 25 homers and 108 RBI in 1957; Pumpsie Green hit .320 and Chuck Tanner hit .319 in 1959; and future Hall-of-Famer Carl Yastrzemski finished second in the league in batting with a .339 mark and 7 homers in 1960.

The Millers took two Junior World Series titles and made the play-offs eleven times in seventeen years, bringing Minnesota, and all fans of number-crunching baseball offense, bruised baseballs and dented fences.

The Minneapolis Millers . . . the original bash brothers.

The Rochester Red Wings

Beginning play in 1877, the Rochester Red Wings have been in operation in the Minors for 114 years, with the exception of 1881 through 1884, and 1890 when they were a Major League franchise, and 1893 and 1894 when fire destroyed their field. But since 1895, when they joined the Eastern League (renamed the International League in 1913), the Red Wings have been a nonstop member of the loop for ninety-five years.

Over the decades, the team has been nicknamed the Rochesters, the Live Oaks, the Brownies (in honor of Rochester resident George Eastman's new camera invention), the Champs, the Jingoes, the Beau Brummels, the Hustlers, the Colts, the Tribe, and the Red Wings (in 1928).

Rochester (nicknamed the Rochesters) debuted in the International League in 1885 (then called the New York State League), and the team initiated what is believed to be the first "Ladies Day," June 10, 1885.

A 73–44 season brought Rochester its first pennant in 1899, the first of fifteen first-place finishes for the franchise.

Rochester spent one year in the Majors, the 1890 season, during which time they were nicknamed the Bronchos.

In 1902, Broncho first baseman Harry O'Hagan registered the first unassisted triple play in professional baseball history against Jersey City. O'Hagan, who was named Rochester manager earlier that day, dove to catch a short bunt off the bat of catcher Johnnie Butler. He then sprinted to first base to catch shortstop Mack Dooley, and raced to second base to nail rightfielder George Shoch, who had wandered past third base.

The 1916 team featured pitcher Carmen Hill, believed to be the first player to wear glasses on the field. He led the team in victories *and* defeats, going 14–16. The next season, pitcher Al Schacht went 12–21.

The 1924 team defeated Newark in one contest by a 30–2 margin, outhitting the Bears 26–6.

In 1928, the St. Louis Cardinals purchased the team, changed the nickname to Red Wings and won the IL flag. The team also won pennants in 1929, 1930, and 1931, copping the Junior World Series titles in '30 and '31 with victories over Louisville and St. Paul, respectively.

In 1939, Billy Southworth returned as manager and went on to defeat the powerful Newark Bears in a twelve-inning thriller (led by Earl Crabtree's three-run homer in the ninth) to capture the Junior World Series.

Luke Easter hit .302 for the team and blasted fourteen homers at the age of forty-five in 1960. Easter made his last appearance for Rochester as a pinch hitter in 1964, at age forty-nine.

In 1971, Joe Altobelli's first year as Red Wings skipper, Rochester took another Junior World Series, taking Denver in the finals.

On opening day, 1982, the Wings fell with a thud, losing 23–1 to Tidewater before a Silver Stadium crowd of 7,147.

Following another Governor's Cup finals appearance—they lost to Richmond—they celebrated a big season by completing a $4.5 million renovation of Silver Stadium, with 12,500 seats, rebuilt foundation, and new wine and beer garden.

One endearing Red Wings tradition is the "Knot Hole Gang," which began in 1927. The Rochester Knot Hole Gang was originated to allow boys and girls under the age of fourteen a chance to come out and see baseball—a dozen games a year at the price of one dollar a year. Members who have Knot Hole cards are allowed in to see special games, and the one price takes care of the entire season. Sixty years ago, that price was a nickel, but even at a buck, this is the greatest bargain in sports.

Rochester has a long history of stars in uniform, a few of whom are presented below.

Frederick Lewis hit .412 in 1887, and teammate Bob Barr followed in 1888 by winning 35 games with a 1.58 ERA.

In 1900, shortstop Frank Bonner committed an unbelievable (unbelievably bad) 104 errors, an all-time, unapproached record.

Wally Pipp blasted 15 homers in 1914.

George "High Pockets" Kelly hit .356 and blasted 15 homers in 1919, Maurice Archdeacon hit .325, .321, and .357 for Rochester, while teammate Albert Head consistently hit over .300.

The 1929 Wings won the IL pennant and set a defensive mark that still stands, completing 225 double plays, thanks to the sure infield gloves of "Rip" Collins at first, "Specs" Torporcer at second, Heinie Sand at short, and Joe "Poison" Brown at third. Collins also hit a ton, driving in 180 runs the following season, at the same time leading the league with a .376 average. Another hero, later to be a beloved Red Wings skipper, was Billy "the Kid" Southworth, who hit .349 in '29, following a .361 mark the previous season.

The 1930 Wings were led by "Rip" Collins, who drove in his 180 runs, and by Pepper Martin, who made lifetime fans by diving headfirst into first base to leg out hits and into other bags to take the extra base while hitting .363. Southworth hit .370.

Stan "The Man" Musial spent 54 games with the 1941 Wings and finished at .326.

Albert "Red" Schoendeinst took the batting title at age twenty by hitting .337 in 1943.

Merv Rettenmund took the MVP in 1968 and hit .331 with 104 RBI in 114 games.

In 1970 and 1971, Don Baylor hit .327 and .313, while hitting a two-year total of 42 homers with 202 RBI.

Bobby Grich was the league's MVP in 1971, thanks to a .336, 32 homers, 83 RBI, and 124 runs scored in 130 games.

Mike Boddicker won 32 games from 1981 to 1983, and a teammate on the '81 squad, Cal Ripken, Jr., won the IL's Rookie of the Year trophy for his .288, 23 homer, 75 ribbie performance.

Jim Traber blasted 21 homers in 1987.

Steve Finley hit .314 and stole 20 bases in 1988 as teammate Craig Worthington belted 16 homers.

Other Rochester heroes include batting leaders George Simmons, Bob Fothergill, Vernal Jones, Don Richmond, Bill Virdon, and Jim Frey.

The San Francisco Seals

Baseball by the Bay probably began with the Eagle Baseball Club, a group of ballplaying tradesmen who engaged a team called the Red Rovers on November 29, 1859. The score was tied at 33-all, when the Rovers forfeited the game by walking off the field in protest of an alleged illegal delivery by an Eagle pitcher.

The legendary Cincinnati Redstockings came to town in 1869 and won two barnstorming games by scores of 35–4 and 58–4, to keep their winning streak alive at 42 games (it eventually ran to 56 games).

Teams from San Francisco bounced back and forth between independent status and membership in the California League and the California State League until 1903, when the Pacific Coast League was formed with San Francisco as a charter member.

The 1909 Seals of the Pacific Coast League went 132–80 to take the crown, their first of twelve flags. Led by pitcher Cack Henley, who won 31 games and won a 24-inning 1–0 pitching duel against Jimmy Wiggs of the Oakland Oaks, the Seals featured Heinie Melchior (the PCL batting leader at .298), Duffy Lewis, Frank "Ping" Bodie (who led the PCL in homers the following year with 30), and Kid Mohler.

Harry Heilmann's clutch hitting (.364) sparked the Seals to their second flag in 1915 (118–89), and Walter "Biff" Schaller led the PCL with twenty dingers.

The 1925 Seals won their third title in four years, with a 128–71 mark, led by Paul Waner who won the batting title (.401); Pitcher Doug McWeeney had the loop's best ERA at 2.70, while going 20–5; and Marty Griffith won 16 and lost only 4.

That same year, the team from Vernon, California, picked up stakes and moved to San Francisco to compete with the Seals. Sharing Recreation Park with the Seals, the new team called itself the Mission Reds. Recreation Park, affectionately called "Old Rec," had a tantalizingly short 235-foot distance from home plate to the right-field wall. But the wall was topped with a 50-foot fence that cut many would-be homers into mere singles.

The 1927 and '28 teams were propelled by Smead Jolley, who won back-to-back batting crowns at .397 and .404 and won the PCL homer title in '28 with 45 roundtrippers and drove in 188 runs.

The 1929 club featured an all-San Francisco-born infield: Gus Suhr at first base, Ike Caveney at second, Babe Pinelli at third, and Frankie Crosetti at short. In one game, Pinelli went 6 for 6 with 3 grand slam homeruns.

On April 7, 1931, the Seals opened a new, million-dollar ballpark, Seals Stadium, and the home team responded by winning the second-half PCL flag, thanks largely to Sam

Gibson's pitching—28–12, 204 strikeouts, and a 2.24 ERA.

The DiMaggio brothers captured the City by the Bay during the 1930s, with Vince, Dom, and Joe taking their turns ripping PCL pitching. Joe, of course, made his mark by going on a record-setting 61-game hitting streak in 1933, en route to a .340 and 169 RBI season, and in four years in San Francisco, never batted below .323. He was PCL MVP in 1935, and Dom was the MVP in 1939. Vince hit .333 in '33. Curiously, Joe DiMaggio only fetched $25,000 in his sale to the New York Yankees. In his final season (1935) with the Seals, Joe D. took manager Lefty O'Doul's batting tips to heart and increased his batting average to .398, only one point off Mission's Ox Eckhardt's league-leading .399 mark. DiMaggio's heroics led the Seals to another second-half crown.

O'Doul, who also starred in the PCL as a hitter, led the Seals to two pennants in seventeen years as skipper, and is generally credited with introducing baseball to Japan in the 1920s. He also took a team of Major League all-stars to Japan in 1934, a team that included Babe Ruth, Lou Gehrig, Charlie Gehringer, Earl Averill, Lefty Gomez, Bing Miller, and a catcher named Moe Berg. The players gave instruction to the Japanese athletes and played exhibitions against Far East teams. And Berg, a journeyman receiver, made history by taking reconnaisance photos of Japanese installations. These photos were later used in Jimmy Doolittle's raids over Tokyo during World War II, with further information on Japan and its culture provided by OSS spy, Moe Berg.

Larry Jansen became the last pitcher to win 30 games in the PCL as he went 30–6 with a 1.57 ERA in 1946. That year, the Seals drew an incredibly high 670,563 fans, who delighted in watching the fine play of Ferris Fain at first, Hugh Luby at second, and Frenchy Uhault and Neill Sheridan in the outfield.

In 1952, following financial reverses, the Seals went

public, as the city of San Francisco took over the team and fans bought shares in "The Little Corporation."

In 1957, manager Joe Gordon piloted the Seals, then a Red Sox affiliate, to a last championship (101–67). Ken Aspromonte led the PCL in batting at .334, and Wil Abernathie went 13–2 on the hill.

The final Minor League game played in San Francisco was a circus. With the pennant won, the Seals played the Sacramento Solons in a doubleheader. In the nightcap, Gordon inserted himself as the starting second baseman (he went 2 for 3, and even came in to pitch an inning), put diminutive center fielder Albie Pearson on the mound as the starting pitcher (he played five positions that game and was the losing pitcher), and generally had the team in stitches during the 14–7 loss.

When the New York Giants made the move west in 1958, Minor League baseball was finished in San Francisco. The Seals moved operations to Phoenix. But, with the proposed move of the San Francisco Giants down the coast to San Jose-Santa Clara, or elsewhere, will Minor League baseball return to town? The outlook seems to be good, with a chance to recapture past glories—if the Oakland A's will concede territorial rights to a Little Show franchise.

Other Seals heroes included: pitcher Charles "Spider" Baum, who won 20 or more games for four consecutive years from 1914 to 1917); third baseman Willie Kamm, who was sold to the Pittsburgh Pirates for the unheard of sum of $125,000 in 1922; Pete Compton, .324 in 1923; Ted Norbert, 30 homers and 163 RBI in 1938; Dick Holder, ten years with the Seals, 24 triples in 1939; and Les Fleming, 25 homers in 1950. Another former Seal was shortstop Leo Righetti, father of Yankee relief pitcher Dave Righetti. In 1991 Dave will follow in his father's spikes playing for San Francisco . . . as Dave signed to hurl for the Giants.

The Buffalo Bisons

With the exception of an eight-year span (1971–78) when they were out of professional baseball, the Buffalo Bisons have operated for 113 years, making the play-offs on nineteen occasions. Beginning with the 1877 independent club that played a series of exhibition games against teams from all over the country, the Bisons have become a Minor League legend.

In 1878, the Bisons joined the International Association—baseball's initial organized Minor League—and, beginning a winning tradition, captured the I.A. crown, going 24–8, thanks to the great pitching of Pud Galvin and the hitting of Dave Force, while also defeating National League teams in 10 of 17 exhibition matches.

In 1879, Buffalo was promoted to the National League where it stayed until 1886.

Returning to the Minors in 1886, the Bisons called Olympic Park their home, a wooden stadium they utilized for 72 years. Early pitching heroes were Mike Walsh (54 wins) in 1886–87, and Mickey Lehane (hit .392) in 1887.

Buffalo made a second run at the Majors by joining the short-lived Players League in 1890. Alas, the circuit that was run by the players flamed out in one season, and by 1891, Buffalo was back in the Little Show with the Eastern Association, a forerunner to the International League.

After a switch to the Western League in 1899, Buffalo had its third strike at the Majors with its 1900 season as a member of the new American League. Once again, it was a one-year shot, and in 1901, Buffalo was back in the Eastern League, where it stayed (the Eastern League became the International League in 1913) until 1970.

A fourth Major League run for Buffalo occurred in 1914 and 1915 as a member of the Federal League, but that team, the Buffalo Feds (also called the Electrics and the Blues), ran in competition to the Bisons, who suffered severe losses but stayed in operation.

The Bisons won titles in four years: 1916 (led by Les Channell at .329 and King Bader, who won 23 games); 1927 (behind Del Bissonette at .365 with 31 homers and 167 RBI, Andy Cohen at .353 and 118 ribbies, and Leo Mangum with 21 wins); 1936 (with John Dickshot at .359 and 112 RBI, Frank McGowan's 23 homers and 45 doubles, and John Wilson's 14 games won) as an independent; and in 1938, when they finally got a Major League Club to act as parent, the Philadelphia A's.

Their first flag for a Big League parent was in 1949 for the A's, who came back after a ten-year absence. The 90–64 team was led by Bob Hooper (19 wins and 3 losses), Coaker Triplett (.322), Gene Markland (25 homers), and Ray Coleman (113 RBI).

In 1961, while finishing third in the International League, the Bisons put it all together in the play-offs to sweep Charleston four games to none, and defeat Rochester four games to one, en route to a Governor's Cup (Junior World Series) championship. That '61 squad had its heroes in Ted Savage (.325, 24 homers, and 31 stolen bases), Don Micher (24 homers), Felix Torrez (24 homers and 32 doubles), and Max Surkont (8–4 record and 3.22 ERA).

In 1970, the franchise was shifted to Winnipeg, and after ninety-three years, Buffalo was without a team.

In 1979, Buffalo reacquired a franchise and was now placed in the new Eastern League, where they remained until joining the Triple-A American Association in 1985.

In 1988, the Bisons' 102nd season, they left friendly War Memorial Stadium for a brand new ballpark, Pilot Field, and set a Minor League attendance mark by drawing 1,186,651 fans during the season. The team has drawn more than one million fans three consecutive years . . . an all-time Minor League record.

Some of the more notable Bisons stars over the years include: Vic Wertz (.301 in 1946), Luke Easter (113 homers and 343 RBI in three seasons from 1956 to 1958), Duke Carmel (35 homers in 1964), Johnny Bench (23 homers and 68 RBI in 98 games in 1967), Rick Lancellotti (41 homers and 107 RBI in 1979), Dwight Taylor (95 stolen bases in 1983), Daryl Boston (.303 and 38 steals in 1986), Fred Hutchinson (26–7 and 2.44 ERA in 1941), Dave Dravecky (13–7, 3.35 ERA in 1980), and Pete Filson (14–3 and 2.27 ERA in 1986), as well as Billy Pierce, Jose De-Leon, Jimmy Walsh, Cleon Jones, Jeff Moronko, Mark

Ryal, Benny Distefano, Otis Nixon, Steve Demeter, and Kelly Gruber.

The Toledo Mud Hens

Long before *"M*A*S*H"* had Corporal Maxwell Q. Klinger (actor Jamie Farr) slinging the virtues of Toledo's Mud Hens, baseball had become one with the Ohio City.

As early as 1876, Toledo had amateur teams playing within its city limits. By 1883, Toledo had entered the re-organized Northwestern League, winning the loop's first championship under the name Toledo Blue Stockings.

The year 1883 was significant in the annals of baseball as Toledo had on its roster the first known black to play Major League ball, Moses Fleetwood "Fleet" Walker. Walker, a tall, lanky catcher, was considered one of the finest all-around athletes in the nation. When the team was promoted to Major League status in 1884 by joining the American Association, Walker became the first black player in the Bigs, sixty-three years before Jackie Robinson. Walker retired from the game in 1891, but he broke new ground while with Toledo.

When Toledo dropped out of the A.A. at the end of the season, the team moved to the Western League, where it lasted only a half-year, beginning a two-and-a-half-year absence from Organized Baseball.

In 1888 as a member of the ten-team Tri-State League, Toledo came back to baseball as the Toledo Maumees (they played ball next to the Maumee River), jumping to the International League in 1889 and to the American Association again in 1890.

In 1892, the team changed its name to the Toledo Black Pirates, which changed to the White Stockings in 1894. The Toledo Terriers were the local team in 1895, and in 1896 the club was known as the Swamp Angels.

It was in 1896 that the Mud Hens officially became the name of the Toledo club, deriving the name from the wild ducks and mud hens that inhabited the marshy and muddy Bay View Park the team called home.

In 1909, Toledo moved to Swayne Field, a structure of wood and concrete, built at a cost of $125,000. The Hens ushered in the park playing an eighteen-inning game, which they lost to Columbus, 12–11 in front of 9,350 fans.

In 1914, the Mud Hens moved to Cleveland to become the Bear Cats and then the Spiders, but in 1916 Toledo had the team again, this time calling itself the Iron Men, only to change back, in 1919, to the Mud Hens. The only deviation from Hens occurred in 1953, when for a year, the team became the Glass Sox. Since then, however, the Mud Hens have ruled the Toledo roost.

Toledo was part of the American Association (Minor League) from 1916 to 1952 before switching to the International League in 1965, where it now resides.

Their first pennant was recorded in 1927 with a 101–67 record under the guidance of future "genius" manager, Casey Stengel. The club was led on the field by outfielders Bobby Veach and Irish Meusel and Everett Scott at short.

In more than 100 years, the Hens have won several league titles with such players wearing their uniforms as: Perry "Moose" Werden (hit .394 in 1889); Red McCall (won 19 games in 1920); Beco Lebourveau (.377 in 1926 and .380 in 1930); Pip Koehler (.323 in 1930); Bill Knickerbocker (69 doubles in 1932); Mike Powers (.336 in 1934, .339 in 1935); Glenn McQuillen (.329 in 1948); Cactus Johnson (12 wins at the age of forty-one in 1937); Jerry Witte (.312 with 46 homers in 1946); Greg "Boomer" Wells (.336, 28 homers, 107 RBI in 1982); Frank Viola (3.88 ERA in 1982); Tim Teufel (27 homers, 100 RBI, 103 runs scored in 1983); Kirk Gibson (a six-game rehab assignment in 1987—.235); Andre David (.328 in 1986); and Steve Searcy (13 wins in 1988).

The Toledo Mud Hens currently call Ned Skeldon Stadium their home and are affiliates of the Detroit Tigers, playing in the International League.

The Columbus Mudcats

Not to be confused with the Columbus, Ohio, Clippers of the International League, this Southern League team is all South, hailing from Georgia and using that Southern influence often in their choice of nicknames.

The nickname Mudcats is relatively new to this Georgia franchise, a moniker that was chosen from more than 600 entries in a "name the team" contest. The name comes from a fish found throughout the Chattahoochie River that borders the westernmost border of Columbus, Georgia. In fact, Golden Park, site of all Mudcat home games, is situated near the banks of the river.

But the current Southern League version of baseball in Columbus has deep roots, roots that go back to 1885, when the city of 20,000 joined Atlanta, Birmingham, New Orleans, Memphis, and others to form a new Southern League.

That early team went through three managers and weathered tough days, but the city and its team prevailed.

The 1910 squad, led by first baseman-manager James C. Fox, won the South Atlantic League (Sally League) title, the first of twelve crowns in 105 years. Nicknamed the Foxes (in honor of Fox), the team repeated as champions in 1911 and 1915, and won the crown again in 1926 in the newly formed Southeastern League. The Foxes were led by pitcher Roy Radabaugh, who won 93 games, including a 25-win campaign in 1909.

Sunday baseball came to Columbus on May 17, 1936, which had previously been an open date on the schedule. The '36 team was led by Howard Christ, who pitched to a 20–9 record.

Night baseball hit town two years later when the parent St. Louis Cardinals insisted that lights be installed at Golden.

The 1939 Columbus Red Birds won the championship and were led by future Dodger manager Walt Alston, who hit .323, and Bill Seinsoth, who went 48–27 during his

Columbus career and pitched an 11-inning no-hitter, which he lost in 13 innings to Augusta.

The 1941 team saw Stan Ferens win 19 games with a 2.58 ERA.

The 1965 Columbus Confederate Yankees won the Southern League championship behind the stellar play of MVP Roy White (.300 with 19 homers).

The 1979 club set an all-time Columbus record with 138 homeruns and won the Eastern Division flag, only to lose the Southern League play-offs to Nashville.

The 1986 Columbus Astros broke a fifteen-year championship drought the hard way, finishing dead last in the first half of the season, then rallying to win the second half title, earning the right to face (and defeat) Jacksonville for the divisional flag, before whipping Huntsville to win the Southern League championship.

Among Columbus' stars were: Enos "Country" Slaughter, who developed his style of hustle there in 1936 while hitting .325 and driving in 118 runs; Herb Bremer hit .305 with 20 homers and 101 RBI in 1937; Bob Gibson, who spent a month there in 1957; Ken Caminiti hit .300 in 1986 and .325 in 1987; Gerald Young stole 54 bases in 1986; Charlie Kerfeld went 14–9 in 1984; Glenn Davis blasted 25 homers in 1983; Erik Anthony hit .300 with 28 homers in 1989; Bill Doran hit .281 in 1981; Johnny Ray hit .324 in 1980; Danny Heep hit .327 with 21 homers in 1979; Joe Sambito went 12–9 with 140 strikeouts over a three-year career; and J.R. Richard; Mark Bailey; Pat Perry; Bert Roberge; and Pete Ladd.

With their distinctive logo, the smiling gray mudcat fish squeezing forward out of the Columbus "C", their colorful name, and long, illustrious past, the Columbus Mudcats have earned their place among Minor League baseball's elite teams to be remembered.

The Denver Bears

The Minor League history of Denver, Colorado, goes back to 1886 and a pennant-winning team in the Western

League (54–26), the first of seven titles covering forty-four teams fielded over the next fifty-eight years.

When the Western League gained steam and began new operations in 1900, the Denver Bears, also called the Grizzlies, won that flag by going 61–44.

One reason that Denver failed to put a team in Organized Baseball every year—indeed, Denver was baseball-less from 1932 to 1947 with the exception of a one-year try in 1941—was that league rivals, tired of losing money on the road, voted both Colorado entries (Denver and Pueblo) out of the Western League.

In 1947, however, Denver baseball witnessed a renaissance in another run with the Western League, with Merchants Park as their home grounds.

Entering into an agreement with the New York Yankees, giving the Bronx Bombers two Bears on the Farm (Newark was the other), Denver was led by Loren Babe, a third baseman who hit .297.

Bears Stadium opened on what was once a landfill in 1948, and the Bears made the play-offs behind Basil Beringhele (.326) and fourteen-game winners Hank Williams and Ken Polivka.

The 1949 Bears moved on to affiliation with the Boston Braves, and Walt Linen (.325) and Chuck Tanner (.313) lead the offense while Ernie Johnson (now a sportscaster for the Atlanta Braves) went 15–5 with a 2.37 ERA to lead the mound corps.

Popular manager Andy Cohen led the 1952 Bears, a Pirates affiliate that year, to a pennant behind the stingy pitching of Alberto Osorio (20–6) and Barney Schultz (17–6), and the power hitting of Bill Pinckard (35 homers and 108 RBI in only 404 at bats). Attendance hit 461,419.

The 1954 season marked Denver's finale in the Western League, and Cohen once again directed the team to a pennant. Top players that year were Pidge Brown (.333 and 109 RBI), Reno DeBenedetti (.329), George Prescott (.311 and 121 RBI), Rocky Ippolito (131 RBI), Earl Weaver (.282

and 102 walks), and pitchers Bob Garber (19–8) and Chuck Garmon (16–7).

In 1955, the Bears moved up to the Triple-A American Association and a re-affiliation with the Yankees. Ralph Houk managed the team that featured sluggers Lou Skizas (.348), Dick Tellebach (.309), Herbie Plews (.302), Marv Throneberry (.273 and a league-leading 36 homers and 117 RBI), and Whitey Herzog (21 homers and 98 RBI). On the hill were Don Larsen, who went 9–1 on the mound and .326 with 6 homers in 46 trips to the plate before being recalled by New York.

The 1956 Bears were awesome, even after the Yankees depleted them with August call-ups. The Bears that year were led by future pinstripe heroes: Tony Kubek (.331); Bobby Richardson (.314); Throneberry (.314, 42 homers and 145 RBI); and Woody Held (35 homers and 125 RBI)— the Bombing Bears hit .298 as a team, while averaging 6 runs a game. Ralph Terry (13–4) and Jim DePaolo (13–5) were the top hurlers.

The 1957 club went on a 32 wins and 6 losses run, during a 46–14 last-half pennant drive, to finish at 90–64 en route to a Junior World Series championship—they swept Minneapolis in four, took St. Paul in six games, and bested Buffalo in five to take the title. Ryne Duren threw a no-hitter in his first Denver appearance and wound up 13–2; Mark Freeman went 12–6; Norm Sieburn hit .349 with 24 homers and 118 RBI; Throneberry blasted another 40 homers; Zeke Bella, Johnny Blanchard, Jim Pisoni, and Curt Roberts all hit better than .300; and Rance Pless slugged 4 grand slams in 33 days.

In 1963, as the American Association disbanded, the Bears moved on to the Pacific Coast League as a Braves affiliate. The team finished 18 games below .500 but hitting was bright with Lou Klimchock at .352, Steve Demeter at .342, and Chico Salmon at .325.

The 1965 Bears were filled with Minnesota Twins prospects, and the team finished 83–62 behind Ted Uhlaender's

PCL-leading .340; Andy Kosco's .327, 27 homers, and 116 RBI; and Jim Merritt's 13–8 mark on the hill.

In 1968 Billy Martin became manager of the Bears, taking over a 7–22 team that went 65–50 with Billy at the helm. The club was led by Graig Nettles (.297, 22 homers, and 83 RBI) and Bob Oliver (.297, 20 homers, 93 RBI) while ageless wonder Art Fowler was the bullpen stopper at age forty-six with a 1.93 ERA.

Back in the American Association in 1969, the team was led by Jim Holt's .339 and Minnie Mendoza's .333, and the name of the home ballpark was changed from Bears Stadium to Mile High Stadium with the expansion from one to three decks in right field.

The 1970 Bears won the A.A. Western Division crown as an affiliate of the Washington Senators. Fowler continued to amaze at age forty-eight, going 9–5 with a 1.59 ERA and 15 saves.

Richie Scheinblum made an assault on .400 in 1971, finishing the season at .388 to lead Denver to an A.A. title.

An affiliation with the Houston Astros brought J.R. Richard to Denver in 1974, and he responded by pitching thirty-two consecutive innings without allowing an earned run.

The Bears went on a three-year tear from 1975 to 1977, winning three pennants. In 1975, Lamar Johnson hit .336 and Steve Dunning went 15–9. In 1976 Roger Freed hit a Denver-record 42 homers, Andre Dawson hit .350 with 12 homers in 13 games, Warren Cromarties hit .311, and Pat Scanlon hit an incredible .786 in the play-offs to help Denver take the crown in six games from Omaha. In 1977 Moose Ortenzio blasted 40 homers and drove in 126 runs and Gary Roenicke hit .321.

The 1980 Bears began the season by winning 32 of its first 40 games and coasted to a pennant at 92–44. Minor League Player of the Year Tim Raines led the Bears with a .354 average, 77 stolen bases, and 105 runs scored, while future Japan League legend Randy Bass connected for 37 homers with 143 RBI, while batting .332. Tim Wallach also supplied power by smashing 36 homers and driving in 124 runs. Other heroes included Danny Briggs at .315, Art Gardner at .316, and Bobby Pate at .323.

Bryn Smith led the Denver play-off win in 1981 with a 15–5 mark and 3.09 ERA, while Terry Francona hit .352 and Dave Hostetler bombed 27 homers and drove in 103 runs, but Briggs beat that with 110 RBI.

In 1984, new owners purchased the Bears and renamed them the Denver Zephyrs. The team, now a member of the American Association, still carried that name with the hopes of transferring the moniker to a Major League team should Denver be selected for Big League status.

Pennants were earned in 1986 and 1987 under Milwaukee Brewers affiliation. The team was led in 1986 by Mike Felder (.363), and in 1987 by second baseman Billy Bates (.316 with 51 steals), Mark Knudsen (7–2 mark), and Paul Mirabella (5–1 with a 2.29 ERA). The Zephyrs seem destined to remain in Denver pending the National League's expansion decision, in which case, expert guessers surmise the nicknames Zephyrs or Bears will adorn the Denver entry into Major League baseball.

The Arkansas Travelers

The Arkansas Travelers, based in Little Rock, Arkansas, is a member of the Texas League and has been a professional franchise since 1901, when manager Mike Finn guided the club to a second-place finish in the Southern Association. They have operated for ninety years, and with the brief exception of three "off-premises" moves, they've called the same field location home since 1932.

Due to their frequent change of leagues—Texas, Southern, Pacific Coast, International, et al.—they have traveled by bus, plane, train, and car to such distant places as Honolulu, Seattle, Lafayette, Louisiana, and Toronto. During a four-year stretch, their opening day opponents were Rochester (New York), Portland (Oregon), Denver (Colorado), and Austin (Texas).

In 1909, the entire franchise was sold to Chattanooga for $12,000, but in 1915, the Montgomery, Alabama, franchise was purchased and brought to Little Rock to resurrect the Travelers.

In 1917, Traveler pitcher Ben Tincup threw a perfect game against Birmingham.

In 1920, the Travs won their first pennant, under the guidance of Norm Eberfield and the field leadership of outfielders Harry Harper (.346) and Bing Miller (.322, 19 homers and 31 steals) and pitchers Rube Robinson (26–12) and Moses Yellowhorse (21–7). Benny Karr and Claude Jounard ran wild on the basepaths as the team stole 184 bases.

In 1932, the Travelers moved from Kavanaugh Field to a steel and concrete facility named Travelers Field. The field was renamed War Memorial Park to honor World War II dead, and renamed Ray Winder Field in 1966 to honor a man who dedicated fifty-two years to the promotion of professional baseball in Little Rock.

It took seventeen years, but pennant number two came to Little Rock in a ninety-seven-win season (1937). The '37 Travs only hit 27 homeruns but banged out 240 doubles and 80 triples. Stars that year included Leo Nonnenkamp (.332, 39 doubles), Lindsey Deal (.340), Al Niemec (.313 and 98 RBI), and Byron Humphreys, who won 16 games.

The third pennant came only five years later, in 1942, thanks to a thirteen-game winning streak near the end of the season. Fibber McGeehee led the '42 squad at .355, while Buck Fausett hit .344, Roy Schalk was the MVP and hit .288, and Jim Trexler was the mound ace at 19–7, backed up by Al Moran at 17–9.

On July 21, 1946, Traveler outfielder Lew Flick collected nine consecutive hits in the first game of a doubleheader. He flied out in his tenth at bat but went 3 for 3 in the second game for a 12 for 13 day.

In 1949, outfielder Hal Simpson banged out 17 homers to lead a mediocre club, and the next year, the Travs lost 21 games in a row from April to May to drop out of contention early.

In 1951, the Travs recovered to win another pennant while setting an all-time attendance high of 225,780. Simpson led the team and was the league MVP at .311 and 23 homers, and Al Yaylian pitched his way to a 16–5 season.

In mid-1956, the Travelers relocated to Montgomery. When the club lost 101 games, it was shifted back to Little Rock without objections from Montgomery.

In 1957, the Travelers could have been sued for nonsupport by pitcher George Brunet. From mid-June to early August, the Travs failed to score a single run for Brunet over eight starts covering 52 1/3 innings. Brunet had a 10–3 record prior to the streak and wound up the season at 14–15 while setting a club record with 235 strikeouts.

Known as the Little Rock Travelers, the team became the Arkansas Travelers in 1961, thus becoming the first professional sports team to be named after an entire state. That year, the Travs were led by enigmatic pitcher Bo Belinsky, who later gained celebrity status as much for his partying and sexual liaisons as for his hurling exploits.

Also in 1961, the Travs went public and became a community-owned franchise for the price of $5 a share. The club now has more than 1,200 stockholders.

In 1962, Arkansas was out of baseball again when the Southern League folded, but in 1963, following a near-appearance in the American Association, the Travs became part of the International League. During that season, Richie Allen became the Travs' first black player. He set a club record for right-handed hitters with 33 homers.

In 1964, the Travs shifted to the PCL and smacked a team-record 208 homers led by Costen Shockley's 36 roundtrippers. Called the "Boom-boom Travs," the team had nine players hit homers in double figures, led by Shockley, Norm Gigon (30), Adolfo Phillips (29), Bill Sorrell (22), and Alex Johnson (21).

In 1966, Arkansas found a home in the Texas League and won a pennant.

In 1973, Keith Hernandez stopped by and hit .260.

In 1977, playing a split season, the Travs finished last the first half then won it all the second half.

Some stars who have worn the Travs' uniform over the years include: Tris Speaker, Baby Doll Jacobson, Charlie Grimm, Travis Jackson, Firpo Marberry, Bill Dickey, Bobo Newsom, Jim Tabor, Ed Lopat, Jim Bunning, Bake McBride, Hector Cruz, and Larry Herndon.

Still toiling in the Texas League, General Manager Bill Valentine has tagged the team with a marketing slogan that says it all: The Arkansas Travelers are "the greatest show on dirt."

The Hollywood Stars

In a wave of nostalgia, a team worthy of fond remembrance, if not as noteworthy as the successful Newark Bears or Rochester Red Wings, are the Hollywood Stars. They were the Minor League equivalent of the Cubs, the early-years Mets, the Indians, the Red Sox . . . teams that were talented enough to win it but rarely seemed to finish high in the standings. A team full of potential and optimism that usually missed the mark. A team you rooted for all year long, and when they broke your heart, you rooted for them again next year.

The Hollywood Stars became a Pacific Coast League entity on January 11, 1926, when Salt Lake City owner Bill Lane was allowed to move his team to the Los Angeles area known as Hollywoodland . . . Hollywood, for short.

On Sunday, July 15, 1928, Hollywood became the first professional team to use air travel—trains, cars, and buses were the accepted mode of transportation in those days. Following a doubleheader in Seattle, Lane, the Stars' owner, arranged for the team to be transported by airplane to Portland so they would arrive in time to catch the southbound train "The Cascade Limited" that evening, for arrival back home in Los Angeles on Tuesday.

Lane, by the way, is a part of the Hollywood Stars' legend. He is the founder of the famed Hollywood Derby restaurant, and reveled in the Tinseltown fishbowl. He recruited stockholders from among movieland's elite, including Bing Crosby and Gary Cooper.

The Hollywood Stars entered the PCL fray again in November 1937, when the previous Hollywood franchise was transferred to San Diego and the Mission team of San Francisco flew south for the summer and took up residence in Hollywood, choosing the nickname "Stars."

The Stars shared stadium facilities, Wrigley Field, with the Los Angeles Angels for a year and then moved into the newly completed Gilmore Field.

When the Los Angeles Dodgers moved to the West Coast from Brooklyn in 1958, the Stars came full circle, packed up and moved to Salt Lake City.

Among the top Stars' teams were the 1929–30–31 pennant winners managed by Ossie Vitt of Newark Bears fame, the 1949 and '52 champs managed by Fred Haney, and the 1953 Stars managed to a pennant by Bobby Bragan.

On the 1930 team, Minor "Mickey" Heath connected for 12 consecutive hits, a PCL record tied in 1953 by Hollywood Star Ted Beard.

The 1930 and '31 teams had PCL homerun champ David Barbee with years of 41 and 47 four-baggers.

The 1949 Stars were 109–78 and were led by PCL MVP Irv Noren.

The '52 squad went 109–71 as pitcher Johnny Lindell went 24–9.

The '53 team went 106–74 and outfielder Ted Beard hit four homers in a single game against San Diego, and Red Munger tossed a no-hitter against Sacramento. Dale Long led the PCL with 35 homers for Hollywood.

Among the lesser teams in terms of record—certainly not talent—was the 1935 version, led by pitcher-manager

Frank Shellenback (14–9 with a 3.42 ERA), first baseman Ray Jacobs (.296, 13 homers, 69 RBI), second baseman Bobby Doerr (.317, 4 homers, 74 RBI), left-fielder Vince DiMaggio (.278, 24 homers, 112 RBI), center-fielder Cedric Durst (.324, 6 homers, 72 RBI) and right-fielder Smead Jolley (.372, 29 homers, and 128 RBI). Also staffed by third sacker Jim Levey, shortstop George Myatt, catcher Gene Desautels, and pitchers Berlyn Horne, Ed Wells, Archie Campbell, Herman "Old Folks" Pillette, and Wally Herbert—the '35 Stars went 73–99.

Some other stars for the Stars included Frank Kelleher (a '37 Newark Bear who led the PCL in homers with 29 for Hollywood in 1944 and 40 in 1950), Dick Stuart (he hit 66 homers for Lincoln in the Western League the year before the Stars got him), Jim Baxes, Dee Fondy, Gus Zernial, Jack Phillips, Dick Smith, Tony Lupien, Roger Bowman, and Frenchy Uhalt.

Local city historians and niche scholars may argue that other cities may have supported teams better and longer, and other teams may have had more heroes and more pennants, but there can be no argument successfully raised to deny that baseball was glorious in the above-mentioned locations. Their stars shone brightly and the excitement generated will always remain a part of the sport.

To those mentioned and those bypassed . . . we salute you.

19
THE PLAYERS: YESTERDAY, TODAY, AND TOMORROW

This chapter extolls the virtues and talents of those athletes who have amazed and entertained us over the years on the Minor League diamonds of America.

Once again, let's not look at who is not represented here, but rather share the joy given us by those we have included.

Reversing history, let's first take a look at the young men who are playing today. These ballplayers are thrilling us in the 1990s and will most likely be the stuff of which legends are made, for their performances in this decade and the decade (and century) to come.

Why look at Minor League stats as a barometer when the Bushes are filled with Big League wannabe's that do well on the Farm but can't handle the pressure, the talent, or the curveball in The Show? Remember that both Nolan Ryan and Dwight Gooden each struck out 300 batters at the Minor League level (more than 100 greater K's than innings pitched), Wade Boggs won a Minor League batting title, Jose Canseco hit better than a homerun every four games, Vince Coleman set a stolen base record, and

Joe DiMaggio hit in sixty-one straight Minor League games . . . some stats are just too good to overlook.

Even though most Major League scouts look at things other than statistics—poise, speed, grace, the "look" of a player, fastball speed, pitching location, and other intangibles—and though many scouts believe that Minor League stats don't tell the entire story, success at lower levels may indicate a winning attitude and a positive climb up the Minor League baseball ladder frequently leads to success in The Show.

Tomorrow's Stars: Players to Watch

The following lists of players to watch are regarded by many scouts and talent judges as the likely Big League stars of tomorrow. This also makes them the Minor League stars of today and part of the skein of players who have been woven into the fabric of greatness and excitement that has been synonymous with Minor League baseball for more than a century.

Many of these diamond stars will endure in the lore that will be handed down through the coming years to generations of yet unborn baseball fans who will be drawn to Minor League ball as a means of satisfying their thirst for the sport and for small-town entertainment.

These athletes toiled in the Minors in 1990 and while some may have short stints with the parent club, demotions to the Bushes and trips to and fro on the Major League-Minor League shuttle before they hit it, they appear destined to provide the small thrills at the Major League level as they have on the Farm.

Remember them for what they accomplished at the Minor League level and look for their potential to become Big League heroes of the '90s and beyond.

Based on stats alone, the thrills of the diamond for these young men are likely only to increase in frequency and baseball importance over the years ahead.

[*Author's note*: Statistical information is accurate as of the time this book went to press. Hitters' stats are listed in order as: average, HR, RBI; Pitching stats are listed in order as: wins-losses, ERA. Major League Baseball Scouting Bureau "Minor League System Prospects" in parentheses following team name—not all prospects listed, as this compilation was confidential.]

American League

Baltimore Orioles (26 prospects)

Ben MacDonald only needed a cup of coffee (or some mustard sardines, his favorite pregame meal) with Rochester (International League-AAA) before the O's brought him up, but Big Ben responded with four wins, a 1.61 ERA, and 17 strikeouts in his first four starts.

Leo Gomez, the third baseman for Rochester, was set to join the Big Club but suffered a separated shoulder. Look for him in '91. Gomez belted 26 homers with 97 RBI. Chris Hoiles, a Red Wings catcher, was hammering away at .348 with 18 homers, and first baseman David Segui got a few looks in Baltimore, and was at .343. Pitching was thin with the exception of Mickey Weston's 1.98 ERA (11–1 mark) in 109 innings pitched.

At Hagerstown (Eastern League-AA), second baseman Pat Austin was at .307, outfielder Scott Meadows hit .293 and outfielder Luis Mercedes was at .334 with 30 steals. On the power front, outfielder Jack Voigt belted 12 homers. Pitching was sharp for the Suns with starter Mike Linskey, who fared well at AA but who got belted (7–9, 3.58 ERA) at Rochester, but for whom great things were predicted; Anthony Telford at 10–2 with a 1.97 ERA; Francisco Delarosa with a 2.06 ERA; reliever Dave Miller 2.81 ERA and 7 saves; reliever Mike Sander at 2.48 ERA; and reliever workhorse Paul Thorpe with a 3.78 ERA and 12 saves.

In the Carolina League (A) at Frederick, righty starter Mike Oquist fanned 170 in 166 innings and had a 2.81

ERA, and starter Zachary Kerr was 12–6 with a 3.13. The Keys were led at the plate by catcher Ed Horowitz, who hit .352 in a limited role through late August.

Boston Red Sox (19 prospects)

In the International League (AAA) with Pawtucket, the Paw Sox boasted of the booming bats of outfielder Phil Plantier and first baseman Mo Vaughn. Plantier slammed 33 homers (despite more than 120 whiffs) and Vaughn 22. Another Sox first sacker, Rick Lancellotti, dh'd, and belted 19 four-baggers. Scott Cooper may be Wade Boggs' third base heir apparent despite a .266 batting average and only 12 homers in his 433 at bats.

At New Britain (Eastern League-AA), twenty-two-year-old Jeff Bagwell (third baseman) was a prized prospect at .333, second in the league in batting, and was thought to be a candidate to leapfrog over Cooper to fill in for Boggs at third in Fenway. Then in late August, he was peddled to Houston for thirty-seven-year-old reliever Larry Anderson for the pennant drive. On the mound, lefty reliever Dan O'Neill blistered the league with a 7–0 record, 0.72 ERA and 11 saves, and Jeff Plympton was at 2.67 and 13 saves.

The Lynchburg Red Sox (Carolina League-A) was led by outfielder Greg Blosser with 18 homers and a familiar Red Sox name at third base, John Malzone, who got off to a quick start at .313.

At Winter Haven (Florida State League-A), outfielder Garrett Jenkins stole 40 bases in his first 209 at bats, and pitcher Al Sanders whiffed 113 in 113 innings while posting a 2.30 ERA.

California Angels (20 prospects)

The Halos shuttled in Devon White (he hit better than .400 during a guest tour) and Jack Howell to Edmonton (Pacific Coast League-AAA), but filled their ranks with several young players who looked even better at the MLB level than they did on the Farm. White is now Toronto property.

Third baseman Pete Coachman, after six years in the Bushes, was hitting .291 (and 22 steals) at Edmonton.

There were times when he never thought he'd be called upon to produce on a Major League diamond. His waiting paid off. He came upon the Angels' scene in August and delivered two hits in each of his first four games, and a .417 clip for his first week in a Halos' uniform.

Lee Stevens was called up earlier in the year, after hitting .293 with 16 homers for the Trappers, filled in for Wally Joyner and hit .297 with 4 homers in his first 23 games. Stevens's play made the injured Joyner trade bait.

Second sacker Kent Anderson was at .283 through 39 games and was called up to Anaheim, and pitcher Joe Grahe was 3–0 in five starts for Edmonton, with a 1.35 ERA before pitching for the Halos in August and September.

First baseman Chris Cron hit .287 with 17 homers for the Trappers. Steve DeAngelis, an outfielder-dh, hit .299, and outfielder Mark Davis hit .373 in his first 31 games and belted 9 roundtrippers for the Trappers in only 128 at bats, after bombing out 12 at Double-A Midland (Texas League) before his promotion. Outfielder Ruben Amaro, Jr., hit .289 with 32 steals in 82 games as a Trapper after hitting .357 in 57 games at Midland.

Rated as "can't miss" by Angels' execs were Edmonton's twenty-four-year-old right-handed hurler Scott Lewis (though only 13–11 with a 3.90), reliever Jeff Richardson (5–0, 10 saves, and 1.86 ERA), and twenty-one-year-old outfielder Tim Salmon, who hit .288 at Palm Springs (California League-A) before being called up to play Double-A ball at Midland.

Also at Midland, Jeff Barns (shortstop) hit .302 and aging Luis Aguayo (third baseman) hit .317 with 10 homers. Outfielder Wiley Lee hit .297.

Pitching was very thin, but reliever David Martinez had 54 K's in 57 innings.

At Quad Cities (Midwest League-A), lefty starter Fili Martinez was 12–4, 2.40 ERA with 172 strikeouts in 146 innings. At the plate, second baseman Chad Curtis hit .307, blasted 11 homers, and stole 63 bases.

Kyle Abbott, the Angels' number one draft pick in 1989, won his first start for Edmonton after being promoted in August—he beat Albuquerque 2–1, and should make the Big League club sometime in 1991.

Daryl Sconiers, former Major Leaguer, was inked by the Angels Texas League affiliate (Midland) and will probably play there or at the Triple-A level until he proves he is ready to return to the Bigs.

At Boise (Northwest League-A), pitcher Hilly Hathaway led the Hawks with an 8–2 mark and 1.46 ERA, while moundmates Randy Powers (7–3, 2.56) and Ken Edenfeld (8–4, 1.66, and 9 saves) sparkled. Outfielder-third base-man Mark Delasandro led the club in hitting at .336.

And right-hander Phillip Leftwich, the Angels' top draft choice in the June 1990 draft, did well in his professional debut, going 8–2 at Boise with a 1.86 ERA and 81 strike-outs in 92 innings covering 15 starts.

Chicago White Sox (23 prospects)

The blaze-through of the Sox's Minor League system was pitcher Alex Fernandez, their first round draft pick and fourth pick overall in the June 1990 draft. Only twenty, Fernandez proved he needed little seasoning by advancing from Rookie League (Sarasota-Gulf Coast League) to the Bigs in less than two months, going 6–1 in three Minor League stops. Fernandez notched wins in his first and third MLB starts, shutting the California Angels down for eight innings, 4–2, in a six-K performance for win num-ber two, just days after his twenty-first birthday.

On the Triple-A level, at Vancouver (Pacific Coast League), pitching was weak, but sometime-Major Leaguer Shawn Hillegas threw for a 1.74 ERA in 67 IP. Outfielder Orsino "Arsenio Hall" Hill, a much-traveled twenty-eight-year-old, was at .284 with 11 homers and could be up in '91. Shortstop Rich Amaral hit .301, and catcher Jerry Willard belted 20 homers.

Also up in Vancouver, catcher Don Wakamatsu hit .303 in the battle with Willard to be Carlton Fisk's eventual replacement, and third baseman Tracy Woodson with 17 homers could give Robin Ventura a run for the ChiSox hot-corner spot.

The ChiSox look good down on the Farm, with Matt Stark, a dh for the Birmingham Bulls (Southern League-AA), belting out 14 homers, a .309 average, and a whopping 109 RBI in 453 at bats.

One young man to watch is Sarasota (Florida State League-A) pitcher Greg Perschke, who went 4–0 in July with a 1.07 ERA and was named the organization's player of the month. He finished at 7–3 with a 1.21 ERA and 107 K's in 111 innings.

At Birmingham, outfielder Willie Magellanes slugged 16 homers, and first sacker Frank Thomas hit .323 with 18 homers. On the Bulls mound, Curt Hasler came in with a 3.27 ERA and reliever Dave Reynolds compiled a 3.09 ERA with Rich Scheid at 2.22.

In the Midwest League (A) for South Bend, first baseman Scott Cepicky hit .312.

Cleveland Indians (18 prospects)

Speedy centerfielder Alex Cole was recalled from Colorado Springs (Pacific Coast League-AAA) and blazed a path toward immediate stardom with a 5 stolen-base performance in only his sixth game, and 12 stolen bases in his first 13 starts, while compiling a .373 average. He was at .308, 33 steals for Colorado Springs.

At Colorado Springs, Beau Allred (outfielder) hit .278, 13 homers; Alan Cockrell (outfielder) .323, 17 homers; and Luis Medina (dh) 18 homers and .272 in the light air of the high altitude. Jeff Manto continued to impress with .297, 18 homers, and a solid third base, and outfielder Jeffrey Wetherby hit .313. Light air and high altitude hurt pitching, and there was little to recommend except reliever Robert Ward at 2.00 with 9 saves.

At Canton-Akron (Eastern League-AA), reliever Bruce Egloff came in with a 1.98 ERA, 15 saves, and 53 K's in 55 IP; starter Tom Kramer 2.03; and Charles Nagy, who was named the No. 3 prospect in the Carolina League in 1989, showed form again in 1990 with a 13–8 record, 2.52, and only 132 hits allowed in 175 IP.

In the Carolina League (A) for Kinston, outfielder Ken Ramos ran away with the batting title at .345, and Garland Kiser won the ERA title at 1.71.

At Watertown (New York-Penn League-A), starter Bill Wertz impressed with a 5–0 mark, 1.49 ERA, and 45 K's in 42 innings; Bob Ryan was at 0.73.

Detroit Tigers (25 prospects)

The Bengals' best youth news came when third baseman Travis Fryman was recalled from Toledo (International-AAA) after posting half-season numbers of .257, 10 homers, and 53 RBI. He responded in Detroit and hit .321 with 4 homers after his first 22 Big League games.

Called up with Fryman was pitcher Steve Searcy, who was 10–5 with a 2.92 ERA at Toledo. Searcy struggled in his first six starts but manager Sparky Anderson remained high on the twenty-six-year-old.

Tim Leiper, the third baseman-outfielder from Brea, California, home of Walter Johnson and Randy Jones, and brother of Dave Leiper (former Padres, A's), is one to watch for in '91. Leiper has hit everywhere he's been and was at .293 for Toledo—he was even chosen as a member of several rotisserie league teams before the season, so his abilities are hardly secret. Also at Toledo, second baseman Torey Lovullo hit 14 homers, and first baseman Jim Lindeman blasted 12 dingers. Outfielder Milt Cuyler showed wheels with 40 steals despite a .258 average. Mud Hen pitching was porous, but lefty Brian Dubois managed a 2.71 ERA in a spot starter-relief role, and reliever Bobby Link was at 2.78 with 8 saves.

At London (Eastern League-AA), first baseman Rico Brogna smashed 21 homers, and, minding the mound, workhouse reliever John Kiely mystified hitters to the tune of a 1.76 ERA and 12 saves. Moundmate, starter Mike

Wilkins, posted a 2.42 ERA and a 13–5 mark and was traded to the Dodgers for lefty reliever Mike Munoz. Rusty Meacham was 15–9.

At Fayetteville (South Atlantic League-A), righty hurler Randy Marshall looked like a shoe-in to move up the Tiger ladder, after going 13–0 with a 1.33 ERA in 102 innings. The topper is that he walked only 9 and gave up only 64 hits while striking out 81.

Kansas City Royals (27 prospects)

At Omaha (American Association-AAA), outfielder Chito Martinez led the Royals with 21 homers, and outfielder Gary Thurman hit .331 with 30 steals. On the hill, Daryl Smith was steady at 3.09 and 56 K's in 64 IP and workhorse Jim Lemasters was at 3.16. Greg Everson came in at 2.35.

According to Ted Tornow, PR Director for the Memphis Chicks (Southern League-AA), some players to watch include Jeff Conine, a first baseman who was in the Top Ten in average (.320), hits, doubles, triples, homers (15), and RBI (95) before being called up to The Show.

Other Chicks to watch are Brent Mayne, the rugged catcher from California State University, Fullerton, who has struggled after overcoming a few injuries, but who has the right stuff and the right tools to play this game at the Major League level; Bobby Moore, the speedy outfielder who was hitting .325 with 31 stolen bases late in the season; Scott Centala, a pitcher with an 85 MPH fastball, a good curve and slider, a respectable 3.22 ERA, and 116 strikeouts in 142 innings pitched; and, of course, Brian McRae, the centerfielder, son of former Royal Hal McRae. Brian burst on the MLB scene in August with a hot .417 average after his first week in the Bigs after the surprise call-up. The young switch-hitter was hitting only .268 when promoted.

And, also at Memphis was Hector Wagner, a reliever, who went 12–4 with a sharp 2.03.

On the Rookie League level, in the Gulf Coast League, pitcher Robert Toth was impressive with a 1.66 ERA in 7 starts covering 38 innings.

And the Royals acquired young pitcher Archie Corbin from the Mets in the Pat Tabler trade. Corbin, pitching for St. Lucie (Florida State League-A), was 7–8 with a respectable 2.97 ERA as a starter.

Milwaukee Brewers (21 prospects)

At Denver (American Association-AAA), outfielder Billy Moore was at .288 and 18 homers hitting in the light air of the Mile-High City; catcher Tim McIntosh also led the Zephyrs with 18 homers and 74 RBI along with a .288 average; Mark Higgins, outfielder, hit 16 homers; and third baseman Joe Redfield belted 17. Mile-high cities are not conducive to low ERAs, so the only pitcher who kept the ball down was lefty reliever Tony Fossas, 1.42 and 3 saves with 26 K's in 19 innings.

At El Paso (Texas League-AA), Jesus Alfaro dh'd to the tune of .301 and 16 homers, and second baseman Mitch Hannahs hit a stand-out .331. On the hill for the Diablos, lefty reliever Ed Puig fashioned a microscopic 1.14 ERA and 8 saves, 24 K's in 23 IP, while bullpenmate Chris George was 1.78 with 13 saves. Starter-reliever Jim Austin went 11–3 and 2.44.

Brewers speed was exhibited with the Stockton Ports (California League-A) by second baseman Pat Listach, with 49 steals in his first 90 games. And late in the year, the Brewers acquired relief pitcher Julio Machado from the Mets in exchange for catcher Charlie O'Brien. Pitching in 27 games for Tidewater, Machado fashioned a neat 1.69 ERA.

Minnesota Twins (19 prospects)

A real prospect star-of-stars may be Denny Neagle, who became the first twenty-game winner in the Minors since 1986, when he notched his twelfth victory for the Orlando

SunRays of the Southern League (AA) in August, raising his record for them to 12–3 with a 2.37 ERA. Those victories occurred after he began the 1990 campaign by going a perfect 8–0 for the Twins' California League (A) franchise in Visalia. Neagle, a six-foot-four-inch, 200-pounder from Gambrills, Maryland, is a left-hander and may see the Metrodome in '91.

The Portland Beavers (Pacific Coast League-AAA) were led by Bernardo Brito (dh), with 25 homers in 376 at bats, and first baseman Paul Sorrento with 19 homers while hitting .302. Outfielder Alonzo Powell led the hitters at .322. The Beaver mound staff took its lumps.

At Orlando, outfielder Kenny Morgan looks like a prospect with 13 homers. And on the SunRays' mound, lefty starter Doug Simons had a 2.54 ERA and had given up only 160 hits in 188 innings while going 15–12.

New York Yankees (33 prospects)

Those who gleefully reported on the demise, the misuse, and the pillaging of the Yankee Farm System may have to eat their words, as reports of the system's death are greatly exaggerated. The same system that has brought the Bronx Bombers a youth movement that includes the smooth-stroking, homerun-hitting (13 homers in his first 110 at bats) Kevin Maas (Columbus, International League-AAA); aggressive batting (.323 through 24 games) Oscar Azocar (Columbus); versatile third baseman-catcher-outfielder (.275 in 54 games) Jim Leyritz (Columbus); shortstop Alvaro Espinoza (Columbus-'88); utility infielder Randy Velarde (Columbus-'89); reliable hitting and fielding centerfielder Roberto Kelly (Columbus-'88); solid defensive catcher Bob Geren (Columbus-'89); reliever Alan Mills (Columbus); and big lefty starter Chuck Cary (Columbus); all of whom wore Yankee pinstripes in 1990, boasts many more prospects in a Minor League organization that has had the best winning percentage in baseball over the past three years.

The Yanks may have traded away Rodney Imes (pitcher) and Hal Morris (first baseman), two stars of the future, to Cincinnati, but they haven't given up on Hensley "Bam Bam" Meulens, the Bomber of tomorrow, whom they switched from third base to the outfield and who responded with 26 homers, and .285 average, 96 RBI at Columbus. Also having hot years in the IL were Mike Blowers, who shuttled to New York and back but hit .339, and Andy Stankewicz, the shortstop who only hit .229 but showed Major League range. Catcher Brian Dorsett hit 14 taters and outfielder Van Snider got 15.

Columbus pitchers included "Wild" Willie Smith with 7 saves and 39 K's in 28 innings, despite a 6.51 ERA; Dave Eiland, 16–5 and 2.87; lefty prospect Steve Adkins, 15–7 with a 2.90; and Rich Monteleone with a 2.24.

At Albany (Eastern League-AA) Bobby Dejardin, shortstop, made a move to climb to New York in '91 with a solid .263 to go with his slick fielding (and may leapfrog over Stankiewicz); catcher Mitch Lyden may get a Bronx look in '91 after a .296, 17-homer performance; first baseman Greg Sparks slammed 19 homers; and outfielder Bernabe Williams, one young player whom the Yanks refused to trade though many offers were made, hit .281 with 30-stolen base potential.

Prospect pitchers include reliever Darrin Chapin 2.73, 21 saves, and 61 K's in 53 IP; Daven Bond, 2.76 ERA; and reliever Don Stanford, 2.15 and 10 saves.

Outfielder Gerald Williams showed power at Ford Lauderdale (Florida State League-A), and after a slow start at Albany, connected for 13 taters.

Oakland A's (21 prospects)

At Tacoma (Pacific Coast League-AAA), first baseman Dan Howitt only hit .265 with 11 dingers but looks like the next big gun in Oakland. With 13 homers was catcher Russ McGinnis. Pitching leaders were Joe Bitker, 26 saves and 52 K's in 56 IP, and Scott Chiamparino, 3.28, 13 wins, who were both shipped to the Texas Rangers in exchange for pennant insurance and Harold Baines. Also at Tacoma, making a brilliant comeback following heart surgery only four months earlier, was relief pitcher Dave Leiper, a former Major Leaguer, who at 28 was 1–0 with a perfect 0.00 ERA in his first nine innings.

At Huntsville (Southern League-AA), outfielder Ozzie Canseco, the twin brother of A's star Jose Canseco, belted 21 homers in only his third year as a hitter—the Yankees had originally drafted Ozzie as a pitcher, and he was without a bat in his hands for three years, until the A's plucked him from the Yankee's farm system. The shortstop for Huntsville, Scott Brosius belted 23 roundtrippers to aid Ozzie in the power department. Ozzie will play in Japan in 1991.

On the mound for the Stars, Steve Chitren had 27 saves and a 1.68 with 61 K's in 54 innings, and lefty starter Johnny Guzman was at 2.37. Starter Dan Eskew knew how to win (14–3) but only fashioned a 3.34 ERA.

And the entire baseball world is watching the A's steal of the year, No. 1 draft pick Todd Van Poppel, who was snatched from high school and began his pro career pitching for the Class-A Southern Oregon Athletics of the Northwest League. Van Poppel has been labeled "can't miss" and should put up some imposing numbers as he rises through the Minor League ranks, before turning his talents to The Show. So far, Van Poppel has done nothing to contradict his label, as he struck out 27 hitters in 19 innings for Medford (Northwest League-A), and went on to whiff 17 more in his first 13 innings for Madison (Midwest League-A).

Seattle Mariners (20 prospects)

At Calgary (Pacific Coast League-AAA), second baseman Todd Haney hit .339; left-handed hitting first baseman Tino Martinez (No. 1 draft pick in 1988) was at .320 with 17 homers, 93 RBI; and Tom Dodd, dh, added 16 homers and 114 RBI.

At Williamsport (Eastern League-AA), starter Mike Gardiner compiled a league-leading 1.90 ERA, and Rich De-Lucia came in at 2.11, while the outfielder with the Hall-of-Fame name, Ted Williams, only hit .227 but stole 34 bases. Third baseman Pat Lennon hit a steady .291.

Switch-hitting third sacker Frank Bolick led the San Bernardino Spirits (California-A) at .324 with 18 homers and 102 RBI. Outfielder Ellerton Maynard showed speed with 65 stolen bases in his first 90 games. On the mound, Roger Sakeld whiffed 134 in 112 IP.

At Peninsula, in the Florida State League-A, pitcher Rod Poissant impressed with a 1.47 ERA and 9 saves in 26 relief appearances.

Texas Rangers (18 prospects)

At Oklahoma City (American Association-AAA), outfielder Juan Gonzales ripped 27 homers and drove in 85 in 417 at bats and was named the American Association's Rookie of the Year. On the mound, relievers Wayne Rosenthal (3.00 ERA and 14 saves) and Jack Hardy (2.34 ERA) were the best the 89ers had to offer, while Gerald Alexander won 19 games working his way up through AA (Tulsa) and AAA (Oklahoma City).

At Tulsa (Texas League-AA), outfielder Kevin Belcher hit .293, outfielder Tony Scruggs was at .317, catcher Bill Haselman drilled 18 shots, and first baseman Rob Maurer socked 21 roundtrippers.

Starter Roger Pavlik was sharp, with a 2.33 ERA for the Drillers.

At Charlotte (Florida State League-A), Robert Brown had a 1.90 ERA, but was shipped to Clearwater and the Phillies.

In a good piece of instant development, the Rangers acquired Joe Bitker, 26 saves and 52 K's in 56 IP, and Scott Chiamparino, 3.28, 13 wins (both men worked at Tacoma—Pacific Coast League-AAA) in a trade for aging Harold Baines.

Toronto Blue Jays (28 prospects)

Steve Karsay, the Blue Jays No. 1 draft choice with a 92 MPH fastball, pitched 2 1/3 innings of hitless relief in his debut for St. Catherine's of the New York–Penn League (A). He looks to rise through the ranks in '91.

At Syracuse (International League-AAA), Stu Pederson, dh, was at .296, and Ed Sprague, third base, led the Chiefs with 20 four-baggers. Toeing the rubber were reliever Tom Gilles with a 2.14 ERA and starter Steve Cummings checking in with at 2.41. Former Yankee and Blue Jay Al Leiter disappointed at Triple A with 3–8, 4.62 season.

At Knoxville (Southern League-AA), first baseman Julian Yan cooked with 15 blasts; third baseman Tom Quinlan also poled 15. Reliever Bob MacDonald picked up 15 saves and had a 1.89 ERA and 54 K's in 57 innings. Starter Pat Hentgen fanned 142 in 153 innings.

In the Florida State League, Class A Dunedin, first baseman Ray Giannelli hit .294 with 14 homers; second baseman Jeff Kent backed him up with 16 blasts. Mike Timlin impressed on the Dunedin hill by posting 21 saves, with a 7–2 mark and a 1.45 ERA before being promoted.

And late in the year, Toronto signed Chris Weinke (St. Paul, Minnesota), considered one of America's best high school football and baseball players. Weinke will make his organized ball debut in 1991.

National League

Atlanta Braves (18 prospects)

At Richmond (International League-AAA), outfielder Geronimo Berroa, belted 12 homers and hit for a .269 average, while infielder Bruce Crabbe was at .268. Outfielder Andy Tomberlin chipped in at .304, and outfielder Dwight Taylor, used sparingly, hit for a .364 mark. On the mound, lefty reliever Brian Snyder was 4–1 with a 2.48, 12 saves; and Bill Laskey was 6–4 with 14 saves.

At Greenville (Southern League-AA), outfielder Brian Hunter hit 14 homers; third baseman Tom Reddington connected for 12 and was claimed by San Diego in an off-season goof by the Braves. First baseman Mike Bell hit .291. Greenville's relief pitcher John Kilner had 15 saves and a 2.75; reliever Matt Turner was 6–4 with a 2.66.

Chicago Cubs (20 prospects)

The Cubbies brought up lefty hurler Lance Dickson from Charlotte (Southern League-AA). Pitching for three Minor League clubs, Dickson posted a 7–3 mark with a 0.94 ERA. Dickson, the Cubs' No. 1 draft selection in 1990, played for five different managers in his first two months of professional baseball. Dickson has claimed to be both a San Diego Padres fan, rooting against the Cubs in the 1984 NL play-offs, and a Cubs fan who cried when Steve Garvey hit a game-winning homer against the Cubs in that same series. Cubs manager Don Zimmer said he doesn't care about the rookie's confusion as long as he keeps confusing hitters.

And Mark Clear, the MLB veteran, was signed and pitched effectively for Iowa (American Association-AAA).

Also at Iowa, outfielder Brad Bierley and catcher Erik Pappas each clubbed 16 homers. Outfielder Cedric Landrum swiped 29 bases on his first 60 hits and 17 walks, and finished at .296. Pitching was problematic at Iowa, but reliever Dave Pavlas notched 96 K's in 99 IP.

At Charlotte (Southern League-AA), catcher Rick Wilkins had 17 dingers for a light-hitting Knights squad, and reliever Fernando Zarranz posted a 2.09 ERA and 13 saves, while Heath Slocumb picked up 12 saves and a 2.15.

In late August, the Cubs looked like they made a good swap of Minor League arms, getting Randy Kramer from the Pirates organization for Greg Kallevig. Kramer's fastball was rated the best in the Pittsburgh system, and he split time in 1990 between the Majors and Buffalo (American Association-AAA). Kallevig was 4–10, 5.67 at Iowa

(American Association-AAA). Kramer was 29, but still considered a prospect though waived just before Christmas to make room for newly acquired Dave Smith.

Cincinnati Reds (17 prospects)

Hal Morris, acquired from the Yankees prior to the season, was recalled by the Reds and responded with a .367 mark in his first 60 games. He won a Minor League batting title at Columbus (International League-AAA) at .326 in 1989.

At Nashville (International League-AAA), outfielder Skeeter Barnes hit .285 and stole more than 30 bases; first baseman Terry Lee hit .304 and 15 homers despite missing a month with a recurrence of a foot injury, and speedy, sure-gloved second baseman Billy Bates, acquired from the Milwaukee Brewers, hit a steady .293. Lefty pitcher Chris Hammond (15–1, 2.17, and 149 K's in 149 IP) was called up for the Reds' pennant push. Scott Scudder won seven of his first eight with a 2.34 before being called up; and Rodney Imes, acquired from the Yankees, delivered 10 wins and a 3.71. Reliever Keith Brown allowed just 3 runs in 23 innings after being promoted to chief stopper and wound up with a 2.39 ERA and 9 saves.

At Chattanooga (Southern League-AA) outfielder Scott Bryant hit .317; first baseman Adam Casillas bettered that at .336; outfielder Benny Colvard came in at .288 with 13 homers (the only real power on the Lookouts), and shortstop Kevin Pearson hit a solid .317.

In the South Atlantic League (A) at Charleston, West Virginia, outfielder Scott Pose hit .298 with more than 30 steals; and starter Tim Pugh went 5–6 with a 1.88 ERA.

Houston Astros (31 prospects)

The Astros' farm may not produce another Eric Anthony but there is some talent down there just the same.

At Tucson (Pacific Coast League-AAA), switch-hitting

shortstop Russell Harris hit .318. His doubleplay partner, second sacker Craig Lee Smajstrla, speedy ten-year Minor Leaguer with the tough-to-pronounce name, hit .313. Outfielder Jose Tolentino provided 21 homers. Ex-Big Leaguer Gerald Young was tearing up the PCL at .333 with 24 RBI in 48 games, but one wonders if he's still a prospect after two very "off" seasons with the 'Stros. Called up in late August, he had begun the season with the parent club, hitting only .177 when sent down May 21.

On the Tucson hill, pitching proved the Toros undoing with little to recommend.

At Columbus (Georgia) in the AA-Southern League, outfielder Jeff Baldwin hit a team-leading .316, shortstop Andujar Cedeno clubbed 13 homers, and first baseman Luis Gonzales topped the Mudcats with 24 homers. Mudcat lefty relief pitcher Al Osuna fashioned 68 strikeouts in only 59 innings, but team ERA, except for Blaise Ilsley's 1.94 in 84 innings (his fourth Minor League stop under 2.00), was high, and pitchers had a tough summer.

At Osceola in the A-Florida State League, righty starter Jeff Juden was 10–1 with a 2.27 ERA after 15 appearances. The six-foot-seven-inch hurler struck out 85 in his first 91 innings. His moundmate Rodney Windes looked sharp with a 1.98 ERA and 4–0 mark after 44 relief appearances. Gabriel Rodriguez finished at 12–5 with a 1.68.

And Houston's best development moves may have occurred in late August, when they traded age for youth. First, they acquired the Eastern League's (AA) leading hitter Jeff Bagwell (third base) from Boston for reliever Larry Anderson. Then they shipped off veteran second baseman Bill Doran to the Cincinnati Reds for Keith Kaiser, Butch Henry, and Terry McGriff.

Los Angeles Dodgers (35 prospects)

The Minor League phenom of the year was shortstop Jose Offerman, the kid with all the abilities and makeup that seem to destine him for stardom. Offerman's heroics for the Albuquerque Dukes (Pacific Coast League-AAA) earned him a shot with the Dodgers, and he responded with a homerun in his first Major League at bat, and four hits in his first two games.

He is labeled as a "can't miss" and should take Alfredo Griffin's shortstop job away in 1991. Still, the Minors are a big step from the Majors and as *Orange County Register* columnist Randy Youngman wrote:

> Let's hold off putting the Dodgers' twenty-one-year-old shortstop Jose Offerman in the Hall of Fame, OK? Offerman is a great prospect who still has a lot to learn. Don't forget, he made 50 errors in one minor-league season, so three errors in his first three big-league games aren't the result of nerves.

Youngman concluded with, "Remember how people raved about a 22-year-old Dodgers shortstop named Mariano Duncan in 1985?"

It is worth noting that Major League teams can quickly sour on young talent, and within two years, Duncan had worn out his welcome and was soon on his way out of Dodgertown.

Offerman was hitting .334 with 60 stolen bases at the time of call-up, while Dukes teammates Butch Davis (out fielder) hit .342, Dave Hansen (third baseman) was at .316, Mike Huff (outfielder) swung for a .325 mark, and Luis Lopez (first baseman) hovered above at .353. Catcher Darrin Fletcher, .291 and 13 homers, was traded to the Phillies for Dennis Cook. One add regarding Offerman: He had failed to hit any homeruns during his Minor League campaign before responding to Big League pressure and connecting for a dinger in his first MLB at bat.

Pitchingwise, the Dukes were led by reliever Mike Christopher with a 1.97 ERA; stopper Dave Walsh at 2.61, 6–0 and 66 K's in 62 IP; lefty fill-in starter Morris Madden, 83 whiffs in 79 IP; and reliever Darren Holmes, 12–2, 99 strikeouts in 93 innings—all who serve to offer Los Angeles some live young arms.

At San Antonio (Texas League-AA), an Offerman sound-alike, Dan Offerman, a first-round draft pick in 1987, won two straight complete games in late August (0.50 ERA) to raise his record to 10–8. Offerman missed the '87 and '88 seasons after undergoing elbow surgery twice, but looks like a comer for '91. He finished '90 at 12–8, 3.41.

San Antonio outfielder Tom Goodwin was considered a top prospect (.278 and 50 steals).

Also with the Missions, Kevin Campbell, with seven saves, a 2.03 ERA and 77 K's in 67 innings looks good; as do first baseman Eric Karros, at .352 and 18 homers and power-hitting outfielder Henry Rodriguez, .291, 28 homers and 109 RBI. All three may jump to Dodger Blue by '92. Karros, by the way, has previously hit .366 at Great Falls and .303 at Bakersfield his first two seasons.

On the Class A front, the Bakersfield Dodgers placed four players on the California League All-Star team: catcher Bryan Bear, dh Brett Magnusson, left-handed pitcher Jason Brosnan, and right-handed pitcher Jim McAndrew, who was promoted to San Antonio earlier in the season.

In the Rookie Leagues, on the Gulf Coast Dodgers, dh Domingo Mota, one of four Minor League Mota brothers (sons of former Dodger Manny Mota), hit .343 and stole 23 bases in 60 games.

And after the season, the Dodgers acquired right-handed pitcher Mike Wilkins (13–5, 2.42 ERA) from the Tigers. Wilkins threw for London in the Double-A Eastern League in 1990.

Montreal Expos (18 prospects)

Acquiring a package of Pirate prospects—Moises Alou, Willie Greene, and Scott Ruskin—in the Zane Smith trade added to the Expos' Minor League talents.

Greene, the Pirates' No. 1 draft choice in 1989, remained with the Pirates' Salem (Carolina League-A) franchise, and Alou, Pittsburgh's No. 1 draft choice in 1986, with the

Bucs' Buffalo (American Association-AAA) club. Alou hit .264 with 5 homers and 37 RBI and had an impressive nine outfield assists, following two .300 seasons (1988 and 1989) in the lower Minors. Alou finished the year at Indianapolis (American Association-AAA).

Up all season at Indianapolis, no regular hit better than .287, and none had hit more than 10 homers or had more than 59 RBI, so hitting help looked bleak at the Triple A level. The top prospect looked to be outfielder Eric Bullock, .281 and 30 stolen bases.

Pitchingwise, reliever Bob Malloy was at 2.70 with 31 K's in 30 innings, and starter Steve Fireovid was at 2.63. Starter Dan Gakeler chipped in at 3.23, and lefty Rich Sauveur was at 1.93.

At Jacksonville (Southern League-AA), catcher Greg Colbrunn paced the Expos at .301 and 13 homers, but the power story was outfielder Terrel Hansen, with 24 homers and 83 RBI. On the mound, watch for lefty starter Brian Barnes to move up. At Jacksonville, he posted a 13–7 mark, 2.77 ERA, and 213 strikeouts in 201 innings with only 144 hits given up. Moundmate Jeff Carter chalked up 15 saves and had a 1.84 ERA; Doug Piatt came in with 5 saves, a 2.58, and 43 whiffs in 38 innings; and Darrin Winston hurled a 2.14 ERA and 7 saves.

At Jamestown (New York-Penn League-A), outfielder Bobby Katzaroff showed poise while leading the league at .364 and stealing 33 bases in his first 70 games.

New York Mets (18 prospects)

Kelvin Torve, the first baseman who tore up the International League at Tidewater with numbers of .303, 11 homers, and 76 RBI, came up with a bang (.400 his first week) and a controversy. He was assigned number 24 in Mets pinstripes . . . the first player to wear that number since Willie Mays retired in 1973. If Torve endures, the above information might become a valued trivia answer. In the meantime, the Mets stemmed the controversy by assigning him a new number, 39, within two weeks.

Also at Tidewater were third baseman Chris Jelic, at .306, and outfielder Darren Reed, with 17 homers. Tides' pitching hopes were propelled by Jeff Innis with 19 saves and 1.71, reliever Ray Soff at 2.38, and starter Manny Hernandez with 157 K's in 173 IP. A Tidewater reliever, Julio Machado (1.69 ERA) was peddled to Milwaukee in the Charlie O'Brien trade.

At Jackson (Texas League-AA), second baseman Joe Dellicarri banged out a .386 mark in his first 44 trips to the plate, and switch-hitting outfielder Chick Carr stole 40 bases. On the hill, Anthony Young was 15–3 with a 1.65 ERA and Terry Bross added 28 saves and a 2.64.

At the A-level, at Columbia (South Atlantic League), speed was the watchword, with shortstop Tito Navarro swiping 40 to go with his .314 average; and outfielder Pat Howell stealing 61 bags by August. Third baseman Tim Howard led the league with a .323 average and 89 RBI, and Dave Telgheder was a top pitcher at 9–3, 1.54 ERA.

At St. Lucie (Florida State League-A), first baseman Nikco Riesgo was the top hitter at .324 with 8 homers and 30 steals, but he was traded to Philadelphia in the Tom Herr deal. Also packaged to the Phils was lefty hurler Rocky Elii, who was 3–3, 3.19 with Jackson (Texas League-AA).

Philadelphia Phillies (18 prospects)

At Scranton/Wilkes-Barre (International League-AAA), third baseman Greg Legg hit .325, and left-handed hitting outfielder Chris Knabenshue, acquired from the San Diego Padres, belted 18 homers to lead the Phillies-in-waiting. And second baseman Mickey Morandini looked like a genuine prospect in the field, while needing to improve his .250 performance at the plate.

On the Red Barons' hill, lefty reliever Steve Sharts was at 2.99 and 6–2 and lefty mop-up man Chuck McElroy had a 2.72 with 78 K's in 76 innings.

At Reading (Eastern League-AA), first baseman Gary Alexander bombed 19 homers and a .254 average, and shortstop Kim Batiste showed speed with more than 20 steals and a .276 average. On the Reading mound, Bob Ayrault went 4–6, with 10 saves and a credible 2.30 ERA, and stopper-reliever Matt Stevens was 3–2 with a great 1.55 ERA.

At Spartanburg (South Atlantic League-A), outfielder Sam Taylor hit .308, and outfielder Al Bennet was over .300 for most of the year. Pitcher Greg Gunderson finished 29 appearances and 55 innings with a 2.11 ERA, and lefty starter Bob Gladdy blazed through 83 innings with 98 strikeouts, a 7–3 mark and 3.35 ERA.

And the Phillies' General Manager George Thomas beat the development process last August by acquiring outfielder Julio Peguero, a .282 hitter at Harrisburg (Eastern League-AA) and outfielder Wes Chamberlain, .250 at Buffalo (American Association-AAA) from Pittsburgh in the Carmelo Martinez trade. Chamberlain was considered the Pirates' top prospect as late as Spring '90 and won the Eastern League's MVP award in 1989.

Not through, Thomas dealt soon-to-be-free-agent second baseman Tom Herr, 34, to the New York Mets for pitcher Rocky Elii and first baseman Nikco Riesgo. Riesgo looked like a comer at .324 with 8 homers and 30 steals at Single A, and lefty starter Rocky Elii was 3–3, 3.19 at Double A. Both players were assigned to Scranton–Wilkes-Barre. And, the Phils picked up catching prospect Darrin Fletcher from the Dodgers (PCL-AAA). Riesgo was then drafted by the Expos at the Winter Meetings and must remain in The Show in 1991 or be offered back to the Phils . . . a gamble or a steal?

Pittsburgh Pirates (25 prospects)

If youth must be served, don't look at the Bucs' Buffalo (International League-AAA) pitching staff for young hurlers. In 1990, the Bisons' pitching staff had an average age of 31.2 years while the parent Pirates' pitching staff averaged 28.6 years of age. Among the aged were Jerry Reuss (41) and Doug Bair (40).

Randy Tomlin was promoted from the Harrisburg Senators (Eastern League-AA) and threw a five-hitter in a 10–1 debut victory over the Philadelphia Phillies. Tomlin said, "I thought if I pitched well this year, I might have a shot at Triple A."

At Buffalo, outfielder Steve Carter hit .303 and first baseman Mark Ryal led the league at .334 and once went 16 games (50 at bats) between strikeouts to lead the bat attack. On the Bisons' mound, starter Randy Kramer was at 6–1 and 2.57, reliever Mark Ross came in at 2.02 and 11 saves, and starter Dorn Taylor was at 2.91, 14–6.

Randy Kramer, who was said to have the best fastball in the Pirates' organization, was up with the big club for a while before being sent back down to Buffalo to learn to change speeds and find some location. The twenty-nine-year-old was expected to be back in Pittsburgh in 1991, but was traded to the Cubs for pitcher Greg Kallevig, 4–10, 5.67 at Iowa (American Association-AAA).

Are Doug Bair (41) and Jerry Reuss (42) prospects? Bair was called up from Buffalo four times in 1990, and Reuss, after pitching twenty-eight consecutive shutout innings for the Bisons, was on the Bucs' forty-man roster at the end of the year before retiring to pursue a broadcasting career.

Switch-hitting catcher Armando Romero at Salem (Carolina League-A), made the most of his hits (.253) and had 73 RBI and 13 homers.

And at Welland in the Single-A New York–Penn League, pitcher David Tellers smoked his way to a 4–2 mark, 1.49 ERA, and 49 strikeouts in only 36 innings after 18 relief appearances.

In an apparent win-or-else-now and to-heck-with-the-future dismantling of the Buc's Minor League system in order to pursue the 1990 flag, Pittsburgh GM Larry

Doughty accidentally waived Wes Chamberlain (Buffalo, American Association-AAA), the 1989 Eastern League MVP who was considered the top player in the Pirates' system before the 1990 season, and outfielder Julio Peguero who hit .282 at Harrisburg (Eastern League—AA), and got Carmelo Martinez from the Phillies for them.

St. Louis Cardinals (23 prospects)

At Louisville (American Association-AAA) switch-hitting second baseman Todd Crosby checked in at .294, outfielder Ray Lankford banged out 10 circuit clouts. Outfielder Bernard Gilkey was on his way to 40 steals. On the Redbirds' hill, starter Omar Olivares remained steady at 2.64, lefty reliever Tim Sherrill was at 2.49, and relief ace Mike Perez, with 33 saves at Double-A Arkansas in 1989, picked up 31 Triple-A saves and 69 K's in 67 IP, despite a 4.28 performance. A 90-MPH fastball is Perez' out pitch; with his good slider and sinker, all should work at the Major League level once he develops his forkball.

But the Redbirds' two most-promising players, according to new Cards manager Joe Torre, seemed to be outfielders Gilkey at .295 and 3 homers, and Lankford at .272 with his 10 roundtrippers, who came on in September.

At Arkansas (Texas League-AA), outfielder Lonnie Maclin checked in at .308, and first baseman Joey Fernandez led the Travelers with 14 four-baggers.

And the Cards acquired third baseman Stan Royer (a No. 1 draft choice in 1988) batting .270 with 6 homers for Double-A Huntsville, Southern League, from the Oakland A's in the Felix Jose-Willie McGee trade.

San Diego Padres (18 prospects)

In Las Vegas (Pacific Coast League-AAA), first baseman Jerald Clark hit a solid .340, switch-hitting shortstop Joey Cora started strong and held steady at .333, second baseman Paul Faries hit .311 and stole 32 bases, outfielder

Thomas Howard hit .328, outfielder Warren Newson (twice a league leader in walks) slugged .304 and 13 homers, and first baseman Rob Nelson banged out 20 roundtrippers.

The Pads called up outfielder Eddie Williams, an Alliance All-Star game starter, from Las Vegas after posting half-season numbers of .316, 17 homers, and 75 RBI.

At Wichita (Texas League-AA), third baseman Greg David led the Wranglers at .299, and outfielder Mike Humphreys bombed 16 four-baggers and stole 23 bases. Switch-hitting outfielder Will Taylor showed speed with 35 steals.

On the Wichita mound, lefty Rich Holsman had 66 K's in 52 innings but staggered home with a 4.15 ERA.

Padre power was delivered for the Riverside Red Wave (California League-A) by third baseman Dave Slaton, who blasted 19 homers in his first 300 at bats.

And in the off-season, the Pads plucked third-sacker Tom Reddington (12 homers, 52 RBI for Greenville in the Southern League) from the ranks of the Atlanta Braves.

San Francisco Giants (26 prospects)

At Phoenix (Pacific Coast League-AAA), Rick Parker, outfielder-third baseman, hit .323, and Mike Laga, infielder, had blasted 20 homers before they were recalled in August.

At Shreveport (Texas League-AA), catcher Steve Decker hit .293 and slugged 15 homers; while on the Captain's mound, Rod Beck, the Ulysses S. Grant High School (Van Nuys, California) graduate—same school that graduated ex-Major League hurler Tom Griffen and actor Tom Selleck—had a 2.23 ERA, Steve Lienhard a 2.50 ERA, and reliever Steve Reed a 1.64 ERA.

The Giants' farm system's most prized prospect seems to be shortstop Andres Santana, the Shreveport field leader, who fielded brilliantly and hit a respectable .292.

Other prospects include Dan Rambo, who came to the rescue with a 12–2 mark, 2.19 ERA, and 142 K's in 144 IP at San Jose (California League-A), and Kevin Rogers, who was 12–5 with 162 whiffs in 149 innings.

Left-handed hitting first baseman Joey James hit .289 for Clinton (Midwest League-A) and blasted 18 homers, and lefty hurler Chris Hancock K'd 123 in 111 innings with a 2.28 ERA and 11–3 mark.

Today's Best

Baseball America, the diamond publication published by Miles Wolff, owner of the Durham Bulls (Carolina League) and Butte Copper Kings (Pioneer League), is generally regarded as a superior judge of talent. According to its mid-August survey of Minor League talent ("Best Tools"), the following selected information was imparted on today's Little Show stars.

[*Author's note*: Player, followed by Minor League team and Major League parent club.]

Best Batting Prospects

Triple-A—Juan Gonzalez (Oklahoma City/Rangers); David Segui (Rochester/Orioles); and Tino Martinez (Calgary/Mariners).

Double-A—Jeff Bagwell (New Britain/Red Sox*); Frank Thomas (Birmingham/White Sox); Jeff Conine (Memphis/Royals); and Henry Rodriguez (San Antonio/Dodgers).

Bagwell traded to the Astros

Single-A—Ray Ortiz (Visalia/Twins); Greg Blosser (Lynchburg/Red Sox); Nikco Riesgo (St. Lucie/Mets*); Reggie Sanders (Cedar Rapids/Reds); and Ryan Kiesko (Sumter/Braves).

Riesgo traded to the Phillies, drafted by the Expos

Best Power Hitters

Triple-A—Juan Gonzalez (Oklahoma City/Rangers); Leo Gomez (Rochester/Orioles); and Mike Laga (Phoenix/Giants).

Double-A—Mitch Lyden (Albany/Yankees); Frank Thomas (Birmingham/White Sox); and Henry Rodriguez (San Antonio/Dodgers).

Single-A—Dave Slaton (Riverside/Padres); Elvin Paulino (Winston-Salem/Cubs); Gerald Williams (Fort Lauderdale/ Yankees); Fred Cooley (Madison/A's); and Mark Thomas (Columbia/Mets).

Best Pitching Prospects

Triple-A—Scott Scudder (Nashville/Reds); Steve Searcy (Toledo/Tigers); and Ray Young (Tacoma/A's).

Double-A—Mike Linskey (Hagerstown/Orioles); Charles Nagy (Canton-Akron/Indians); Scott Erickson (Orlando/ Twins); and Anthony Young (Jackson/Mets).

Single-A—Chris Johnson (Stockton/Brewers); Arthur Rhodes (Frederick/Orioles); Jeff Juden (Osceola/Astros); Alan Newman (Kenosha/Twins); and Randy Marshall (Fayetteville/Tigers).

Most Exciting Player

Triple-A—Bernard Gilkey (Louisville/Cardinals); Mark Whiten (Syracuse/Blue Jays); and Joe Offerman (Albuquerque/Dodgers).

Double-A—Luis Mercedes (Hagerstown/Orioles); Frank Thomas (Birmingham/White Sox); and Chuck Carr (Jackson/Mets).

Single-A—Darrell Sherman (Riverside/Padres); Russ Davis (Prince William/Yankees); Nikco Riesgo (St. Lucie/ Mets*); Reggie Sanders (Cedar Rapids/Reds); and Pat Howell (Columbia/Mets).

*Riesgo traded to the Phillies, drafted by the Expos

1990s Minor League Most Valuable Players
(for the eleven full-season Minor Leagues)

Triple-A

American Association—Juan Gonzalez, outfielder, Oklahoma City (Rangers)

International League—Hensley "Bam Bam" Meulens, outfielder, Columbus (Yankees)

Pacific Coast League—Jose Offerman, shortstop, Albuquerque (Dodgers)

Double-A

Eastern League—Jeff Bagwel, third baseman, New Britain (Red Sox; traded to the Astros)

Southern League—Jeff Conine, first baseman, Memphis (Royals)

Texas League—Henry Rodriguez, outfielder, San Antonio (Dodgers)

Single-A

California League—Frank Bolick, third baseman, San Bernardino (Mariners)

Carolina League—Gary Scott, third baseman, Winston-Salem (Pirates)

Florida State League—Nikco Riesgo, first baseman, St. Lucie (Mets; traded to the Phillies, drafted by the Expos)

Midwest League—Reggie Sanders, outfielder, Cedar Rapids (Reds)

South Atlantic League—Tim Howard, third baseman, Columbia (Mets)

Yesterday's Stars: Minor League Then, Major League Now

Without apology, the following players were chosen for their Minor League records or their Major League prowess, returning to where it all began, in The Little Show.

Some telltale Minor League stats of the past should have shown perceptive Major League experts that their young troops were future "can't miss" stars (be sure to check out Nolan Ryan, Jose Canseco, Rickey Henderson, Don Mattingly, Ron Kittle, Steve Balboni, Mike Marshall, and Rob

Deer in the American League, and Dwight Gooden, Sid Fernandez, Gary Redus, Vince Coleman, Donnell Nixon, Tony Gwynn, and Mark Grant in the National League).

Once again, some of these "career" years or successive years' performances were just too good to overlook, despite the level of competition. These Minor League stats proved MLB worthiness. Some current Major Leaguers' Minor League totals worth noting follow.

American League

Baltimore Orioles

Jeff Ballard: 10–2, 1.41 ERA at Newark in 1985, 1.85 ERA for Hagerstown in 1986; Phil Bradley: three straight seasons over .300; Pete Harnisch: first two seasons under 2.50 ERA and better than a strikeout per inning; Randy Milligan: 29 homers, 103 RBI, 91 walks and .326 for Tidewater in 1987; Cal Ripken, Jr.: played every game and hit 25 homers for Charlotte in 1980.

Boston Red Sox

Wade Boggs: five consecutive seasons over .300, won International League batting title at .335 at Pawtucket in 1981 after losing The Silver Bat by .0007 the year before; Tom Brunansky: blasted 70 homers and a .307 average over three years from 1979–81 for Salinas, El Paso, and Salt Lake City; Roger Clemens: ERAs of 1.24 at Winter Haven in 1983, 1.38 at New Britain in 1983, and 1.93 at Pawtucket in 1984; Danny Heep: hit .340 at Daytona Beach in 1987, .327 at Columbus in 1979, and .343 at Tucson in 1980; Mike Marshall: hit .373, 34 homers, and 137 RBI at Albuquerque in 1981, and hit .388 for the Dukes in '82; Phil Plantier: hit .300, 27 homers, and 105 RBI at Lynchburg in 1989; Jeff Reardon: 17–4, 2.54 ERA at Jackson in 1978 and a 2.09 ERA at Tidewater in 1979.

California Angels

Chili Davis (now with the Twins): .350 and 19 homers in
88 games at Phoenix in 1981; Bryan Harvey: 111 strikeouts in 81 innings at Quad City in 1985; 68 K's in 57
innings for Palm Springs in 1986 and 78 whiffs and a 2.04
ERA in 54 innings at Midland in 1987; Lance Parrish: 25
homers in 115 games for Evansville in 1977; Luis Polonia:
four seasons over .300 and 55 steals at Madison in 1984;
Max Venable: 12 1/2 seasons in the Minors . . . at least give
him a break for perseverance and makeup.

Chicago White Sox

Ivan Calderon: .365 for Salt Lake in 1984, two seasons
with 20 or more homers; Ozzie Guillen: .347 at Reno in
1982; Ron Kittle (released): 40 homeruns, 102 RBI, and
.324 at Glens Falls in 1981, 50 homers, 144 RBI, and .345
at Edmonton in 1982, before being called up; Dan Pasqua:
33 homers for Nashville in 1984, 18 homers in 78 games
(on the Yankee shuttle up-and-down) for Columbus in
1985; Bobby Thigpen: 1.78 ERA and 74 K's in 52 innings
at Niagara Falls in 1985.

Cleveland Indians

Tom Candiotti: six consecutive seasons under 2.92 ERA;
Keith Hernandez: .351 and .300 for Tulsa in 1974–75;
Candy Maldonado: 70 homers, 302 RBI in three seasons at
Albuquerque, 1981–83—25 and 102, 21 and 104, and 24
and 96; Ken Phelps: blasted 46 homers, 141 RBI, 108
walks, and .333 for Wichita in 1982.

Detroit Tigers

Cecil Fielder: hit .322, 20 homers and 68 RBI in 69 games
for Butte in 1982, and .302 with 38 homers in 106 games
in 1989 for Hanshin of the Japanese Central League; Gary
Pettis: three consecutive seasons over 50 steals; Larry

Sheets: 25 homers for Charlotte in 1983; Lou Whitaker: amassed 76 steals in two seasons.

Kansas City Royals

Mark Davis: 19–6, 2.47, and 185 K's in 193 innings for Reading in 1980; Jim Eisenreich: .311, 23 homers, 27 doubles, and 99 RBI at Wisconsin Rapids in 1981; Steve Farr (now with the Yankees): 13–1, 1.61, 108 K's in 112 innings at Buffalo in 1983; Tom Gordon: 16–5, 11.62, and 263 strikeouts in 183.2 innings; Danny Tartabull: 43 homers, 109 RBI, and .300 for Calgary in 1985.

Milwaukee Brewers

Chris Bosio: 17–6, 2.73 for Beloit in 1984 and 16 saves, 7–3, 2.28 for Vancouver in 1986; Greg Brock: 105 homers and 339 RBI in three seasons—1980/Lodi-29 and 95 RBI, 1981/San Antonio-32 with 106 RBI, 1982/Albuquerque-44 with 138 RBI; Rob Deer (now with the Tigers): 126 homers in four seasons—1981/Fresno-33, 1982/Shreveport-27 homers, 1983/Shreveport-35 homers, and 1984/Phoenix-31 homers; Terry Francona: .351 in 1981 for Memphis and Denver; Dave Parker: .358 at Monroe in 1971; Greg Vaughn: 87 homers in three seasons—1987/Beloit-33, 1988/El Paso-28, and 1989/Denver-26.

Minnesota Twins

Gary Gaetti (now with the Angels): 30 homers for Orlando in 1981; Dan Gladden: seven seasons over .300, including .397 at Phoenix in 1984, two years over 50 steals; Brian Harper: 28 homers, 45 doubles, and .350 at Salt Lake City in 1981; Kent Hrbek: 27 homers, 111 RBI, and .379 at Visalia in 1981; Tim Laudner: 42 homers for Orlando in 1981; Kirby Puckett: .382 for Elizabethton in 1982, and 91 steals in his first 203 games, Paul Sorrento: 27 homers for Orlando in 1989; David West: 194 K's in 150 innings at Columbia in 1985, 186 K's in 166 innings at Jackson in 1987, and 12–4 with a 1.80 ERA for Tidewater in 1988.

New York Yankees

Kevin Maas: 28 homeruns for Albany and Prince William in 1988; Steve Balboni: 151 homers and 480 RBI in five years—1979/Fort Lauderdale-26, 1980/Nashville-34, 1981/Columbus-33, 1982/Columbus-32 in only 83 games, and 1983/Columbus-27 in only 84 games on the Yankee shuttle; Mel Hall: 1981/Midland-24 homers, 1982/Iowa-34; Dave LaPoint: 1979/Stockton-208 strikeouts in 180 innings; Don Mattingly: five seasons over .300—1979/Oneonta-.349, 1980/Greensboro-.358, 1981/Nashville-.314, 1982 Columbus .315, and 1983 Columbus-.340; Dave Righetti (now with the Giants): 127 K's in 91 innings at Tulsa in 1978 and 122 K's in 109 innings in '79 for West Haven and Columbus; Steve Sax: .346 and 34 steals at San Antonio in 1981.

Oakland Athletics

Jose Canseco: .333, with 36 homers, 127 RBI, and 70 walks in 118 games for Huntsville and Tacoma in 1985 (25 of those dingers in 58 games with Huntsville); Dave Henderson: 27 homers and .300 for San Jose in 1979; Rickey Henderson: four great Minor League seasons—1976/Boise-.336 with 29 steals, 1977 Modesto-.345 with 95 steals, 1978/Jersey City-.310 with 81 steals, and 1979/Ogden-.309 with 44 steals in 71 games; Carney Lansford: .332 and 18 homers for El Paso in 1977; Mark McGwire: 24 homers for Modesto in 1985; Gene Nelson: 20–3, 1.97 ERA for Fort Lauderdale in 1980; Dave Stewart: 17–4, 2.15 ERA for Clinton in 1977.

Seattle Mariners

Mickey Brantley: 30 homers, .318 at Calgary in 1986 before being called up; Jay Buhner: 31 homers for Columbus in 1987; Ken Griffey, Jr.: .320 at Bellingham in 1987 and .338 at San Bernardino in 1988; Randy Johnson: 133 K's in 120 innings for West Palm Beach in 1986, 163 K's in 140 innings for Jacksonville in 1987; Jeffrey Leonard: .365 for Albuquerque in 1978 and .401 for Phoenix in 1981; Edgar Martinez: .363 for Calgary in 1988 and .345 in '89.

Texas Rangers

Brad Arnsberg: 12–5 and 2.95 at Greensboro in 1984, 14–2 and 1.59 for Albany in 1985; Julio Franco: five consecutive seasons over .300; Nolan Ryan: 17–4, 2.31, and 307 strikeouts in 202 innings for Greenville and Williamsport in 1966, after fanning 115 in 78 innings a year earlier for Marion. Ryan, the all-time fewest-hits-per-inning leader, gave up only 118 hits in 202 innings during that '66 Minor League season.

Toronto Blue Jays

John Cerutti: 120 K's in 107 innings at Medicine Hat in 1981 and 136 whiffs in 113 innings at Kinston in 1982; Mike Flanagan: 181 K's in 187 innings and 2.01 ERA for Miami and Asheville in 1974; Tom Henke: 100 strikeouts in 87 innings for Tulsa in 1982; Glenallen Hill: 31 homers for Knoxville in 1986, but as a hitter, he fanned 211 times in 131 games for Kinston, with 20 homers and 42 steals in 1985—the high number of K's, when compared to his production at that level, indicates aggressiveness and is not necessarily a negative stat (Hill fanned 665 times over four Minor League seasons but blasted 83 homers, drove in 284 runs and stole 112 bases while hitting .242); Mookie Wilson: 99 steals over two seasons at Tidewater—1979–80.

National League

Atlanta Braves

Nick Esasky: 30 home runs for Waterbury in 1980 and 27 dingers in 105 games for Indianapolis in 1982; Ron Gant: 26 homers, 102 RBI for Durham in 1986; Andres Thomas: .315 for Anderson in 1983; Dave Justice: 22 homers and 105 RBI for Sumter and Durham in 1986.

Chicago Cubs

Mike Bielecki: 19–3 with Hawaii in 1984; Andre Dawson: hit .352 with 28 homers in 114 games with Quebec and Denver in 1976; Shawon Dunston: three straight seasons of .310 or better to start his career, 58 steals for Quad City in 1983; Mark Grace: won batting title at Peoria (.342) in 1986, was Eastern League MVP at Pittsfield (.333, 17 homers, 101 RBI) in 1987; Jerome Walton: won Eastern League batting title in 1988 (.331) and stole 42 bases, after stealing 49 and hitting .335 at Peoria in 1987; Mitch Williams: 175 strikeouts in 132 innings for Salem and Tulsa in 1985.

Cincinnati Reds

Glen Braggs: hit a lofty .390 and 16 homers for Paintsville in 1983, .360 for Vancouver in 1986; Hal Morris: hit .378 at Oneonta in 1986, .326 for Albany in '87, and won International League title at .326 for Columbus in '89; Jose Rijo: 15–5 with a 1.68 ERA and 152 strikeouts in 160 innings for Ft. Lauderdale in 1983.

Houston Astros

Eric Anthony: blasted 29 homeruns for Asheville in 1988 and bombed 31 for Columbus and Tucson in '89; Glenn Davis (now with the O's): knocked out 25 homers for Columbus in 1983; Franklin Stubbs (now with the Brewers): hit 32 homers for Albuquerque in 1986; Eric Yelding: 62 steals for Kinston in 1985, 83 steals for Knoxville and Myrtle Beach in '87, and 59 for Syracuse in '88.

Los Angeles Dodgers

Kal Daniels: hit .367 for Billings in 1982; Jeff Hamilton: hit .360 at Albuquerque in 1987; Ramon Martinez: went 16–5, 2.17 ERA at Vero Beach in 1987 and 10–2, 2.79 ERA and 127 strikeouts in 113 innings at Albuquerque in 1989.

Montreal Expos

Dennis "Oil Can" Boyd: 7–1, 2.48 ERA, and 79 K's in 69 innings for Elmira in 1980; Andres Galarraga: 27 homers for Jacksonville in 1984, 25 blasts for Indianapolis in '85; Otis Nixon: four times stole more than 60 bases, including 94 steals for Columbus in 1983; Tim Raines (now with the ChiSox): hit .354 and stole 77 bases for Denver in 1979.

New York Mets

Sid Fernandez: 1.54 ERA and 128 strikeouts in 76 innings at Lethbridge in 1981 and 1.91 ERA and 137 K's in 84 innings at Vero Beach in '82; Dwight Gooden: 300 strikeouts in 191 innings, while going 19–4 with a 2.50 at Lynchburg in 1983; Gregg Jefferies: .354 at Lynchburg in 1986 and .367 and 20 homers at Jackson in 1987; Dave Magadan: .350 at Lynchburg in 1984; Kevin McReynolds: hit .376 and 28 homers at Reno in 1982, .352 at Amarillo in '82, and .377 and 32 homers at Las Vegas in '83; Darryl Strawberry (now with the Dodgers): belted 34 homers, 97 RBI, and stole 45 bases at Jackson in 1982.

Philadelphia Phillies

Lenny Dykstra: hit .358 with 105 stolen bases, 107 walks, and only 35 strikeouts for Lynchburg in 1983; Von Hayes: hit .329, 90 RBI and 51 stolen bases for Waterloo in 1980; John Kruk: hit .341 at Beaumont in 1983, and a league-leading .351 for Las Vegas in 1985; Randy Ready: hit a league-leading .376 at Butte in 1980, a league-leading .375 at El Paso in '82 and at five other Minor League stops he hit at .308 or better.

Pittsburgh Pirates

Sid Bream: 32 homers, 118 RBI at Albuquerque in 1983, 20 clouts and .343 for the Dukes in '84; John Cangelosi: 87 steals for Appleton in 1983 and 65 stolen bases for Glens Falls in '85; Bob Kipper: 18–8 and a 2.04 ERA for Redwood in 1984; Carmelo Martinez: hit 79 homers over three seasons—1981–83 at Midland and Iowa; Gary Redus: Led Pioneer League in batting, runs, hits, total bases, and steals for Billings in 1978 . . . and his .462 average was the second highest in Minor League history (Walter Malmquist hit a disputed .477 in the Nebraska State League in 1913), stole 40-plus bases, and hit 16 or more homers for 5 straight seasons.

St. Louis Cardinals

Vince Coleman (now with the Mets): hit a league-leading .350 and recorded a professional baseball record 145 steals in 113 games for Macon in 1983, 101 steals for Louisville in 1984; Pedro Guerrerro: hit .345 for Danville in 1975, 305 for Waterbury in '76, 403 for Albuquerque in '77, .337 and 116 RBI for Albuquerque in '78, and .333 and 103 RBI for the Dukes in '89; Greg Mathews: fashioned a microscopic 1.11 ERA and 13–1 mark with St. Petersburg in 1985.

San Diego Padres

Roberto Alomar: hit a league-leading .346 for Reno in 1986; Jack Clark (now with the Red Sox): drove in 117 RBI in 131 games for Fresno in 1974; Jerald Clark: five consecutive years hitting over .300; Mark Grant: 243 strikeouts in 198 innings, 16–5 with a 2.36 ERA for Clinton in 1982; Tony Gwynn: hit .462 for Amarillo in 1981, never hit below .328 at any Minor League stop over three years; Garry Templeton: hit .401 in 42 games for Arkansas in 1975.

San Francisco Giants

Brett Butler (now with the Dodgers): hit .366 for Durham in 1980, and .335 and .363 for Richmond in 1981–82; Mike Laga: 31 homers for Birmingham in 1981, 34 homers for Evansville in '82, 30 more dingers for Evansville in '84, and three other Minor League seasons with 20-or-more blasts; Donnell Nixon: stole 144 bases and hit .321 for

Bakersfield in 1983, stole 102 bases for Chattanooga in '84, and five times hit better than .300; Rick Reuschel: 1.32 ERA at Wichita in 1972; Matt Williams: hit .320 with 26 homeruns in 76 games for Phoenix in 1989.

Great Players of the Past: Minors and Majors

The above statistics may seem to be quite impressive, but they pale considerably when compared to the early glimpses of greatness shown by the following athletes . . . or, at least after the highlighted seasons, these young men looked as though they were ready for the jump to the Majors.

Once again, prospects are evaluated, not on statistics alone, but on potential and value to the parent ballclub. But some of the years put together by those diamond stars that follow are years for the ages . . . and certainly an indication that these men were ready to stand the Big Leagues on its ear.

Henry Aaron—Hank Aaron, the all-time Major League homerun king for the Milwaukee Braves, began his work in style as he excelled at Eau Claire in 1952, after being purchased from the Indianapolis Clowns of the Negro American League with a .336 average and only 19 strikeouts in 87 games. He followed that up in 1953 with a .362 mark at Jacksonville, with a league-leading 208 hits in 137 games, 22 homers, 36 doubles, and 125 RBI. He began his assault on the National League with the Milwaukee Braves in 1954.

Grover Cleveland Alexander—The Hall-of-Fame pitcher who threw 90 shutouts and won 373 games in the Bigs, won 29 games and fired an amazing 14 Minor League shutouts for the Syracuse Chiefs of the New York State League in 1910. Six years later, he threw a Major League record 16 blankings for the Philadelphia Phillies.

Earl Averill—The Hall-of-Fame outfielder for the Cleveland Indians demolished the Pacific Coast League with the San Francisco Seals in 1928 by hitting .356 (his third straight .300 season), 36 homers, and 173 RBI. He hit .378 with the Tribe in 1936.

Johnny Bench—The Hall-of-Fame catcher for the "Big Red Machine" Cincinnati Reds earned his "can't miss" label when he belted 22 homers in 98 games for the Peninsula Grays of the Carolina League in 1966. Peninsula retired his uniform, as did the Cincy Reds. Bench blasted 45 dingers for the Reds in 1970.

Oscar Charleston—A twenty-three-year performer at first base and in the outfield in the Negro Leagues, during which time he hit .357. "The Hoosier Comet" showed his abilities in 1921 when, with the St. Louis Giants, he hit .434, with 15 homeruns (dead ball era), and 34 stolen bases. He again rose to the top and displayed his talents— he was considered by many to be the greatest Negro Leagues player of that era—in 1924 and '25 for the Harrisburg Giants when he hit .411 and .445, also leading the league in homeruns both years with 11 and 20. Charleston's career ended in 1941 (he was 45), before he would have been allowed to play in the Majors.

Dizzy Dean—Hall-of-Fame pitching whiz, "Ol' Diz" led the 1931 Texas League with Houston by compiling a 26–10 mark with 303 strikeouts and a 1.57 ERA. Dean backed up his Minor League marks in the Majors, as he won 20 with the St. Louis Cardinals in 1933, improved to 30 wins in '34, won 28 in '35, and 24 more in '36 before an injury overtook him.

Joe DiMaggio—Joltin' Joe, "The Yankee Clipper," exhibited his grace and style in a San Francisco Seals uniform in the Pacific Coast League of 1933 as he hit in a record 61 consecutive games. DiMag finished the season at .340 with 169 RBI. Four years later, DiMaggio drove in 167 runs with the Yankees, and in 1941, hit in an MLB record 56 straight games with the Bronx Bombers en route to his enshrinement as a Hall-of-Fame centerfielder. Joe D. finished with eleven .300 seasons in a thirteen-year-career which was interrupted by three years of military service.

Vince DiMaggio—Joe's older brother, a top Minor League player in his own right who also played for ten years in the Majors, Vince led the American Association with 46 homers and 136 RBI for Kansas City in 1939. After his MLB days were over, at age thirty-six, Vince led the California League in homers with 30 for Stockton in 1948.

Lou Gehrig—The Hall-of-Fame-bound "Iron Horse" for the New York Yankees, Gehrig amassed a slugging percentage of a whopping .720 for Hartford of the Eastern League in 1924. Three years later, the slugging first baseman won the American League MVP award by finishing with a slugging percentage of .765, a batting average of .373, 47 homers, 52 doubles, 18 triples, and 175 RBI for the Yanks.

Josh Gibson—A Hall-of-Fame catcher who was not allowed to play in the Major Leagues because of his skin color (he died at the age of 35 soon after Jackie Robinson broke the MLB color line), Gibson showed he was ready for The Show when he hit 20 homers in 38 games and batted .457 for the Pittsburgh Crawfords in 1936; batted .453 in the Dominican Republic in 1937; .467 for Vera Cruz of the Mexican League in 1940; a loop-leading 33 roundtrippers, 124 RBI and a .754 slugging percentage in 94 games in '41; .480 in the Puerto Rican Winter League in 1941; 20 homers in 42 games and .452 for the Homestead Grays in '42; and he hit .474 for the Homestead Grays in 1943. He led the Mexican League in homers and RBI in 1941 with 33 four-baggers and 124 runs driven in.

Hank Greenberg—The Hall-of-Fame slugging first baseman for the Detroit Tigers got it all started with the Beaumont Exporters of the Texas League in 1932, for whom he hit 39 homers and drove in 131 runs. Greenberg drove in 139 runs for the Tigers two years later and knocked in 170 in 1935. He won four American League homerun titles and slammed 58 in 1938.

Tony Lazerri—The classy second baseman for the New York Yankees showed he was ready for pinstripes when, in 1925, playing for Salt Lake City of the Pacific Coast League, "Poosh 'em Up Tony" set the Coast on fire with an atmospheric then-Minor League record 60 home runs (two years before Babe Ruth hit the same magic number in the Bigs), 222 RBI (also a record at the time), and 202 runs scored (still a Minor League mark). As a Yankee rookie in 1926, Lazerri drove in 114.

Mickey Mantle—Arguably the greatest switch-hitter in baseball history, "The Mick" finished his final Minor League season with the Kansas City Blues of the American Association in 1951, hitting .361 with 11 homers and 55 RBI in 166 at bats. Mantle finished his Big League career with 536 homeruns. Minor League stats often tell: Mantle proved he was not a Major League *shortstop* by committing 55 errors at short with Kansas City in 1950; he was converted to an outfielder, where he played with Hall-of-Fame skill for sixteen years before moving to first base in an effort to save his legs and prolong his career.

Roger Maris—One-half of the Yankees' famed "M&M Boys," Maris, the MLB single-season homerun leader—with 61 in 1961—showed he had that sweet swing, taught to him by coach Jo Jo White, when he blasted 32 four-baggers for Keokuk in 1954. When he finally made the Majors with Cleveland in 1957, Maris went 3 for 5 in the season opener against the White Sox, and the next day, his second as a Major Leaguer, showed what he could do by slamming a game-winning grand slam homer in the top of the 11th.

Christy Mathewson—The Hall-of-Fame pitcher known as "Big Six" won 373 games during his seventeen-year Big League career. He displayed what was to come by fashioning a 20–2 mark for Norfolk of the Virginia League in 1900. He followed that up in 1901, in the National League, by going 20–17 with a 2.41 ERA as a rookie for the New York Giants.

Willie Mays—Often called the best all-around player in the game, "Say Hey" showed he was ready for the Bigs and the New York Giants when, during a 35-game stint with the Minneapolis Millers of the American Association in 1951, he demolished Triple-A pitching for a .477 average. Mays went on to a Hall-of-Fame career and ten .300 seasons for a 22-year-career average of .302 and 660 home runs.

Willie McCovey—"Stretch" was a Hall-of-Fame first baseman who broke in with the San Francisco Giants in 1959 and lasted 22 years, hitting 521 homeruns in the process. Willie Mac ended his Minor League career with a flourish and began his MLB stay the same way. In 1959, playing for Phoenix in the Pacific Coast League, McCovey showed he was ready for Big League pitching as he blasted 29 homeruns in just over half-a-season—a total that was good enough to win the PCL home run crown that season. He came up to the newly relocated San Francisco Giants and in 52 games, hit 13 more homers while batting .354, totals that were good enough to get him named National League Rookie of the Year in the same year he won a Minor League homerun title.

Stan "The Man" Musial—Musial impressed scouts both as a pitcher and as a hitter, and it was as the latter for which he was enshrined in the Hall of Fame. The "Danora Greyhound" pitched for Daytona Beach in 1940 and went 18–5, and he also played the outfield that season and hit .352. Musial hit better than .300 for 18 of his 22 years, won seven batting titles, and hit .331 for his career.

Lefty O'Doul—Belted out 309 hits and scored 185 runs for Salt Lake of the Pacific Coast League in 1925, hitting .375. He followed that up by hitting a National League-leading .398 for the Philadelphia Phillies in 1929. O'Doul hit .352 in 3253 at bats in the Minors and .349 in 3264 at bats in the Majors.

Jackie Robinson—Regularly called "The Black Jim Thorpe," this all-around athlete led the International League in batting at .349 for Montreal in 1946, the year before he was called up to play for the Brooklyn Dodgers. He also led second basemen in fielding percentage at .985— only 10 errors in 656 chances—and runs scored (113), and he was second in stolen bases with 40. Robinson also hit .387 in 1945, as a shortstop playing for the Kansas City Monarchs of the Negro American League.

Babe Ruth—Originally signed as a pitcher, and one who ranks as one of the best lefty hurlers to ever take the mound, Ruth went 22–9 for Baltimore and Providence of the International League in 1914. Known more for his bat than his arm (714 career homers and a .342 batting average), Ruth compiled a .671 winning percentage and a 2.28 career ERA in the Bigs, winning 23 games in 1916 and 24 in 1917 before his conversion to the outfield on a full-time basis.

Herb Score—Touted as the best fireballing mound ace in baseball (Cleveland Indians) before an unfortunate incident—a line drive off the bat of classy Yankee infielder Gil MacDougald that struck him in the eye—in 1957 robbed him of his perception, Score set the American Association on fire with a 330-strikeout performance while going 22–5 for Indianapolis in 1954. Score led the American League in strikeouts as a rookie in 1955, and again in 1956, and won 20 games in that '56 season.

Dick Stuart—Known as "Dr. Strangeglove," a power-hitting, no-field first baseman for the Pittsburgh Pirates, belted out 66 homers for Lincoln of the Western League in 1956 but didn't make the Majors until 1958. Stuart blasted 222 homers during his Minor League career and 228 more in the Majors.

Gorman Thomas—A player who won two American League homerun titles and who hit more than 30 round-trippers five times in 13 seasons showed he had power by slamming out 51 four-baggers while playing in a bandbox park for Sacramento of the Pacific Coast League in 1974. Thomas banged out 45 for the Milwaukee Brewers in 1979.

Virgil Trucks—A durable pitcher who lasted for 17 years in the Majors (Detroit Tigers, et al.), showed he could plow through a lineup by fanning 418 hitters while playing for Andalusia of the Alabama-Florida League in 1938. Trucks earned one American League strikeout crown by whiffing 153 batters in 1949.

Dazzy Vance—The righty pitcher who won 196 games with the Dodgers and others, threw out a clue to his worth by going 22–11 with New Orleans of the Southern League in 1921. He followed that up by winning 18 games and leading the National League in strikeouts as a rookie for Brooklyn the next year.

Paul "Big Poison" Waner—A reliable, if oft-intoxicated Hall-of-Fame slugger with the Pittsburgh Pirates, Waner completed a three-year reign of terror on Pacific Coast League pitchers by hitting .369, .356, and .401 for the San Francisco Seals from 1924–26. In 1925, Waner connected for a league-record 75 doubles. As a rookie for Pittsburgh in 1926, after being called up in May, Waner blistered the National League to the tune of a .336 average, which he increased to a league-leading .380 in his sophomore season.

Ted Williams—A man who has been called "the greatest hitter who ever lived," Williams, the Boston Red Sox Hall-of-Fame right fielder who was affectionately called "The Splendid Splinter" and "Teddy Ballgame," annihilated the American Association for Minneapolis in 1938 as a nineteen-year-old, batting .366. After hitting American League pitching for .327 and .344 his first two seasons in the Bigs, "The Thumper" hit .406 in 1941.

Jud Wilson—A stand-out third baseman in the Negro Leagues, Wilson won back-to-back batting championships in the Cuban Winter Leagues with averages of .430 and .424 in 1925 and 1926. He also hit .469 for the Baltimore Black Sox of the NAL in 1927. Wilson spent 24 years in the Black Leagues, compiling a .345 average.

Carl Yastrzemski—Yaz, the right fielder-first baseman Hall-of-Fame symbol of the Boston Red Sox from 1961 to 1983, made his presence felt as a second baseman for the Raleigh Capitals in 1959 when he was selected Rookie of the Year and Player of the Year in the Carolina League. Yaz won the batting title at .377 and led the league in doubles with 34. Yastrzemski won the American League batting crown for the BoSox in 1963 at .321.

Minor League Stars, Major League Busts

For many reasons, there have been ballplayers who excelled at the Minor League level but either failed in the Majors or never really got a fair shot to perform in The Show. Call it promise unfulfilled or promises unkept, big fishes in little ponds sinking once they get to the Major League ocean, or examples of burnout, but many Minor League heroes never waxed heroic in the Bigs.

Why?

One may argue that the competition, or lack thereof, is the main factor. Minor Leaguers just aren't as good as Major Leaguers and once a kid comes up to face athletes on the Big League level, he may have exceeded his level of competence and must be relegated forever to the Little Show. Former Dodgers executive Fresco Thompson said, "At the Minor League level, players reach their level of competency; at the Major League level, players reach their level of incompetency."

Another oft-told argument is that Minor League hitters face Minor League fastballs and very few curves, which are, at best, Minor League curves. Once they face Major League pitchers with an assortment of pitches—Big League heat and Big League benders—that can all be spotted and controlled, a hitter of Minor League talent is soon exposed and sent packing. Cliff Mapes, who wore number 3 for the New York Yankees before it was retired for Babe Ruth, switched to number 13 (the first Yankee to wear that one), then wore number 7 before it was given to Mickey Mantle, said, "In the American Association, pitchers who knew my weaknesses would throw against me once in a series. In the American League, I'd see them every day."

A third reason for great Minor League stats is that in the old days particularly, though not as much today, the home teams in small towns played in tiny, bandbox ballparks with diminutive dimensions, clearly hundreds of feet shorter than the parks they'd have to play in in the Majors. They could reach short seats on soft pitching but couldn't manage to do the same in larger yards against tougher throwers.

A fourth reason for not making the Bigs might have been the fewer number of teams and players in the Majors. Eight teams and 200 active players in each league didn't leave much room for any kid on his way up. There was little use of disabled lists, no concept of Minor League shuttles, and a minimum of optioning players to the Farm. And as there was no free agency until relatively recently—a player belonged to his parent team for life (with a few exceptions)—a player was stuck in a certain organization. If he was a first baseman for the Yankees in the '20s and '30s, how was he going to break in when Lou Gehrig didn't miss a game for fourteen years? How was a raw talent going to supplant Eddie Collins at second? Or Luke Appling at short? Or Gabby Hartnett behind the plate? Or play ahead of a Ruth or Musial? These everyday players were the rule, rather than the exception, and that circumstance served to bury talented athletes in the Minors for years with no avenue for extrication . . . or promotion to the Majors.

A fifth situation that kept some hot hitters down on the farm was a porous glove. In the pre-designated-hitter days, a bad glove was enough to banish even the most talented slugger to life imprisonment in the Minors. Some good-hit, no-field types made it up to The Show for a short time, but rarely did they enjoy long careers in the Bigs.

A sixth item that kept certain players down was "attitude" or perceived attitude. What that boils down to is that if someone in the organization didn't like a guy for whatever real or imagined reason—an argumentative nature, poor work habits, nonconforming habits, religion, ethnic background, or looks alone—the athlete was easily forgotten and pushed down year after year in the Minors.

A seventh put-down is lack of wheels. If a guy has no speed, it can be reasoned that he has no range and can't play a position in the field; can't run out a base hit and is limited in his appeal to a Major League club. Of course, today, if a guy has fifty-homerun potential there's a spot for him. But in the old days, no legs meant no call to the Majors, and bad knees caused the premature end to scores of promising careers.

An eighth blackball is the "poor arm syndrome." That ranges from the fielders who can't break a pane of glass with their cutoffs, to pitchers whose fastball fails to impress or hurlers who come to the Bigs with one pitch (usually a fastball) and nothing else to set it up; either that or lack of ability to change speeds—not necessary in lower leagues but essential for success higher up. In the Majors, mastery of several pitches is needed, and without that, a star Minor Leaguer is just a one-pitch wonder, in-and-out, in The Show. Add to that the likelihood that in the Majors a pitcher has to face nine different guys capable of taking him "downtown" or at least nine spots that can give a hurler trouble, where in the Minors he can usually pitch around anyone who can cause damage, and you have the probability of many early showers for one who was once a Minor League mound ace. And, of course, injured arms on the Minor League level have ruined more careers than can be calculated. Often a kid on the way up blew out an arm trying to impress his coaches, and while piling up good numbers, he threw out his career in the process.

A ninth means of Major League failure is that some players just didn't have the makeup . . . the mental acumen to handle the pressures of the limelight. In many cases, small-town boys played the boys' game near their family and friends, and once away from home, exposed to bright lights and big cities, longed for the more comfortable confines of Minor League competition. It is a clear case of "You can take the boy out of the farm, but you can't take the farm out of the boy." And in the same "comfort" scenario, money was a factor in some cases of long Minor League-short Major League careers. In some cases, Bush League stars who were community heroes actually made much more money on the Farm than they would have playing for tight-fisted Major League owners in the days before megabuck contracts.

A tenth consideration is the factor of race. Without further belaboring the point made elsewhere in this book, the bigotry of baseball past kept many deserving and talented ballplayers off Major League ballfields for many years, regardless of how skillful the victim-athlete was. That bigotry still exists today, but it seems as though today's baseball powers would rather win than keep a worthy human being on the Farm because of his race, ethnic makeup, religious persuasion, or sexual preference. If a player can win you a ball-game, make the clutch play, steal the needed base, drive in the crucial run, or strike out an opposing hitter with the game on the line, it matters not what color, religion, ethnicity, sexual preference, or odd behavioral traits are present.

One prejudice still very much alive in Major League clubhouses today—and Minor League locker-rooms as well—is that of gender. There are no female players in the Big Leagues today, and there are no female ballplayers on Minor League diamonds today. Whether that is due to lack of talent, strength, size, ability or mental toughness or a result of the lack of opportunity is an arguable point. But it remains clear that females certainly suffer from lack of credibility in the eyes of the male-run kingdom of baseball. When a female ballplayer with the necessary skills makes it through the Minor League system—and probably the court system as well, because it seems likely that jurisprudence will have to intercede on her behalf before she is ever allowed to take the field—she may then be allowed to compete with her peers, other ballplayers with the talent and mental strength, to try and succeed both on the Minor

League and Major League levels. It seems likely that in this age of physical pursuit, nutrition, and workout science, eventually some females will come along (if some overlooked women haven't already) with stature and abilities and grit worthy of playing on an even keel with men. That's not to say there are female Cecil Fielders and Jose Cansecos or Nolan Ryans out there, but if there are 1,026 jobs (26 teams times the 40-*man* roster) up for grabs, there certainly will come a time when some women will have what it takes to play the game if only they are allowed to. Certainly some female athletes will surface whose fielding and throwing is better than some weak male defensive infielders and outfielders, and who's to say if there's not another Jackie Mitchell—the seventeen-year-old girl who struck out Babe Ruth and Lou Gehrig—out there (see Chapter 9: Southern League). And on the Minor League level, if there are about 200 teams currently in operation, averaging 25 players per roster, that means there are some 5,000 positions to be filled. Surely there will come a time when women can no longer be excluded—on talent alone— from that number.

The logic is simple. If in tennis, Steffi Graf, Monica Seles, Gabriela Sabatini, and Martina Navratilova are among the best the women's ranks have to offer, even if none of them could regularly compete with the top male players, they could almost certainly compete with those ranked in the low 100s who eventually break through to win top prize money.

On the Women's golf tour, there are certainly some women who may not hit it long enough off the tee but whose approach game and short game are equal to that of the men (Nancy Lopez, Betsy King, Julie Inkster, and Pat Bradley?) and who could pick up more winnings than many of the middle-ranked males. If you drive for show and putt for dough, women can certainly play the links with the men.

The same goes for baseball, where fundamentals, bat control, reflexes, good fielding, and sharp, accurate throws are qualities exhibited by valued players. If a female is allowed to progress throughout the ranks from Little League to Babe Ruth League to American Legion (that will be the day), to High School to College to the Minors, eventually some will rise to the top and be capable of filling important roles on Major League clubs. It seems as inevitable as was the eventual breaking down of the color barrier in professional baseball.

There are other possible rationales for lack of Big League exposure afforded to Minor League stars, but for whatever reasons or excuses offered, the evidence is clear . . . some players enjoyed enormous success and legendary recognition for Ruthian feats on the Farm yet barely had "a cup of coffee" in The Show.

Fifteen of these Minor League legends, chosen for the spotlight on the pages that follow, are a few of those dream field legends who never became household words to America's Major League baseball fans. More's the pity that they aren't included in the skein of Big League fabric, but they are part and parcel of what makes Minor League lore just as bright as the mythic Major League tales of Babe Ruth, Ty Cobb, Cy Young, Walter Johnson, Jackie Robinson, Mickey Mantle, Willie Mays, Sandy Koufax, Nolan Ryan, Jose Canseco, and other diamond heroes who were afforded the opportunity to perform on Big League diamonds.

These men are not Walter Mittys, but rather are skillful athletes who attained their niche in American sports history by exhibiting marvelous abilities on the playing fields of the Minor Leagues. The following fifteen—just tips of the iceberg, but glorious nonetheless—were certainly not as famous nor as lucky as Ruth, Cobb, Young, Johnson, Robinson, Mantle, Mays, Koufax, Ryan, and Canseco, but perhaps, in certain ways, were as talented.

Why these particular fifteen? We find these men to be representational of the kind of men who have generated special excitement on the Minor League level for more than a hundred years. These fifteen were chosen for the thrills, the stats, their talent and the dominating way in which they used it.

"Buzz" Arlett—Russell Louis Arlett was considered the top switch-hitter in the Minor Leagues for nearly fifteen years. In a story that parallels that of Babe Ruth's, but on the Minor League level, the good-looking six-foot-three, 225-pounder began his career in 1918 as a spitball pitcher with the Oakland Oaks of the Pacific Coast League and ended with the Syracuse Chiefs of the International League in 1937. Arlett won 29 games and pitched 427 innings for the Oaks in 1920 and won 25 in 374 innings in 1922.

When an injury reduced his pitching effectiveness in 1923, Arlett converted to the outfield (a conversion with which he never looked quite comfortable) and became an accomplished hitter, garnering three homerun titles—including 54 taters for Baltimore of the International League in 1932—and two RBI crowns. During that '32 campaign, Arlett hit four homers in a game on June 1, and duplicated the feat on July 4.

Over an eight-year period with Oakland, Arlett drove in 101 or more runs each season, and 1,100 runs all told for the run

After spending a strong 1931 season with the Philadelphia Phillies (.313 with 18 homers and 72 RBI in 121 games), he was banished to the Minors and five more consecutive 100-RBI seasons.

One reason for his short stint with the Phillies was Chuck Klein, the Hall-of-Fame rightfielder who spent fifteen years with the club, averaging .326. Another might have been his uneasy or casual appearance in the outfield . . . at least when compared to the polished, businesslike moves of Klein.

Comfortable on the Farm, before and after his fling in Philadelphia, Arlett finished with thirteen years in the PCL (all with the Oaks) before his MLB stop, three years in the International League, and three years in the American Association—all at the Triple-A level after the Philly fiasco.

RUSSELL LOUIS (BUZZ) ARLETT

Born January 3, 1899, in Oakland, CA. Died May 16, 1964, in Minneapolis, MN.
Batted left and right. Threw right. Height, 6.03. Weight: 225.

YEAR	CLUB	LEA	POS	G	AB	R	H	2B	3B	HR	RBI	SB	PCT
1918	Oakland	P. C.	P-2-1	26	71	9	15	4	0	1	8	1	.211
1919	Oakland	P. C.	P	58	144	15	42	8	2	1	19	2	.292
1920	Oakland	P. C.	P-1B	64	178	26	45	5	4	5	26	2	.253
1921	Oakland	P. C.	P	64	128	12	28	5	1	3	14	1	.219
1922	Oakland	P. C.	P-OF	74	174	23	42	9	4	4	21	0	.241
1923	Oakland	P. C.	OF-P	149	445	76	147	31	5	19	101	9	.330
1924	Oakland	P. C.	OF-P	193	698	122	229	57	19*	33	145	24	.328
1925	Oakland	P. C.	OF	190	710	121	244	49	13	25	146	26	.344
1926	Oakland	P. C.	OF-1B-P	194	667	140	255	52	16	35	140*	26	.382
1927	Oakland	P. C.	OF-P	187	658	122	231	54*	7	30	123	20	.351
1928	Oakland	P. C.	OF-P	160	561	111	205	47	3	25	113	10	.365
1929	Oakland	P. C.	OF-1B-P	200	722	146	270	70*	8	39	189	22	.374
1930	Oakland	P. C.	OF-P	176	618	132	223	57	7	31	143	8	.361
1931	Philadelphia	Nat.	OF	121	418	65	131	26	7	18	72	3	.313
1932	Baltimore	Int.	OF	147	516	141*	175	33	4	54*	144*	11	.339
1933	Baltimore	Int.	OF-1B	159	531	135*	182	40	3	39*	146	20	.343
1934	Brimingham	South	OF	35	128	28	42	9	4	7	23	3	.328
	Minneapolis	A. A.	OF	116	430	106	137	32	1	41*	132	8	.319
1935	Minneapolis	A. A.	OF	122	425	90	153	26	2	25	101	6	.360
1936	Minneapolis	A. A.	OF	74	193	55	61	10	4	15	52	1	.316
1937	Syracuse	Int.	PH	4	4	0	0	0	0	0	0	0	.000
			Majors	**121**	**418**	**65**	**131**	**26**	**7**	**18**	**72**	**3**	**.313**
			Minors	**2390**	**8001**	**1610**	**2726**	**598**	**107**	**432**	**1786**	**200**	**.341**

PITCHING RECORD

YEAR	CLUB	LEA	G	IP	W	L	H	R	ER	BB	SO	ERA
1918	Oakland	P. C.	21	153	4	9	150	60	46	43	34	2.70
1919	Oakland	P. C.	57*	348	22	17	315	172*	116	112	79	3.00
1920	Oakland	P. C.	53	427*	29*	17	430	162	137	134	105	2.89
1921	Oakland	P. C.	55	319	19	18	371	180	155	115	101	4.37
1922	Oakland	P. C.	47	374*	25	19	396	171	115	112	128	2.77
1923	Oakland	P. C.	28	125	4	9	182	106	84	47	34	5.76
1924	Oakland	P. C.	2	4	0	0	9	7	6	3	0	13.50
1925	Oakland	P. C.	1	4	0	0	1	0	0	2	0	0.00
1926	Oakland	P. C.	5	14	2	0	13	2	2	3	4	1.29
1927	Oakland	P. C.	1	9	1	0	10	6	3	4	4	3.00
1928	Oakland	P. C.	7	27	1	0	19	2	2	8	7	0.67
1929	Oakland	P. C.	17	61	1	4	83	46	40	17	17	5.76
1930	Oakland	P. C.	3	3	0	0	3	3	3	1	0	9.00
		Minors	**297**	**1868**	**108**	**93**	**1982**	**917**	**709**	**601**	**513**	**3.42**

Source: SABR
* = led league

Arlett also spent part of a Double-A season at Birmingham in the Southern League, near the end of his career; remaining constant by hitting .328—he hit better than .300 for fifteen consecutive full seasons to end his career.

Arlett's career Minor League marks include a .341 average, 432 homers, 1,786 RBI, 1,610 runs scored, 598 doubles, and 1,137 extra-base hits in 2,390 games.

Renowned as a terrible, or at least lackadaisical, fielder, he more than made up for his glove misadventures with his steady bat, and he set career PCL records for home runs (251) and RBI (1,188).

Despite being considered a slow runner, Arlett managed to swipe 200 bases during his career. His was the right stuff; the stuff that managed to accomplish whatever was necessary on a particular day to win a ballgame. Major League stuff in a Minor League setting.

Joe Bauman Joe Willis Bauman was a big (six-foot-five, 235-pound) left-handed hitting first baseman with thunder in his swings. Bauman set an organized baseball record in 1954 by demolishing all pitching competition and winning the triple crown as he clouted an amazing 72 home runs, driving in 224 runs (the second highest total ever accumulated in a single season), and batting an even .400 in 138 games for the Roswell Rockets of the Longhorn League; and with 456 total bases in 498 at bats, set another professional baseball mark with a .916 slugging percentage.

Bauman went on a four-year Longhorn League tear by bashing 221 homers, driving home 654 runs and batting .371. Yet no Major League action came the way of the huge first baseman, who retired after the 1956 season at the young age of thirty-four as the only player ever to lead the entire Minor Leagues in homeruns for four different years, and three years in a row (1946, 1952–54).

In only eleven seasons (he lost four years to military service during World War II and he held out for more money from 1949–51), Bauman belted 337 homers in 1,019 games (one homer every 10.27 at bats); drove in better than a run a game, with 1,057 RBI; and hit .337.

Bauman played virtually his entire career below the Single-A level. Why didn't he go any higher?

Part of the reason might have been comfort and another might have been money. Bauman was an Oklahoma boy who liked the Southwest and saw little reason to leave. Additionally, with tightwad Major League owners paying as little as the traffic would bear in the Bigs, $5,000 to $10,000 were average salaries, and even less in the Minors, $200 a month to $500 a month were about all one could expect to earn—Bauman probably made more dough by sticking close to home, with grateful owners, city businessmen and friends making Bauman's stay worthwhile. That and a small business or two he ran (including a gas station in Roswell) could have earned him three times or more what he might have made in another area in a higher league. And, it has been reported that Bauman was invited to play higher-level ball—possibly even at the Major League level—but he declined.

JOE WILLIS BAUMAN

Born, April 17, 1922, at Welch, OK.
Batted left. Threw left. Height, 6.05. Weight 235.

YEAR	CLUB	LEA	POS	G	AB	R	H	2B	3B	HR	RBI	SB	PCT
1941	Newport	N.E Ark.	1B	59	195	29	42	5	1	3	26	1	.215
	Little Rock	South.	1B	3	10	0	0	0	0	0	0	0	.000
1942				(Not in O.B.)									
1943–45				(Military Service)									
1946	Amarillo	W.T.-N.M.	1B	136	499	137	150	22	4	48*	159*	3	.301
1947	Amarillo	W.T.-N.M.	1B	130	432	142	151	45	2	38	127	3	.350
1948	Milwaukee	A. A.	1B	1	1	0	0	0	0	0	0	0	.000
	Hartford	Eastern	1B	98	276	38	76	13	3	10	53	0	.275
1949–51				(Not in O.B.)									
1952	Artesia	Longhorn	1B	139	469	144	176	21	0	50*	157*	2	.375
1953	Artesia	Longhorn	1B	132	463	135*	172	43	1	53*	141	4	.371
1954	Roswell	Longhorn	1B	138	498	188*	199	35	3	72*	224*	4	.400*
1955	Roswell	Longhorn	1B	131	453	118	152	32	3	46	132	1	.336
1956	Roswell	So'west.	1B	52	167	51	48	5	0	17	38	0	.287
			Minors	1019	3463	982	1166	221	17	337	1057	18	.337

Source: SABR
* = led league

Whatever the case, the Majors just might have missed out on a real hero. Even if he hit his 50 and 53 homers (with Artesia in 1952–53) and his record 72 and 46 (for Roswell in 1954–55) in bandbox ballparks of the Southwest, it can be argued that no one else in his era (or ever, for that matter) approached his success rate. The possible exception was Bobby Crues, a big outfielder who played in some of the same parks and put together a two-year run at Amarillo in 1947–48, poking out 52 and 69 homeruns (69 is second to Bauman on the all-time single-season list) and knocked in 178 and a record 254 RBI. But when the right-handed hitting Crues played in the Longhorn League for three years (1949–51) he managed only 28, 32, and 10 homers—end of competition.

Hitting lefty, with that power swing, Bauman could have been something at short-porched Ebbets Field, the Polo Grounds, or Yankee Stadium. The Show missed out on some exciting days.

Steve Bilko—Thick-muscled, thick-waisted Stephen Thomas Bilko was a first baseman who endeared himself forever to Los Angeles fans by virtue of a three-year reign of terror with the old Angels of the Pacific Coast League. At six-foot-one, 240 pounds (he may have, at times, weighed closer to 270), Bilko at the plate struck fear in the hearts of opposing pitchers as he bombed 148 homers playing at Los Angeles' Wrigley Field (site of TV's "Home Run Derby") for the PCL Angels in three years. He hit 37 dingers, drove in 124 runs, and batted .328 in 1955; followed that up by winning the PCL triple crown in '56 with totals of 55, 164, and .360; and finished his reign with 56 homers, 140 ribbies, and .300 in 1957.

In all, Bilko blasted out 313 Minor League homers in 13 seasons, batted .312, and drove in 1,157 runs. He managed to stay in the Majors for 600 games over ten seasons, and was the power threat for the original expansion Los Angeles Angels of the American League, returning to Wrigley Field to blast out 20 four-baggers in 1961 in only 294 at bats.

STEPHEN THOMAS BILKO

Born, November 13, 1928, at Nanticoke, PA. Died March 7, 1978, Wilkes-Barre, PA.
Batted right. Threw right. Height, 6.01. Weight, 240.

YEAR	CLUB	LEA	POS	G	AB	R	H	2B	3B	HR	RBI	SB	PCT.
1945	Allentown	Int. St.	OF	1	1	0	1	0	0	0	1	0	1.000
1946	Allentown	Int. St.	PH	1	1	0	0	0	0	0	0	0	.000
	Salisbury	East. Sh.	1B	122	441	73	121	28	4	12	90	6	.274
1947	Winston-Salem	Carolina	1B	116	438	109	148	26	3	29	120	12	.338
1948	Rochester	Int.	1B	12	41	5	6	1	0	0	3	0	.146
	Lynchburg	Piedmont	1B	128	463	89	154	34*	6	20*	92	3	.333*
1949	Rochester	Int.	1B	139	503	101	156	32	5	34	125*	1	.310
	St. Louis	National	1B	6	17	3	5	2	0	0	2	0	.294
1950	St. Louis	National	1B	10	33	1	6	1	0	0	2	0	.182
	Rochester	Int.	1B-2B	109	334	71	97	18	6	15	58	1	.290
1951	Columbus	A. A.	1B	26	74	13	21	2	0	1	6	0	.284
	Rochester	Int.	1B	73	273	41	77	14	6	8	50	0	.282
1951	St. Louis	National	1B	21	72	5	16	4	0	2	12	0	.222
1952	Rochester	Int.	1B	82	286	55	92	22	5	12	55	0	.322
	St. Louis	National	1B	20	72	7	19	6	1	1	6	0	.264
1953	St. Louis	National	1B	154	570	72	143	23	3	21	84	0	.251
1954	St. L.-Chi.	National	1B	55	106	12	24	8	1	4	13	0	.226
1955	Los Angeles	P. C.	1B	168	622	105	204	35	3	37*	124	4	.328
1956	Los Angeles	P. C.	1B	162	597	163*	215*	18	6	55*	164*	4	.360*
1957	Los Angeles	P. C.	1B	158	536	111*	161	22	1	56*	140*	8	.300
1958	Cin.-L.A.	National	1B	78	188	25	44	5	4	11	35	0	.234
1959	Spokane	P. C.	1B	135	478	76	146	24	1	26	92*	2	.305
1960	Detroit	Amer.	1B	78	222	20	46	11	2	9	25	0	.207
1961	Los Angeles	Amer.	1B	114	294	49	82	16	1	20	59	1	.279
1962	Los Angeles	Amer.	1B	64	164	26	47	9	1	8	38	1	.287
1963	Rochester	Int.	1B	101	261	41	68	17	1	8	37	1	.261
			Majors	**600**	**1738**	**220**	**432**	**85**	**13**	**76**	**276**	**2**	**.249**
			Minors	**1533**	**5349**	**1053**	**1667**	**293**	**47**	**313**	**1157**	**42**	**.312**

Source: SABR
* = led league

One reason for Bilko's lack of opportunity in the Bigs
was that, as St. Louis Cardinals' chattel, he played behind,
at various times, Stan Musial, Dick Sisler, and Nippy
Jones. Another was that he broke his arm during his first
stint with the Cards in 1952 and was often in pain. A third
was his proclivity for striking out . . . 125 times for the
Cards in 1953 and 81 times (once every 3.6 at bats) for the
Angels in '61.

"Ike" Boone—Isaac Morgan Boone was a solidly-built
(six-foot, 200-pound) outfielder who could hit, hit with

power, and steal a base if he had to. The all-time top hitter (career) in Minor League history at .370 was another good-hit, no-field type—or in his case, a great-hit no-field type. With no dh rule in effect, Boone had to be content with short stays in the Majors. While with Boston, he was not the fielder or complete player Ira Flagstead was, and with the Brooklyn Dodgers, he was a substitute behind Babe Herman.

In the Minors, Boone won five batting titles and hit better than .400 four times.

With the San Antonio Missions of the Texas League, in

ISAAC MORGAN (IKE) BOONE

Born, February 7, 1897, at Samantha, AL. Died, August 1, 1958, at Northport, AL. Batted left. Threw right. Height, 6.00. Weight, 200.

YEAR	CLUB	LEA	POS	G	AB	R	H	2B	3B	HR	RBI	SB	PCT
1920	Cedartown	Ga. St.	O-I-P	72	290	63	117	23	10	10	—	10	.403
1921	New Orleans	South.	OF	156	574	118	223	46*	27*	5	126	28	.389*
1922	New York	Nat.	OF	2	2	0	1	0	0	0	0	0	.500
	Toledo	A. A.	OF	26	88	9	24	5	1	0	13	0	.273
	Little Rock	South.	OF	83	307	60	101	17	10	6	—	11	.329
1923	San Antonio	Texas	OF	148	600	134*	241*	53*	26*	15	135*	7	.402*
	Boston	Amer.	OF	5	15	1	4	0	1	0	2	0	.267
1924	Boston	Amer.	OF	127	481	70	160	29	3	13	95	2	.333
1925	Boston	Amer.	OF	133	476	79	157	34	5	9	68	1	.330
1926	Missions	P. C.	OF	172	626	140	238	55	3	32	137	16	.380
1927	Chicago	Amer.	OF	29	53	10	12	4	0	1	11	0	.226
1928	Port.-Miss.	P. C.	OF	166	594	92	210	46	1	9	104	8	.354
1929	Missions	P. C.	OF	198	794	195	323*	49	8	55*	218*	9	.407*
1930	Missions	P. C.	OF	83	310	76	139	22	3	22	96	5	.448
	Brooklyn	Nat.	OF	40	101	13	30	9	1	3	13	0	.297
1931	Brooklyn	Nat.	OF	6	5	0	1	0	0	0	0	0	.200
	Newark	Int.	OF	124	469	82	167	33	9	18	92	2	.356*
1932	Brooklyn	Nat.	OF	13	21	2	3	1	0	0	2	0	.143
	Jersey City	Int.	OF	135	491	102	157	29	4	16	95	9	.320
1933	Toronto	Int.	OF	157	558	100	199	36	7	11	103	1	.357
1934	Toronto	Int.	OF	136	500	87	186	32	9	6	108	8	.372*
1935	Toronto	Int.	OF	130	437	82	153	23	8	9	85	3	.350
1936	Toronto	Int.	OF	71	169	22	43	8	2	3	22	3	.254
			Majors	**355**	**1154**	**175**	**368**	**77**	**10**	**26**	**191**	**3**	**.319**
			Minors	**1857**	**6807**	**1362**	**2521**	**477**	**128**	**217**	**1334**	**120**	**.370**

Source: SABR

* = led league

1923, Boone hit .402, 15 homers, 26 triples, and 53 doubles. In 1929, with Mission of the PCL, Boone had the ultimate season, winning the triple crown, batting a robust .407, slamming 55 homers, bopping 49 doubles, 112 extra-base-hits, setting a Minor League mark with 553 total bases. He did this while slapping out the second-highest single-season hit total in Minor League annals with 323 and posting a fourth-best ever total of 218 RBI and a fourth-highest runs scored figure of 195.

He followed that up in 1930 with a .448 average, 22 homers, and 96 RBI in 83 games before being purchased by the Brooklyn Dodgers.

But Boone, a slow runner and suspect fielder, played himself out of Brooklyn by failing to hit up to his promise, as the Dodgers relied on Babe Herman, Lefty O'Doul, and Hack Wilson for their hitting and fielding needs, dropping Boone down to Toronto of the International League where he regained his stroke and hit .357, .372, and .350 from 1933–35.

"Bunny" Brief—Anthony Vincent Brief, who was born with the name Antonio Bordetski, was another tough first baseman, who stood six-feet tall and weighed 185 pounds. He set career American Association records for runs scored (1,342), hits (2,196), doubles (458), homeruns (276), and RBI (1,451). During his entire Minor League career, he became the eighth top run scorer in history (1,776). Brief was up for a stint with the Browns in 1912–13, White Sox in 1915, and the Pirates in 1917. His best years were to come later when he went on binge from 1920 to 1926 by demolishing American Association pitching for eight straight 100 RBI seasons, winning five RBI titles, and five homerun crowns. During that span he belted 227 four-baggers and knocked in 1,128 ribbies, including 191 in 1921. Brief won eight homerun titles during his nineteen-year Minor League run and hit over .300 for each of the last ten years of his career, which ended at Milwaukee of the American Association in 1928.

Brief had speed (247 Minor League steals), good defen-

ANTHONY VINCENT (BUNNY) BRIEF (Real name: Antonio Bordetski)

Born, July 3, 1892, at Remus, MI. Died, February 10, 1963, at Milwaukee, WI.
Batted right. Threw right. Height, 6.00. Weight, 185.

YEAR	CLUB	LEA	POS	G	AB	R	H	2B	3B	HR	RBI	SB	PCT
1910	Tra. City	Mich. St.	OF	95*	354	51	100	19	10*	2	—	12	.282
1911	Tra. City	Mich. St.	OF-1B	118*	482*	97*	169*	26	8	10*	—	32	.351
1912	Tra. City	Mich. St.	1B-OF	119*	431	74*	152*	31	11*	13*	—	40	.353
	St. Louis	Amer.	OF-1B	15	42	9	13	3	0	0	5	2	.310
1913	St. Louis	Amer.	1B-OF	84	258	24	56	11	6	1	26	3	.217
	Kansas City	A. A.	1B	37	120	7	29	3	2	0	—	5	.225
1914	Kansas City	A. A.	1B	169	645	117	205	51	16	12	123	38	.318
1915	Chicago	Amer.	1B	48	154	13	33	6	2	2	17	8	.214
	Salt Lake City	P. C.	1B	82	328	63	119	23	3	8	—	16	.363
1916	Salt Lake City	P. C.	1B	195	723	149*	227	38	5	33*	133	23	.314
1917	Pittsburgh	Nat.	1B	36	115	15	25	5	1	2	11	4	.217
	Louisville	A. A.	1B	48	156	23	45	8	2	1	19	1	.288
1918	Kansas City	A. A.	1B	74	260	32	68	6	2	4	36	3	.261
1919	Kansas City	A. A.	1B	152	564	89	183	30	11	13	101	13	.324
1920	Kansas City	A. A.	1B-OF	165	615	99	196	41	9	23*	120*	15	.319
1921	Kansas City	A. A.	1B	164	615	166*	222	51*	11	42*	191*	12	.361
1922	Kansas City	A. A.	1B	130	519	133	176	40	7	40*	151*	7	.339
1923	Kansas City	A. A.	1B-OF	166	640	161*	230	47	15	29	164*	9	.359
1924	Kansas City	A. A.	OF	159	601	106	203	58	12	17	104	5	.338
1925	Milwaukee	A. A.	OF	167	618	134	221	45	13	37*	175*	2	.358
1926	Milwaukee	A. A.	OF-1B	161	583	130	205	38	10	26*	122	9	.352
1927	Milwaukee	A. A.	OF-1B	126	432	89	133	27	4	14	86	3	.308
1928	Milwaukee	A. A.	OF-1B	90	259	56	80	12	3	18	59	2	.309
			Majors	**183**	**569**	**61**	**127**	**25**	**9**	**5**	**59**	**17**	**.223**
			Minors	**2426**	**8945**	**1776**	**2963**	**594**	**154**	**342**	**1584**	**247**	**.331**

Source: SABR
* = led league

slve skills at both first base and the outfield, and a good
bat, but he failed to impress Big League clubs during his
three short stints and, thought of as a first baseman, was
overshadowed by many big hitting Big League first sack-
ers of the day.

Nick Cullop—Heinrich Nicholas "Tomato Face" Cullop
was a muscular, six-foot, 200-pound outfielder who started
his career as a pitcher—went 49–50—and was moved to
the outfield to utilize his powerful swing. The third top
all-time Minor League home run hitter (420), he is *numero
uno* in RBI, topping the Minor League career list with

HEINRICH NICHOLAS (NICK) CULLOP

Born, October 16, 1900, at Weldon Spring, MO. Died December 8, 1978, at Westerville, OH.
Batted right. Threw right. Height, 6.00. Weight, 200.

YEAR	CLUB	LEA	POS	G	AB	R	H	2B	3B	HR	RBI	SB	PCT.
1920	Madison	S. Dak. St.	P-O-2B	66	182	20	62	6	2	3	33	3	.341
	Minneapolis	A. A.	P	3	8	2	3	0	1	0	1	0	.375
1921	St. J.-Tulsa	Western	P-2B	38	70	8	16	1	1	0	14	0	.228
1922	Des Moines	Western	P-OF-1B	55	149	27	44	8	1	6	32	1	.295
1923	Omaha	Western	O-1-P-2	114	350	57	98	19	7	12	81	7	.280
1924	Omaha	Western	OF-1B-P	154	596	131	192	46	8	40	155	6	.322
1925	Atlanta	South.	OF-1B-P	137	522	120	162	36	18	30*	139	28	.310
1926	New York	Amer.	PH	2	2	0	1	0	0	0	0	0	.500
	St. Paul	A. A.	OF	125	449	92	141	22	7	22	68	32	.314
1927	Wash.-Clev.	Amer.	OF-P	47	91	11	21	4	3	1	9	0	.231
1928	Buffalo	Int.	OF	15	45	6	14	8	0	0	6	1	.311
	Atlanta	South.	OF	75	250	54	88	22	6	17	62	11	.352
1929	Atlanta	South.	OF	113	402	63	117	23	4	17	54	7	.291
	Brooklyn	Nat.	OF	13	41	7	8	2	2	1	5	0	.195
1930	Minneapolis	A. A.	OF	139	515	150*	185	28	9	54*	152*	8	.359
	Cincinnati	Nat.	OF	7	22	2	4	0	0	1	5	0	.182
1931	Cincinnati	Nat.	OF	104	334	29	88	23	7	8	48	1	.263
1932	Rochester	Int.	OF	9	30	5	8	3	0	1	4	0	.267
	Columbus	A. A.	OF	128	442	97	154	37	4	26	99	8	.348
1933	Columbus	A. A.	OF	150	587	110	184	37	22*	28	143	5	.313
1934	Columbus	A. A.	OF	147	587	97	178	34	13	27	130	8	.303
1935	Columbus	A. A.	OF	145	559	102	190	40	14	24	128	4	.340
1936	Columbus	A. A.	OF	145	560	108	181	30	11	24	114	4	.323
1937	Sacramento	P. C.	OF	151	532	83	165	45	4	19	127	4	.312
1938	Sacramento	P. C.	OF	138	485	72	124	19	1	20	66	7	.256
1939	Houston	Texas	OF	157	554	97	176	29	5	25*	112*	5	.318
1940	Houston	Texas	OF	125	423	73	115	18	5	21	96	2	.272
1941	Asheville	Piedmont	OF	75	188	25	50	10	4	2	28	3	.266
1942	Pocatello	Pioneer	OF-P	28	35	3	10	0	0	1	4	0	.286
1943	Columbus	A. A.	OF	42	45	5	10	2	0	1	8	0	.222
1944	Columbus	A. A.	PH	10	6	0	3	0	0	0	1	0	.500
		Majors		173	490	49	122	29	12	11	67	1	.249
		Minors		2484	8571	1607	2670	523	147	420	1857	154	.312

Source: SABR
* = led league

1,857 plus some uncounted games. His 1,090 extra-base hits rank him among the Game's all-time best. He hit over .300 on fifteen stops along the way, topped 20 home runs twelve times, and drove in 100-or-more runs nine times during his twenty-three-year-career on the Farm.

His best year might have been 1930 with Minneapolis of the American Association, when he hit .359, with a league-leading 152 RBI, 54 homers, and 150 runs scored in 139 games.

Cullop was an aggressive and popular player and a talented outfielder.

He had a two-game shot with the 1926 Yankees playing behind Babe Ruth, Earl Combs, and Bob Meusel and made a two-year run with the Cincinnati Reds in 1930–31 before Babe Herman was obtained by the Reds in 1932.

Perhaps the Majors were turned off to him because he led the National League in strikeouts with Cincy in 1931, fanning 84 times in 104 games while banging out only 8 homers.

Steve Dalkowski—The Nolan Ryan of his era—in terms of speed, strikeouts and wildness, but little additional similarity—Steven Louis Dalkowski, a five-foot-ten, 170-pound lefty, blazed through the Minors (and etched his name into Minor League lore) in the mid-'50s and mid-'60s with an unimpressive 46–80 won-lost record, but an amazing 1,396 strikeouts and 1,354 walks in only 995 innings pitched. But while Ryan is usually credited with throwing the fastest clocked fastball in the Majors (at 100.9 MPH in Anaheim, August 20, 1974), Dalkowski threw a heater for Elmira, in the Single-A Eastern League in 1962 that was measured at a blinding 108 MPH. And this man was no Sidd Finch . . . he is real.

Dalkowski, a project within the Baltimore Orioles organization, was all potential . . . all raw talent, blinding speed and frightful wildness. He got up to Triple-A with Rochester and Columbus but could never put it all together. Hitters—usually afraid to stand in against him—connected for only 682 hits, an average of 6.16 every nine innings. That stat is lower than Ryan's 6.57 mark, the lowest hits-per-innings ratio in MLB history. His strikeout average is an astronomical 12.63 per nine innings as compared with Ryan's MLB record of 9.54, but his walk ratio is an awful 12.24 as compared with Ryan's 4.77.

STEVEN LOUIS DALKOWSKI

Born, June 3, 1939, at New Britain, CT.
Threw left. Batted left. Height, 5:10. Weight, 170.

YEAR	CLUB	LEA	G	IP	W	L	H	R	ER	BB	SO	ERA
1957	Kingsport	Appal.	15	62	1	8	22	68	56*	129*	121	8.13
1958	Knoxville	So. Atl.	11	42	1	4	17	41	39	95	82	7.93
	Wilson	Carol.	8	14	0	1	7	19	19	38	29	12.21
	Aberdeen	North.	11	62	3	5	29	50	44	112	121	6.39
1959	Aberdeen	North.	12	59	4	3	30	43	37	110	99	5.64
	Pensacola	Ala.-Fla.	7	25	0	4	11	38	36	80	43	12.96
1960	Stockton	Calif.	32	170	7	15*	105	120	97	262*	262	5.14
1961	Kennewick	No'west.	31	103	3	12	75	117	96	196*	150	8.39
1962	Elmira	Eastern	31	160	7	10	117	61	54	114	192	3.04
1963	Elmira	Eastern	13	29	2	2	20	10	9	26	28	2.79
	Rochester	Int.	12	12	0	2	7	8	8	14	8	6.00
1964	Elmira	Eastern	8	15	0	1	17	12	10	19	16	6.00
	Stockton	Calif.	20	108	8	4	91	40	34	62	141	2.83
	Columbus	Int.	3	12	2	1	15	11	11	11	9	8.25
1965	Kennewick	No'west	16	84	6	5	84	60	48	52	62	5.14
	San Jose	Calif.	6	38	2	3	35	25	20	34	33	4.74
	Minors		**236**	**995**	**46**	**80**	**682**	**723**	**618**	**1354**	**1396**	**5.59**

Source: SABR
* = led league

While Ryan's ERA is a very credible 3.15 against Major League hitters, Dalkowski's ERA was a horrible 5.59 versus Farm system types—and that high figure was *all* due to his wildness. Finally, of course, Ryan is 30 games over .500 after twenty-four years in the Bigs, while Dalkowski was a miserable 34 games under .500 in his nine years in the Bushes.

Still, Dalkowski thrilled every crowd that paid to see him from 1957 with Kingsport in the Appalachian League— 121 strikeouts and 129 walks in only 62 innings with a microscopic 22 hits allowed; to Stockton of the California League in 1960—262 strikeouts and 262 walks in only 170 innings while allowing only 105 hits; to Elmira in 1962–63—where he was under control with 192 K's and 114 walks in 160 innings and only 117 hits allowed, to bring his ERA down to 3.04 in '62 and 2.79 in '63; to his final stint with San Jose in the California League in 1965, when he could throw no more . . . the twenty-six-year-old arm thrown out; dead before its time.

He was an unharnessed supernova who burned brightly and then burned out, leaving gasps and heads shaking in amazement along the diamonds of Minor League baseball.

Ray Dandridge—A victim of the times and the discrimination within the baseball world, Ray Dandridge was not permitted to exhibit his considerable talents against the best Minor Leaguers and Major Leaguers of the 1930s and '40s because of his race. Dandridge, elected to the Hall of Fame in 1987, played ball nevertheless and compiled impressive numbers playing in the Negro Leagues and the Mexican League.

Dandridge, a five-foot-five, 175-pound third baseman, was the Brooks Robinson of his day, a sure-handed quick-gloved infielder with a strong arm and graceful style. As a

RAYMOND DANDRIDGE

Born August 31, 1913, at Richmond, VA.
Batted right. Threw right. Height 5.06. Weight 185.
Played in the Negro National League 1933–38, 1942 and 1944, and the Negro American League in 1949.

YEAR	CLUB	LEAGUE	POS	G	AB	R	H	2B	3B	HR	RBI	SB	BA
1940	Vera Cruz	Mexican	3B	27	127	27	44	8	3	1	27	6	.346
1941	Vera Cruz	Mexican	3B-SS	101	430	94	158	32	5	8	86	12	.367
1942	Vera Cruz	Mexican	3B	35	142	27	44	7	1	4	37	8	.310
	Nowark	Neg Nat		(Record not available)									
1943	Vera Cruz	Mexican	3B	90	370	67	131*	24	4	8	70*	17	.354
1944	Newark	Neg Nat	3-2-S	47	189	38	70	12	5	2	21	8	.370
1945	Mexico City	Mexican	3B-SS	83	344	67	126	29	4	1	58	20	.366
1946	Mexico City	Mexican	3B	98	418	79	135	24	0	7	51	24	.323
1947	Mexico City	Mexican	3B-SS	122	514	90	169*	24	6	2	65	23	.329
1948	Mexico City	Mexican	3B	88	370	65	138*	22	6	3	52	10	.373*
1949	New York	Neg Amer		(Record not available)									
	Minneapolis	A A	3B-2B	99	398	60	144	22	5	6	64	4	.362
1950	Minneapolis	A A	3B-2B	150	627*	106	195*	24	1	11	80	1	.311
1951	Minneapolis	A A	3B	107	423	59	137	24	1	8	61	1	.324
1952	Minneapolis	A A	3B	145	618	86	180	27	1	10	68	3	.291
1953	Sac/Oakland	P C	2B-3B	87	254	32	68	10	1	0	13	1	.268
	Minors			1232	5035	859	1669	277	38	69	732	130	.331

Source: SABR
* = led league

hitter, Dandridge, nicknamed "Hooks," could hit to all fields, exhibited Rod Carew-like bat control and rarely struck out.

In nine seasons in the Mexican League, Dandridge averaged .343, while in the Negro Leagues hit better than .335 (records incomplete) and led the Negro National League in batting in 1938 with a .404 mark for the Newark Eagles. He also topped .400 in 1934, batting .436 for the Newark Dodgers. His best season in Mexico was his final year with Mexico City, in 1948, when he led the league at .373, banging out 138 hits in 88 games. And while in the Mexican League, Dandridge led the circuit in hits three times (1943, 1947, 1948) and set a league mark for longest hitting streak—33 consecutive games in 1947—that was broken a year later by Roberto Ortiz (Gonzalez) who increased the mark to 35 games. He led the league in RBI with 70 in 1943.

In 1990, forty-two years after his final Mexican League game, Dandridge still ranks forty-seventh on the all-time stolen base list (120).

Finally allowed to play Triple-A ball in 1949, he was signed by the New York Giants—he could have gone directly to the Cleveland Indians and a Major League spot but refused to leave Mexico unless the Tribe offered a bonus . . . which they didn't—and assigned to play for Minneapolis of the American Association. Dandridge responded by hitting a robust .362 with 144 hits and 64 RBI in 99 games, earning him Rookie-of-the-Year honors at the age of thirty-six.

In 1950, he led the Millers to the American Association championship by hitting .311 with 11 homers, 106 runs scored and 80 RBI, as he led the Association in hits with 195 in 150 games en route to winning the league's MVP award.

He reportedly declined the opportunity to play in the Majors the following year because of age. He said he wouldn't be at his best—besides, the Giants refused to pay

Dandridge a bonus for making the Majors—and he decided to spend the next two seasons at Minneapolis.

He retired following the 1953 season, which he spent at Sacramento and Oakland in the Pacific Coast League.

Luke Easter—Lucious Luke Easter was a big (six-foot-four, 240-pound) first baseman who spent thirteen years in the Minors, playing until the age of forty-nine, following a decorated career in the Negro Leagues. In between he served for six seasons with the Cleveland Indians of the American League and fared well, hitting 86 homers and driving in 307 runs during his first three years in the Bigs; and he powered a legendary 477-foot blast out of Cleveland Municipal Stadium—a shot considered the longest drive ever hit there.

But in the Minors, particularly in the International League, he shined as brightly as anyone has ever shone. During a four-year stretch at the Triple-A level (Charleston of the American Association in 1955, and Buffalo of the International League from 1956–58), Easter hit 143 homers and drove in 445 runs . . . and he was in his forties at the time.

During his eight full years in the International League following his MLB career, when most considered his best days behind him, Easter blasted 180 homers and drove in 622 runs.

"Ox" Eckhardt—Oscar Eckhardt was a brawny outfielder who stood six-foot-one and weighed 190. He set a career PCL record for batting average at .382, going 1542 for 4032. He finished his Minor League career as the No. 2 all-time batter at .367. He had a taste of the Bigs with Brooklyn in 1936, but was shipped out after failing to match his Minor League success against Major League curves.

He was considered an outstanding hitter (five batting titles and a .414 mark for Mission of the PCL in 1933) with little power, but his slashing swing and ability to take the extra base got him 27 triples for Wichita-Amarillo in the Western League in 1928 and 55 doubles for Beaumont in

LUSCIOUS LUKE EASTER

Born April 4, 1915, at St. Louis, MO. Died March 29, 1979, at Euclid, OH.
Batted left. Threw right. Height 6.04½. Weight 240.

YEAR	CLUB	LEAGUE	POS	G	AB	R	H	2B	3B	HR	RBI	SB	BA
1949	San Diego	P C	1B	80	273	56	99	23	0	25	92	1	.363
	Cleveland	Amer	OF	21	45	6	10	3	0	0	2	0	.222
1950	Cleveland	Amer	1B-OF	141	540	96	151	20	4	28	107	0	.280
1951	Cleveland	Amer	1B	128	486	65	131	12	5	27	103	0	.270
1952	Indianapolis	A A	1B	14	50	13	17	2	0	6	12	1	.340
	Cleveland	Amer	1B	127	437	63	115	10	3	31	97	1	.263
1953	Cleveland	Amer	1B	68	211	26	64	9	0	7	31	0	.303
1954	Cleveland	Amer	PH	6	6	0	1	0	0	0	0	0	.167
	Ottawa	Int	1B	66	230	49	80	10	0	15	48	1	.348
	San Diego	P C	1B	56	198	43	55	8	1	13	42	1	.278
1955	Charleston	A A	1B	144	477	78	135	25	5	30	102	1	.283
1956	Buffalo	Int	1B	145	483	75	148	20	3	35*	106*	0	.306
1957	Buffalo	Int	1B	154	534	87	149	27	2	40*	128*	0	.279
1958	Buffalo	Int	1B	148	502	89	154	33	0	38	109	1	.307
1959	Buf/Rochester	Int	1B	143	478	68	125	32	2	22	76	0	.262
1960	Rochester	Int	1B	115	275	36	83	12	1	14	57	0	.302
1961	Rochester	Int	1B	82	203	24	59	13	1	10	51	0	.291
1962	Rochester	Int	1B	93	249	39	70	11	1	15	60	0	.281
1963	Rochester	Int	1B	77	188	20	51	8	1	6	35	0	.271
1964	Rochester	Int	PH	10	10	0	2	0	0	0	1	0	.200
		Majors		491	1725	256	472	54	12	93	340	1	.274
		Minors		1327	4150	677	1227	224	17	269	919	6	.296

Source: SABR
* = led league

the Texas League in 1930. He also recorded 10 or more triples on seven other occasions and 30 or more doubles seven additional times.

During a four-year span with Mission, following his demotion from the Boston Red Sox in 1932, Eckhardt won three PCL batting crowns, smashed out 1,065 hits, drove in 445 runs, scored 500 runs and hit a cumulative .392.

In the years before the dh, his poor fielding was probably a determining factor in keeping him out of the Majors. That, and the fact that Boston had Smead Jolley ahead of him.

Hector Espino—Hector Espino (Gonzales) was a five-foot-eleven, 185-pound, power hitting first baseman who

OSCAR GEORGE (OX) ECKHARDT

Born, December 23, 1901, at Yorktown, TX. Died, April 22, 1951, at Yorktown, TX.
Batted left. Threw right. Height, 6.01. Weight, 190.

YEAR	CLUB	LEA	POS	G	AB	R	H	2B	3B	HR	RBI	SB	PCT
1925	Austin	Tex. A.	OF	2	7	1	2	0	0	0	0	0	.286
1926-27				(Not in O. B.)									
1928	Wich.-Amar.	Western	OF	127	490	91	184	32	27*	3	—	20	.376
1929	Seattle	P. C.	OF	161	571	84	202	35	17*	7	70	16	.354
1930	Beaumont	Texas	OF	147	573	99	217*	55*	5	8	83	19	.379*
1931	Mission	P. C.	OF	185	745	129	275*	52	10	7	117	9	.369*
1932	Boston	Nat.	PH	8	8	1	2	0	0	0	1	0	.250
	Mission	P. C.	OF	134	539	80	200	33	13	5	82	15	.371*
1933	Mission	P. C.	OF	189*	760	145	315*	56	16	12	143	15	.414*
1934	Mission	P. C.	OF	184	707	126	267	36	11	6	106	7	.378
1935	Mission	P. C.	OF-P	172	710	149	283*	40	11	2	114	8	.399*
1936	Brooklyn	Nat.	OF	16	44	5	8	1	0	1	8	0	.182
	Indianapolis	A. A.	OF	128	541	95	191	26	11	4	69	3	.353
1937	Indianapolis	A. A.	OF	142	589	97	201	20	8	7	79	14	.341
1938	Toledo	A. A.	OF	55	201	29	46	9	3	2	29	3	.229
	Beaumont	Texas	OF	72	279	43	108	19	7	0	43	4	.387
1939	Memphis	South.	OF	124	482	61	174	26	4	2	80	6	.361
1940	Dallas	Texas	OF	104	369	46	108	16	3	1	22	1	.293
			Majors	**24**	**52**	**6**	**10**	**1**	**0**	**1**	**7**	**0**	**.192**
			Minors	**1926**	**7563**	**1275**	**2773**	**455**	**146**	**66**	**1037**	**140**	**.367**

Source: SABR
* = led league

is the all-time leader in Minor League homeruns. Espino is credited with having blasted out 484 roundtrippers (disputed by Mexican League official records, which place him with 453) during his 2,500-game career and is eighth on the all-time RBI list (1,631).

Espino was a good-fielding first-sacker—he led the Mexican League in assists for four straight years from 1967 to 1970—but was known for his bat. He is among the career leaders in the Mexican League in eight offensive categories: batting average—sixth at .335; hits—first with 2.752; doubles—second with 373; homeruns—first with 453; runs scored—first with 1,505; RBI—first with 1,573; total bases —first with 4,582; and slugging percentage—first at .558.

HECTOR ESPINO (GONZALEZ)

Born, June 8, 1939, at Chihuahua, Mexico.
Batted right. Threw right. Height, 5:11. Weight, 185.

YEAR	CLUB	LEA	POS	G	AB	R	H	2B	3B	HR	RBI	SB	PCT
1960	San Luis Pot.	Mex. Cen.	OF	63	229	58	83	20	2	20	60	0	.363
1961	San Luis Pot.	Mex. Cen.	OF	17	71	19	33	4	2	8	30	0	.465
1962	Monterrey	Mexican	OF	126	444	106*	159	20	12	23	105*	3	.358
1963	Monterrey	Mexicqn	OF	99	393	79	136	20	6	24	80	3	.346
1964	Monterrey	Mexican	1B	126	448	118*	166	22	3	46*	117	5	.371*
	Jacksonville	Int.	1B	32	100	15	30	6	0	3	15	0	.300
1965	Monterrey	Mexican	1B	67	215	38	72	10	4	17	48	1	.335
1966	Monterrey	Mexican	1B-OF	120	393	84	145	16	4	31	75	2	.369*
1967	Monterrey	Mexican	1B	123	419	106	159	29	3	34	89	6	.379*
1968	Monterrey	Mexican	1B-OF	109	351	59	128	18	1	27*	79	4	.365*
1969	Monterrey	Mexican	1B	147	461	101*	140	22	2	37*	97	5	.304
1970	Monterrey	Mexican	1B	136	432	86	138	17	2	18	47	3	.319
1971	Tampico	Mexican	1B	104	341	65	106	11	2	20	58	4	.311
1972	Tampico	Mexican	1B	129	433	101*	154	23	1	37*	101	0	.356
1973	Tampico	Mexican	1B	116	422	82	159	20	2	22	107*	3	.377*
1974	Tampico	Mexican	1B	109	374	66	117	20	0	17	61	3	.313
1975	Tampico	Mexican	1B	119	428	73	153	18	0	17	75	3	.357
1976	Tampico	Mexican	1B	96	337	49	100	7	0	20	65	1	.297
1977	Tampico	Mexican	1B	97	332	57	112	14	1	14	51	1	.337
1978	Tampico	Mexican	1B	119	441	64	141	20	0	12	82	4	.320
1979	Leon–U. L.	Mexican	1B	94	355	48	120	17	0	15	70	1	.338
1980	U. L.-Mva-Salt.	Mexican	1B	62	230	27	84	12	1	10	33	0	.365
	Saltillo	Mex. #2	1B	35	110	23	36	6	0	1	18	0	.327
1981	M. C. Reds-Mont.	Mex.	1B	95	319	40	93	13	0	4	46	0	.292
1982	Monterrey	Mexican	1B	70	233	16	63	11	1	4	41	1	.270
1983	Monterrey	Mexican	1B	70	244	14	60	7	0	2	20	1	.246
1984	Monterrey	Mexican	1B	20	50	3	11	0	0	1	8	0	.220
			Minors	**2500**	**8605**	**1597**	**2898**	**403**	**49**	**484**	**1678**	**54**	**.337**

Source: SABR
* = led league

He led his league in batting four times (for Monterrey in 1964, 1966–68) with a career best of .371 in '64, and won four homerun titles (in 1964, 1968–69, and 1972) while capturing seven slugging percentage crowns.

Comfortable at home in Mexico, and making good money there ($18,000), he declined several offers to jump to the Major Leagues (the Cardinals, Mets, and Padres dangled contracts in front of him) and several other offers to play Minor League ball in the United States.

He did play for Jacksonville of the International League in 1964—and hit .300—but sickened by what he saw as racial discrimination, swore he would never again play in the United States.

He nearly signed a contract with the California Angels sometime in the late '60s, but again, patriotic pride (and perhaps tight money) kept him at home.

Joe Hauser—Joseph John "Unser Choe" Hauser was a strong, five-foot-ten, 175-pound first baseman who bombed out left-handed drives and ended his twenty-four-year career as the number five all-time Minor League homerun hitter (399). On his way to that total, he became the only player in professional baseball history to twice top the 60-homerun mark in a season, crashing 63 roundtrippers (in 617 at bats) for Baltimore of the International League in 1930, and slamming 69 (in only 570 at bats) for the Minneapolis Millers of the American Association in 1933.

It can certainly be argued that Hauser took full advantage of parks tailor-made to his swing, as he blasted 50 of his 69 four-baggers in 1933 in Minneapolis' Nicollet Park, a stadium with a short porch, 279 feet down the right field line and 328 to the right-centerfield power alley—perfect for his left-handed swing. Still, no one else ever accomplished what he did, and he was head-and-shoulders above his contemporaries, so whatever the boundaries were, Hauser succeeded in a way no player has either before or after him.

During a five-year onslaught in the Triple-A arena, from 1930–34, Hauser won four consecutive homerun crowns and clouted 245 roundtrippers while driving in 672 runs.

Hauser was one who *did* impress on the Major League level, as he was a decent fielder with average speed, and a swing that was sweet and strong.

Following a 20-homerun, 110 RBI, .316 season for Milwaukee of the American Association in 1921, Connie Mack offered him a Major League contract with the Philadelphia A's.

Hauser bombed 27 homers and drove in 115 runs for the

JOSEPH JOHN (UNSER CHOE) HAUSER

Born, January 12, 1899, at Milwaukee, WI
Batted left. Threw left. Height, 5.10½. Weight, 175.

YEAR	CLUB	LEA	POS	G	AB	R	H	2B	3B	HR	RBI	SB	PCT
1918	Providence	Eastern	OF	39	130	17	36	5	6	1	—	4	.277
1919	Providence	Eastern	OF	107	385	64	105	20	21*	6*	—	11	.273
1920	Milwaukee	A. A.	OF	156	549	94	156	22	16	15	79	7	.284
1921	Milwaukee	A. A.	1B	167	632	126	200	26	9	20	110	12	.316
1922	Philadelphia	Amer.	1B	111	368	61	119	21	5	9	43	1	.323
1923	Philadelphia	Amer.	1B	146	537	93	165	21	10	16	94	6	.307
1924	Philadelphia	Amer.	1B	149	562	97	162	31	8	27	115	7	.288
1925	Philadelphia	Amer.	1B	(Did not play; Broke leg April 7)									
1926	Philadelphia	Amer.	1B	91	229	31	44	10	0	8	36	1	.192
1927	Kansas City	A. A.	1B	169	617	145	218	49	22*	20	134	25	.353
1928	Philadelphia	Amer.	1B	95	300	61	78	19	5	16	59	4	.260
1929	Cleveland	Amer.	1B	37	48	8	12	1	1	3	9	0	.250
	Milwaukee	A. A.	1B	31	105	18	25	2	0	3	14	2	.238
1930	Baltimore	Int.	1B	168*	617	173*	193	39	11	63*	175	1	.313
1931	Baltimore	Int.	1B	144	487	100	126	20	6	31*	98	1	.259
1932	Minneapolis	A. A.	1B	149	522	100	158	31	3	49*	129	12	.303
1933	Minneapolis	A. A.	1B	153	570	153*	189	35	4	69*	182*	1	.332
1934	Minneapolis	A. A.	1B	82	287	81	100	7	3	33	88	1	.348
1935	Minneapolis	A. A.	1B	131	409	74	107	18	1	23	101	3	.262
1936	Minneapolis	A. A.	1B	125	437	95	117	20	2	34	87	1	.268
1937	Sheboygan	+Wis. St.	1B	37	131	—	45	12	3	81	38	—	.344
1938	Sheboygan	+Wis. St.	1B	49	172	55	55	19	2	10	54	—	.320
1939	Sheboygan	+Wis. St.		—	—	—	—	—	—	—	—	—	—
1940	Sheboygan	Wis. St.	1B	79	204	48	53	16	3	7	32	11	.260
1941	Sheboygan	Wis. St.	1B	77	233	53	67	13	5	11	54	10	.288
1942	Sheboygan	Wis. St.	1B	77	242	57	73	17	4	14	70	7	.302
			Majors	**629**	**2044**	**351**	**580**	**103**	**29**	**79**	**356**	**19**	**.284**
			Minors	**1854**	**6426**	**1430**	**1923**	**340**	**116**	**399**	**1353**	**109**	**.299**

+ Not affiliated with Organized Baseball.
Source: SABR
* = led league

A's in 1924 (second in the American League only to Babe Ruth), but broke his kneecap in 1925, and, wearing a knee brace, he lost the ability to run and move quickly in the field—his worth was diminished.

After sitting out 1925, he had a poor 1926 and returned to the Minors in '27 where, with Kansas City of the American Association, he regained his swing to the tune of .353 with 22 triples (not bad for a guy with a knee brace) and 20 homers and 134 RBI.

Promoted to the A's again in 1928, he battled with Jimmie Foxx for the first base job, and by hitting 16 homers to Foxx's 13, kept the battle close.

But during the '28 season, an odd thing happened . . . he took some advice.

Teammate Ty Cobb, arguably the greatest hitter of all-time, and also arguably the meanest man ever to play the game, was admittedly jealous that Hauser was taking attention away from him. He took Hauser aside and convinced him to change his swing—to abandon his pull-hitting for a spray technique. Hauser listened, changed, and flopped, slumping from over .300 to a season-finishing .260, losing his position to Foxx and his spot on the team via a trade to Cleveland.

His swing awry, he fell even further to .250 in 1929, with virtually no power. Hauser was soon in the Minors, a move he agreed with as he said, "Who wants a guy who can't run, *or* hit?"

His Major League career over by 1930, Hauser rediscovered his swing as he set out to pull every ball he swung at until his stroke returned. He soon went on to mythic Minor League status laying seige to pitchers at the Triple-A level for seven years (302 homers and 860 RBI) prior to his move to Sheboygen in his home state Wisconsin State League, where he played and managed on four pennant-winners. Even at the age of forty-three, Hauser belted out 14 homers in 242 at bats, with 70 RBI for Sheboygen in 1942.

His nickname, "Unser Choe," is German-American for "Our Joe," and that, he was.

Smead Jolley—Smead Powell Jolley was a power-packed outfielder who stood in at six-foot-three, 202 pounds. A player who was as deficient with his glove as he was proficient with his bat, Jolley finished his sixteen-year Minor League career as the third top hitter in history at .366. He was also ninth in doubles (612 plus some unavailable stats), and ninth in RBI (1,631 plus some uncounted games), and blasted 334 homers along the way.

He became a San Francisco legend, playing for the Seals from 1925 to 1929, ripping apart all comers and most pitchers, and had compiled successive batting marks of .397, .404, and .387 before he got a call from the Chicago White Sox in 1930.

He was up for four years with the White Sox and Red Sox, and hit a credible .305. But his fielding betrayed him (44 errors in 413 outfield games) and by 1934, he was back in the PCL after Boston replaced him with Roy Johnson.

His fielding was so bad, that a story—undocumented but

SMEAD POWELL JOLLEY

Born, January 14, 1902, at Wesson, AR.
Batted left. Threw right. Height, 6.03½. Weight, 202.

YEAR	CLUB	LEA	POS	G	AB	R	H	2B	3B	HR	RBI	SB	PCT
1922	Greenville	Cot. St.	P	39	86	7	27	11	0	0	—	0	.314
	Shreveport	Texas	P	3	8	2	2	0	0	0	2	0	.250
1923	Shreveport	Texas	P-OF	76	196	24	65	19	1	1	32	1	.331
1924	Shreveport	Texas	OF	6	14	2	5	0	0	0	3	0	.357
	Texarkana	E. Tex.	OF-P	112	429	85	159	46	1	14	—	7	.370
	Bartlesville	West. A.	OF-P	11	45	15	23	7	0	4	24	0	.511
1925	Corsicana	Tex. A.	OF-P	126	495	95	174*	11	2	24*	—	9	.352
	San Francisco	P. C.	OF-P	38	132	31	59	16	1	12	43	1	.447
1926	San Francisco	P. C.	OF-P	174	575	79	199	45	3	25	132	3	.346
1927	San Francisco	P. C.	OF-C	168	625	106	248	33	7	33	163*	3	.397*
1928	San Francisco	P. C.	OF	191	765	143	309*	52	10	45*	188*	9	.404*
1929	San Francisco	P. C.	OF-P	200	812	172	314*	65	10	35	159	6	.387
1930	Chicago	Amer.	OF	152	616	76	193	38	12	16	114	3	.313
1931	Chicago	Amer.	OF	54	110	5	33	11	0	3	28	0	.300
1932	Chi.-Boston	Amer.	OF-C	149	573	60	179	30	5	18	106	1	.312
1933	Boston	Amer.	OF	118	411	47	116	32	4	9	65	1	.282
1934	Hollywood	P. C.	OF	171	631	117	227	49	7	23	133	7	.360
1935	Hollywood	P. C.	OF	159	599	113	223	44	3	29	128	0	.372
1936	Albany	Int.	OF	155*	592	109	221*	52*	9	18	105	2	.373*
1937	Jersey City	Int.	OF	12	42	5	14	1	0	1	5	0	.333
	Nashville	South.	OF	53	205	39	61	11	1	6	37	0	.298
1938	Holly-Oak.	P. C.	OF	119	414	48	145	25	9	6	54	2	.350*
1939	Oakland	P. C.	OF	140	499	60	154	39	2	9	76	4	.309
1940	Spokane	W. Int.	OF-P	145	601	117	224*	56*	5	25	181*	2	.373*
1941	Spokane-Van.	W. Int.	OF-P	133	533	86	184	30	4	24	128*	5	.345*
			Majors	**473**	**1710**	**188**	**521**	**111**	**21**	**46**	**313**	**5**	**.305**
			Minors	**2231**	**8298**	**1455**	**3037**	**612**	**75**	**334**	**1593**	**61**	**.366**

Source: SABR
* = led league

oft-told—about him has become legend. According to the tale, he was credited with three errors on the same play: filling his position in right field, a line drive off an enemy bat took several hops and bounded through his legs (error number one); as he turned to watch the ball strike the wall behind him, the ball ricocheted and returned from whence it came, again going through Jolley's legs (error number two); when he finally caught up with the errant sphere, he picked it up and overthrew his intended target, allowing the batter to score (error number three).

He had no such joking references made about his strong arm or his quick, powerful bat.

Beginning his career as a pitcher, going 41–34, Jolley discovered his bat was even more valuable than his arm, and he used it to annihilate Minor League pitching and grab six batting titles (including a .404 mark for the San Francisco Seals in a triple crown year of 1928—.404, 45 homers, and 188 RBI); four RBI crowns; two homerun championships; five league-leading hit totals; and two doubles leaderships.

He enjoyed as much success after his Major League days as he had before, hitting .360 and .372 for the Hollywood Stars of the PCL; then he moved on the International League, hitting .373 for Albany in 1936.

Jolley hung on until 1941, when, playing for Spokane and Vancouver as a thirty-nine-year-old, he blasted Western-International League pitching for 24 homers, 128 RBI, and a league-leading .345 average.

"Jigger" Statz—Arnold John Statz was a pepperpot outfielder with a good glove, excellent speed, and a quick bat. Standing in at five-foot seven, 150 pounds, Statz gained a reputation for being a real "gamer" who worked hard and did what was necessary to help his team win.

Moving directly off the campus of Holy Cross College to the fields of the Major League's New York Giants in 1919–20, Statz didn't get a real shot at the starting lineup in two years with the club and began seasoning himself with the Los Angeles Angels of the PCL. The centerfielder eventually spent a record eighteen years with the same club, the Angels, and set career PCL records for games (2,790), runs scored (1,996), hits (3,356), doubles (595), and triples (137). He wound up fourth on the all-time Minor League runs list and sixth in hits.

Statz got another Major League opportunity and spent four years with the Cubs and two years with the Brooklyn Dodgers, acquitting himself well enough, but after uncharacteristically leading the league in errors in 1924, and

ARNOLD JOHN (JIGGER) STATZ

Born, October 20, 1897, at Waukegan, IL. Died, March 16, 1988, at Corona Del Mar, CA.
Batted right. Threw right. Height, 5.07½. Weight, 150.

YEAR	CLUB	LEA	POS	G	AB	R	H	2B	3B	HR	RBI	SB	PCT
1919	New York	Nat.	OF	21	60	7	18	2	1	0	6	2	.300
1920	New York	Nat.	OF	16	30	0	4	0	1	0	5	0	.133
	Boston	Amer.	OF	2	3	0	0	0	0	0	0	0	.000
	Los Angeles	P. C.	OF	101	386	42	91	14	5	0	—	11	.236
1921	Los Angeles	P. C.	OF	153	584	126	181	21	7	2	34	52	.310
1922	Chicago	Nat.	OF	110	462	77	137	19	5	1	34	16	.297
1923	Chicago	Nat.	OF	154	655	110	209	33	8	10	70	29	.319
1924	Chicago	Nat.	OF	135	549	69	152	22	5	3	49	13	.277
1925	Chicago	Nat.	OF	38	148	21	38	6	3	2	14	4	.257
	Los Angeles	P. C.	OF	130	545	90	144	27	7	2	45	17	.264
1926	Los Angeles	P. C.	OF	199	823	150	291*	68	18*	4	59	19	.354
1927	Brooklyn	Nat.	OF	130	507	64	139	24	7	1	21	10	.274
1928	Brooklyn	Nat.	OF	77	171	28	40	8	1	0	16	3	.234
1929	Los Angeles	P. C.	OF	195	799	173	246	41	7	3	75	37	.308
1930	Los Angeles	P. C.	OF-3B	161	558	95	201	43	12	5	84	37	.360
1931	Los Angeles	P. C.	OF	184	748	141*	248	42	13	6	107	45*	.332
1932	Los Angeles	P. C.	OF	188	737	153*	256	43	12	6	93	21	.347
1933	Los Angeles	P. C.	OF	182	767	144	249	29	8	10	73	17	.325
1934	Los Angeles	P. C.	OF	183	760	168	246	39	13*	6	66	61	.324
1935	Los Angeles	P. C.	OF	171	716	132	236	40	7	2	65	53*	.330
1936	Los Angeles	P. C.	OF	158	631	134*	203	37	7	3	62	43*	.322
1937	Los Angeles	P. C.	OF	154	558	90	162	32	5	2	57	18	.290
1938	Los Angeles	P. C.	OF	167	630	131*	200	41	4	2	44	12	.317
1939	Los Angeles	P. C.	OF	145	557	89	173	38	5	4	62	9	.311
1940	Los Angeles	P. C.	OF	144	453	97	131	30	3	1	48	11	.289
1941	Los Angeles	P. C.	OF	75	142	8	38	3	1	0	21	1	.268
1942	Los Angeles	P. C.	OF	100	263	33	60	9	2	2	22	2	.228
			Majors	683	2585	376	737	114	31	17	215	77	.285
			Minors	2790	10657	1996	3356	597	136	60	1017	466	.315

Source: SABR
* = led league

showing no power, the Cubbies replaced him with Mandy Brooks the next year. The Dodgers started Statz in 1927 and he played the field well. But when he slumped in '28, the Brooks brought in Max Carey and then it was back to the PCL for fourteen more years with the Angels.

Statz showed his consistency and determination, hitting .300 in ten of the next eleven years; and he showed his speed, winning back-to-back theft crowns with 53 in 1935 and 43 in 1936, the latter at the age of thirty-nine.

Statz finished up his career in 1942 with what was then the most games ever played in organized baseball . . . 3,473 games (683 in the Majors, 2,790 in the Minors), which stood until Henry Aaron and Pete Rose passed him more than thirty years later.

George Whiteman—The all-time Minor League leader in games played with 3,282, of which 3,103 were played in the outfield, George Whiteman was a magnificent glove man, but was unimpressive at the stick, which is why his run in the Majors was a short one—85 games over two seasons with the Yankees and Red Sox. The five-foot-seven, 160-pound speedster actually did hit well as a fill-in for the 1913 Yankees (the Highlanders changed their name to Yankees that year, with a move to the Polo Grounds), at .344, but as he was thirty years old, the Yankees called him a non prospect and he was sent down to Montreal of the International League, where he won a homerun title with 14 four-baggers in 1915.

The BoSox took a shot with him in 1918, but with Babe Ruth in left field (Ruth started 59 games in left, 13 at first base, and 20 on the mound), Whiteman was relegated to 71 games as a thirty-five-year-old sub. In that role, he achieved Boston immortality when in the final game of the 1918 World Series, Whiteman, playing left field, made a somersaulting catch in the eighth inning to preserve a 2–1 Red Sox victory over the Chicago Cubs, wrapping up the Red Sox's last World Championship. By 1919, however, he was back in the International League, this time with Toronto.

He never really settled in with any one club, and he instead moved around, playing for eighteen teams over his twenty-five-year career.

But he showed glimmers of brilliance at bat with one doubles crown (53 in 1921 for Houston of the Texas League), two triples titles (14 for Houston in 1912 and 18 for the Buffs in 1913), and one homerun championship (14 for Montreal in 1915), and at the age of forty-two, hit 26 roundtrippers for Ardmore of the Western Association in 1925.

On the basepaths, Whiteman stole 50 bases for Houston in 1912 and stole 30 or more bases eight times.

His hitting claim to fame may be that he won the Texas League batting championship with the lowest total ever recorded by a Minor League leader, at .281 for Cleburne in 1906, but he did manage to hit .300 or better at nine stops along his way, including .320 in 146 games for Salisbury of the Piedmont League as a forty-four-year-old in 1927.

And these are only fifteen of yesterday's heroes of the Farm who didn't, couldn't, or wouldn't repeat their successes in the Bigs. Woven into the Minor League fabric are these fifteen plus the likes of pitchers Tony Freitas (the top-winning Minor League lefty, at 340 victories), Oyster Joe Martina, Ben Tincup, Shelly Shellenback, Grasshopper Mains, Rube Eldridge, Chester Covington, Satchel Paige, Bullet Joe Rogan, Luis Tiant, Sr., George Brunet (the top all-time Minor League strikeout ace with more than 3,200) and Bill Thomas (the all-time leader in games pitched: 1,015 games, winning 383, against 346); and hitters including Cool Papa Bell, Perry Werden, Frank Carswell, Buster Chatham, Judge Pyle, Zip Payne, Clarence Kraft, Prince Oana, Spencer Harris (the all-time Minor League leader in hits: 3,617, scoring 2,287 runs, and hitting 743 doubles), Moose Clabaugh, Frank Grant, Simon Rosenthal, Buck Frierson, Bobby Crues, Jack Harshman, Tony So-

GEORGE WHITEMAN

Born, December 23, 1882, at Peoria, IL Died, February 10, 1947, in Houston, TX.
Batted right. Threw right. Height, 5.07. Weight, 160.

YEAR	CLUB	LEA	POS	G	AB	R	H	2B	3B	HR	RBI	SB	PCT
1905	Waco	Texas	OF-2B-3B	124	464	33	112	12	3	0	—	29	.241
1906	Cleburne	Texas	OF	120	466	75	131*	29	10	3	—	33	.281*
1907	Houston	Texas	OF	135	508	67	118	27	7	6	—	31	.232
	Boston	Amer.	OF	3	11	0	2	0	0	0	1	0	.167
1908	Houston	Texas	OF	139	509	88	138	17	6	6	—	48	.271
1909	Montgomery	South.	OF-3B	128	434	54	103	13	8	2	—	20	.237
1910	Montgomery	South.	O-3-S-2	141	484	61	109	15	10	3	—	17	.204
1911	Missoula	Union A.	OF	23	81	3	18	2	0	0	4	1	.222
	Houston	Texas	OF	117	378	41	78	11	3	0	—	39	.206
1912	Houston	Texas	OF	144	511	76	155	25	14*	3	—	50	.303
1913	Houston	Texas	OF	155	563	71	143	29	18*	4	—	36	.254
	New York	Amer.	OF	11	32	8	11	3	1	0	2	2	.344
1914	Montreal	Int.	OF	149	562	92	176	20	15	8	—	32	.313
1915	Montreal	Int.	OF	141	526	106*	164	27	13	14*	—	25	.312
1916	Louisville	A. A.	OF	125	450	63	123	20	11	3	—	10	.273
1917	Louisville	A. A.	OF	3	11	1	3	0	0	0	2	1	.273
	Toronto	Int.	OF	140	530	104	181	32	10	7	—	23	.342
1918	Boston	Amer.	OF	71	214	24	57	14	0	1	28	9	.267
1919	Toronto	Int.	OF	149	592	102	179	39	9	4	—	25	.302
1920	Toronto	Int.	OF	128	458	74	124	27	6	6	—	18	.271
1921	Houston	Texas	OF	147	547	73	153	53*	8	6	96	22	.280
1922	Houston	Texas	OF-3B-2B	130	468	81	142	31	12	3	75	10	.303
1923	Oakland	P. C.	OF	25	92	14	25	4	1	2	7	2	.272
	Wi. Falls-Gal.	Texas	OF	75	255	35	75	16	5	4	57	5	.294
1924	Galveston	Texas	OF	146	564	80	161	34	5	9	77	2	.285
1925	Ardmore	West. A.	OF	147	569	129	197	47	4	26	138	11	.346
1926	Ardm.-Joplin	West. A.	OF	143	540	126	157	34	6	18	—	14	.291
1927	Salisbury	Pied.	OF	146	513	74	164	36	3	8	102	32	.320
1928	Salisbury	Pied.	OF	126	452	73	135	37	3	7	83	7	.299
1929	Win. Salem	Pied.	OF	136	464	69	124	34	6	10	84	13	.267
			Majors	**85**	**257**	**32**	**70**	**17**	**1**	**1**	**31**	**11**	**.272**
			Minors	**3282**	**11991**	**1865**	**3388**	**671**	**196**	**162**	**725**	**556**	**.283**

(*Source:* SABR)* — led league

laita, Manuel Magallon, Bevo LeBourveau, Quiet Joe
Knight, Fuzzy Hufft, Stubby Greer, Double Dwyer (451
career two-baggers), Count Campeau, Lyman Lamb,
George Hogriever (the all-time leader with 948 stolen
bases), Elliot Bigelow, Zeke Bonura, Paul Easterling, Carlton East, Pete Hughes, Pooch Puccinelli, Frosty Kennedy,
Big Boy Kraft, Pud Miller, Howitzer Howie Moss, Muscle

Shoals, Buck Leonard, Jim Thorpe, and several thousand other athletes who have thrilled home-town fans in communities stretching from Havana to Vancouver, from Mexico City to Fargo, from Honolulu to Jersey City, from San Diego to Bangor, and everywhere in between.

All of these men boomed in the Minors but busted in the Majors (if they even got there). But can one legitimately call a Minor League star a Major League bust? One can, but the phrase really doesn't do the athlete justice. Suffice it to say that the above fifteen (plus the fifty additional names listed after them as well as the thousands of others that space did not permit naming) were genuine heroes to countless American baseball fans who lived and died by their every play during the long years the players toiled on the Farm.

These men were just as famous and just as cherished within the small towns, villages, and communities they represented as were the Mayses, Mantles, Bankses, Williamses, and Greenbergs to the metropolises in which they performed. The fact that the above fifteen didn't perform as well or as long on the Major League level does not diminish their contribution to American baseball lore. The Minor Leagues are privileged to have had them . . . it's baseball's gain, the Minor Leagues' gain, and perhaps the Major Leagues' loss.

They've done the game proud.

Thanks for the memories, guys.

20
MINOR LEAGUES IN OPERATION 1877 – 1900

Total: 70 leagues

(*Sources:* Bob Hoie, Bob McConnell, John Pardon, Ray Nemec and Jerry Jackson, and SABR.)

Arkansas
Atlantic
Atlantic Assn.
California
California St.
Canadian
Central
Central Interstate
Central New Jersey
Central Pennsyl-
   vania
Colorado
Connecticut St.
Cumberland Valley
Eastern
Eastern Interstate
Eastern Iowa

Eastern New En-
   gland
Florida St.
Hudson River
Illinois-Indiana
Illinois-Iowa
Indiana St.
International
International Assn.
Interstate
Interstate Assn.
Iron & Oil
Keystone
Kootenay &
   Washington
Lehigh Valley
Maine St.
Michigan St.

Michigan-Wisconsin
Middle States
Montana St.
Naugautuck Valley
Nebraska St.
New England
New England Assn.
New England
Interstate
New Jersey St.
New York-Penn-
   sylvania
New York St.
Northwest
Ohio-Michigan
Ohio St.
Ohio Valley
Ohio-West Virginia

Ontario
Pacific
Pacific Interstate
Pacific Northwest
Pennsylvania St.
Puget Sound
Red River Valley
Rhode Island

South Atlantic
Southeastern
Southeast Virginia
Southern
Southern New
England
Southwestern
Texas

Tri State
Virginia St.
Western
Western Assn.
Western Interstate
Western
Pennsylvania
Wisconsin St.

21
MINOR LEAGUES
IN OPERATION
1901 – 1990

Total: 239 leagues

(*Sources:* Bob Hoie, Bob McConnell, John Pardon, Ray Nemec, and Jerry Jackson, and SABR).

CLASS	MINOR LEAGUE	YEARS IN OPERATION
D	Alabama State	1946–50
D	Alabama-Florida	1936–41, 1951–62
D	Alabama-Mississippi	1936
D	Alabama-Tennessee	1921
AAA	American Association	1902–62, 1969–
D	Anthracite	1928
D-R	Appalachian	1911–14, 1921–25, 1937–55, 1957–
R	Arizona League	1988–
D	Arizona State	1928–30
C	Arizona-Mexico	1955–58
D-C	Arizona-Texas	1931–32, 1937–41, 1947–50, 1953–54
D	Arkansas	1908–09

D	Arkansas State	1934–35
D	Arkansas-Missouri	1936–40
D	Arkansas-Texas	1905
D	Atlantic Association	1908
D	Atlantic	1907–08, 1914
D	Bi-State (NC-VA)	1934–42
D	Bi-State (WI-IL)	1915
B	Big State	1947–57
D	Blue Grass	1908–12, 1922–24
D	Blue Ridge	1915–18, 1920–30, 1946–50
D	Border (MI)	1912
C	Border (NY-Canada)	1946–51
D	Buckeye	1915
C-A	California	1913–15, 1941–42, 1946–
B-D	California State	1901–02, 1903–09, 1910, 1929
C-D	Canadian	1905, 1911–15
C	Canadian-American	1936–42, 1946–51
D-C	Cape Breton Colliery	1937–39
D	Carolina Association	1908–12
C-B-A	Carolina	1945–
D-B-C	Central Association	1908–17, 1947–49
D	Central	1903–17, 1920–22, 1928–30, 1934, 1948–51
D	Central California	1910–11
D	Central Kansas	1908–12
C	Central International	1912
C	Central Mexican	1956–57
C	Central New York	1910
D	Central Texas	1914–17
D	Coastal Plain	1937–41, 1946–52
R	Cocoa Rookie	1964
C-B	Colonial	1914, 1915, 1947–50
D	Connecticut Assn.	1910
D	Connecticut (Conn St.)	1901–12
D	Copper Country-Soo	1905
D-C	Cotton States	1902–08, 1910–13, 1922–32, 1936–41, 1947–55
D	Dakota (SD L.)	1921–22
D	Delta	1904–05

C	Dixie Association	1971
D	Dixie	1916–17, 1933
R	Dominican Summer	1990–
AAA	Dominican Winter	1990–
B	Eastern Association	1913–14
B	Eastern	1901–11, 1916–32, 1939–
B	Eastern Canada	1922–23
D	Eastern Illinois	1907–08
D	Eastern Kansas	1910–11
D	Eastern Shore	1922–28, 1937–41, 1946–49
C	East Dixie	1934–35
D	East Michigan (Border)	1913
D-C	East Texas	1916, 1923–26, 1931, 1934–40, 1946, 1949–50
D	Eastern Carolina	1906, 1908–11, 1928–29
D	Empire State (GA)	1913
C	Empire State (NY)	1905–07
D-C	Evangeline	1934–42, 1946–57
D	Far West	1948–51
D	Florida East Coast	1940–42, 1972
C-B	Florida International	1946–54
R	Florida Rookie	1965
D-C	Florida State	1917–27, 1936–41, 1946–
D	F.L.A.G. (FL, LA, AL, GA)	1915
D	Georgia State	1906, 1914, 1920–21, 1948–56
C	Georgia-Alabama	1913–17, 1928–30, 1946–51
D-A	Georgia-Florida	1935–42, 1946–58
D	Gulf Coast (LA)	1907–08, 1926, 1950–53
R	Gulf Coast (FL)	1964–
R	Gulf States	
D	Hudson River	1903–07
B	Illinois State	1947–48
D	I-I-I	1901–17, 1919–32, 1935, 1937–42, 1946–61
D	Illinois-Missouri	1908–14
D	Indiana State	1911–12
D	Indiana-Michigan	1910

D	Indiana-Ohio	1907
D	Inland Empire	1902, 1908
R	Inter-American	
D	Intermountain	1909
D	International	1908, 1913–
D	Interstate Assn. (IN, MI, OH)	1906
C-D	Interstate*	1905–08, 1913–16, 1932, 1939–52

*Author's note: Three different regions had Interstate
                  Leagues: Mostly in PA, CT, MD, OH and
                  VA

D	Iowa State	1904–07, 1911
D	Iowa & South Dakota	1902–03
D	Kansas State	1905–06, 1909–14
D	K-O-M (KS, OK, MO)	1946–52
D	Keystone	1935*
D	KITTY (KY, IL, TN)	1903–06, 1910–14, 1916, 1922–24, 1935–42, 1946–55
D-C	Lone Star	1927–29, 1947–48
D-C	Longhorn	1947–55
D	Louisiana State	1920
D	MA-CT	1912
D	Maine State	1907–08
AAA	Mexican	1955–
A	Mexican Center	1960–
AAA	Mexican National	1946
A	Mexican Northern	1968–71
AAA	Mexican Pacific Winter	
R	Mexican Rookie	1968
B	Mexican Southeast	1964–70
D	Michigan State	1902, 1911–14, 1926, 1940–41
B	Michigan-Ontario	1919–25
D	Middle Atlantic	1925–42, 1946–51
D	Middle Texas	1914–15
D	M.I.N.K. (MO, IA, NE, KS)	1910–13
D-A	Midwest	1956–
D-C	Minnesota-Wisconsin	1909–12

D	Mississippi-Ohio Valley League	1949–55
D	Mississippi State	1921
D-B	Mississippi Valley	1922–33
D	Missouri State	1911
D	Missouri-Kansas	1912
D	Missouri Valley	1902–05
D	Mountain State	1938–42
D	Mountain States	1911–12, 1937, 1948–54
D-R	Nebraska State	1910–15, 1922–23, 1928–38, 1956–59
D	New Brunswick-Maine	1913
B	New England	1901–15, 1919, 1925–30, 1933, 1946–49
D	New Hampshire	1907
B	New York State	1901–17
D	New York-New Jersey	1913
D-A	New York-Penn	1939–
D	North Carolina Assn.	1913–17
D	North Carolina	1902
D	North Carolina State	1937–42, 1945–52
D	North Atlantic	1946–50
D	Northeast Arkansas	1909–11, 1936–41
A	Northeastern	1934
C	Northern Association	1910
D-C-A	Northern	1902–05, 1908, 1913–17, 1933–42, 1946–71
C	Northern Copper	1906–07
D	Northern Indiana	1909–10
D	Northern Maine	1920
D	Northern New York	1902
D	North Dakota	1923
D	North Texas	1906–07
B	Northwest	1955–
B	Northwestern	1905–17
D	Ohio State	1908–16, 1936–41
D	Ohio Valley	1912
D	Ohio-Indiana	1907, 1936–41, 1944–51
D	Ohio & Pennsylvania	1905–12
D	Oklahoma State	1912, 1922–24, 1936
D	O-A-K (OK, AK, KS)	1907

D	Oklahoma-Kansas	1908
D	Old Dominion (VA)	1908
D	Ontario (CAN)	1930
D	Oregon State	1904
AAA	Pacific Coast	1903–
B	Pacific Coast Int.	1919–21
C	Pacific National	1903–04
D	Pacific Northwest	1901–02
D	Palmetto	1931
D	Panhandle-Pecos Val.	1923
D	Penn. State Assn.	1934–42
D	Penn. State	1902, 1916
D	P-O-M (PA, OH, MD)	1906–07
D	P-O-N-Y (PA, ONT, NY)	1939–56
D	Penn.-West Virginia	1908–09, 1914
D-C-B	Piedmont	1920–55
C-A-R	Pioneer	1939–42, 1946–
D	Potomac	1916
C	Provincial	1944–49, 1950–55
AAA	Puerto Rican Winter	
B	Quebec-Ontario-Vt.	1924
B	Quebec Provincial	1940
D	Rio Grande Assn.	1915
C	Rio Grande Valley	1931, 1949–50
D	Rocky Mountain (CO)	1912
D	San Joaquin Valley	1910–11
R	Sarasota Rookie	1964
D	Sooner State	1947–57
D	Sophomore	1958
D-C	South Atlantic	1904–17, 1919–30, 1936–42, 1946–63
D	South Carolina	1907–08
D	South Central	1906, 1912
D	South Dakota	1920, 1923
	South Texas	1903–06, 1912
D	Southeastern	1910–12, 1926–30, 1932, 1937–42, 1946–50
D	Southeastern Kansas	1911
A	Southern Association	1901–61
AA	Southern	1964–70, 1972–
D	Southern California	1913

D	So. Calif. Trolley	1910
D	Southern Illinois	1910
C	Southern Michigan	1906–15
D	Southern N.H.	1907
C-D	Southwest	1921–26
C	Southwest Int.	1951–52
D	Southwest Iowa	1903
D	Southwest Texas	1910–12
D	Southwest Washington	1903–06
B	Southwestern (NM, TX)	1904, 1956–57
C	Sunset	1947–50
D	Tar Heel	1939–40, 1953–54
D	Tennessee-Alabama	1904
D	Texas Association	1923–26
A-AA	Texas	1902–42, 1946–70, 1972–
D	Texas Valley	1927–28, 1938
D	Texas-Oklahoma	1911–14, 1921–22
D	Tobacco State (NC)	1946–50
D	Tri-State (MS)	1925–26
D	Tri-State (NE)	1924
D	Tri-State (PA)	1904–06, 1907–14
B	Tri-State (NC)	1946–55
D	Twin State	1911
E	Twin Ports (MN)	1943
	Utah (Intermountain)	1901
D	Utah-Idaho	1926–28
D	Union Association	1911–14
AAA	Venezuelan Winter	
C-D	Virginia	1906–28, 1939–42, 1948–51
D	Virginia Mountain	1914
D	Virginia Valley	1910
D	Virginia-North Car.	1901, 1905
D	Washington State	1910–12
C	West Dixie	1934–35
D	West Michigan	1910
D	West Pennsylvania	1907
D	West Texas	1920–22, 1928–29
D-C	West Texas-New Mex.	1937–42, 1946–55
D	West Virginia	1910

C-B	Western Association	1901, 1905–11, 1914–17, 1920–32, 1934–42, 1946–54
A-D	Western	1901–37, 1939–41, 1947–58
C-B	Western Canada	1907, 1909–14, 1919–21
D-C	Western Carolina	1948–52
D-A	Western Carolinas	1960–
B-A	Western International	1922, 1937–42, 1946–54
D	Western Tri-State	1912–14
D	Wisconsin State	1905–06, 1940–42, 1946–53
D	Wisconsin-Illinois	1907–14

22
MINOR LEAGUE CITIES IN OPERATION 1877–1990

Total: 1414 cities

(*Sources:* Bob Hoie, Bob McConnell, John Pardon, Ray Nemec and Jerry Jackson, SABR, and *Baseball America*)

United States (1247)

Alabama (36)

Abbeville	Enterprise	Opelika
Alabama City	Eufaula	Opp
Albany	Evergreen	Ozark
Alexander City	Florence	Russelville
Andalusia	Gadsden	Selma
Anniston	Geneva	Sheffield
Attalla	Greenville	Talladega
Bessemer	Headland	Tallassee
Birmingham	Huntsville	Troy
Brewton	Lanett	Tuscumbia
Decatur	Mobile	Tuskegee
Dothan	Montgomery	Union Springs

Arizona (12)

Bisbee	Miami	Scottsdale
Douglass	Nogales	Tempe
Globe	Peoria	Tucson
Mesa	Phoenix	Yuma

Arkansas (23)

Argenta	Fort Smith	Osceola
Batesville	Helena	Paragould
Bentonville	Hot Springs	Pine Bluff
Blytheville	Huntsville	Rogers
Brinkley	Jonesboro	Siloam Springs
Camden	Little Rock	Texarkana
El Dorado	Marianna	Van Buren
Fayetteville	Newport	

California (63)

Alameda	Napa	San Bernardino
Anaheim	Oakland	San Diego
Bakersfield	Ontario	San Francisco
Berkeley	Orange	San Jose
Calexico	Oroville	San Leandro
Coalinga	Palm Springs	San Pedro
Coronado	Pasadena	San Rafael
El Centro	Petaluma	Santa Ana
Elmhurst	Pittsburg	Santa Barbara
Fresno	Pomona	Santa Clara
Fruitvale	Porterville	Santa Cruz
Hanford	Redding	Santa Rosa
Hayward	Redondo Beach	Stockton
Healdsburg	Redwood	Tulare
Hollywood	Richmond	Vallejo
Lodi	Riverside	Ventura
Long Beach	Rohnert Park	Vernon
Los Angeles	Roseville	Visalia
Marysville	Sacramento	Watsonville
Merced	St. Helena	Willows
Modesto	Salinas	Yuba City

Colorado (6)

Canon City	Denver	Leadville
Colorado Springs	La Junta	Pueblo

Connecticut (17)

Ansonia	Meriden	Stamford
Bridgeport	Middletown	Torrington
Bristol	New Britain	Waterbury
Danbury	New Haven	West Haven
Derby	New London	Willimantic
Hartford	Norwich	

Delaware (6)

Dover	Milford	Seaford
Laurel	Rehoboth Beach	Wilmington

District of Columbia (1)

Washington

Florida (47)

Bartow	Graceville	Pensacola
Baseball City	Hollywood	Pirate City
Bradenton	Jacksonville	Plant City
Charlotte	Jacksonville Beach	Pompano Beach
Clearwater	Key West	St. Augustine
Cocoa	Kissimmee	St. Petersburg
Crestview	Lakeland	St. Lucie
Daytona Beach	Leesburg	Sanford
Deerfield Beach	Melbourne	Sarasota
DeLand	Miami	Tallahassee
Dunedin	Miami Beach	Tampa
Fort Lauderdale	Ocala	Twin Lakes
Fort Myers	Orlando	Vero Beach
Fort Pierce	Osceola	West Palm Beach
Fort Walton Beach	Palatka	Winter Haven
Gainesville	Panama City	

Georgia (38)

Albany	Dublin	Rome
Americus	Eastman	Sandersville
Atlanta	Fitzgerald	Savannah
Augusta	Griffin	Sparta
Bainbridge	Hazlehurst	Statesboro
Baxley	Jesup	Thomasville
Brunswick	LaGrange	Thomson
Carrollton	Lindale	Tifton
Cedartown	Lyons	Valdosta
Columbus	Macon	Vidalia
Cordele	Moultrie	Waycross
Donalsonville	Newman	West Point
Douglas	Quitman	

Hawaii (1)

Honolulu

Idaho (8)

Boise	Idaho Falls	Pocatello
Caldwell	Lewiston	Twin Falls
Gate City	Magic Valley	

Illinois (53)

Alton	East Moline	McLeansboro
Aurora	Eldorado	Macomb
Beardstown	Elgin	Marion
Belleville	Freeport	Mattoon
Bloomington	Galesburg	Moline
Cairo	Harrisburg	Monmouth
Canton	Havana	Mount Vernon
Centralia	Herrin	Murphysboro
Champaign	Jacksonville	Ottawa
Charleston	Joliet	Pana
Chicago	Kankakee	Pekin
Clinton	Kewanee	Peoria
Danville	LaSalle	Peru
Decatur	Lincoln	Quincy

Rockford   Staunton   Urbana
Rock Island   Sterling   Waukegan
Shelbyville   Streator   West Frankfort
Springfield   Taylorville

Indiana (25)

Anderson   Goshen   Matthews
Auburn   Huntington   Michigan City
Bluffton   Indianapolis   Muncie
Decatur   Kokomo   Portland
Elkhart   Lafayette   Richmond
Evansville   Linton   South Bend
Fort Wayne   Logansport   Terre Haute
Gary   Marion   Vincennes
                                    Wabash

Iowa (28)

Bettendorf   Davenport   Mason City
Boone   Des Moines   Muscatine
Burlington   Dubuque   Oskaloosa
Cedar Rapids   Emmettsburg   Ottumwa
Charles City   Estherville   Quad Cities
Clarinda   Fort Dodge   Rock Rapids
Clear Lake   Keokuk   Sheldon
Clinton   LeMars   Shenandoah
Council Bluffs   Marshalltown   Sioux City
                                    Waterloo

Kansas (43)

Abilene   El Dorado   Iola
Arkansas City   Ellsworth   Junction City
Atchison   Emporia   Larned
Beloit   Eureka   Leavenworth
Blue Rapids   Fort Scott   Lyons
Chanute   Great Bend   McPherson
Chapman   Hiawatha   Manhattan
Cherryvale   Holton   Marysville
Clay Center   Horton   Minneapolis
Coffeyville   Hutchinson   Mulberry
Concordia   Independence   Newton

Norton   Sabetha   Seneca
Parsons   Salina   Topeka
Pittsburg   Scammon   Wellington
                                            Wichita

Kentucky (32)

Ashland   Jenkins   Owensboro
Bowling Green   Lawrenceburg   Paducah
Catlettsburg   Lexington   Paintsville
Cynthiana   Louisville   Paris
Dawson Springs   Madisonville   Pikeville
Frankfort   Mayfield   Pineville
Fulton   Maysville   Princeton
Harlan   Middlesboro   Richmond
Hazard   Mount Sterling   Shelbyville
Henderson   Newport   Winchester
Hopkinsville   Nicholasville

Louisiana (23)

Abbeville   Jeanerette   Oakdale
Alexandria   Lafayette   Opelousas
Baton Rouge   Lake Charles   Rayne
Crowley   Leesville   Shreveport
DeQuincy   Monroe   Thibodaux
DeRidder   Morgan City   Twin Cities
Hammond   New Iberia   West Monroe
Houma   New Orleans

Maine (13)

Auburn   Brewer   Old Orchard Beach
Augusta   Calais   Old Town
Bangor   Lewiston   Pine Tree
Biddeford   Millinocket   Portland
                                            York Beach

Maryland (14)

Baltimore   Crisfield   Federalsburg
Cambridge   Cumberland   Frederick
Centreville   Easton   Frostburg

Hagerstown	Pocomoke City	Westernport
Lonaconing	Salisbury	

Massachusetts (24)

Attleboro	Holyoke	Quincy
Berkshire	Lawrence	Salem
Boston	Lowell	Springfield
Brockton	Lynn	Taunton
Fall River	Malden	Waltham
Fitchburg	New Bedford	Watertown
Gloucester	Northampton	Wayland
Haverhill	Pittsfield	Worcester

Michigan (36)

Adrian	Hancock	Mount Clemens
Battle Creek	Holland	Muskegon
Bay City	Houghton	Niles
Belding	Ionia	Pontiac
Benton Harbor	Iron Mountain	Port Huron
Berrien Springs	Jackson	Saginaw
Boyne City	Kalamazoo	St. Joseph
Cadillac	Lake Linden	Saulte St. Marie
Calumet	Lansing	Tecumseh
Detroit	Ludington	Traverse City
Flint	Manistee	Wyandotte
Grand Rapids	Menominee	Ypsilanti

Minnesota (17)

Bloomington	Little Falls	St. Cloud
Brainerd	Mankato	St. Paul
Breckenridge	Minneapolis	Virginia
Crookston	Moorhead	Winona
Duluth	Red Wing	Worthington
East Grand Forks	Rochester	

Mississippi (19)

Aberdeen	Canton	Columbus
Biloxi	Clarksdale	Corinth
Brookhaven	Cleveland	Greenville

Greenwood   Jackson   Natchez
Gulfport   Laurel   Tupelo
Hattiesburg   Meridian   Vicksburg
                                    Yazoo City

Missouri (24)

Brookfield   Joplin   Poplar Bluff
Cape Girardeau   Kansas City   Portageville
Carthage   Kirksville   St. Joseph
Caruthersville   Macon   St. Louis
Cassville   Maryville   Sedalia
Chillicothe   Monett   Springfield
Hannibal   Neosho   Webb City
Jefferson City   Nevada   West Plains

Montana (5)

Billings   Great Falls   Missoula
Butte   Helena

Nebraska (22)

Auburn   Hastings   Nebraska City
Beatrice   Holdrege   Norfolk
Columbus   Humboldt   North Platte
Fairbury   Kearney   Omaha
Falls City   Lexington   Red Cloud
Fremont   Lincoln   Seward
Grand Island   McCook   Superior
                                    York

Nevada (2)

Las Vegas   Reno

New Hampshire (8)

Concord   Fremont   Nashua
Dover   Kingston   Newton
Epping   Manchester

New Jersey (13)

Asbury Park	Camden	New Brunswick
Atlantic City	Jersey City	Paterson
Bloomfield	Long Branch	Perth Amboy
Bloomingdale	Newark	Trenton
		Washington

New Mexico (6)

Albuquerque	Clovis	Las Cruces
Artesia	Hobbs	Roswell

New York (62)

Albany	Jamestown	Peekskill
Amsterdam	Johnson City	Penn Yan
Auburn	Johnstown	Plattsburgh
Batavia	Kingston	Port Chester
Beacon	Little Falls	Potsdam
Binghamton	Lockport	Poughkeepsie
Brooklyn	Lyons	Rochester
Buffalo	Malone	Rome
Catskill	Massena	St. Albans
Corning	Middleton	Saugerties
Cortland	Newark	Schenectady
Elmira	Newburgh	Seneca Falls
Endicott	New York	Syracuse
Fulton	Niagara Falls	Troy
Geneva	Nyack	Utica
Glens Falls	Ogdensburg	Walden
Gloversville	Olean	Watertown
Herkimer	Oneida	Waverly
Hornell	Oneonta	Wellsville
Hudson	Ossining	Yonkers
Ilion	Oswego	

North Carolina (71)

Albermarle	Ayden	Charlotte
Angier	Belmont	Clinton
Ashville	Burlington	Conover

Cooleemee
Dunn
Durham
Edenton
Elizabeth City
Elkin
Erwin
Fayetteville
Forest City
Fuquay Springs
Gastonia
Goldsboro
Graham
Granite Falls
Greensboro
Greenville
Henderson
Hendersonville
Hickory
High Point
Kannapolis

Kinston
Landis
Leaksville-Spray-
    Draper
Lenoir
Lexington
Lincolnton
Lumberton
Marion
Mayodan
Moorsville
Morganton
Mount Airy
New Bern
Newton
North Wilkesboro
Raleigh
Red Springs
Reidsville
Roanoke Rapids
Rockingham

Rocky Mount
Rutherfordton
Salisbury
Sanford
Selma
Shelby
Smithfield
Snow Hill
Spencer
Spindale
Statesville
Tarboro
Thomasville
Wadesboro
Warsaw
Weldon
Whiteville
Williamston
Wilmington
Wilson
Winston-Salem

North Dakota (10)

Bismarck
Cavalier
Devils Lake

Fargo
Grand Forks
Jamestown

Minot
Valley City
Wahpeton
Warren

Ohio (42)

Akron
Alliance
Canton
Chillicothe
Cincinnati
Cleveland
Columbus
Coshocton
Dayton
Dover

East Liverpool
Findlay
Fostoria
Fremont
Gallipolis
Girard
Hamilton
Ironton
Lancaster
Lima

Mansfield
Marion
Massillon
Middleport
Middletown
Mount Vernon
Newark
New Philadelphia
Niles
Piqua

Pomeroy	Sebring	Toledo
Portsmouth	Springfield	Warren
Salem	Steubenville	Youngstown
Sandusky	Tiffin	Zanesville

Oklahoma (37)

Ada	Durant	Muskogee
Altus	El Reno	Oklahoma City
Anadarko	Enid	Okmulgee
Ardmore	Eufaula	Pauls Valley
Bartlesville	Guthrie	Pawhuska
Blackwell	Henryetta	Ponca City
Bristow	Holdenville	Sapulpa
Chickasha	Hugo	Seminole
Clinton	Lawton	Shawnee
Cushing	McAlester	Tulsa
Drumright	Maud	Vinita
Duncan	Miami	Wewoka
		Wilson

Oregon (12)

Baker	Eugene	North Bend
Bend	Klamath Falls	Pendleton
Central Oregon	La Grande	Portland
Coos Bay	Medford	Salem

Pennsylvania (67)

Allentown	Coatesville	Homestead
Altoona	Connellsville	Jeanette
Bangor	Coudersport	Johnsonburg
Beaver Falls	Donora	Johnstown
Berwick	DuBois	Kane
Braddock	Erie	Lancaster
Bradford	Franklin	Lansdale
Butler	Gettysburgh	Lebanon
Carbondale	Greensburg	McKeesport
Chambersburg	Hanover	Mahonoy City
Charleroi	Harrisburg	Monessen
Chester	Hazleton	Mount Carmel

New Castle
Nazareth
Norristown
Oil City
Patton
Philadelphia
Pittsburgh
Pottstown
Pottsville
Punxsutawney

Reading
Ridgway
St. Clair
St. Mary's
Scottdale
Scranton
Shamokin
Sharon
Shenandoah
Slatington

Stroudsburg
Tamaqua
Uniontown
Vandegrift
Warren
Washington
Waynesboro
Waynesburg
Wilkes-Barre
Williamsport
York

Rhode Island (6)

Cranston
Newport

Pawtucket
Providence

Taunton
Woonsocket

South Carolina (14)

Anderson
Bennettsville
Charleston
Chester
Columbia

Darlington
Florence
Greenville
Greenwood
Myrtle Beach

Orangeburg
Rock Hill
Spartanburg
Sumter

South Dakota (10)

Aberdeen
Flandreau
Huron
Madison

Miller
Mitchell
Redfield
Sioux Falls

Watertown
Wessington
  Springs

Tennessee (27)

Alcoa
Bristol
Chattanooga
Clarksville
Cleveland
Columbia
Dyersburg
Elizabethton
Erwin

Greensville
Harriman
Jackson
Johnson City
Kingsport
Knoxville
Lexington
Maryville
Memphis

Milan
Morristown
Nashville
Newport
Oak Ridge
Paris
Springfield
Trenton
Union City

Texas (103)

Abilene	Galveston	Odessa
Alpine	Georgetown	Orange
Amarillo	Gladewater	Palestine
Arlington	Gorman	Pampa
Austin	Graham	Paris
Ballinger	Greenville	Plainview
Bartlett	Hamlin	Port Arthur
Bay City	Harlingen	Ranger
Beaumont	Henderson	Refugio
Beeville	Hillsboro	Rio Grande Valley
Belton	Houston	Robstown
Big Spring	Italy	Rusk
Bonham	Jacksonville	San Angelo
Borger	Kaufman	San Antonio
Brenham	Kilgore	San Benito
Brownsville	Kingsville	Schulenburg
Bryan	La Feria	Sequin
Cisco	Lamesa	Sherman
Clarksville	Lampasas	Stamford
Cleburne	Laredo	Sulphur Springs
Coleman	Longview	Sweetwater
Corpus Christi	Lubbock	Taft
Corsicana	Lufkin	Temple
Crockett	McAllen	Terrell
Dallas	McKinney	Texarkana
Del Rio	Marlin	Texas City
Denison	Marshall	Tyler
Donna	Mexia	Vernon
Eastland	Midland	Victoria
Edinburg	Mineral Wells	Waco
El Paso	Mission	Waxahachie
Ennis	Monahans	Weslaco
Fort Worth	Mount Pleasant	West
Gainesville	Nacogdoches	Wichita Falls
		Wink

Utah (5)

Logan	Ogden	Salt Lake City
Murray	Park City	

Vermont (3)

Burlington   Montpelier   Rutland

Virginia (47)

Abingdon   Galax   Penninsula
Alexandria   Halifax   Petersburg
Bassett   Hampton   Portsmouth
Big Stone Gap   Harrisonburg   Prince William
Blackstone   Hopewell   Pulaski
Bluefield   Lawrenceville   Radford
Bristol   Lynchburg   Roanoke
Cape Charles   Marion   Richmond
Charlottesville   Martinsville   Salem
Clifton Forge   Narrows   Schoolfield
Colonial Heights   Newport News   South Boston
Covington   Norfolk   Staunton
Danville   Northampton   Suffolk
Emporia   Norton   Tidewater
Fieldale   Parksley   Wytheville
Franklin   Pennington Gap

Washington (26)

Aberdeen   Kelso   South Bend
Ballard   Kennewick   Spokane
Bellingham   Longview   Tacoma
Centralia   Montesano   Tri-Cities
Chehalis   Olympia   Victoria
Clarkston   Pasco   Walla Walla
Everett   Raymond   Wenatchee
Gray's Harbor   Richland   Yakima
Hoquiam   Seattle

West Virginia (18)

Beckley   Fairmont   Logan
Bluefield   Follansbee   Mannington
Charleston   Grafton   Martinsburg
Clarksburg   Huntington   Montgomery

| Parkersburg | Point Pleasant | Welch |
| Piedmont | Princeton | Williamson |

Wisconsin (18)

Appleton	Janesville	Oshkosh
Beloit	Kenosha	Racine
Eau Claire	La Crosse	Sheboygan
Fond du Lac	Madison	Superior
Freeport	Marinette	Wausau
Green Bay	Milwaukee	Wisconsin Rapids

Wyoming (3)

| Cheyenne | Jackson | Laramie |

Puerto Rico (6)

| Aguadilla | Mayaguez | San Juan |
| Caguas | Ponce | Santurce |

Cuba (2)

| Almendaris | Havana |

Panama (1)

Panama City

Venezuela (2)

| Caracas | Maracaibo |

Dominican Republic (1)

Santo Domingo

Canada (65)

| Acton Vale, | Bassano, Alberta | Brandon, Manitoba |
| Quebec | Berlin, Ontario | Brantford, Ontario |

Brockville, Ontario
Burlington, Ontario
Calgary, Alberta
Cap de la Madeleine, Quebec
Cornwall, Ontario
Dominion, Nova Scotia
Drummondville, Quebec
Edmonton, Alberta
Farnham, Quebec
Fort William, Ontario
Fredericton, New Brunswick
Glace Bay, Nova Scotia
Granby, Quebec
Guelph, Ontario
Hamilton, Ontario
Hull, Quebec
Ingersoll, Ontario
Kingston, Ontario
Kitchener, Ontario
Lethbridge, Alberta
London, Ontario
Medicine Hat, Alberta

Montreal, Quebec
Moose Jaw, Saskatchewan
New Waterford, Nova Scotia
New Westminster, B.C.
Niagara Falls, Ontario
Outermont, Quebec
Ottawa, Ontario
Perth, Ontario
Peterborough, Ontario
Port Arthur, Ontario
Quebec, Quebec
Red Deer, Alberta
Regina, Saskatchewan
St. Boniface, Manitoba
St. Catherines, Ontario
St. Croix, New Brunswick
St. Hyacinthe, Quebec
St. Jean, Quebec

St. John, New Brunswick
St. Stephen, New Brunswick
St. Thomas, Ontario
Sarnia, Ontario
Saskatoon, Saskatchewan
Saulte St. Marie, Ontario
Sherbrooke, Quebec
Smiths Falls, Ontario
Sydney, Nova Scotia
Sydney Mines, Nova Scotia
Thetford Mines, Quebec
Three Rivers, Que. (Trois Rivieres)
Toronto, Ontario
Valleyfield, Quebec
Vancouver, B.C.
Victoria, B.C.
Welland, Ontario
Windsor, Ontario
Winnipeg, Manitoba
Woodstock, Ontario

Mexico (90)

Acambaro
Agua Prieta, Sonora
Aguascalientes, Aguas.
Aguila

Arandas
Caborca, Sonora
Campeche, Camp.
Cananea, Sonora
Celaya, Guan.
Cerro Azul

Chihuahua, Chih.
Ciudad del Carmen, Camp.
Ciudad de Valles, S.L.P.

Ciudad Juarez, Chih.

Ciudad Madero, Tam.

Ciudad Mante, Tam.

Ciudad Monclava, Coah.

Ciudad Obregon

Ciudad Valles

Ciudad Victoria, Tam.

Coahuila

Coatzacoalcos, Vera.

Cordoba, Vera.

Cortazar

Culican

Diaz Ordaz

Durango, Durango

Elbano, S.L.P.

Ensenada, Baja California

Fresnillo, Azc

Gomez Palacio, Durango

Guadalajara, Jalisco

Guadalupe

Guamuchil

Guanajuato, Guan.

Guasave

Guayamas

Hermosillo

Jalisco

Juarez

La Barra

Las Choapas, Vera.

Lagos de Moreno

Leon, Guan.

Los Mochis

Matamoros

Mazatlan

Merida, Yuc.

Mexicali, Baja California

Mexico, D.F.

Mexico City

Miguel Aleman

Minatitlan, Vera

Monclova

Monterrey, N.L.

Morelia, Michoacan

Moroleon

Narajo, Vera.

Navojoa

Nogales, Sonora

Nuevo Laredo, Tam.

Orizaba, Vera.

Parras

Poza Rica, Vera.

Puebla, Puebla

Puerto Penasco, Sonora

Reynosa, Tem.

Sabinas, N.L.

Salamanca, Guan.

Saltillo, Coah.

San Luis Potosi, S.L.P.

San Luis Rio Colorado, Son.

San Pedro de las Colonias, Coah.

Silao

Tabasco

Tampico, Tam.

Tamuin, S.L.P.

Teocaltiche

Tijuana, Baja, CA

Toluca

Torreon, Coah.

Union Laguna

Uriangato

Veracruz, Vera.

Villahermosa, Tab.

Yucatan

Zacatecas, Zac.

BIBLIOGRAPHY

The research phase of this book could not have been completed without the information contained in the following books, newspapers, magazines, newsletters, articles, and media guides, some of which were paraphrased and/or provided statistical or historical matter used verbatim.

Asociacion de Equipos Professionales de Beisbol de la Liga Mexicana (The Mexican League). *A.C. Quien es Quien en el Beisbol Liga Mexicana 1990.* Mexico City, Mexico, 1990.

Bailey, Jim. *Arkansas Travelers: 79 Years of Baseball.* Little Rock, AK: Arkansas Travelers Baseball Club Inc., 1980.

Baseball America, information and statistics from numerous editions. Durham, NC: 1990 American Sports Publishing Inc., 1990.

Baseball America. *Baseball America's 1989 Directory.* Durham, NC: American Sports Publishing Inc., 1990.

Baseball America. *Baseball America's 1990 Directory.* Durham, NC: American Sports Publishing Inc., 1990.

Baseball America. *Baseball America's 1990 Almanac.* Durham, NC: American Sports Publishing Inc., 1990.

Dixon, Phil. *The Negro Baseball Leagues: A Photographic History.* Mattituck, NY: Ameron House, 1990.

Fuselle, Warner. *Baseball: A Laughing Matter.* St. Louis, MO: The Sporting News, 1987.

Gutman, Dan. *It Ain't Cheatin' If You Don't Get Caught.* New York: Penguin Books, 1990.

Hershberger, Chuck. *Old Tyme Baseball News,* numerous articles from several editions. Pleasant Ridge, MI: Where Sports Network, 1987–90.

Kleinknecht, Merl F. *Blacks in 19th Century Organized Baseball,* several editions, several home locations for SABR. Garrett Park, MD: SABR Baseball Research Journals.

Kleinknecht, Merl F. *Integration of Baseball After World War II,* several editions. Garrett Park, MD: SABR Baseball Research Journals.

The Los Angeles Times, many clips from numerous editions. Los Angeles, CA: 1989–90.

Lowry, Philip J. *Green Cathedrals,* Manhattan, KS: SABR, Ag Press, 1986.

Maravetz, Steven. *A Love Affair With the Bush Leagues.* Waterloo, Iowa: Waterloo Royals, 1977.

Major League Baseball. *The Major League Baseball Newsletter,* editions of April, May, June, July. New York: Commissioners Office, 1990.

Mayer, Ronald A. *1937 Newark Bears: A Baseball Legend.* East Hanover, NJ: Vintage Press, 1980.

McCarthy, William E. *Rochester Diamond Echoes.* New York: Scheible Press, 1949.

Mote, James. *Everything Baseball.* New York: Prentice Hall Press, 1989.

Nash, Bruce and Allan Zullo. *The Baseball Hall of Shame*™. New York: Pocket Books, 1985.

Nash, Bruce and Allan Zullo. *The Baseball Hall of Shame*™ *2.* New York: Pocket Books, 1986.

Nash, Bruce and Allan Zullo. *The Baseball Hall of Shame™ 3.* New York: Pocket Books, 1987.

Nash, Bruce and Allan Zullo. *The Baseball of Shame™ 4.* New York: Pocket Books, 1990.

Obojski, Robert. *Baseball's Strangest Moments.* New York: Sterling Publishing Co., 1988.

Obojski, Robert. *Bush League: A History of Minor League Baseball.* New York: Macmillan Publishing Co. Inc., 1975.

Okrent, Daniel and Steve Wulf. *Baseball Anecdotes.* New York: Harper & Row (reprinted by permission of Oxford University Press), 1989.

O'Neil, Bill. *The Texas League: A Century of Baseball.* Austin, Texas: Eakin Press, 1987.

The Orange County Register, many clips from numerous editions. Santa Ana, CA: 1989–90.

Peary, Danny. *Cult Baseball Players.* New York: Simon and Shuster, 1990.

Rains, Rob. *1990 Top 150 Minor League Prospects.* St. Louis, MO: The Sporting News, 1990.

Reichler, Joseph L., editor. *The Baseball Encyclopedia (7th Edition),* New York: Macmillan Publishing Co., 1988.

SABR (Society for American Baseball Research). *Minor League Baseball Stars.* Manhattan, KS: Ag Press Inc., 1978.

SABR (Society for American Baseball Research). *Minor League Baseball Stars, Volume II.* Manhattan, KS: Ag Press Inc., 1985.

SABR (Society for American Baseball Research). *The National Pastime: A Review of Baseball History.* Birmingham, AL: EBSCO MEDIA, 1990.

SABR (Society for American Baseball Research). *The SABR Bulletin (Newsletter), Vol. 20, No. 1; Volume 20, No. 2; Volume 20, No. 3.* Garrett Park, MD: SABR, 1990.

SABR (Society for American Baseball Research). Various *SABR Journals,* numerous articles bylined by: Thomas S. Busch ("Seaching for Victory"); David K. Anderson ("All-Time College All-Star Teams"); George W.

Hilton ("The Evangeline League Scandal of 1946"). Garrett Park, MD: SABR, 1980–90.

Shlain, Bruce. *Oddballs.* New York: Penguin Books, 1989.

Shyer, Brent. *Dodgers Alumni News, Volume 6, No. 2.* Los Angeles, CA: Los Angeles Dodgers, 1990.

The Sporting News, many clips from numerous editions. St. Louis, MO: 1987–90.

Townsend, Bob. *The Night They Played Until 4 A.M.* Boston, MA: Howe About That Newsletter, Howe Sportsdata International Inc., March 1990.

Weiss, William J. *Your California League Record Book 1989.* San Mateo, CA: 1989.

Wolff, Rick, editor. *The Baseball Encyclopedia (8th Edition).* New York: Macmillan Publishing Co., 1990.

Woodford Associates. *A History of Baseball in the San Francisco Bay Area.* San Francisco, CA: San Francisco Giants, 1985.

⚾   ⚾   ⚾   ⚾

And the Media Guides and team magazines supplied by the following organizations:

Major League Baseball:
The 1990 Major League Baseball Media Information Guide—The Commissioners Office, 1990.

American League:
American League Red Book, Baltimore Orioles, Boston Red Sox, California Angels, Chicago White Sox, Cleveland Indians, Detroit Tigers, Milwaukee Brewers, Minnesota Twins, New York Yankees, Oakland A's, Seattle Mariners, Texas Rangers, Toronto Blue Jays.

National League:
National League Green Book, Atlanta Braves, Chicago Cubs, Cincinnati Reds, Houston Astros, Los Angeles Dodgers, Montreal Expos, New York Mets, Philadelphia Phil-

lies, Pittsburgh Pirates, St. Louis Cardinals, San Diego Padres, San Francisco Giants.

Minor League:

Albuquerque Dukes, American Association, Arkansas Travelers, Buffalo Bisons, Carolina League, Chattanooga Lookouts, Columbus Mudcats, Denver Zephyrs, Eastern League, Florida State League, Greenville Hornets, International League, Louisville Redbirds, Nashville Sounds, Northwest League, Oklahoma City 89ers, Pacific Coast League, Phoenix Firebirds, Quad City Angels, Rochester Red Wings, San Jose Bees, San Jose Giants, South Atlantic League, Southern League, Toledo Mud Hens, Waterloo Diamonds.

ABOUT THE AUTHOR

Mike Blake took his shot at "The Show" and "The Little Show" as an outfielder for Van Nuys High School in Southern California—home of such athletes as Don Drysdale, Bob Waterfield, Rob Scribner, Anthony Cook, Robert Redford, and Charlton Heston. He earned his varsity letter for VNHS, before moving on to college where he made his mark—at California State University, Northridge—as a switch-hitting shortstop-outfielder, setting a freshman team record for walks in a season. This prompted his coach to say, "Go up there and walk." But his approach to hitting also provoked his mentor to remark, "Blake, you hit equally as bad both ways."

Realizing his baseball career was in jeopardy, Blake hung up his spikes—except for his thrice-weekly softball games—to embark on a writing career. He has toiled for such now-defunct newspaper giants as the Los Angeles *Herald Examiner* and the electronic newspaper arm of the Los Angeles *Times* (Times-Mirror Videotex), as well as several dozen other newspapers and magazines from New York to Japan (where he is often translated into Japanese), providing more than 500 published articles in 14 years.

Blake has also written three films for the United States Air Force, two theatrical screenplays, two teleplays, and three books.

But baseball is his true love, and writing from his office, on a spot where Babe Ruth faced Walter Johnson in a barnstorming exhibition game in 1924, Blake says, "Minor League ball is the heart that pumps the talent and spirit into the grassroots arteries of America. It is the glorious and pure game that keeps America young and innocent . . . between the white lines, for nine innings at a time."

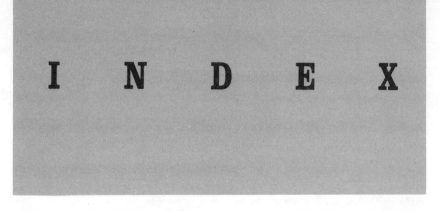

INDEX

NOTE: A number in italics references a page of the photographic insert; boldfaced page numbers indicate charts.